Chinese Woodcut:
The Art of Liu Chunjie

ACC ART BOOKS

Contents

Preface

For 38 years, I've been creating woodcuts. During this time, the world and the lives of people in it have undergone tremendous changes, becoming vibrant and diverse. Yet, my passion for woodcut art has remained steadfast, akin to eating, sleeping, sipping tea, socialising, and periodic solace-seeking. Continuous creation and perpetual evolution have become my daily routine.

I've dabbled in stone, copper and silk-screen printing, but it's woodcut that captivates me the most. For me, it is the *śarīra* of art. The crunching sound of carving into wood, the graceful dance of swirling wood shavings, the scent of sunlight emanating from the boards – all converge into a symphony. The brilliance of ink under the pressure of rolling and the heartbeats of anticipation while hand printing, the moment of revelation when unveiling a finished piece – all akin to the climax of a perfect concert.

Woodcut art is my way of life, a ritual, a refuge, a belief. Just as devotees meditate, sit in contemplation or recite scriptures, I engage ancient tools and materials, devoutly creating works that embody modern concepts. The accumulated imagery becomes my scripture, and the bound volumes become my religious books.

Over the past decade or so, I've also experimented with coloured ink, installation art, and mixed-media painting. However, the spirit of woodcut remains the foundation of my art: sharp, resolute and boldly delineated with vivid contrasts. I struggle constantly with the materials, grappling with familiar traditional methods. Innovation doesn't just depend on a shift in form; it's about elevating the essence of the artwork to a new height, transforming the certainty of 'having a bamboo picture in mind' into a state of 'having no picture in mind' [*]. I no longer sketch; instead, I pick up my tools without a plan, responding to the moment, following my instincts, letting creativity flow naturally, creating from nothing. It's a journey from abstraction to representation, and from representation back to abstraction, until the act of 'painting' no longer exists.

---

* Translator's note: Here the author utilises a Chinese idiom '胸有成竹', which literally means 'having a bamboo picture in mind' and figuratively means 'having a well-thought-out plan'. The author indicates that in the final phase of creating art, one should not have any clear picture in mind.

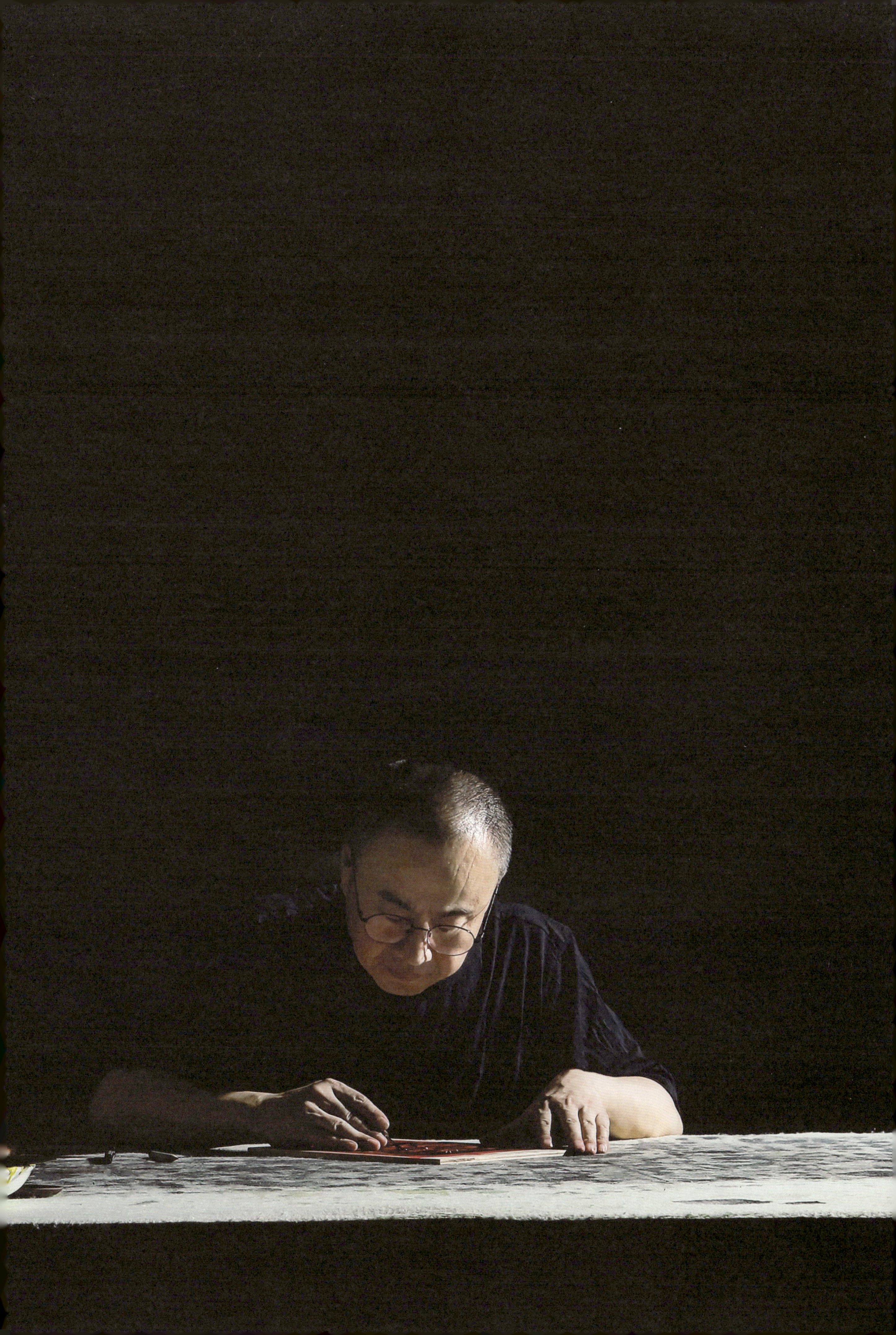

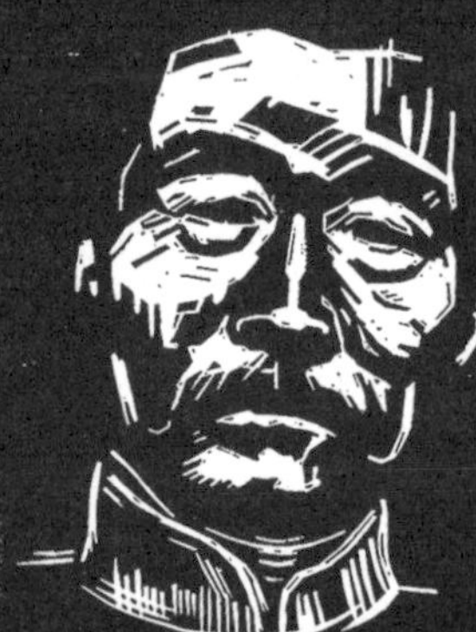

他已经是鲁迅了

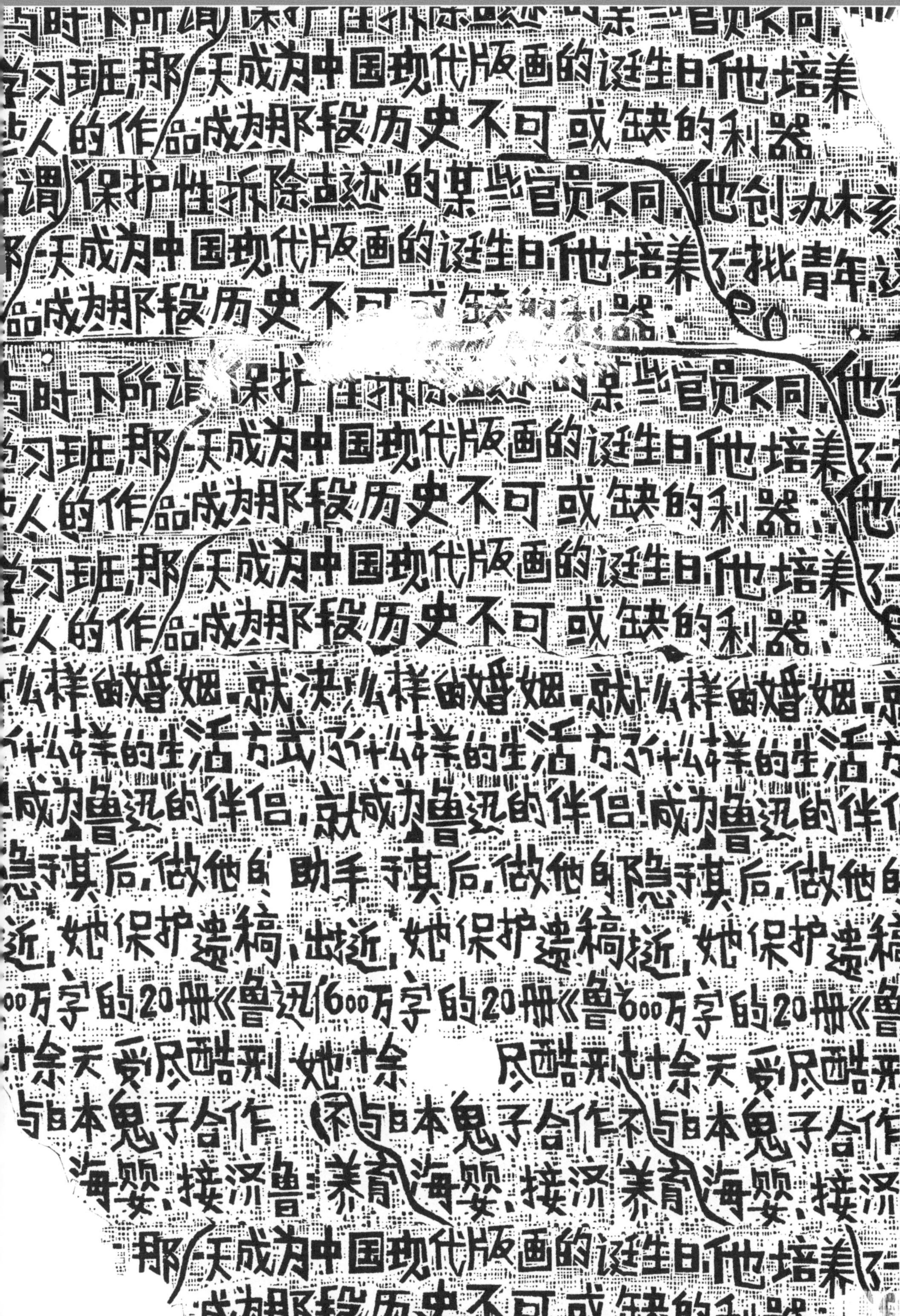
与时下所谓"保护性拆除古迹"的某些官员不同，
学习班，那一天成为中国现代版画的诞生日。他培养
些人的作品成为那段历史不可或缺的利器；
谓"保护性拆除古迹"的某些官员不同，他创办木刻
那一天成为中国现代版画的诞生日。他培养了一批青年
品成为那段历史不可或缺的利器；
与时下所谓"保护性拆除古迹"的某些官员不同，他
学习班，那一天成为中国现代版画的诞生日。他培养了一
些人的作品成为那段历史不可或缺的利器；他
学习班，那一天成为中国现代版画的诞生日。他培养了
些人的作品成为那段历史不可或缺的利器；
么样的婚姻，就决么样的婚姻，就么样的婚姻，就
什么样的生活方式了什么样的生活方了什么样的生活方
成为鲁迅的伴侣，就成为鲁迅的伴侣，成为鲁迅的伴
隐于其后，做他的助手于其后，做他的隐于其后，做他的
逝，她保护遗稿，出逝，她保护遗稿逝，她保护遗稿
00万字的20册《鲁迅600万字的20册《鲁600万字的20册《鲁
十余天受尽酷刑，她十余 尽酷刑七十余天受尽酷刑
与日本鬼子合作，不与日本鬼子合作不与日本鬼子合作
海婴，接济鲁美育海婴，接济养育海婴，接济
一那一天成为中国现代版画的诞生日。他培养了一
成为那段历史不可或缺的利器；

我的木刻经

从古至今的修行人，最初皆为修苦行，木刻创作亦然，它是一条孤独寂寞[illegible]之路。屈指一算，我从事木刻创作已有二十六年，世界已经天翻地覆多姿多彩，我也不再年轻，但我于木刻却日久生情，生活中已然不能缺少它。打坐，佛法叫坐禅，它可以让人心平气和地与自己的身体沟通，体内循环处于最佳状态，五脏六腑得到休息。宗教讲，通过冥想可以开启智慧，内心清静，明心见性，摆脱苦恼。每日，我只要立于画案前，无需敲木鱼捻佛珠，也不需有菩萨像，更不要正襟危坐，拿起刻刀，举刀向木，手起刀落，游刃自如，虔诚发自内心，不被物所系，不为名所累，画板上呈现出万千气象，如经书之于信徒，倘有烦恼与不快，定会随着木屑纷飞而去。

木刻于我是一种仪式，是精神的寄托，是生活的方式。木刻是我的信仰，我刻木刻就如同信徒参禅、打坐、诵经，我虔诚地刻，这些日积月累的图像就是我的经文，这些装订成册的刻本就是我的经书。

春杰谨记

1. *Beidahuang Prints*

I was born in Beidahuang in the mid-1960s, vast and fertile, poetic and mysterious. Long winters draped the land in ice and snow, rendering the silent wilderness desolate yet teeming with wildlife. After 1958, several hundred thousand demobilised soldiers, border-support youths, and educated youths gathered there to reclaim the wilderness. Among them were intellectuals, writers and painters, many of whom were considered 'socially disadvantaged' or 'politically backward', voluntarily seeking to reform themselves in the most arduous of places. Their arrival brought Beidahuang opportunities for cultural development. Later, some said that during that era, Beidahuang was a place of cultural exile. In my youth, I could see a huge chimney from my window, painted with rows of large characters: 'emancipate mankind first, then emancipate oneself' and 'keep the country in your heart and the whole world in your mind'. I didn't understand the meaning of these words, but they instilled in me a sense of boldness and grandeur.

Due to the intensity of labour required, life was tough for the pioneer team members. Under the pressure, they sought solace in artistic nourishment, leading to a flourishing of literature and painting. Bordering Russia, Beidahuang's special relationship with the Soviet Union in the 1950s fostered an artistic atmosphere filled with passion, melancholy and romance. In an era that had been devoid of poetry, Beidahuang was now imbued with it. It was here that the vibrant chapter in history of contemporary Chinese printmaking, known as Beidahuang Prints, was born. This artistic community, named after its region, bore distinct imprints of its time and became my first spiritual wellspring.

In the 1970s, people lived in mud-and-thatch houses, but the land reclamation workers let us children have the best and grandest brick houses to study in. My first painting class took place in one such house, taught by a mathematics teacher. He placed an enamel basin against the blackboard, drew a large circle with chalk, coloured it in red, and told us it was the sun.

In 1985, I had the honour of participating in a woodcut workshop in Beidahuang. Three elder artists were mentors, and the students were amateurs from over a hundred farms. There was no formal syllabus or any theoretical courses; instead, they took the traditional master–apprentice hands-on approach. Students would first sketch drafts, receive feedback and sometimes revisions, then proceed to enlarge the designs onto woodblocks, learn to carve with knives, and finally learn the printing. It took about a month to complete one piece, and after getting the hang of it, we moved on to our second and third works, gradually becoming more proficient. There were already some veteran students who had created numerous works, serving as role models for newcomers. I often pondered how to differentiate my work from theirs. After studying the early works of our teachers, depicting agricultural scenes with a bold style, I decided to depict the life and environment of farm work. While my teachers' work was meticulous, mine was relaxed; while their forms were realistic, I opted for a childlike style. I created dozens of whimsical, hopeful pastoral scenes, with innocence, romance, serenity, sweetness and warmth, expressive and enthusiastic. For this difference, my works often had the honour of being exhibited and published. Though somewhat naïve, these works were imbued with traces of growth; in those years, I tried hard to take off, experiencing ups and downs, before soaring into the skies.

In an article, a media professional Zheng Yun described my colour woodcut work *When the Evening Breeze is Passing* (2003) as follows: 'By the year 2000, China had long been engulfed in materialism and hedonism. Who else could evoke such a romantic yet melancholic, sweet yet tranquil, and pure yet powerful sentiment? The dream-like golden background represents nostalgia for days gone by. The leisurely long skirts and braids, freely roaming pigs and sheep, smiling and tender sunflowers, the mature yet youthful crane, undisturbed tadpoles and fish, wooden houses and distant mountains – everything is stirred gently by the evening breeze. I don't know what contemporary artists accustomed to the blurred lines of flesh and blood would think, and I don't care how contemporary critics scorn or rage. When the gentle breeze passes by, worldly matters have nothing to do with me. If one must ascribe meaning to the work, then its indifference and disdain towards materialism are the most powerful critique of the times' (Zheng Sun, 2014).

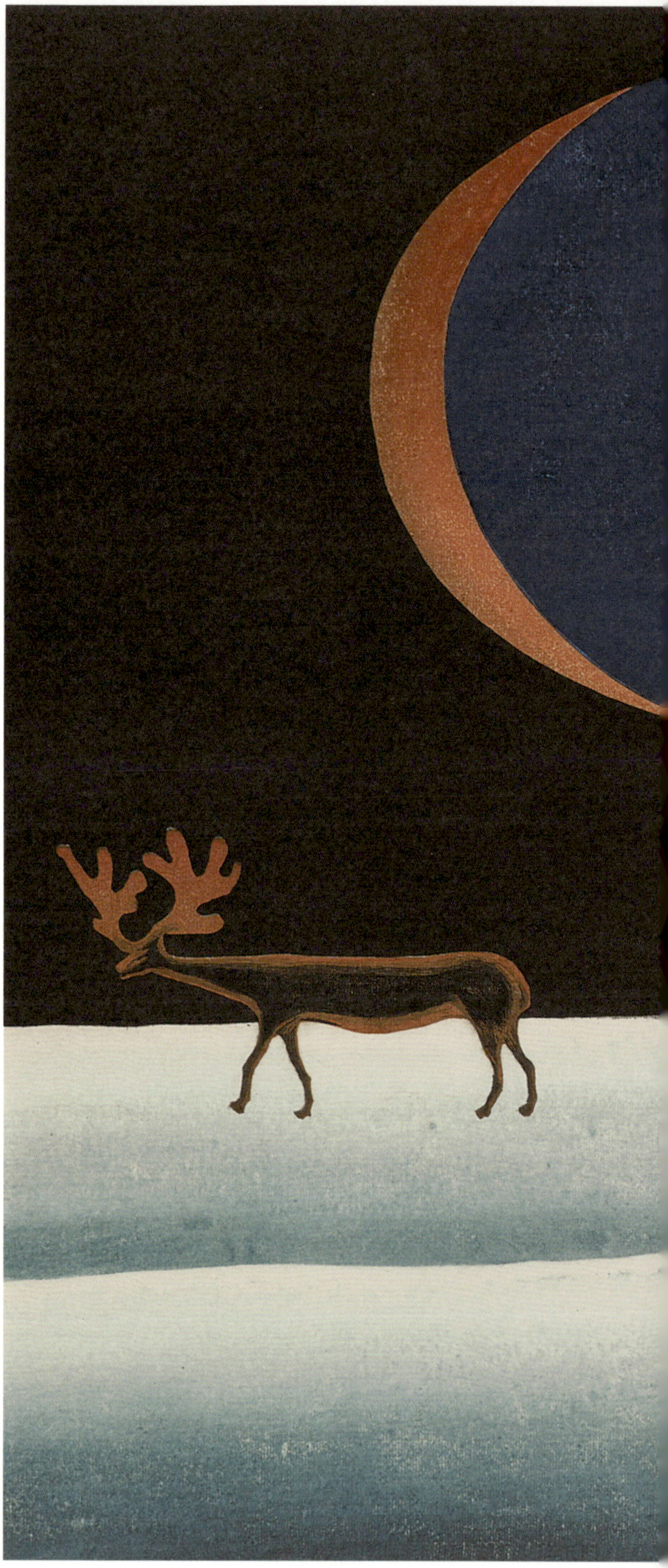

Revolving Moon
60cm × 80.5cm　Woodcut　1992

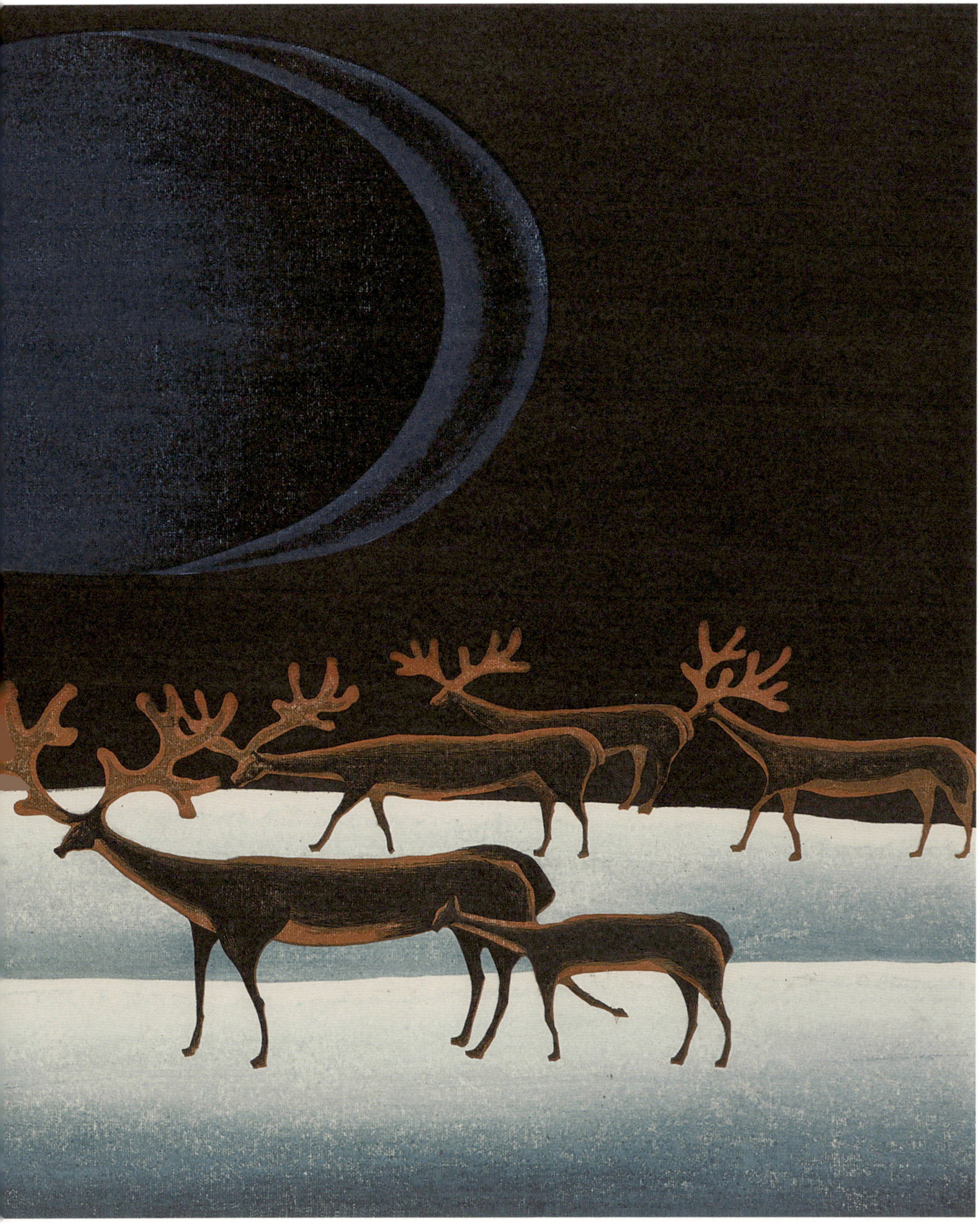

The Cry of Deer 60cm × 73cm Woodcut 1993

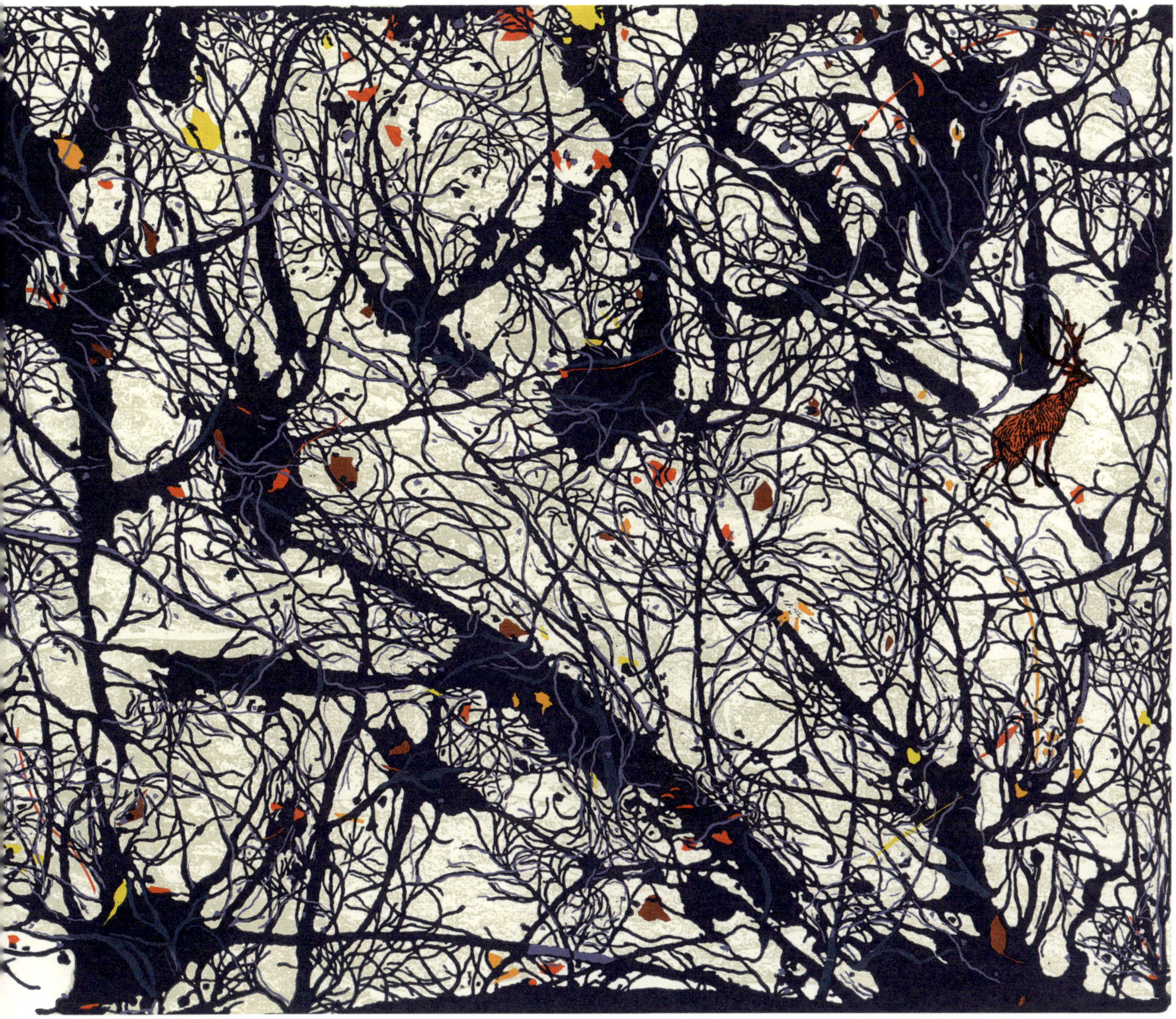

What a Cool Autumn! 72.5cm × 68cm Woodcut 1994

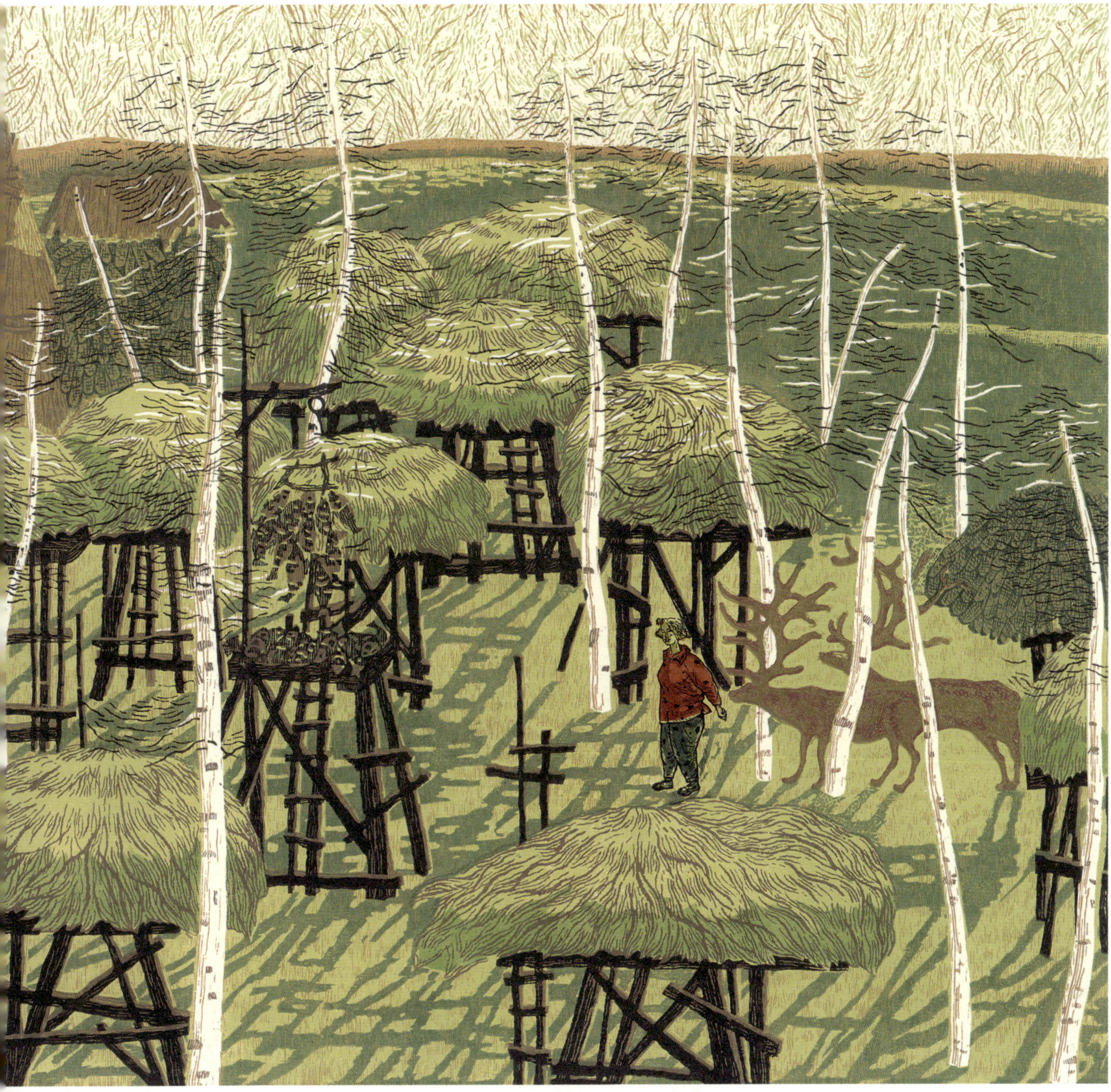

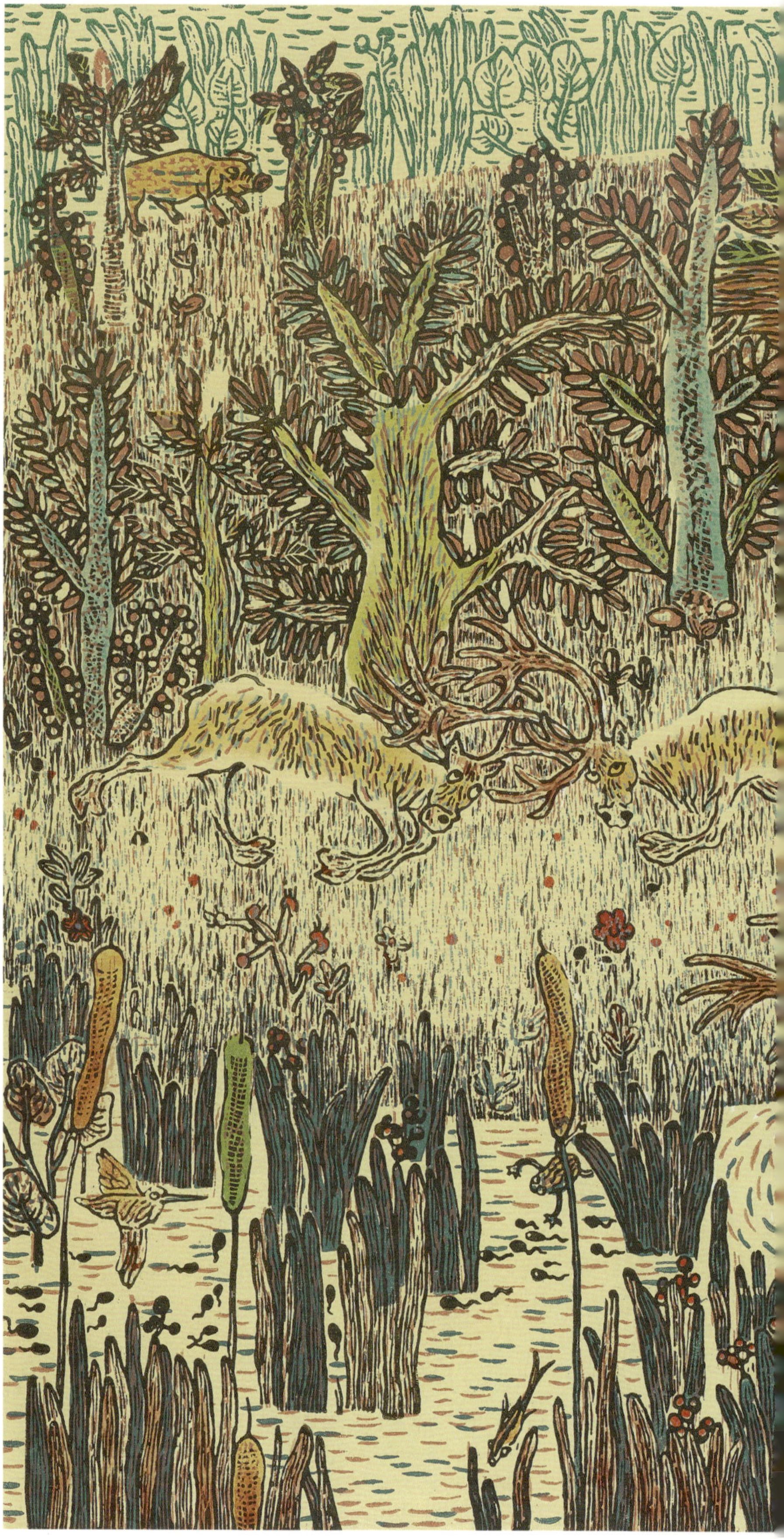

The Light Dance of the Wind
80.5cm × 59cm Woodcut 1995

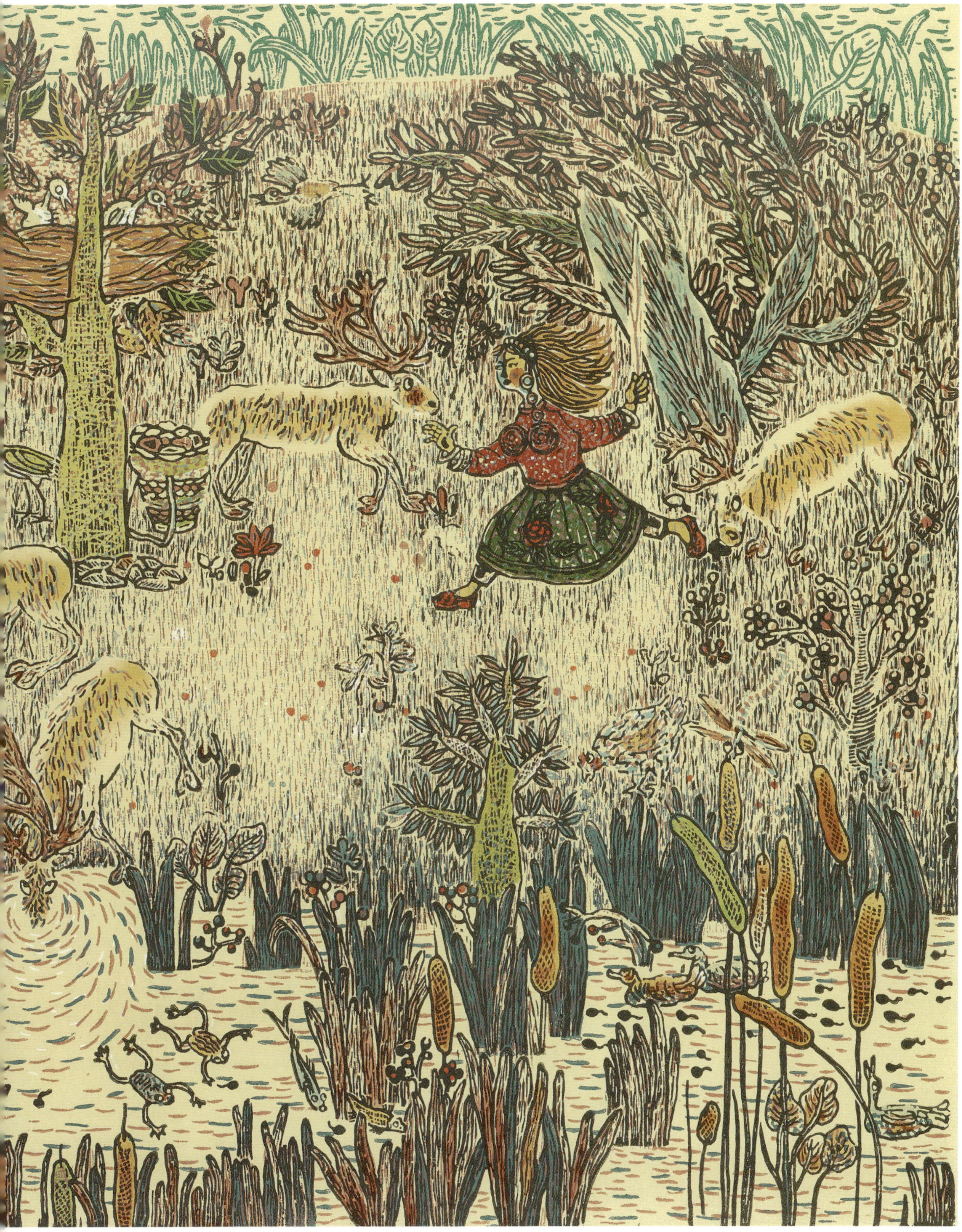

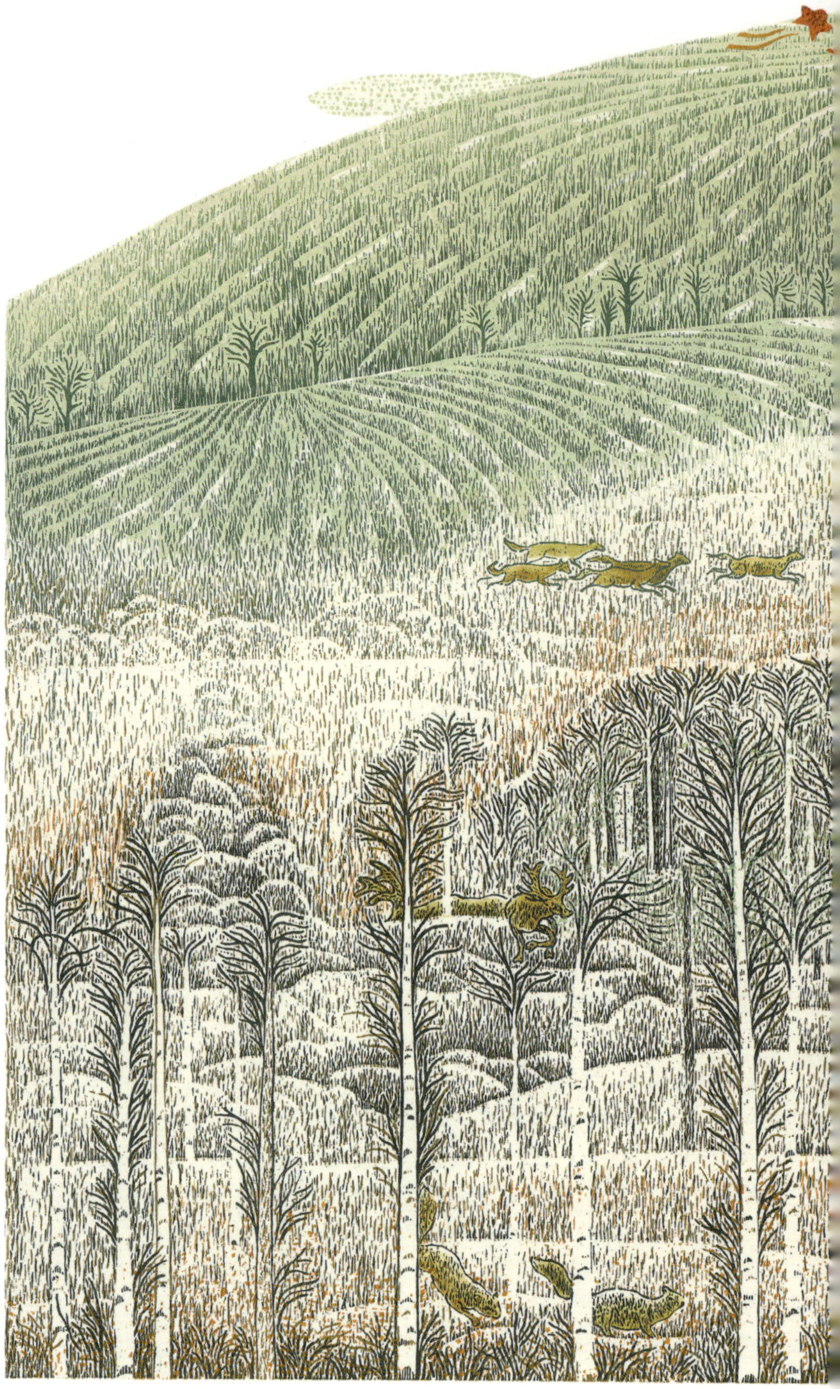

A Paradise with Favourable Weather
77cm × 49cm Woodcut 1997

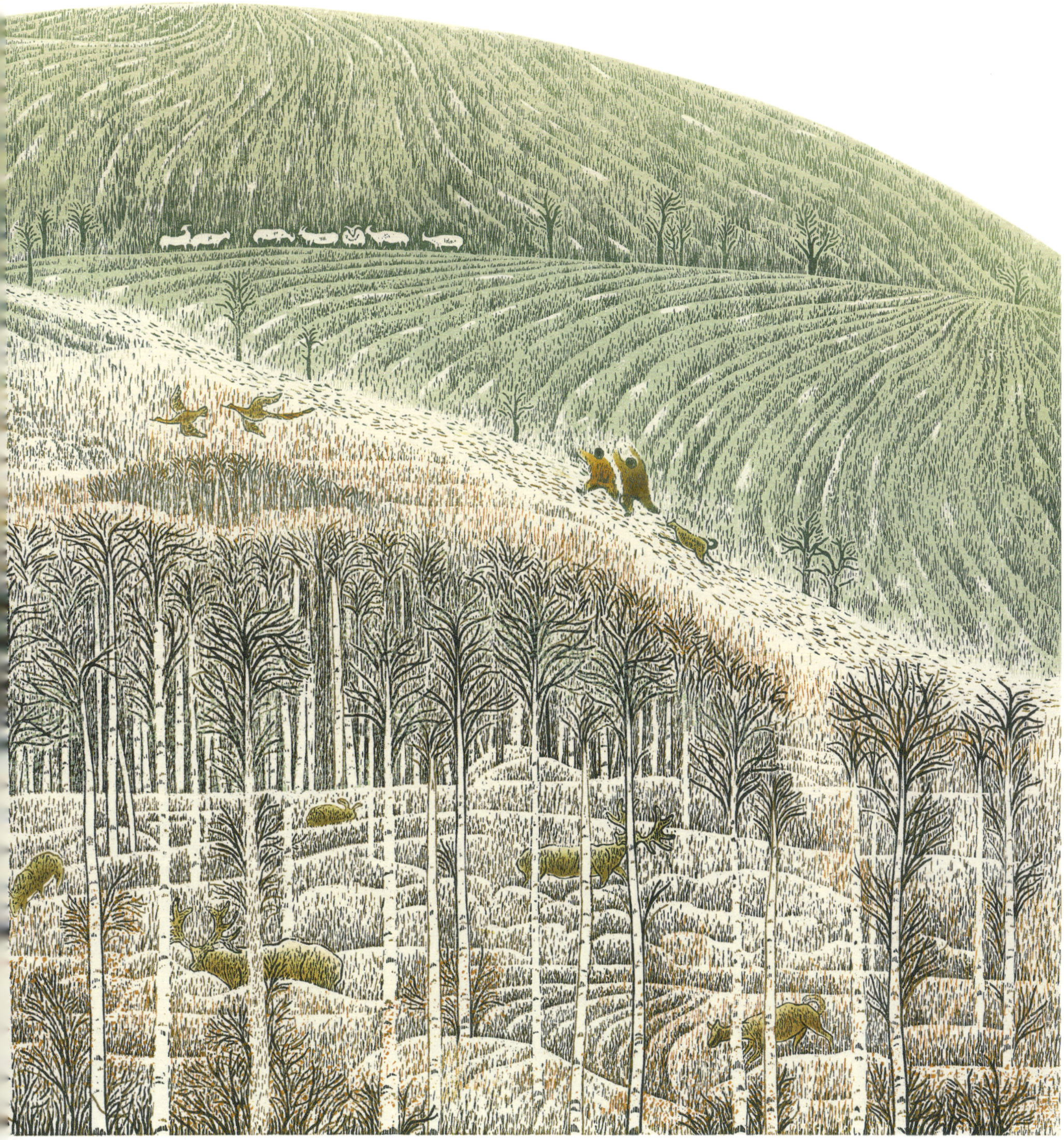

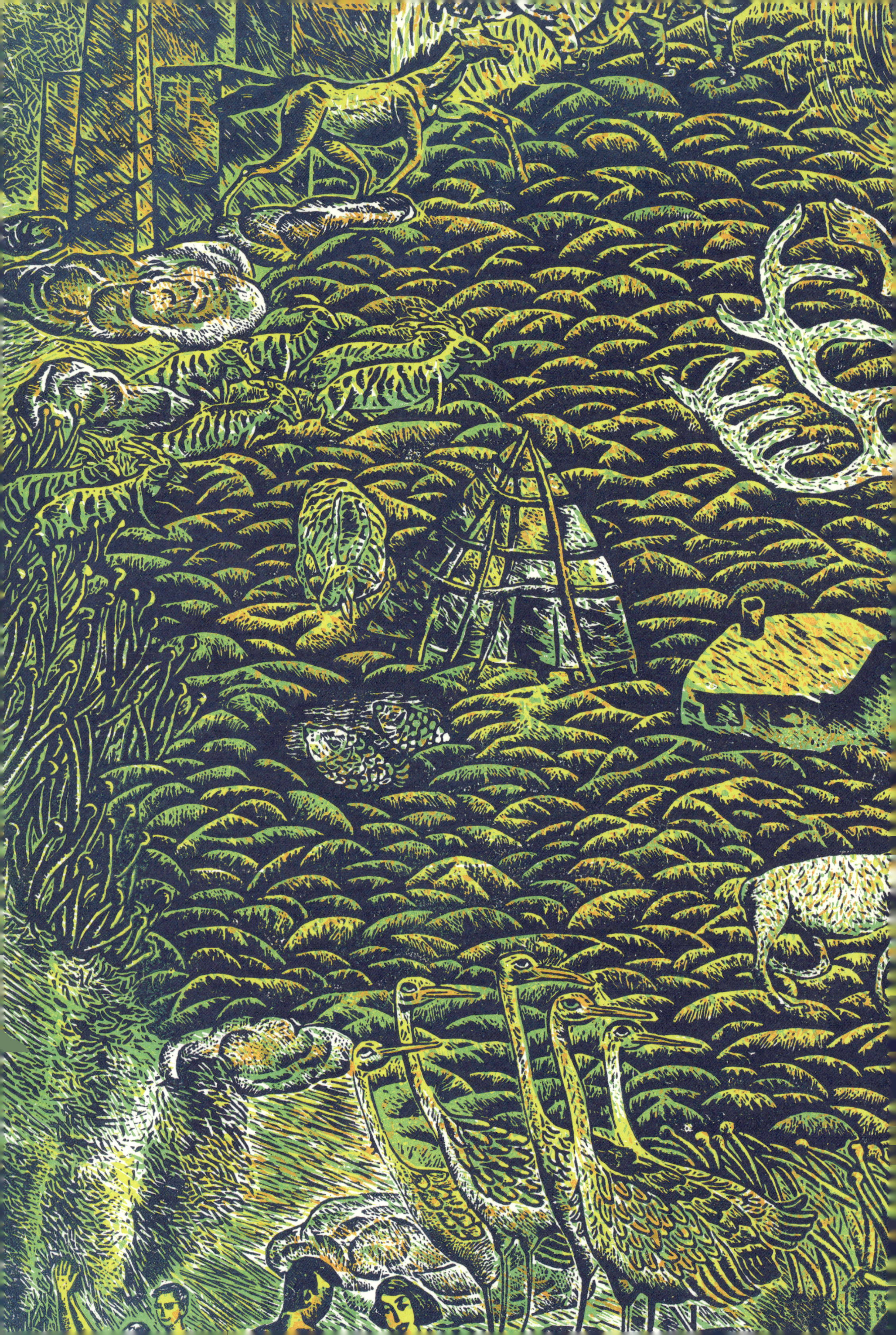

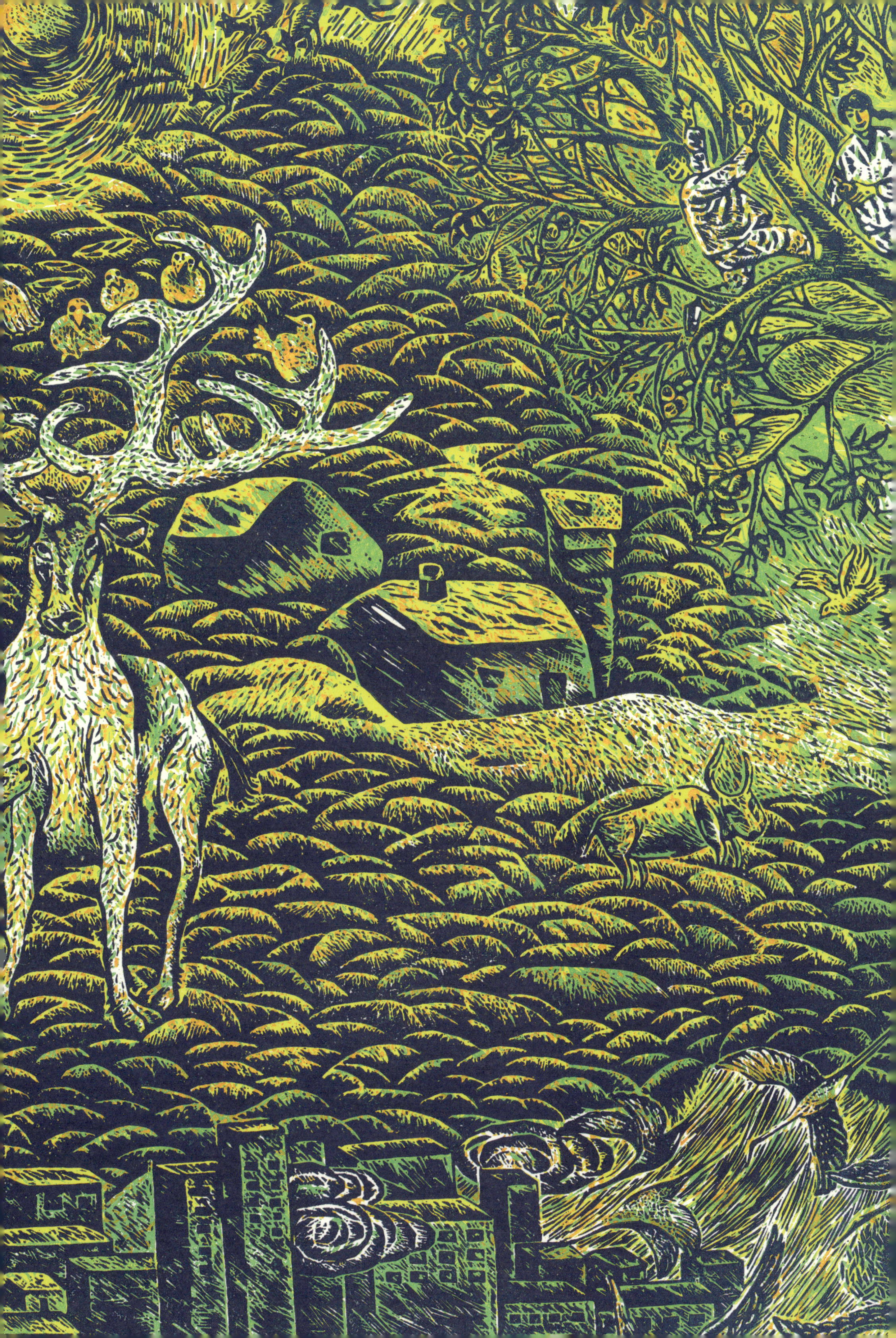

Golden Dreams in the Old Garden 79cm × 70cm Woodcut 1998

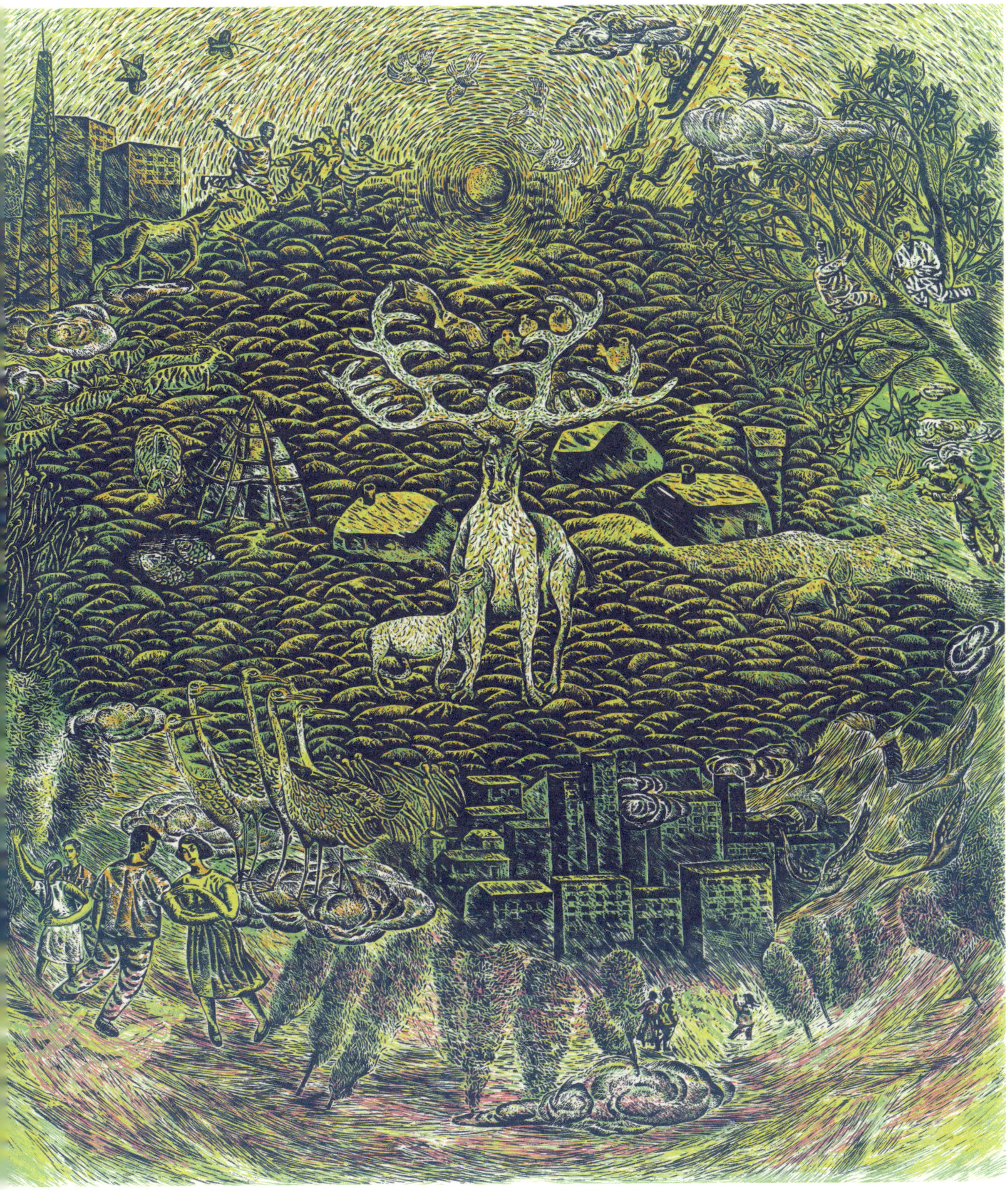

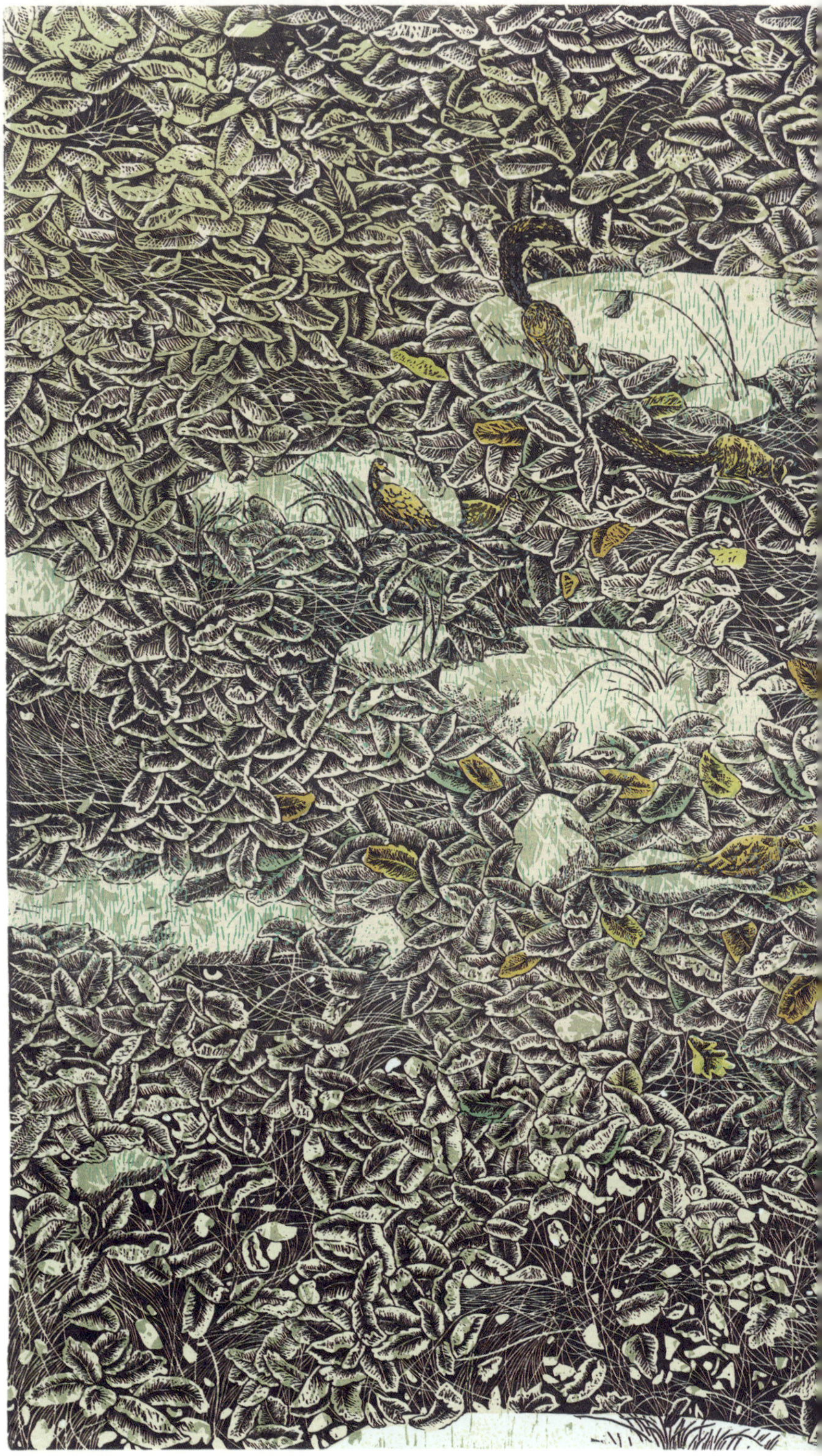

Fallen Autumn Flower
80cm × 53cm　Woodcut　1998

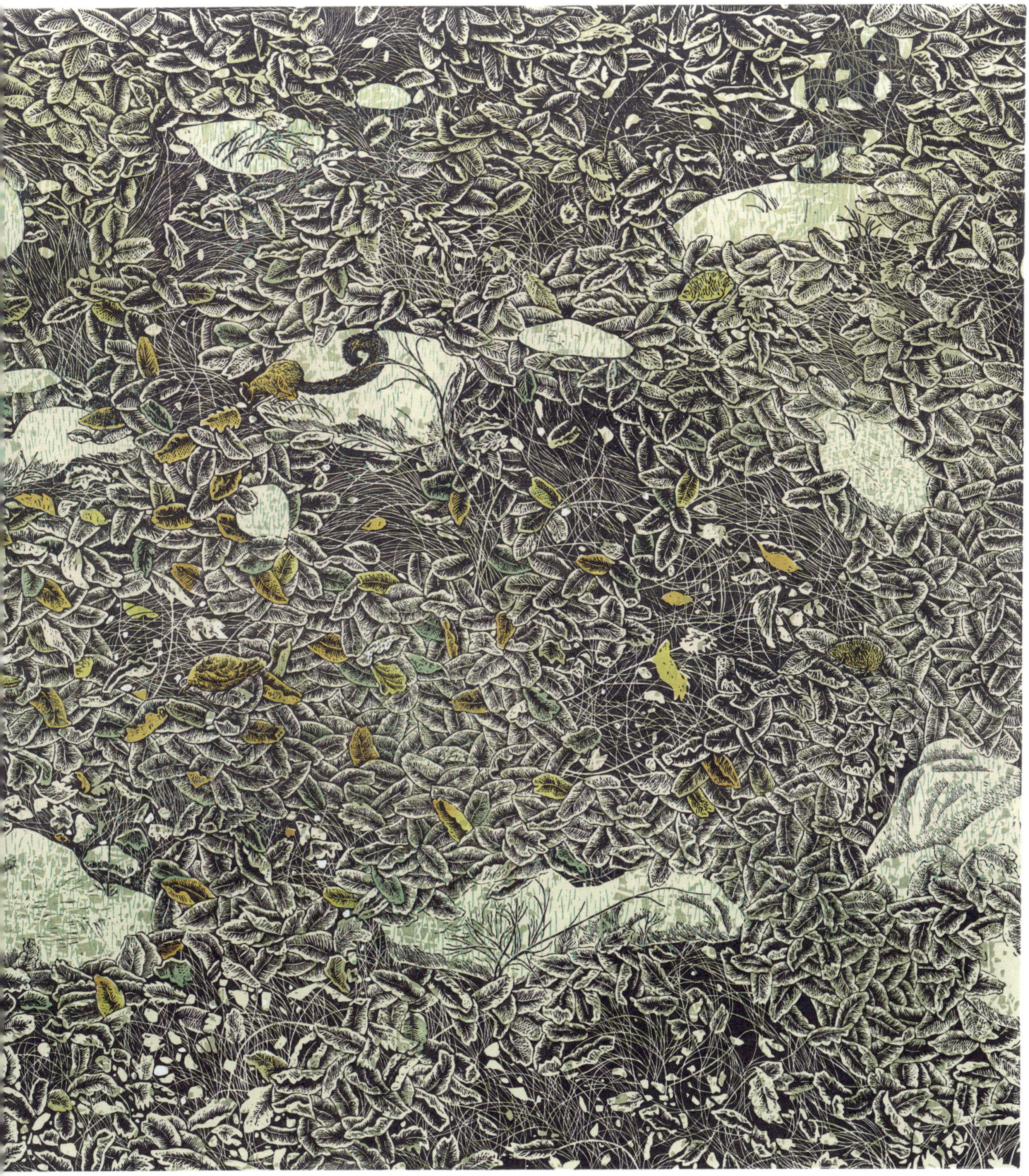

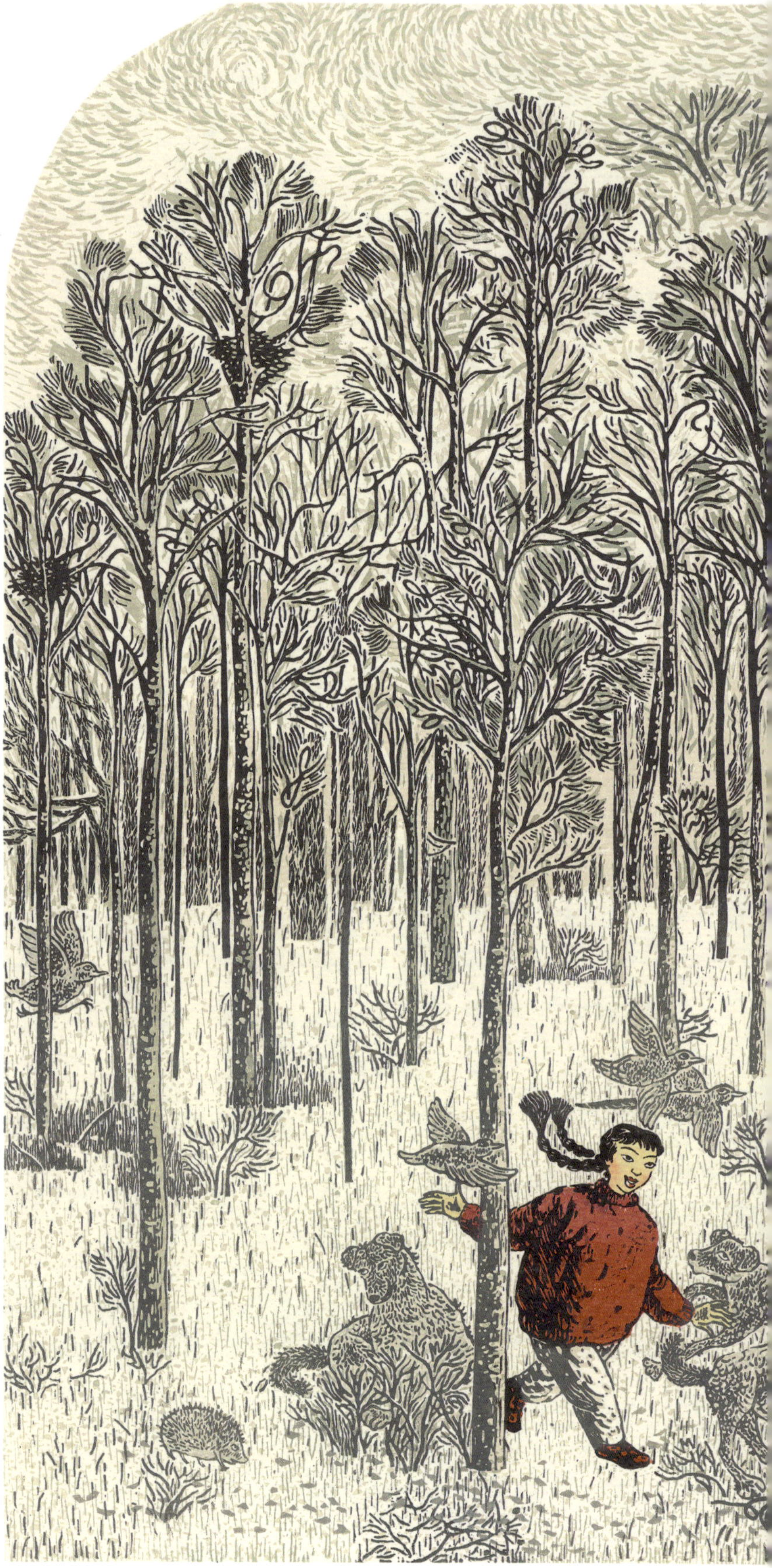

Dreamlike Children's Ballads
82cm × 62cm Woodcut 1998

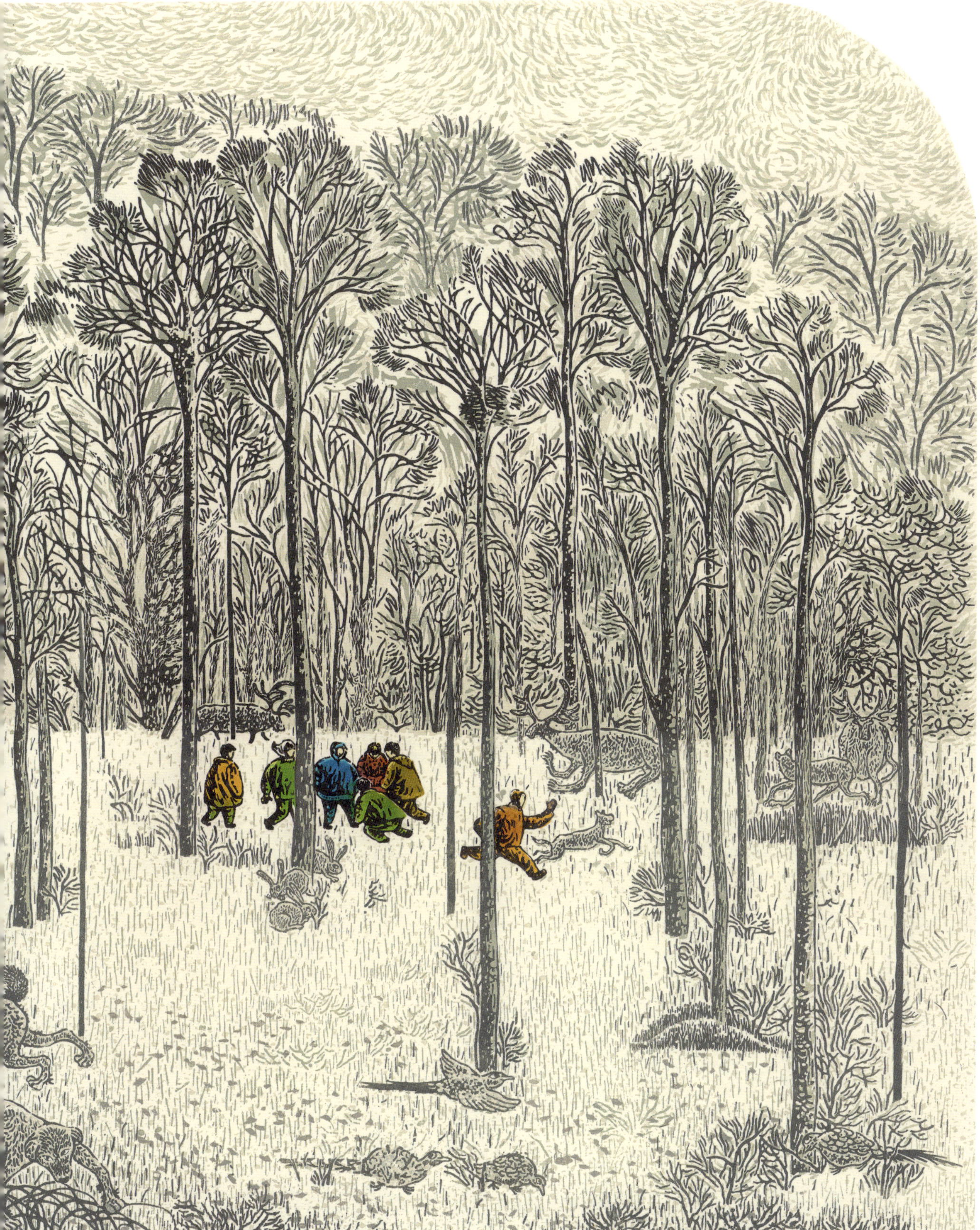

Together Forever 75cm × 61cm Woodcut 2001

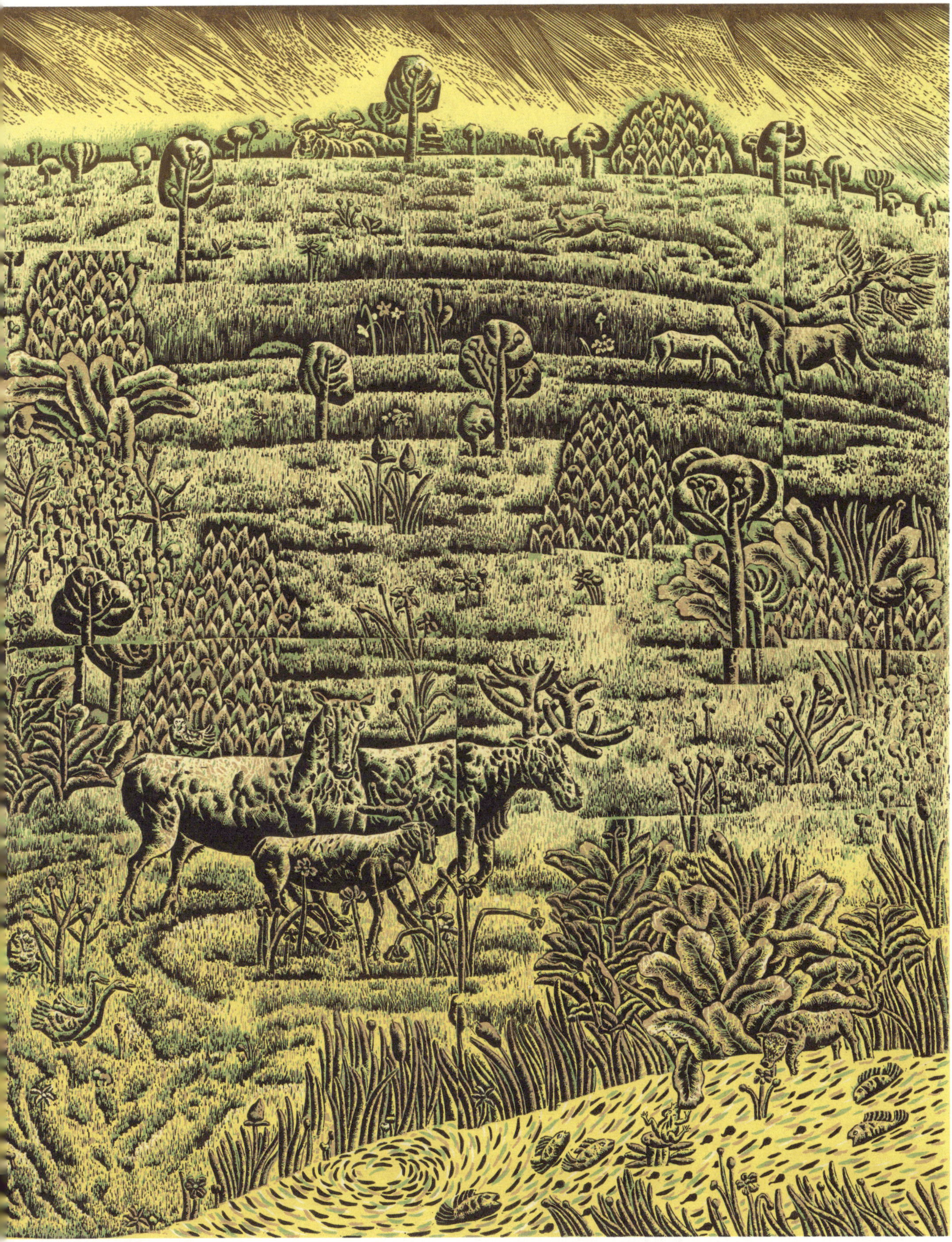

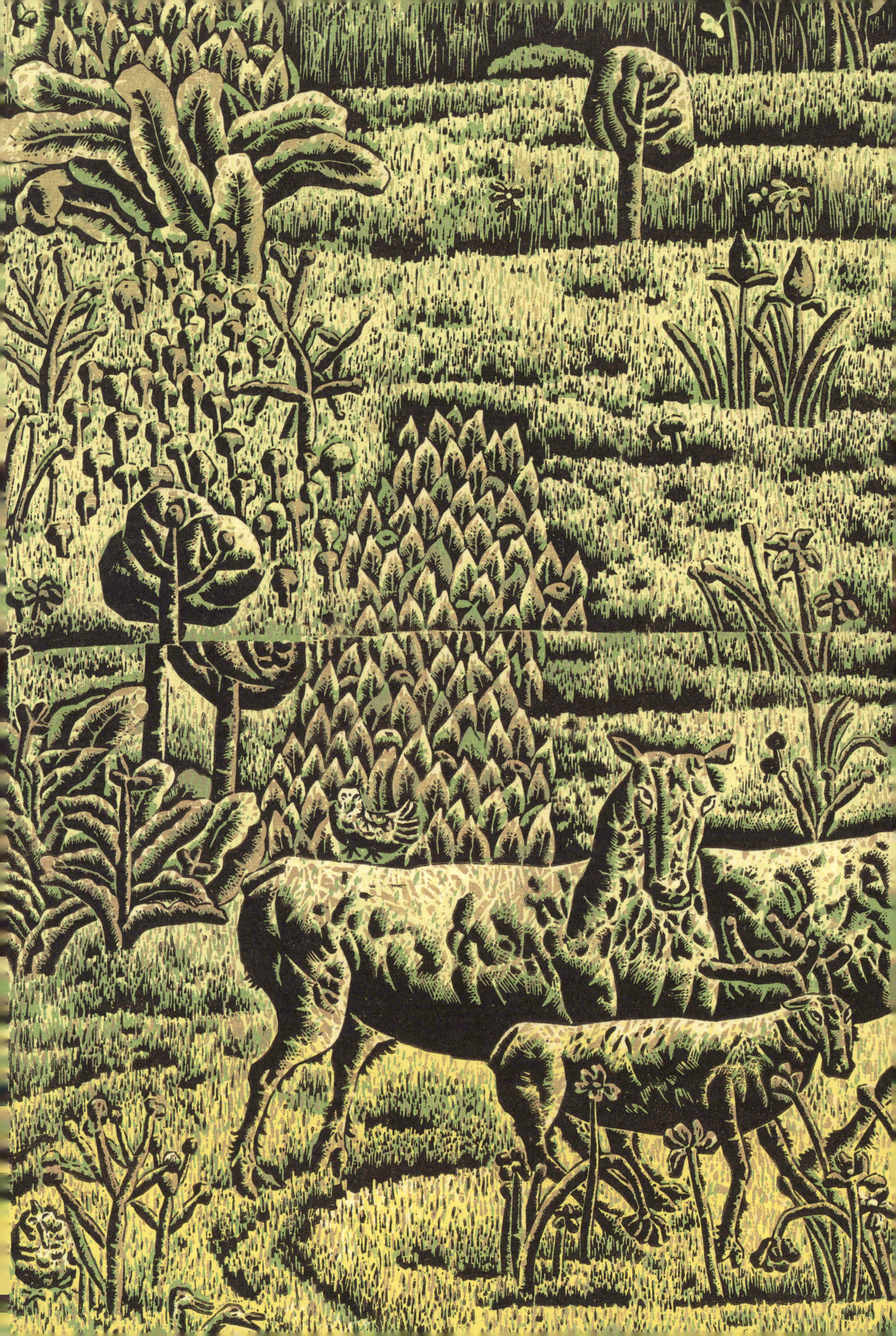

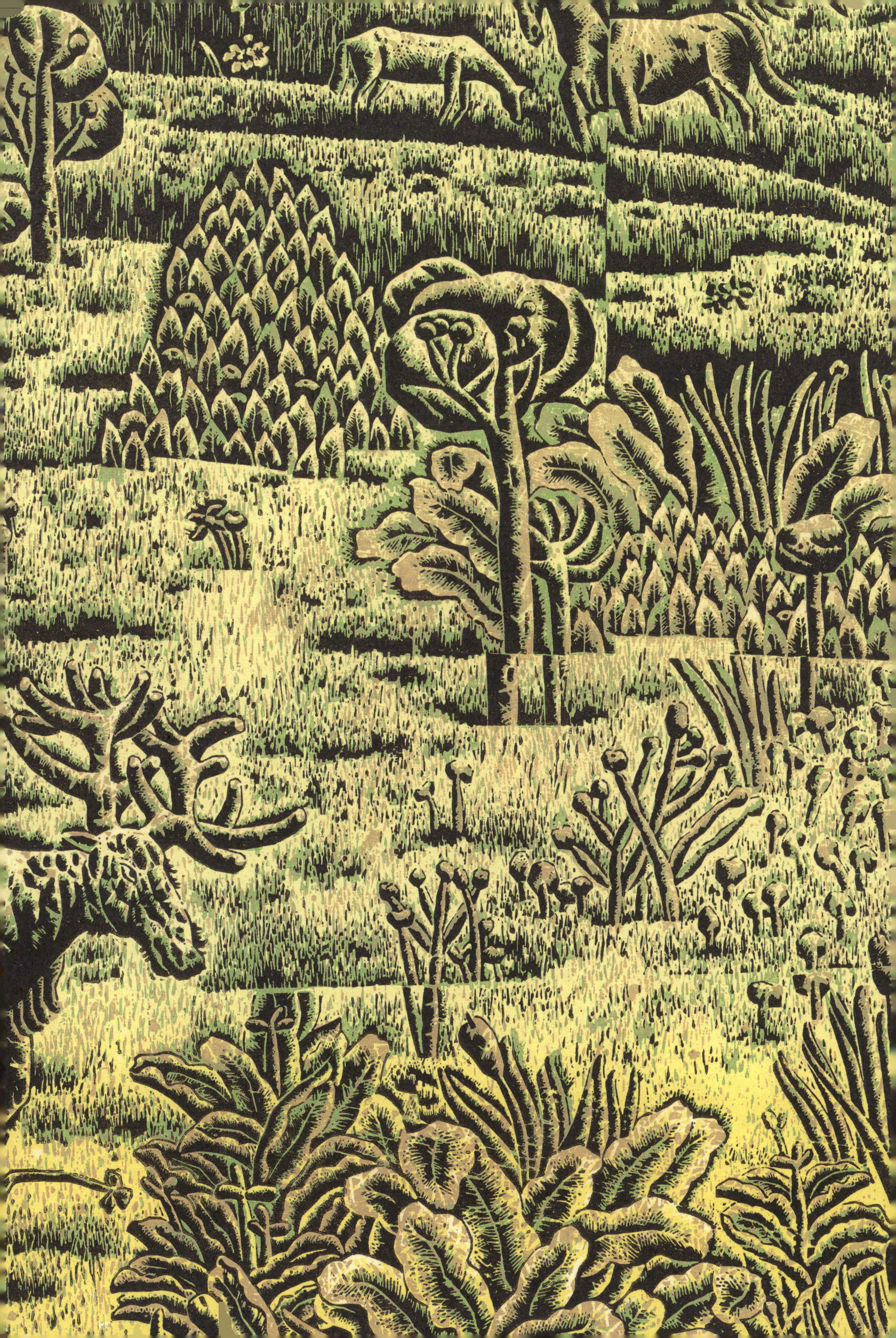

Traceless Snow 85cm × 60cm Woodcut 2001

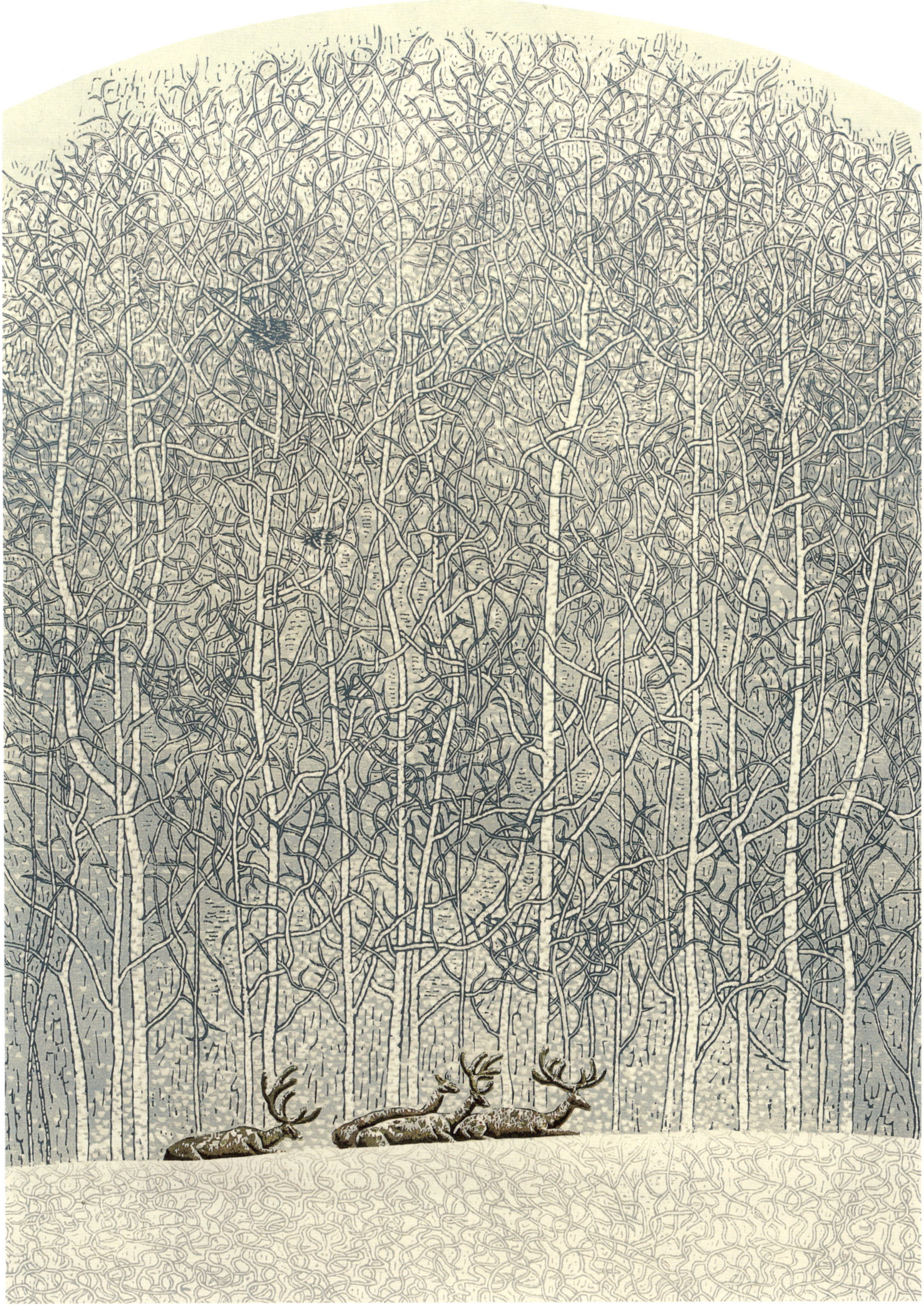

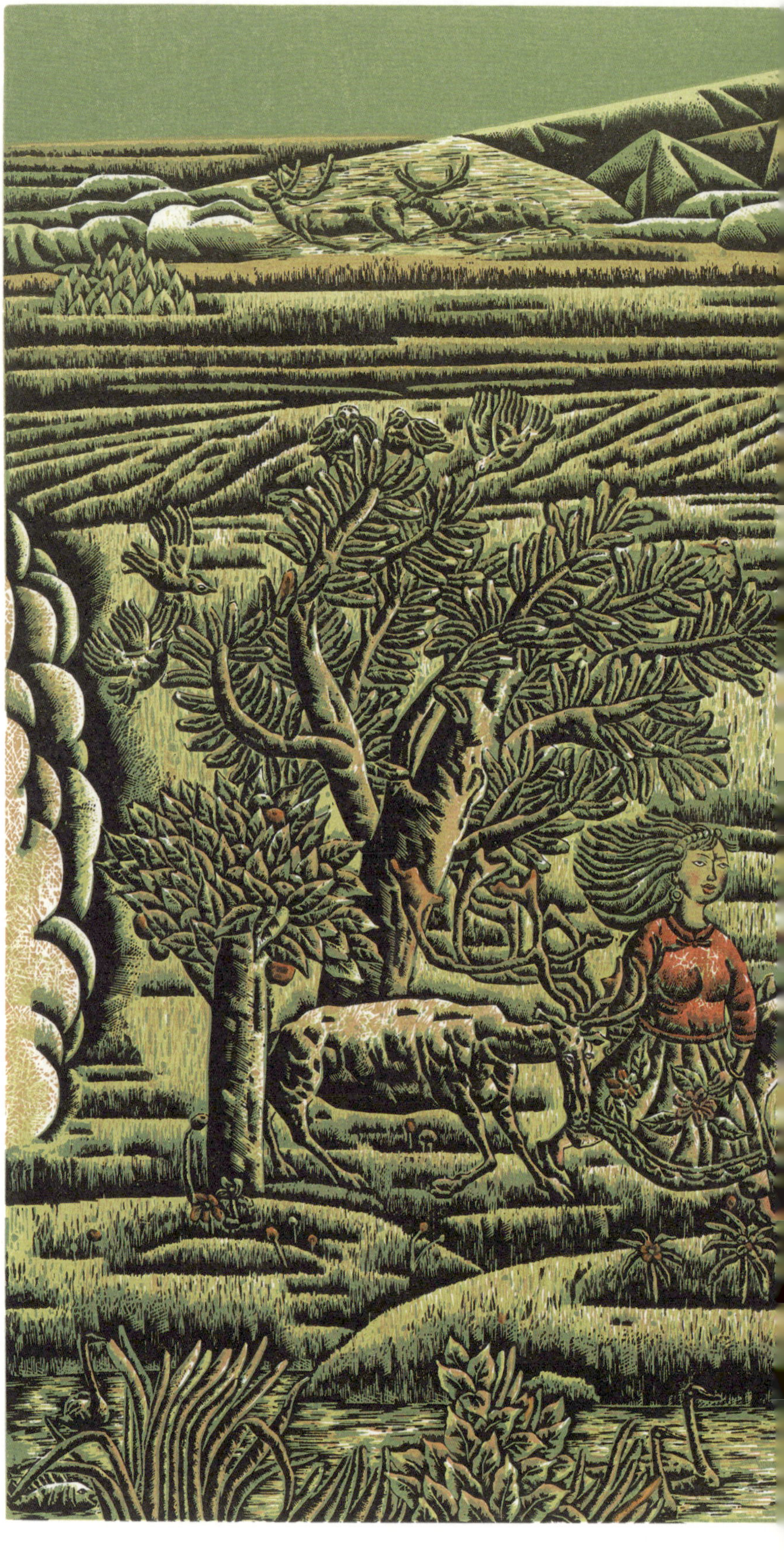

Singing in the Setting Sun
86cm × 60cm Woodcut 2003

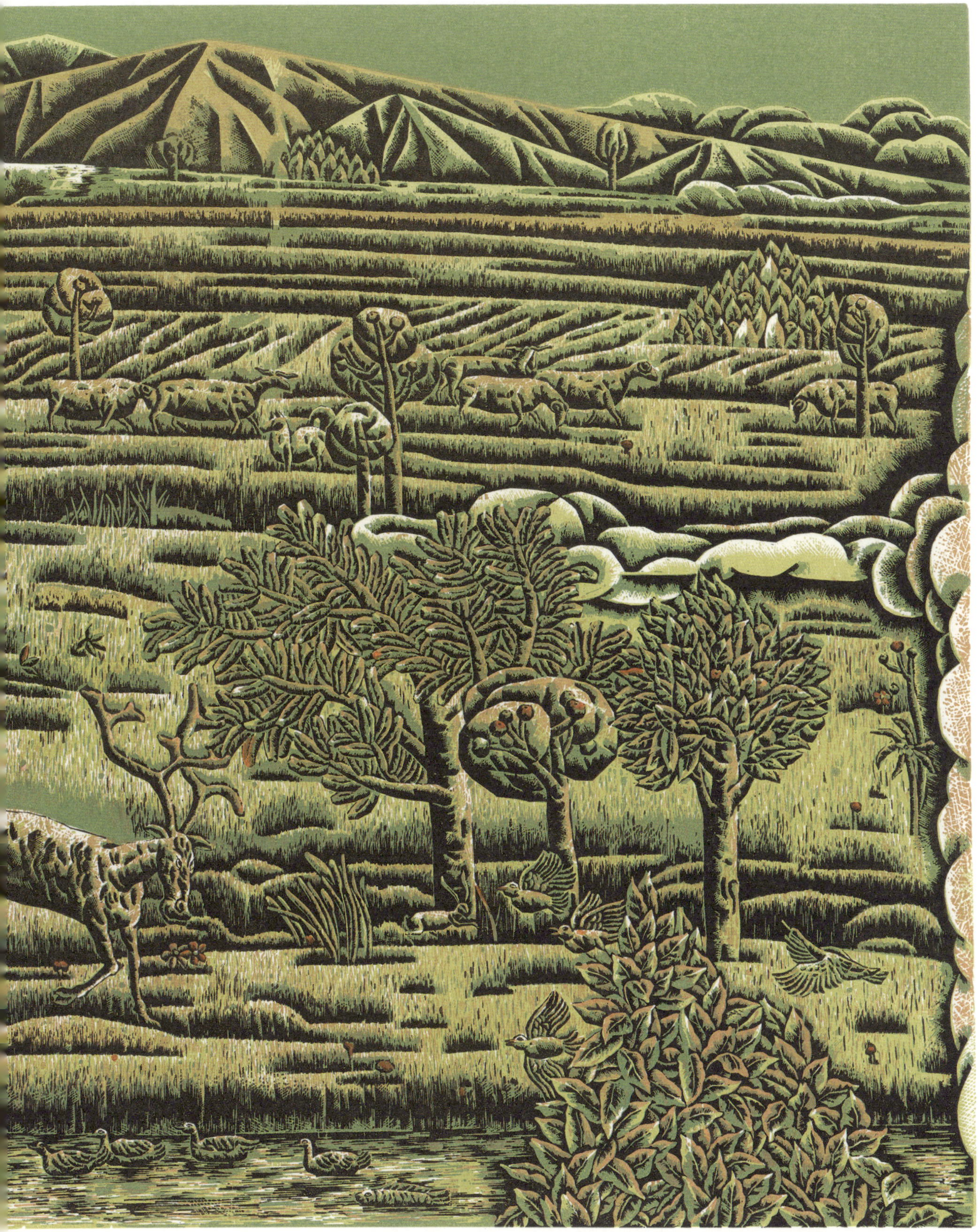

When the Evening Breeze is Passing
83cm × 64cm Woodcut 2003

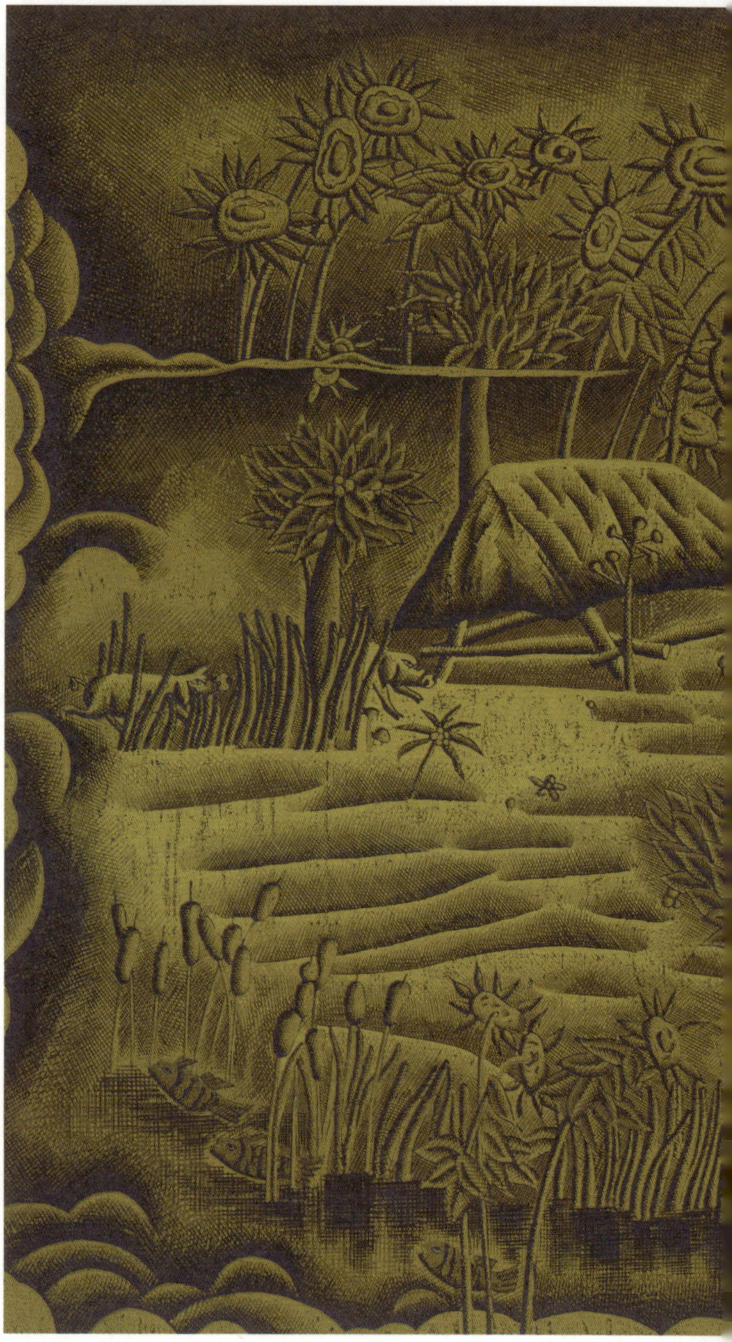

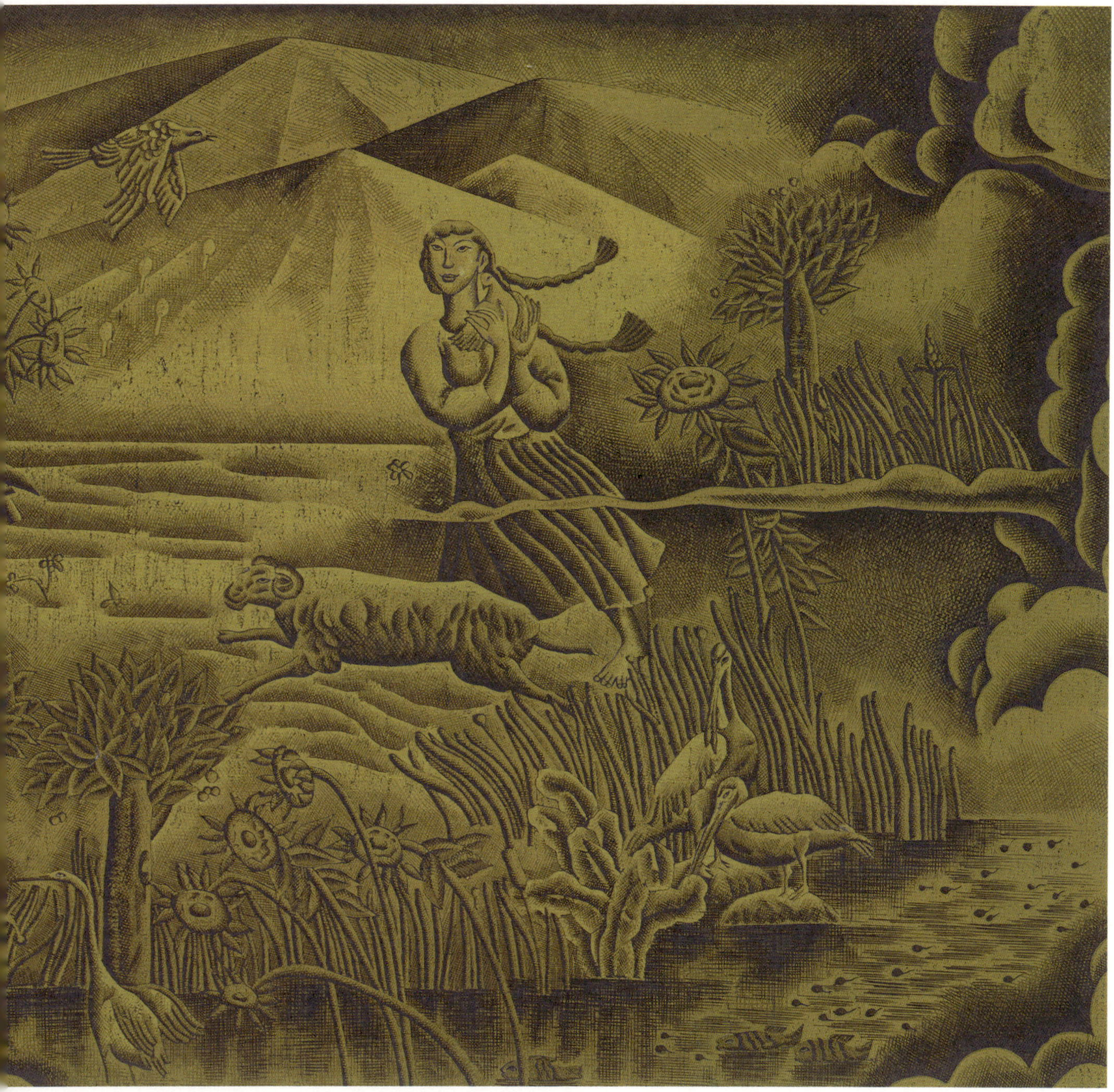

Wandering through Hundreds of Rivers
79cm × 59cm Woodcut 1998

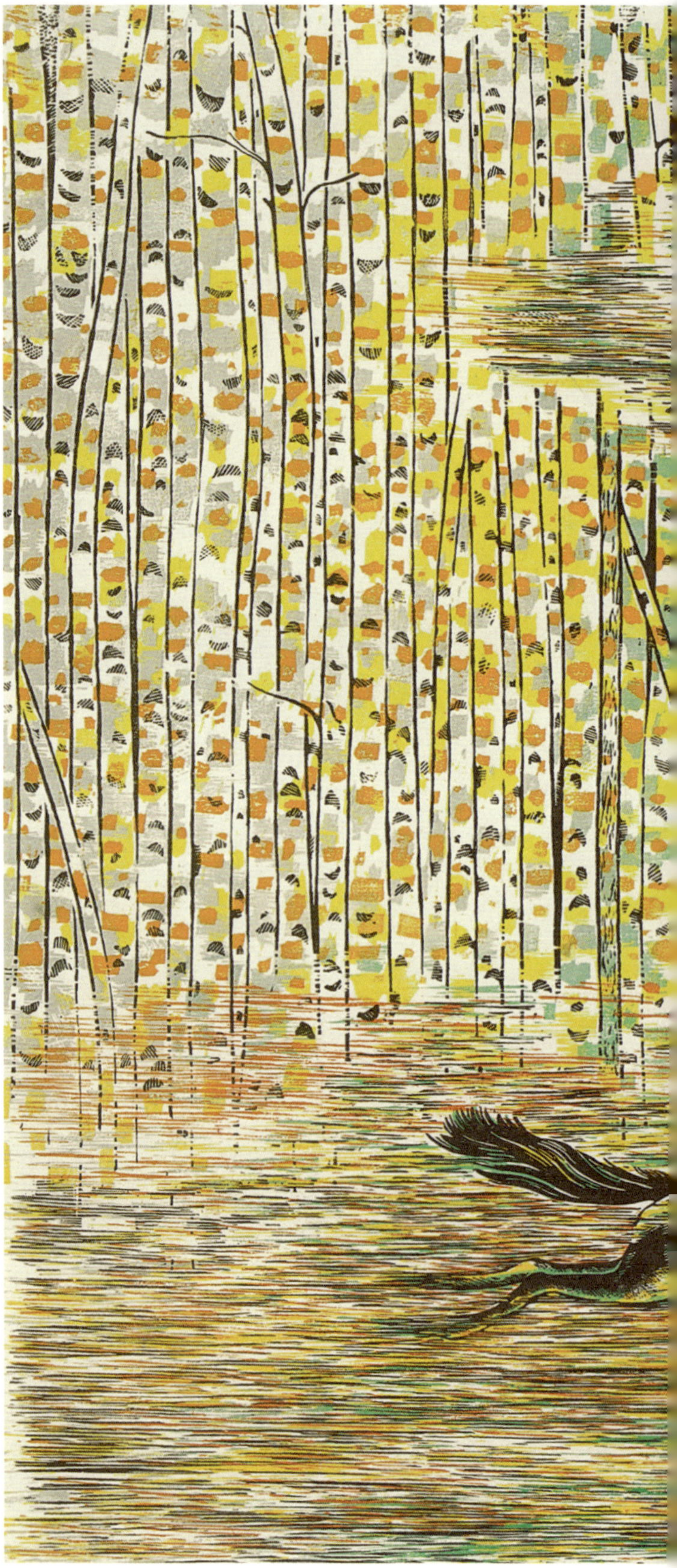

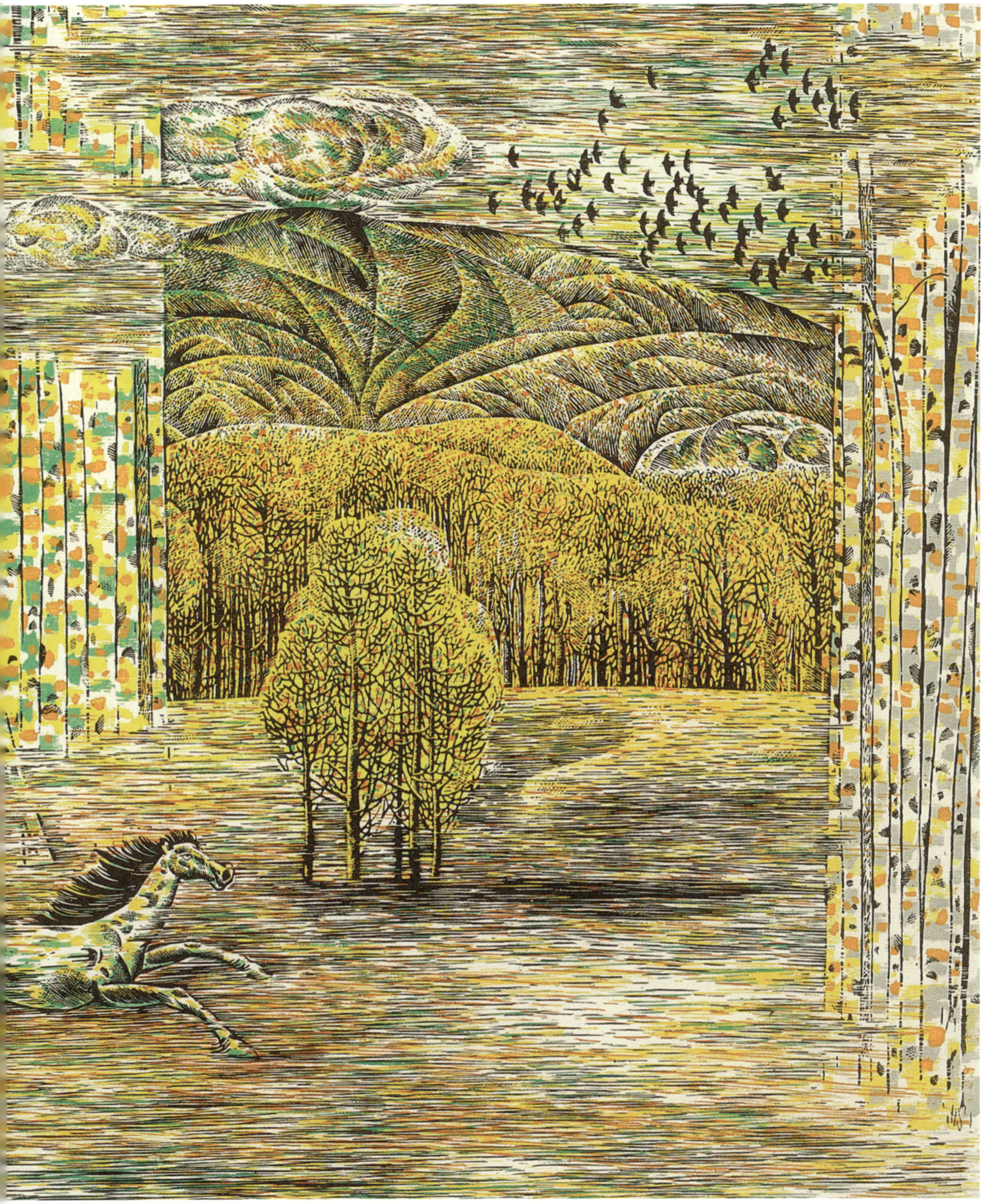

Happy Hometown 75cm × 61cm Woodcut 2002

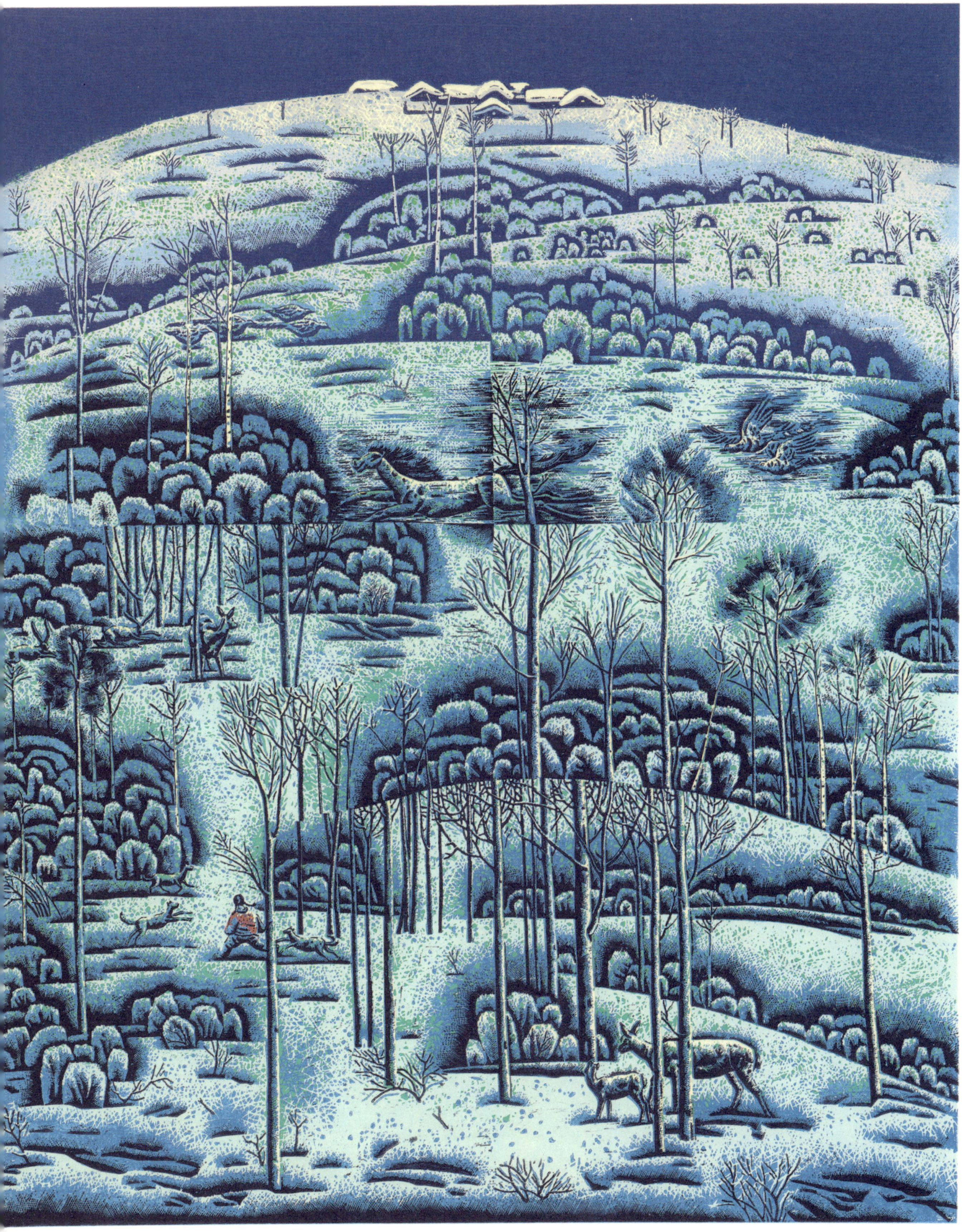

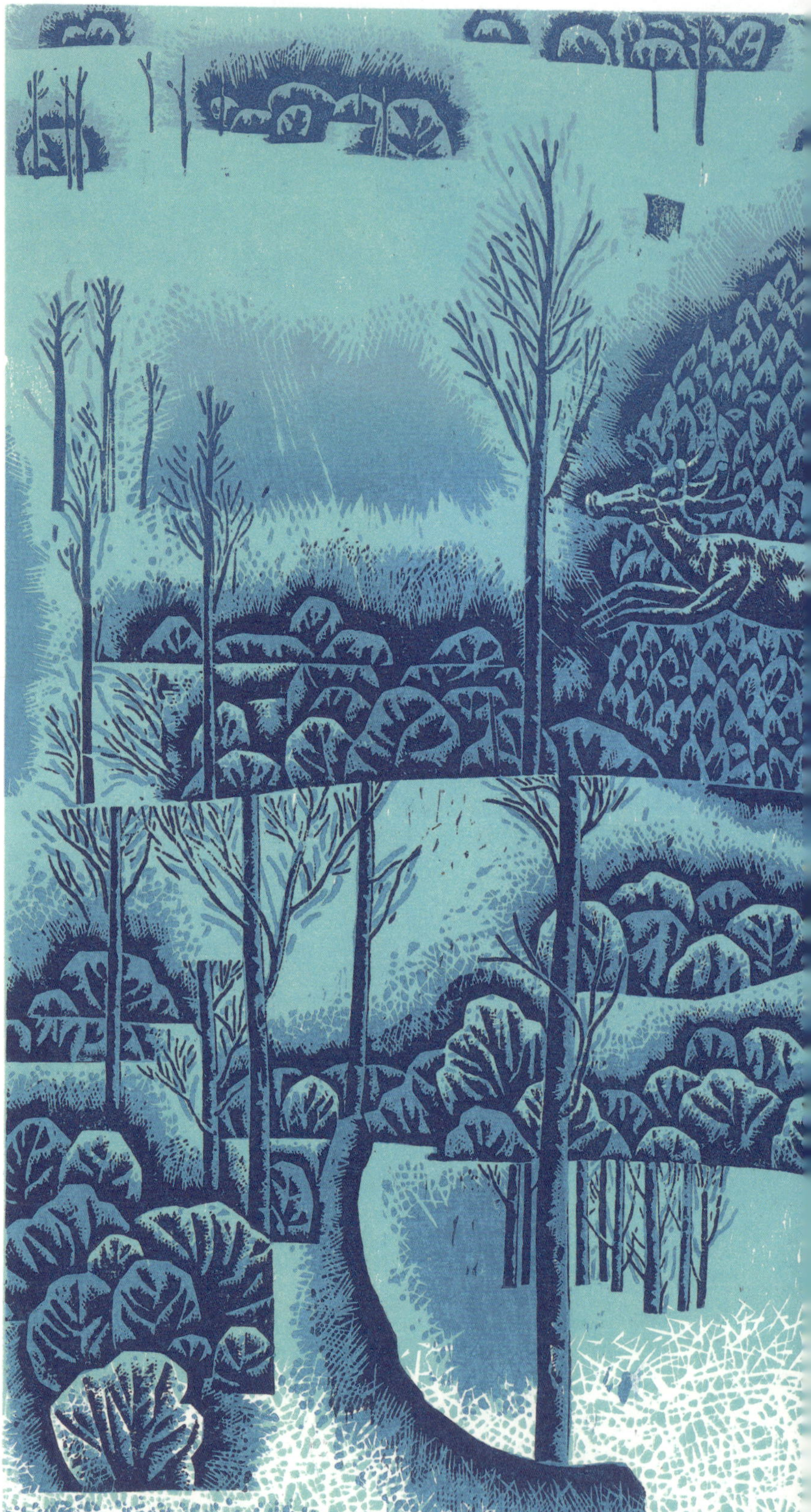

Years Passed like a Song
78cm x 56cm Woodcut 2001

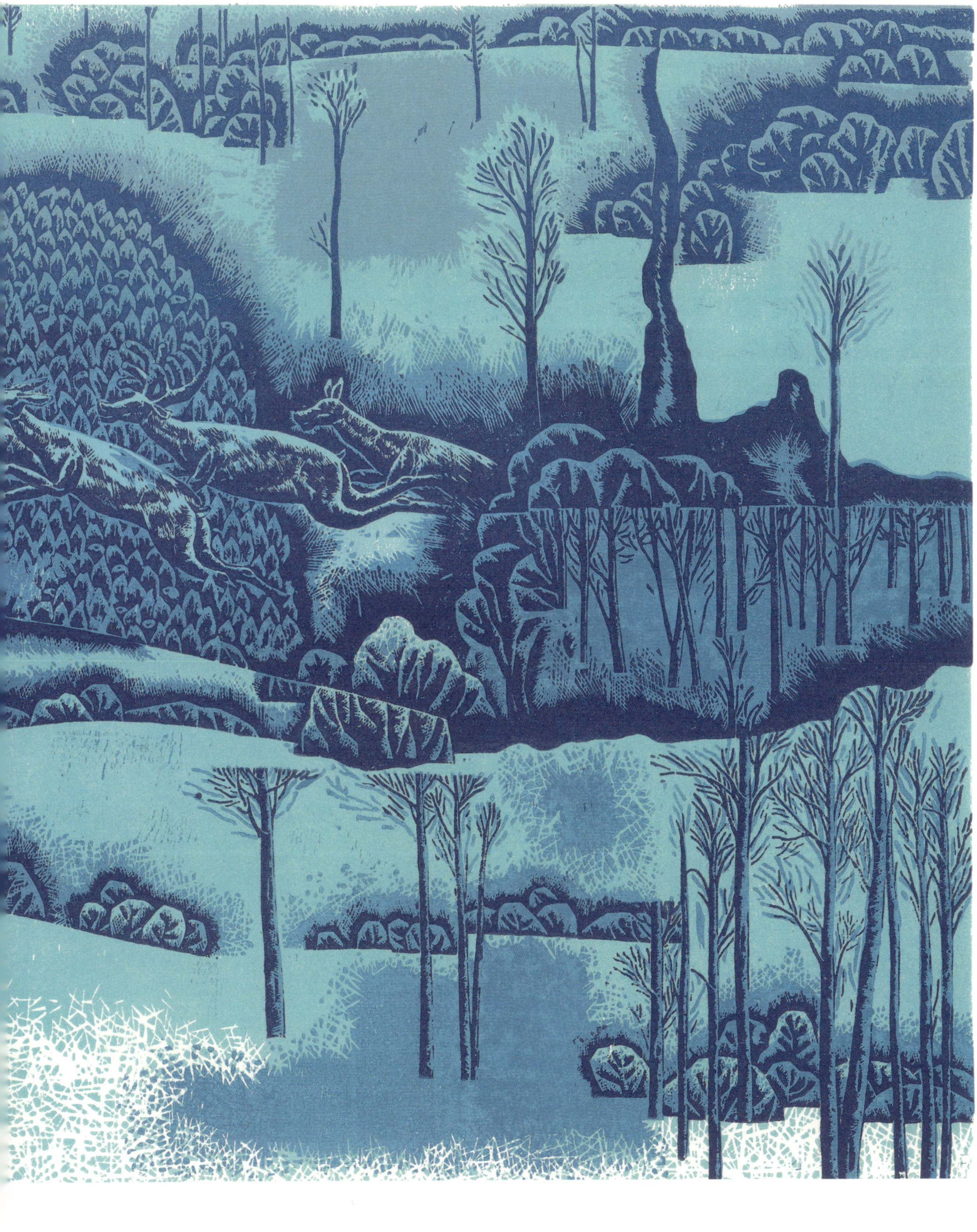

Undoubtedly, Beidahuang woodcut prints carry the genes of collectivism, with aesthetic empathy as their underlying tone. As I grew older and was more exposed to the complex outside world, I gradually realised that no matter how beautiful those paintings were back then, they were merely embellishments of life. There was no true power. The deer, rabbits and partridges, once running across the canvas under the azure sky, were all gone. Even we had changed; could art remain unchanged? In fact, many renowned artists have explicitly stated multiple times that Beidahuang Prints were decorative items with regional characteristics. For someone as passionate as myself, this was a devastating blow. However, deep down I understood that old experiences cannot guide new practices. If we keep following the methods taught by teachers at the workshop and we fail, it is not the teachers' fault.

I became obsessed with figuring out how to break away and find a new path. For quite a long time, I didn't even want to mention Beidahuang.

2.
Private Thoughts and Lu Xun

In 2004, I moved from the icy city of Harbin to Nanjing, one of the four furnaces of China, where I squeezed into a small office with six or seven other people. Fortunately, there was a desk for me. Coming from a farm, the environment didn't bother me too much; as long as there was a desk, I could paint.

I shifted away from creating large-scale colour woodcuts and turned to simpler woodcut sketches. Instead of depicting fantastical nursery rhymes, I began portraying people around me and writing about everyday life, distancing myself from the collective consciousness of the past and pursuing personal expression of individual thought. For example, I started with a simple circle drawn with a brush, aiming for the awkward beauty and simplicity of geometric shapes. The moon in the water resembled a small boat, so I added a man and a woman to it. With just a few strokes, a sentence naturally came to mind: 'Seen from afar, such a scene in life is beautiful, but when you get closer, you may find that it isn't true.' I immediately titled the work *Moon in the Water, Beautiful Picture* (2005) , arranging the characters like an inscription on traditional Chinese paintings.

The Private Thinker series consists of 100 small woodcuts in shades of grey or black, markedly different from my previous style. I felt I had found a new direction for my creativity. At that moment, I also formulated my own manifesto: while great minds ponder, ordinary people dare not discuss ideas. Therefore, we could only fantasise, imagine, dream, daydream – all done privately... Thus, private thinkers are not philosophical thinkers.*

* 'Private thinkers (私想者)' and 'philosophical thinkers (思想者)' are both pronounced *Sixiang Zhe* in Chinese.

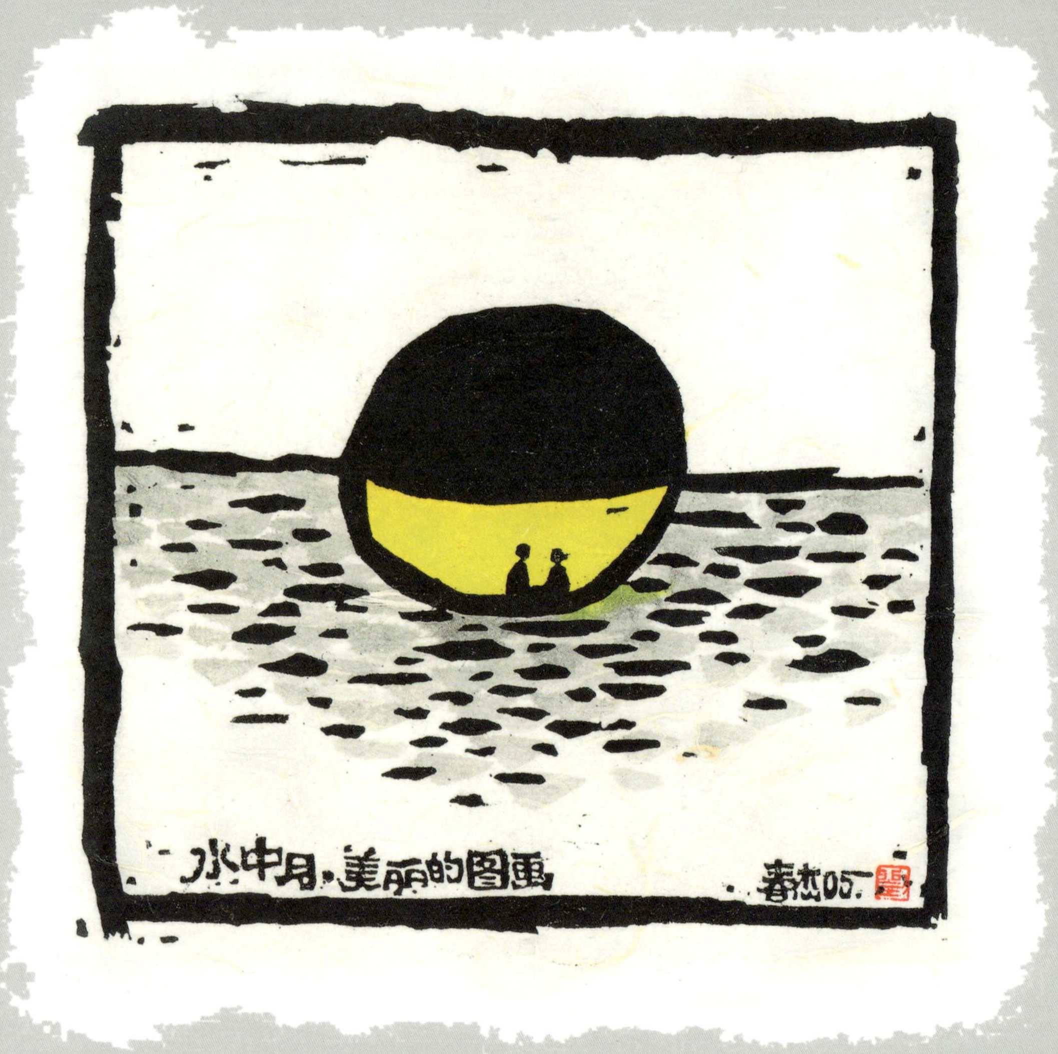

Moon in the Water, Beautiful Picture 15cm × 15cm Woodcut 2005

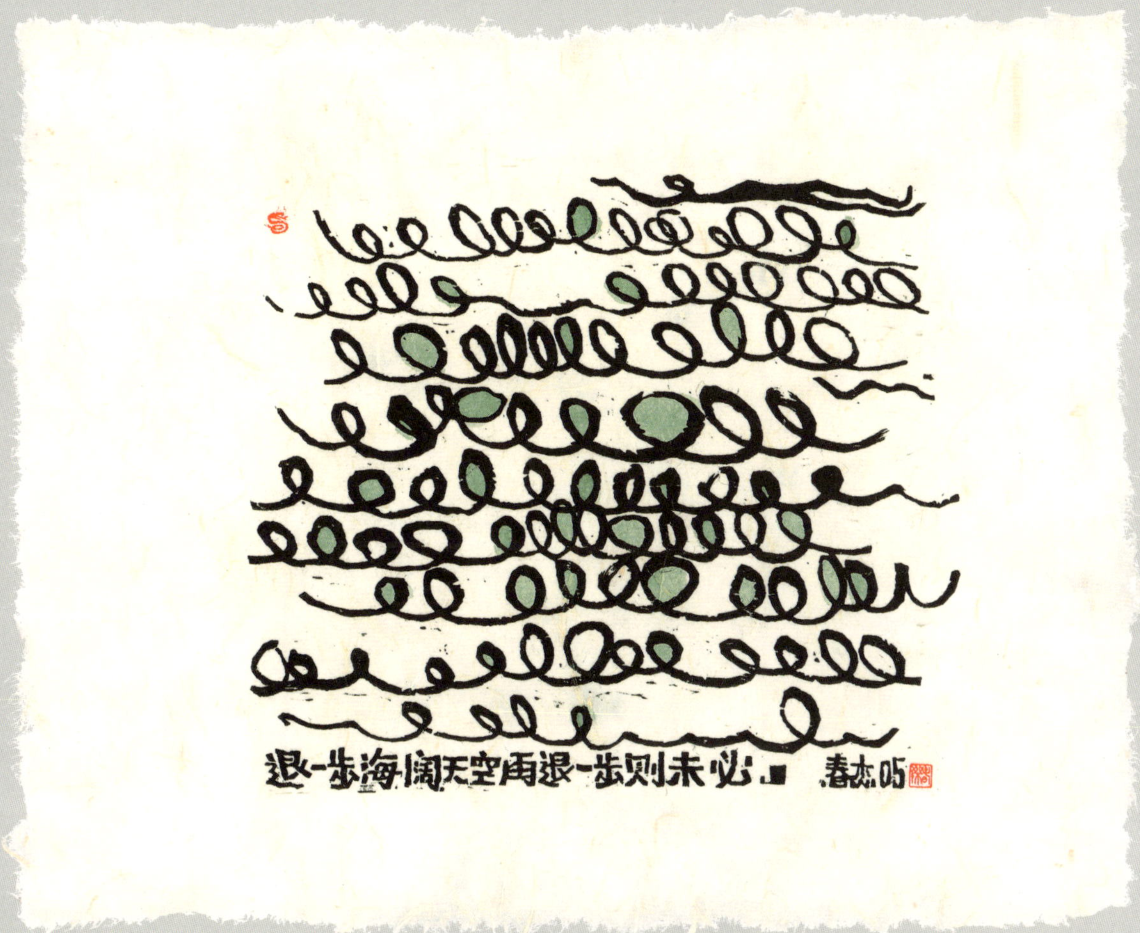

What If We Step Back Further 20cm × 16cm Woodcut 2005

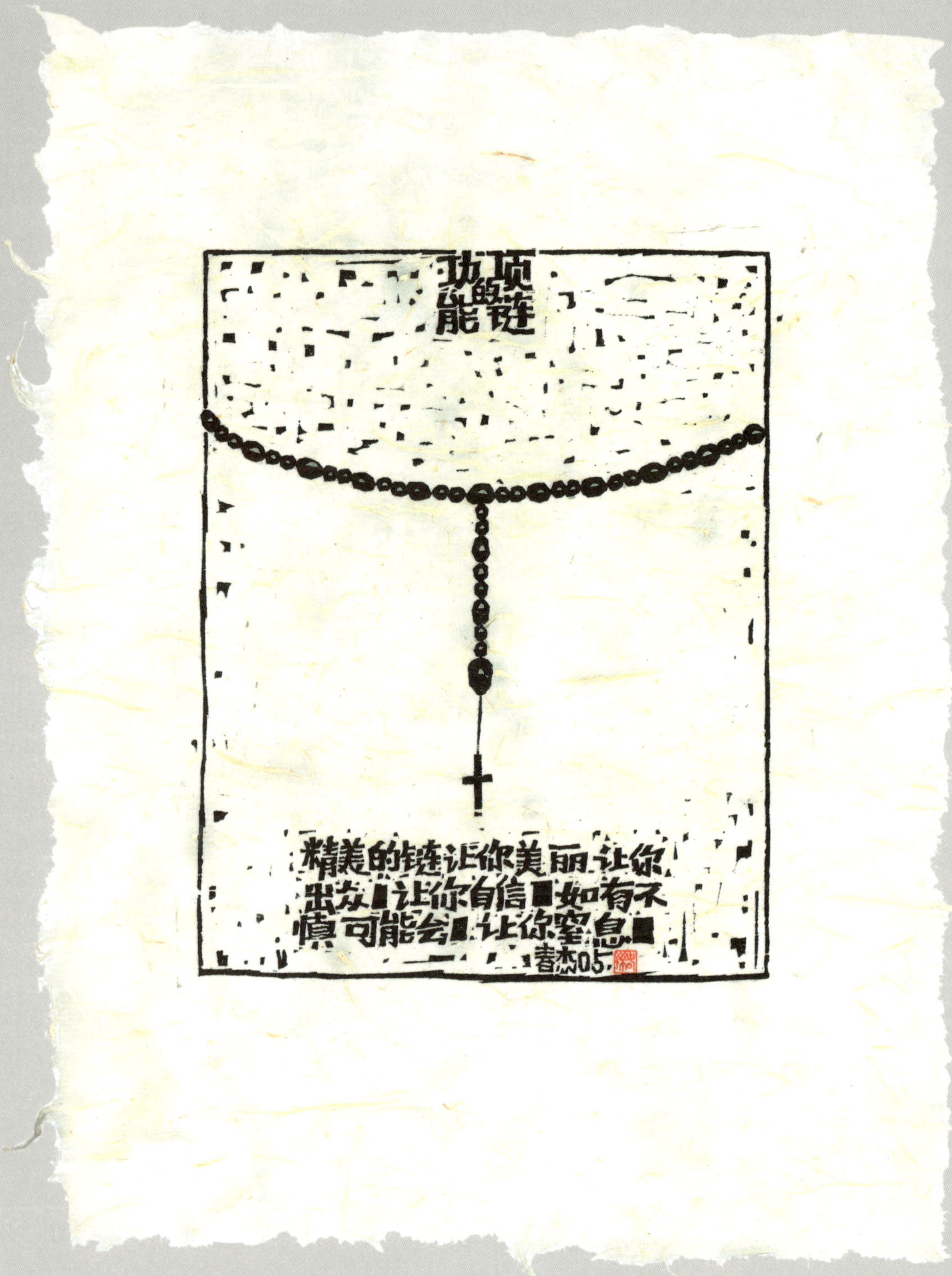

The Function of a Necklace 20cm × 16cm Woodcut 2005

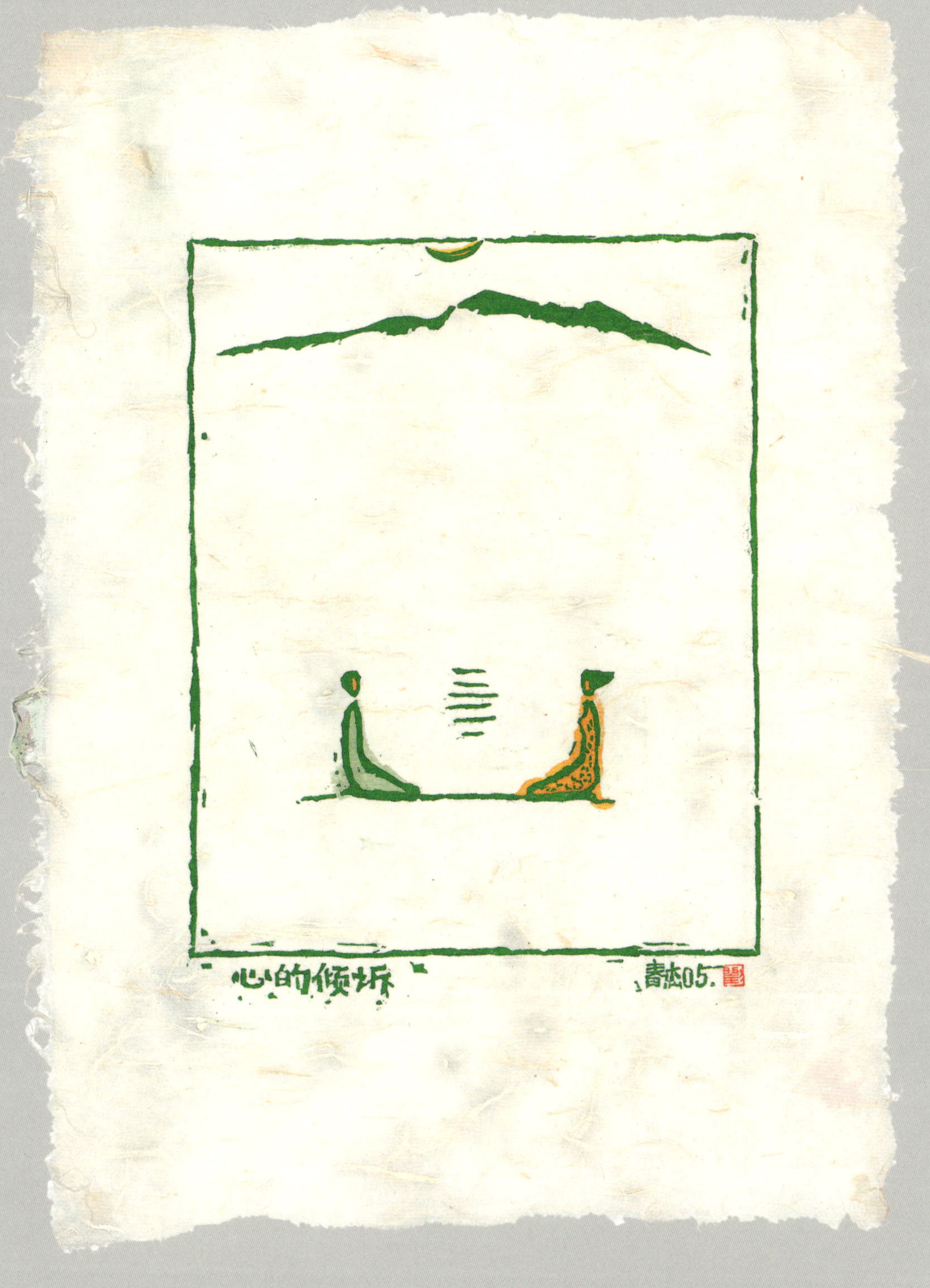

The Heart's Confession 20cm × 16cm Woodcut 2005

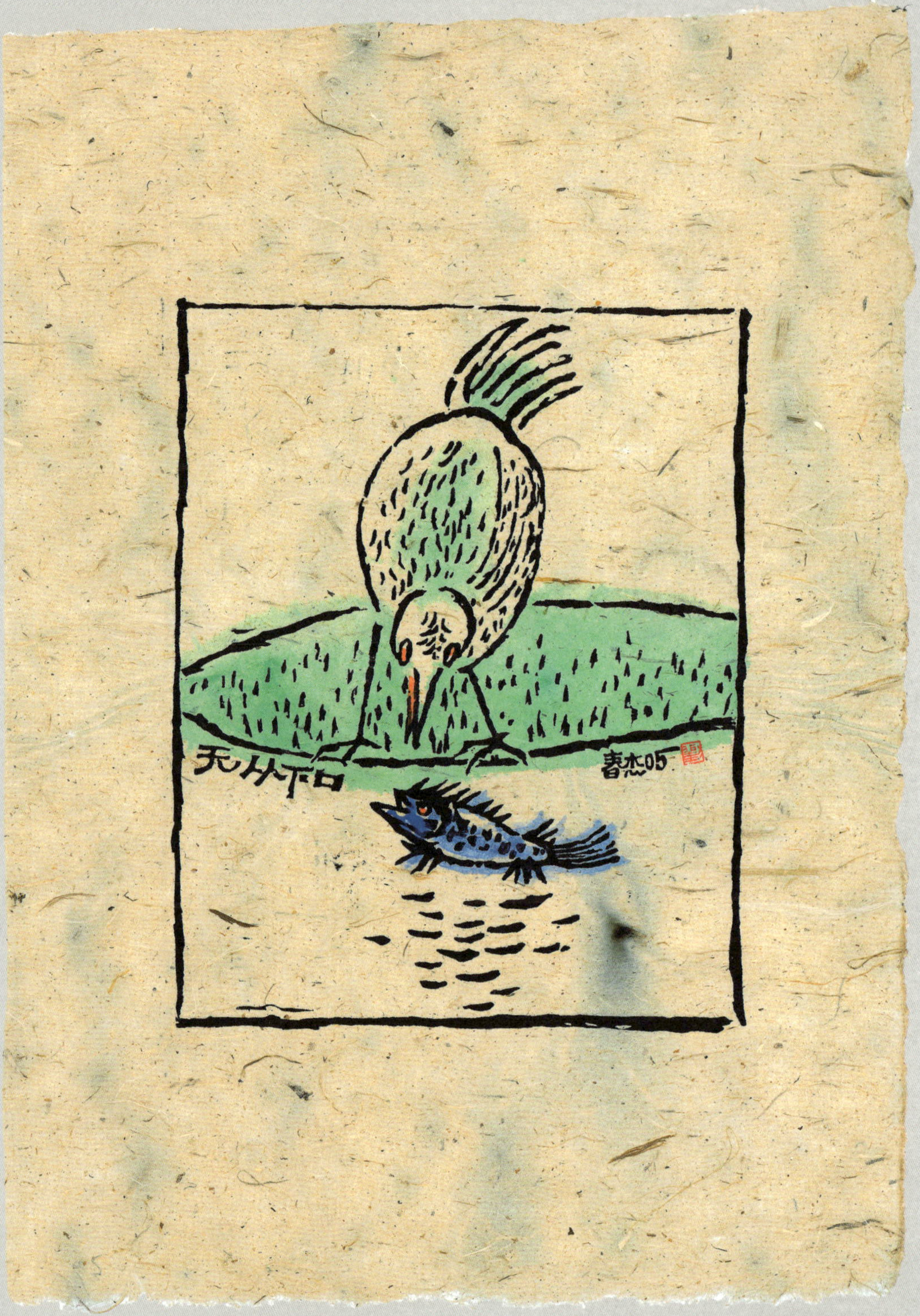

Can't Start Eating 20cm × 16cm Woodcut 2005

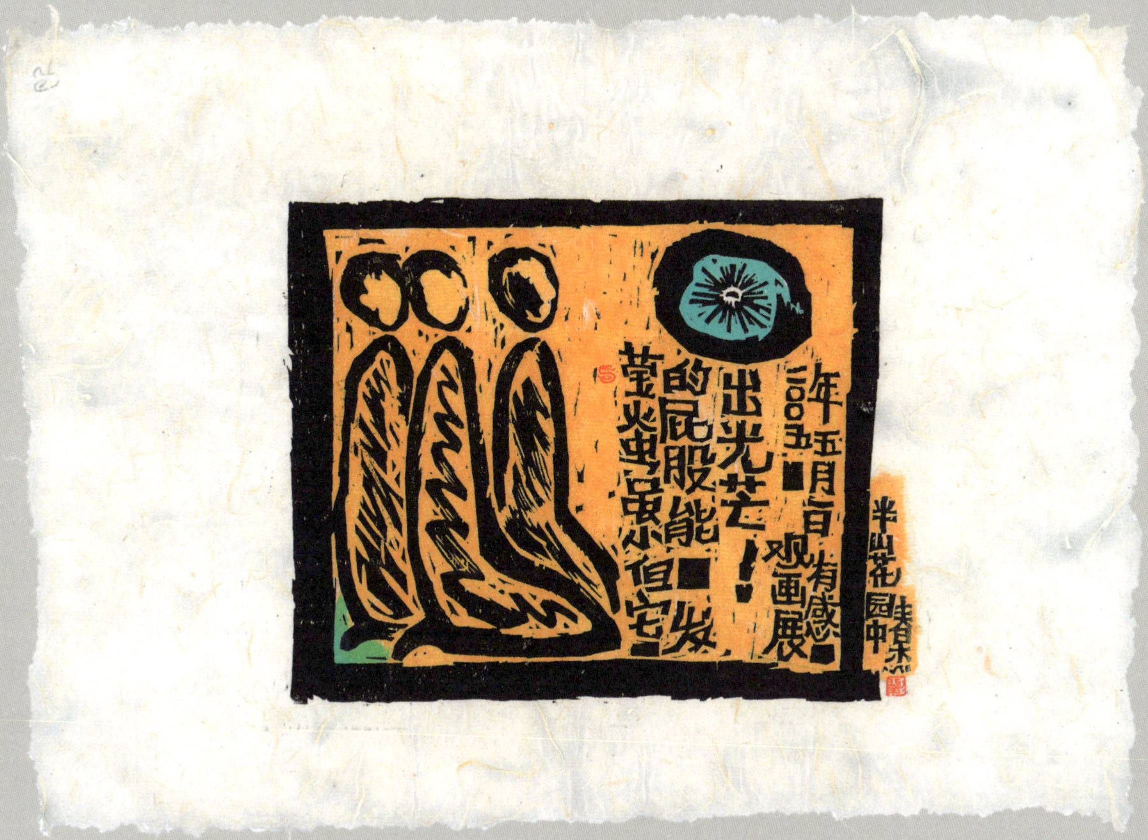

Ode to Fireflies 20cm × 16cm Woodcut 2005

——*The Private Thinker*

The World Is Noisy, Even the Heavens Are Noisy 28cm × 21.5cm Woodcut 2007

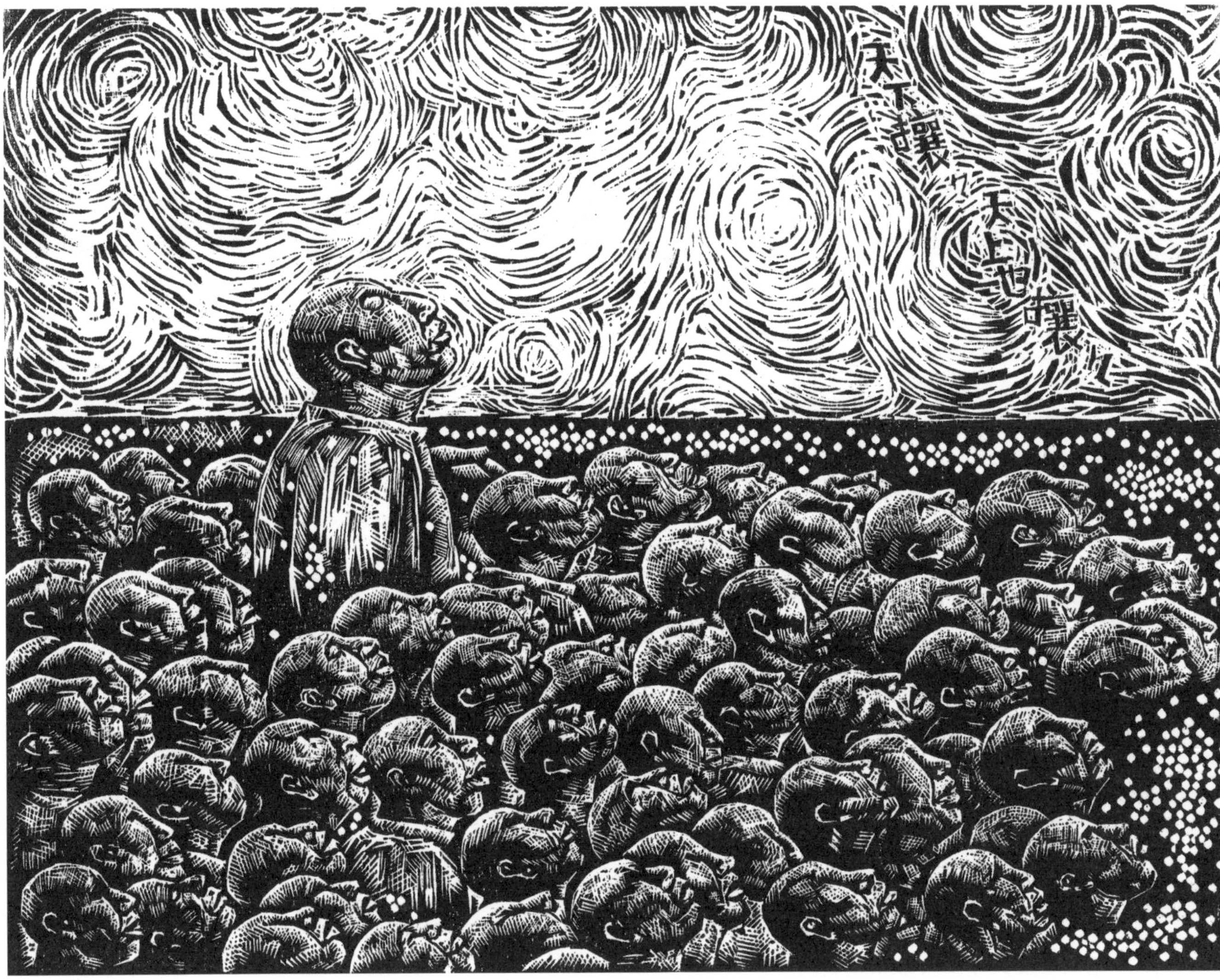
天下嚷々
天上也嚷々

Loudly Speaking Small Matters 28cm × 21.5cm Woodcut 2007

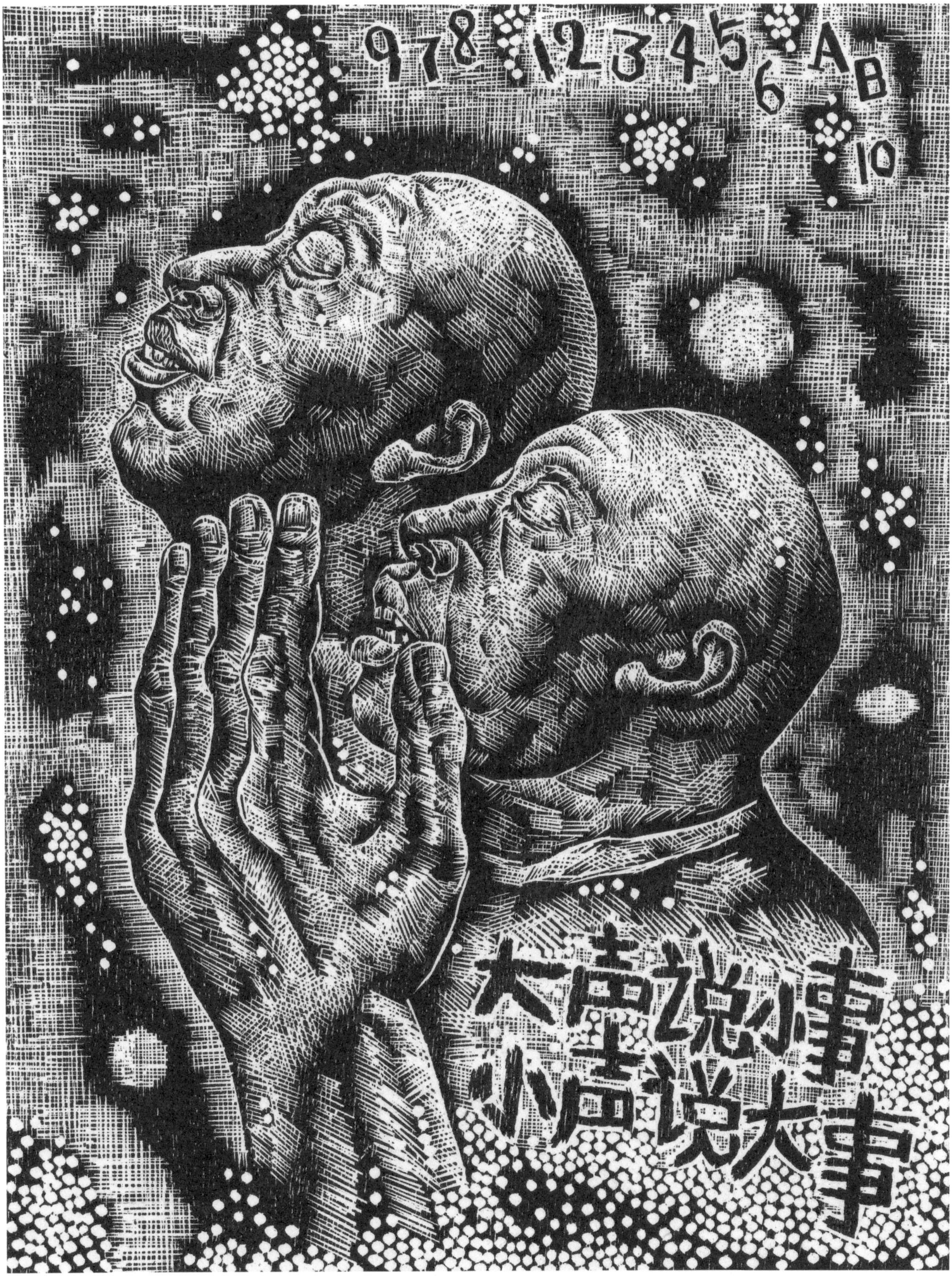
978 123456 AB 10
大声说小事
小声说大事

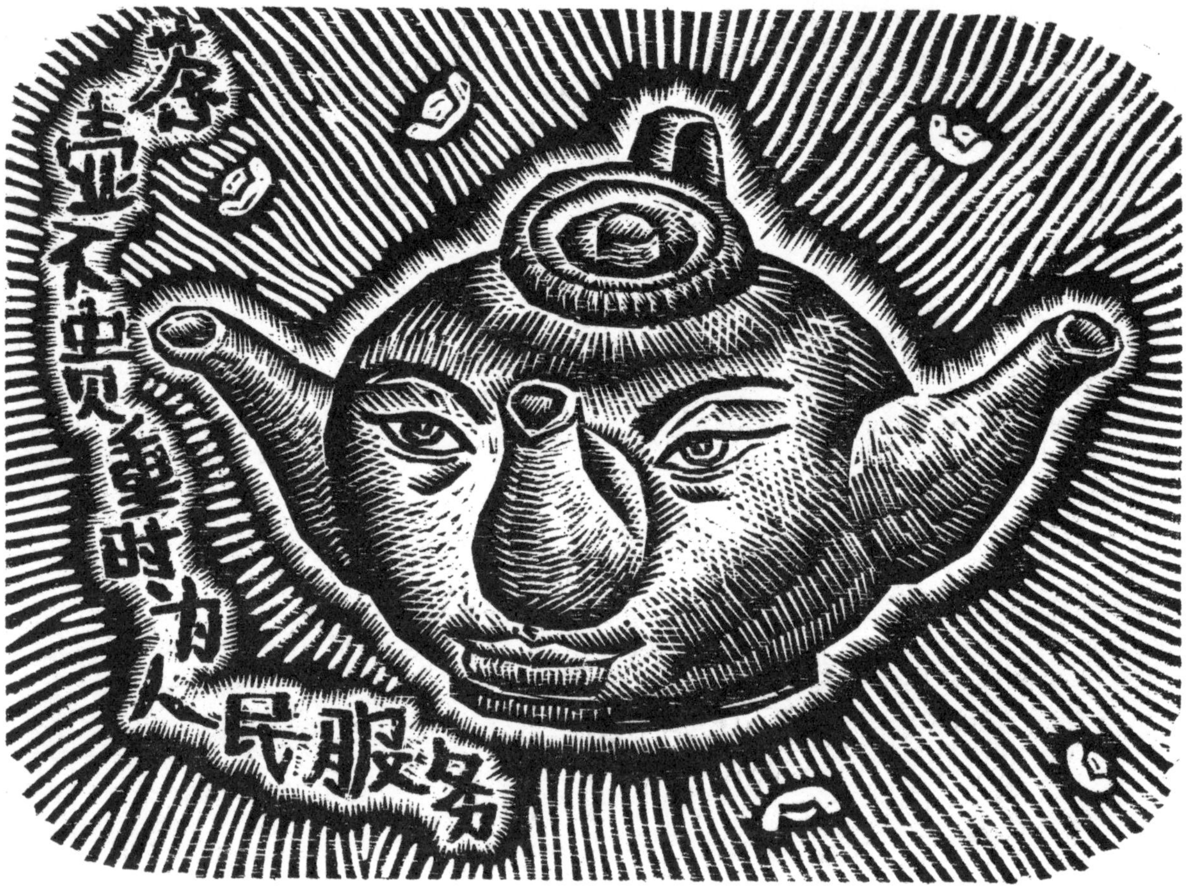

The Fellow with Many Mouths 28cm × 21.5cm Woodcut 2007

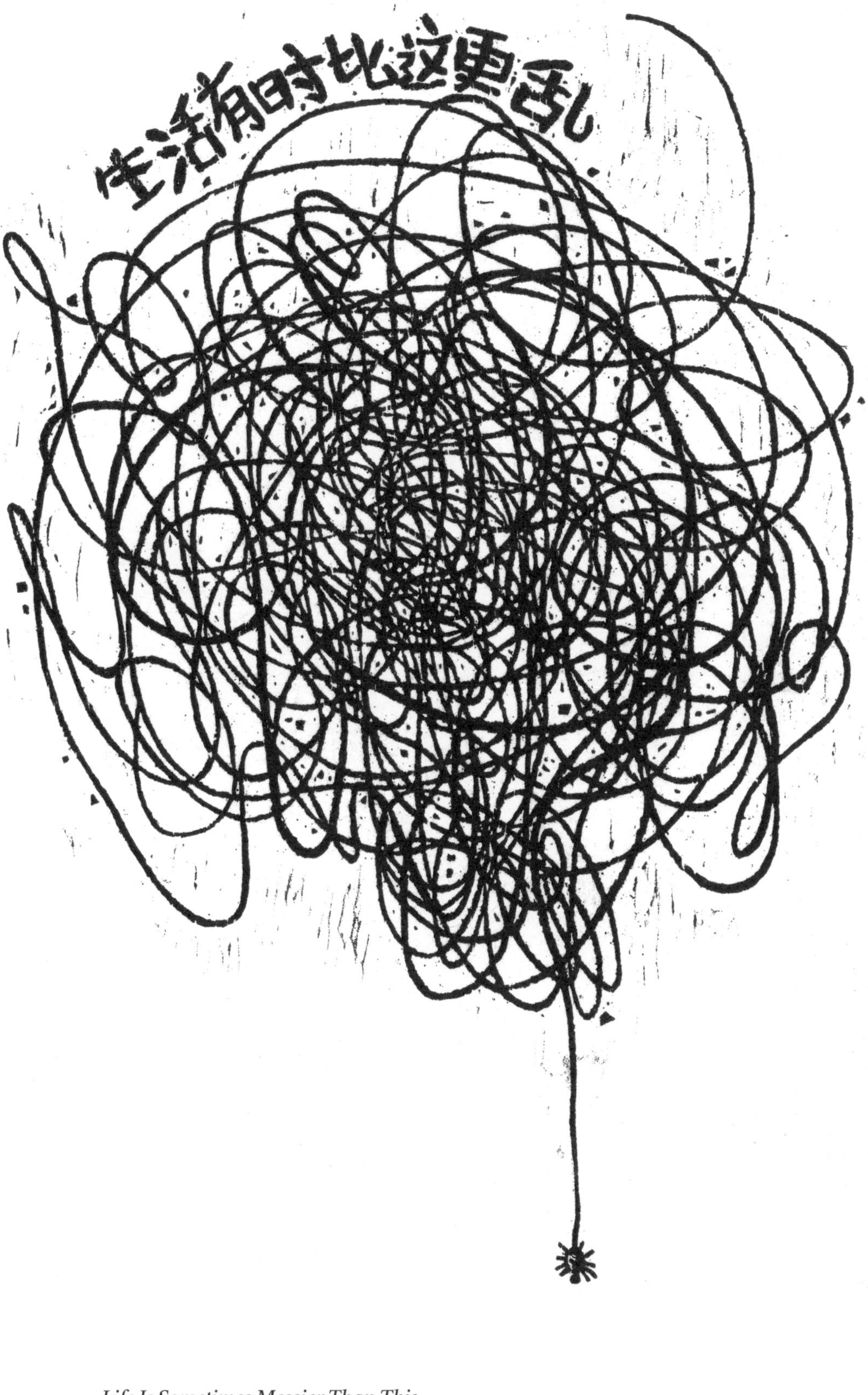

Life Is Sometimes Messier Than This
26cm × 19cm Woodcut 2007

Can't Stand the Heat 28cm × 21.5cm Woodcut 2007

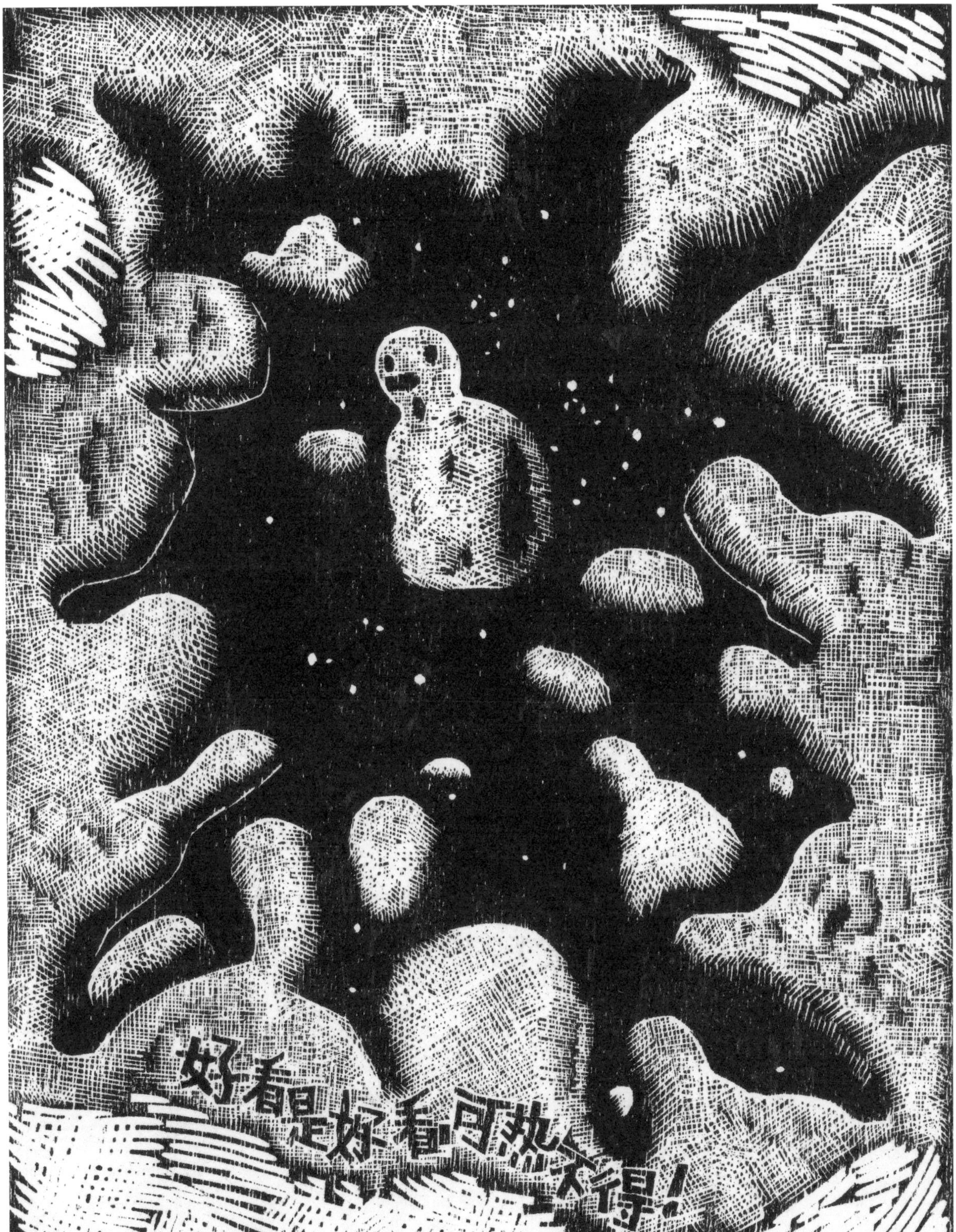
好看是好看可热人得!

He Said It So Well   28cm × 21.5cm   Woodcut   2007

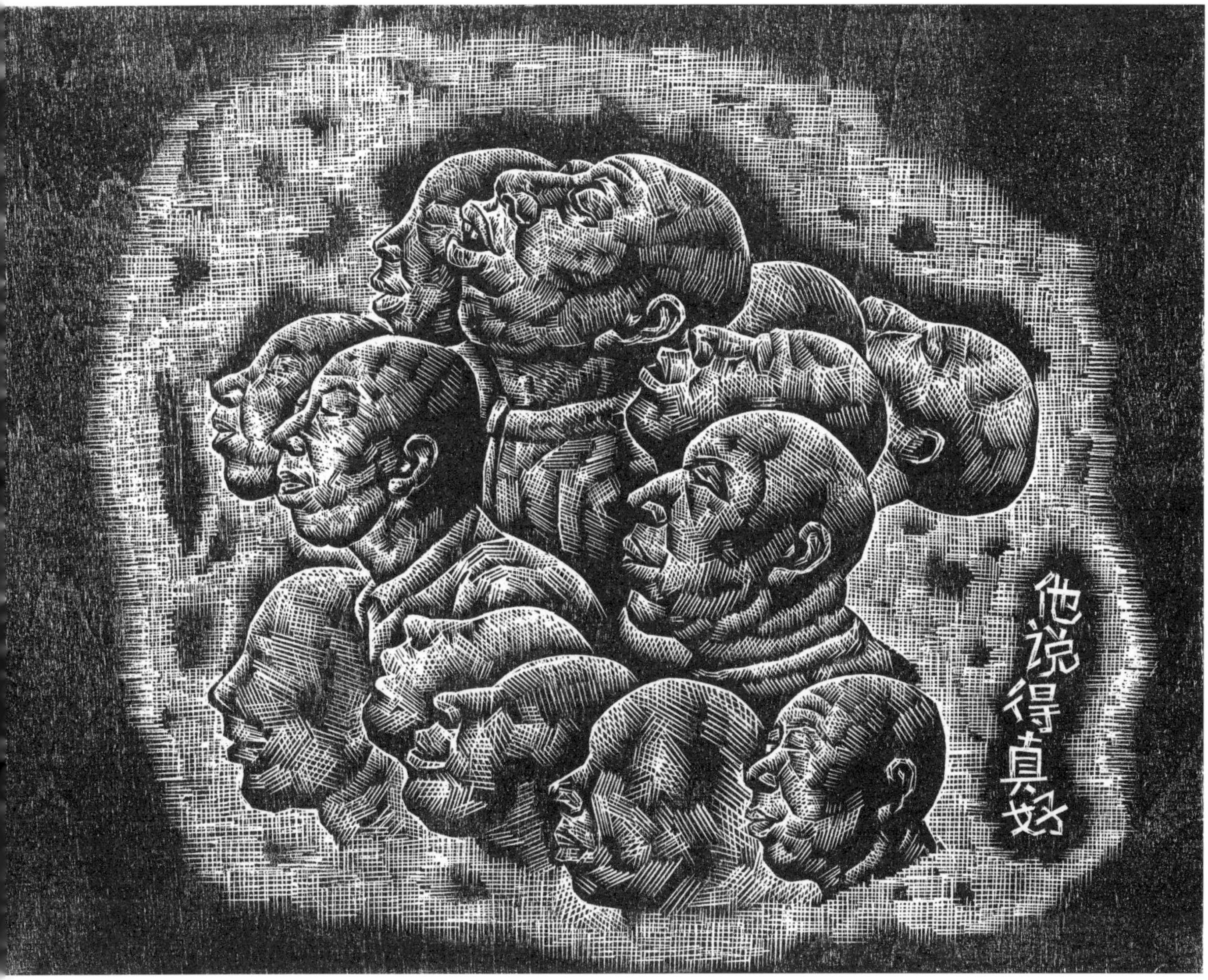
他说得真好

Truly Popular 28cm × 21.5cm Woodcut 2007

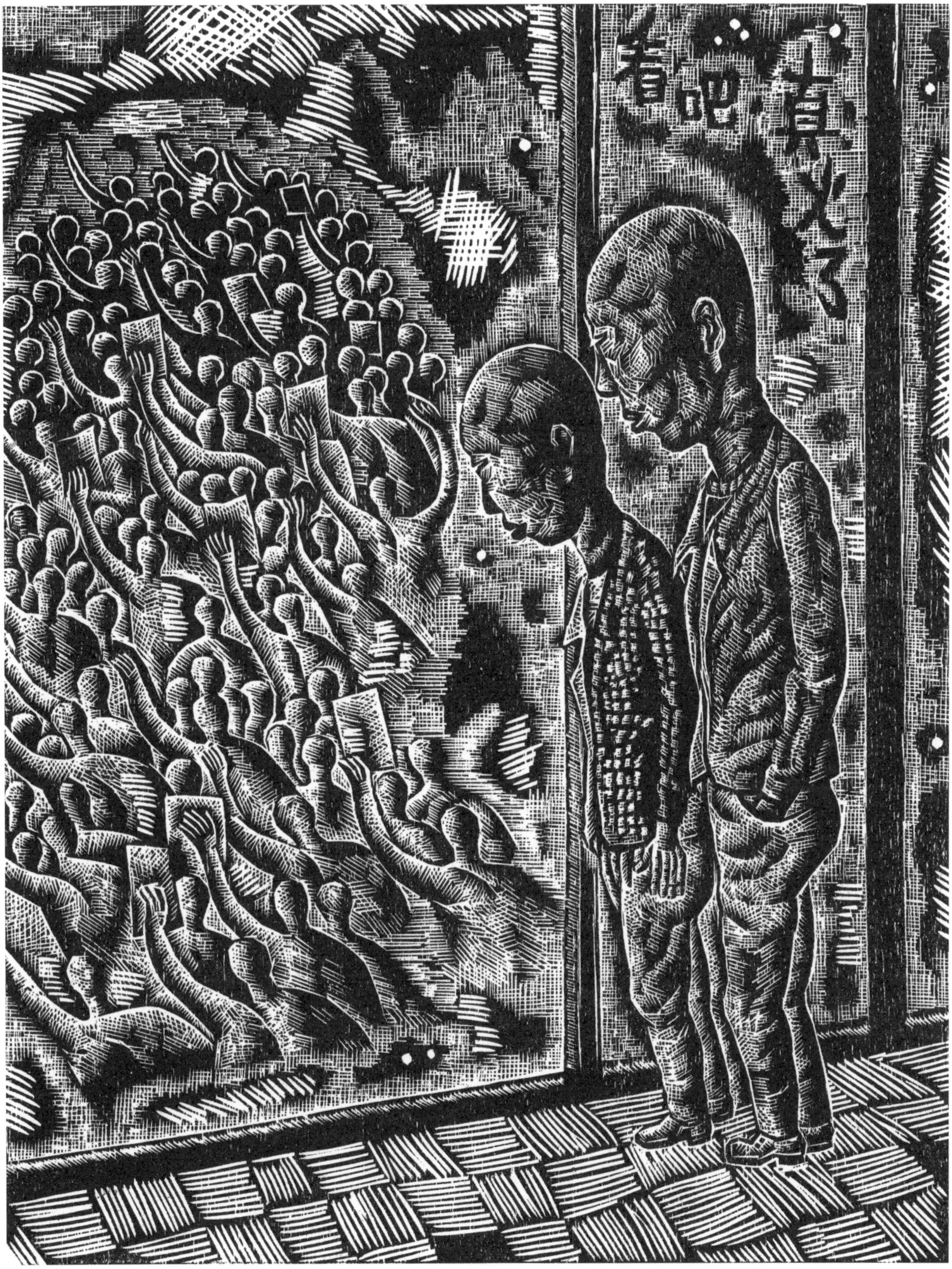
看吧·真火了

On and Off the Stage 28cm × 21.5cm Woodcut 2007

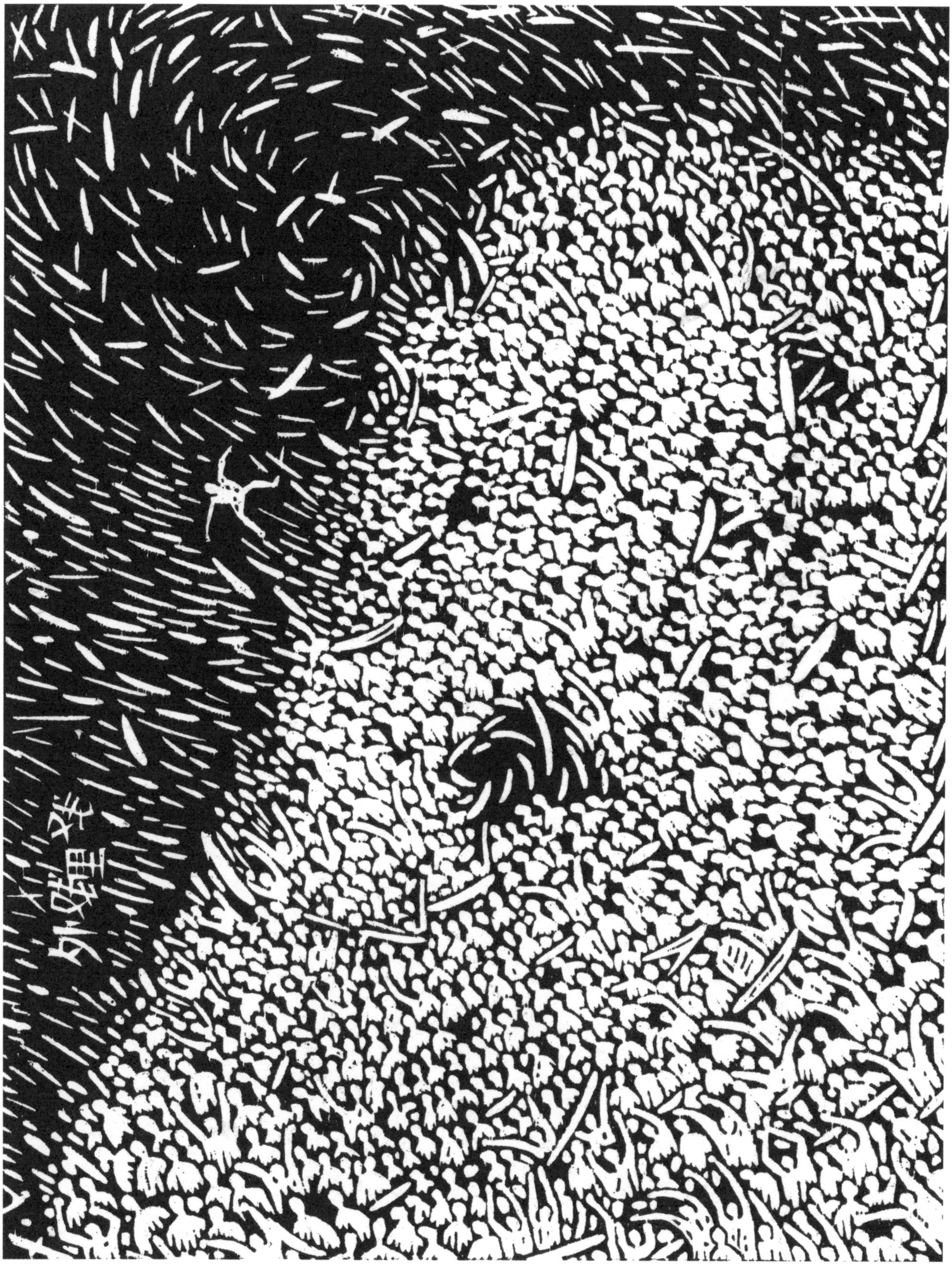

Lu Xun (1881–1936) was a renowned Chinese writer, educator and democratic fighter, and is considered as one of the founding figures of modern Chinese literature. He made significant contributions to literature, literary criticism, historical research, translation and art theory, earning him the title of 'the most widely known writer of the 20th century in East Asia'. Despite living for only 56 years, he was also a predecessor for Chinese woodcut art, and it was through his advocacy and support that traditional woodcut art experienced a revival.

There are countless art works about Lu Xun, with tens of thousands of prints depicting him. However, no printmaker has yet used woodcut combined with text to depict his life, which presented me with an opportunity. I portrayed Lu Xun as proactive, nihilistic, just, eerie and complex, inviting the great figure to merge with the cycles of time. I deconstructed the idolised Lu Xun, traversing the myriad mazes surrounding him, reconstructing a 'man' stepping down from the pedestal. I placed him back among his neighbours, bringing him back to everyday life. Lu Xun observed reality with his black eyes, confronting darkness and enlightening the masses. He refused to yield, hoping to build ideals in ruins, seeking the future where there seemed to be no way out. I used large black and white blocks to portray him, shaping numerous new images of Lu Xun with laughter and anger, nihilism and positivity. Woodcut interweaves with his dialogues, and text serves as a structure, enriching the composition of black, white and grey. Sharp knives break through stable order, with bold, free-spirited knife marks filled with passion, resonating with Lu Xun's novel *Call to Arms* (1922).

I leaned on him, carrying my personal thoughts and using his mouth to speak my words. Lu Xun evolved from an idol into my personal self-portrait, diverse, humorous and playful; he became another spiritual wellspring for me.

——— *Lu Xun*

The Skeptic 32cm × 26cm Original Woodcut 2012

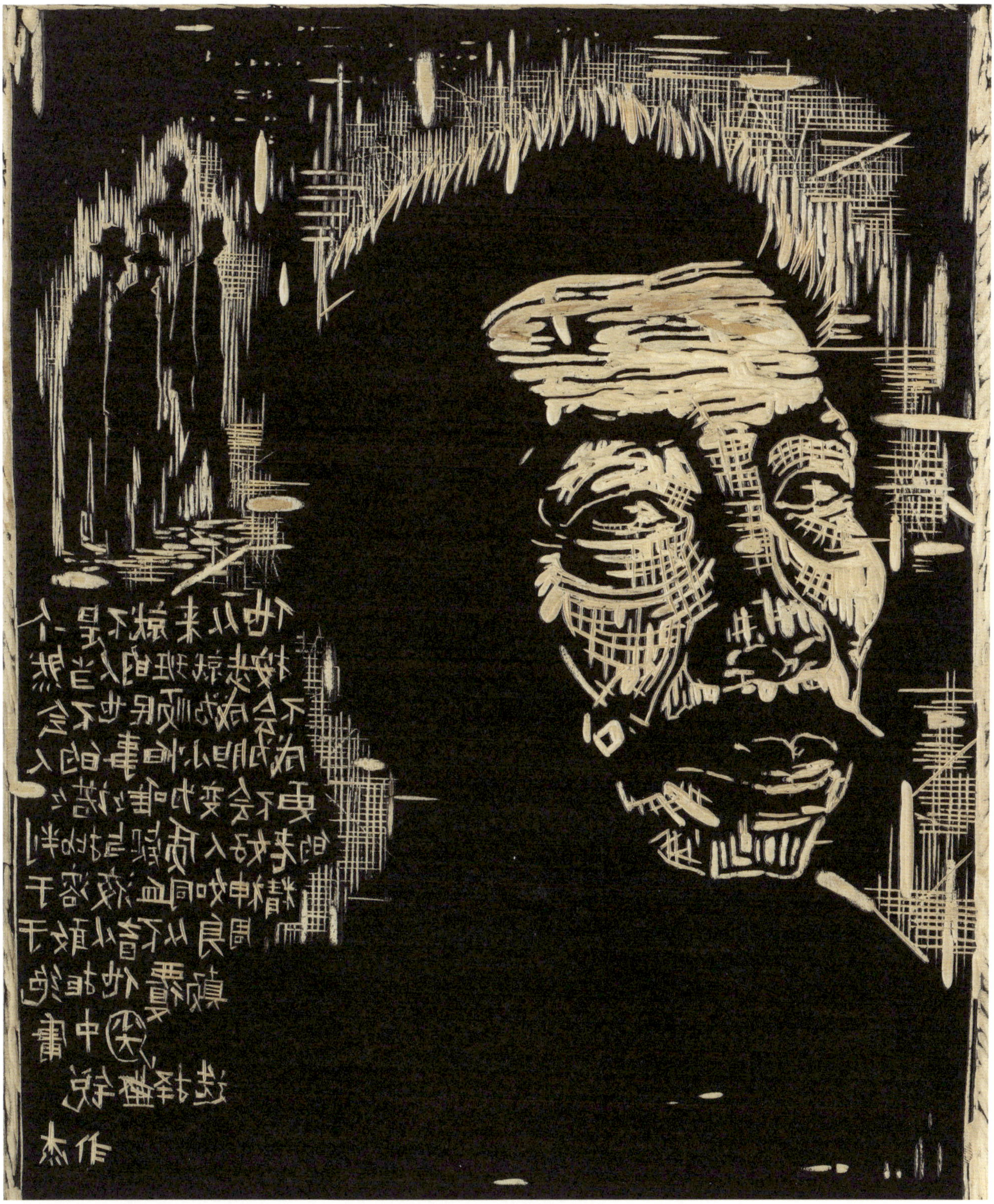
他从来就不是一个
按步就班的人当然
不会成为顺民也不会
成为胆小怕事的人
更不会变为唯唯诺诺
的老好人质疑与批判
精神如同血液溶于
周身以不言以敢于
颠覆他拒绝
中庸
选择尖锐
杰作

The Pain of Orphans and Widows 26cm × 32cm Original Woodcut 2012

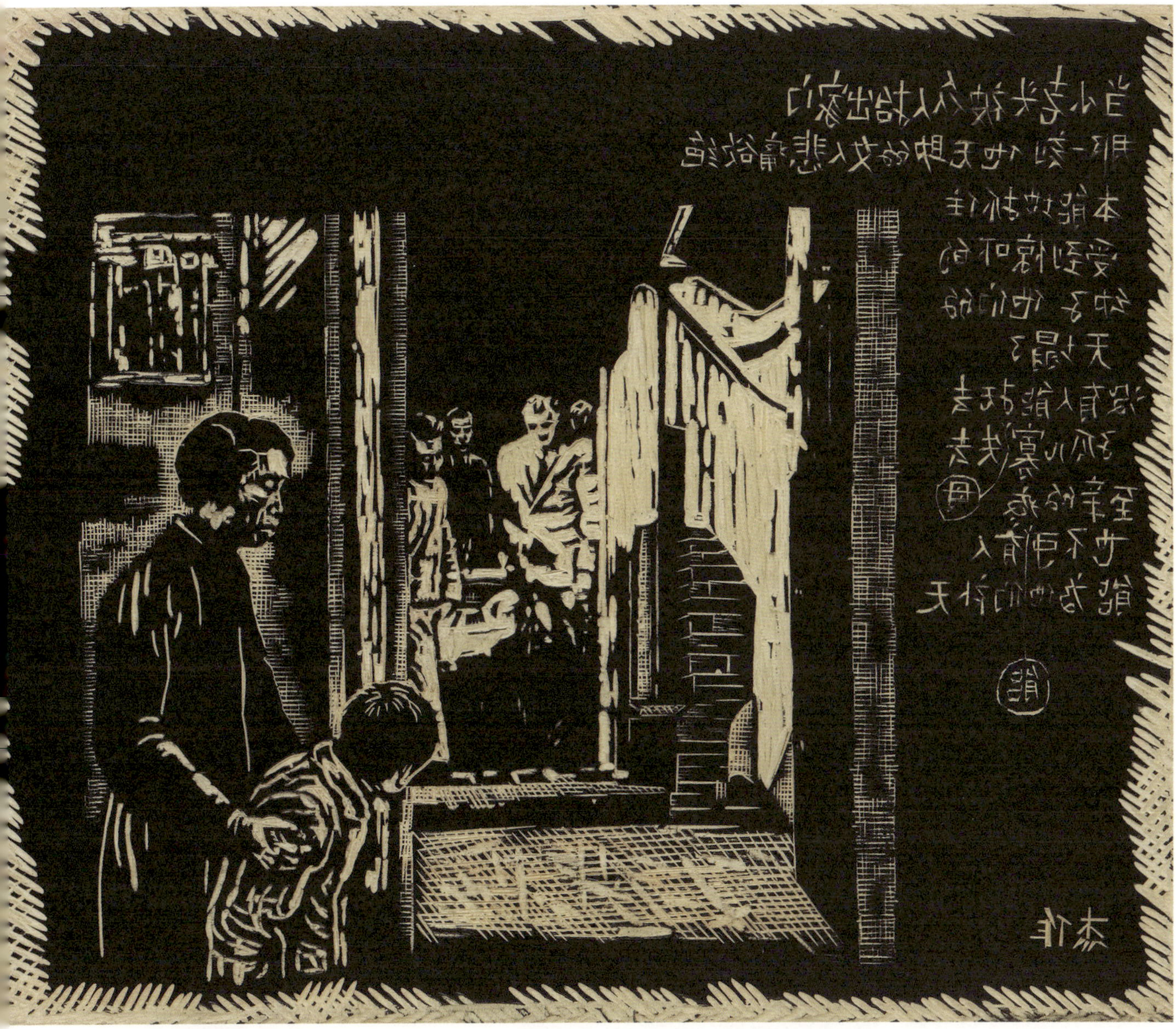

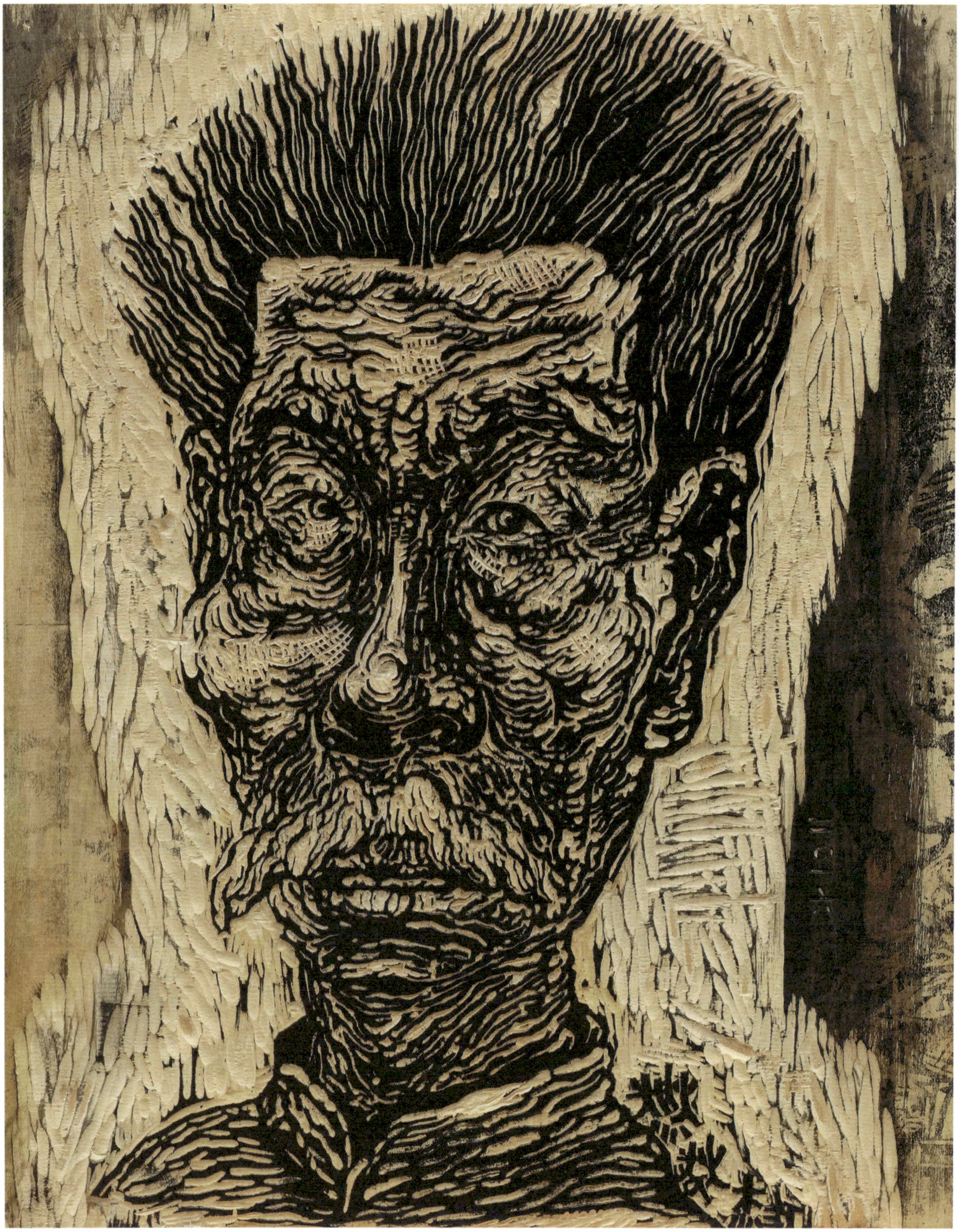

Portrait 1 39.2cm × 49cm Original Woodcut 2016

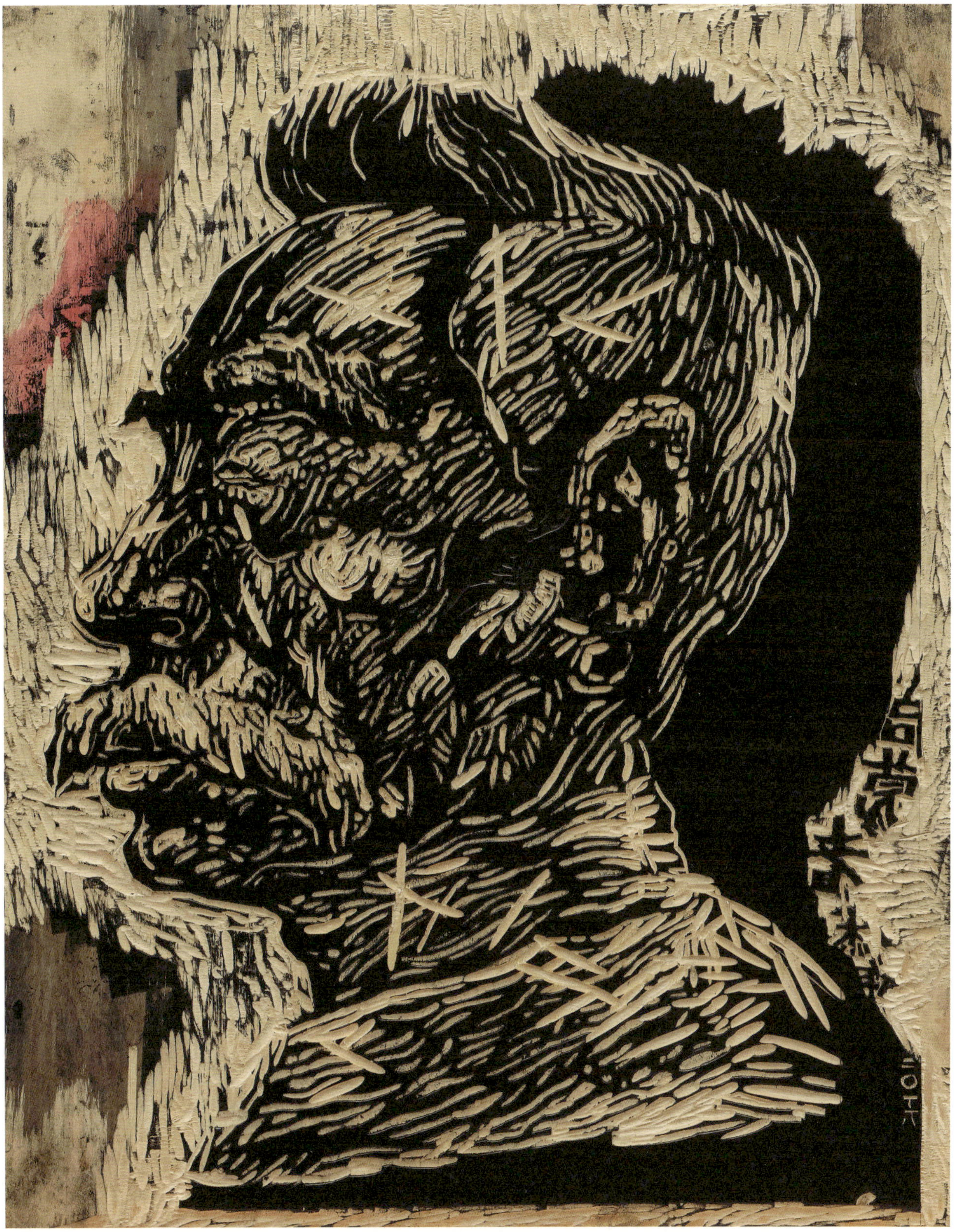

Portrait 2 39.2cm × 49cm Original Woodcut 2016

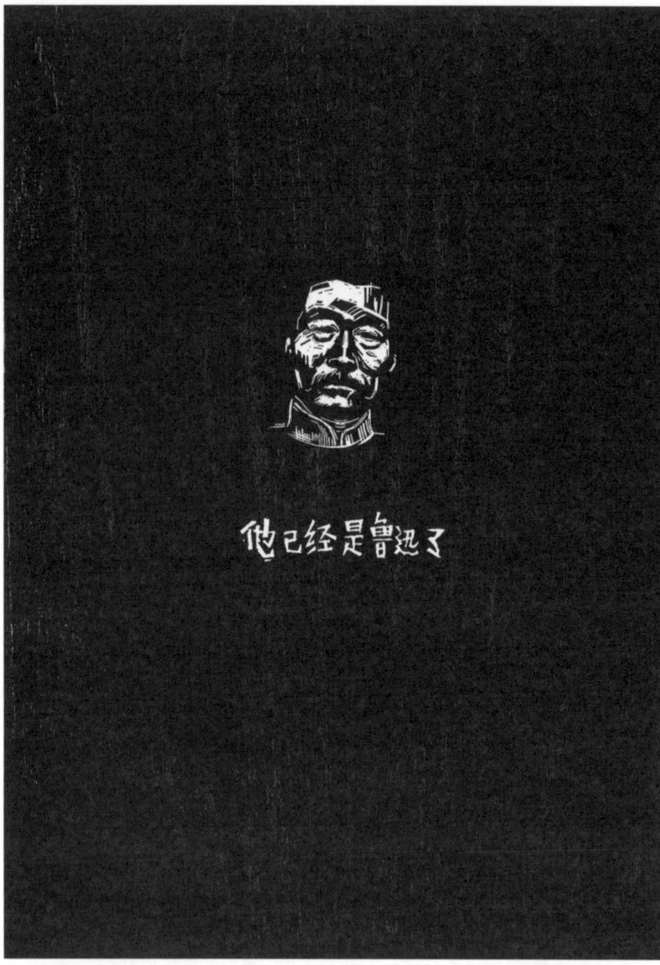
他已经是鲁迅了

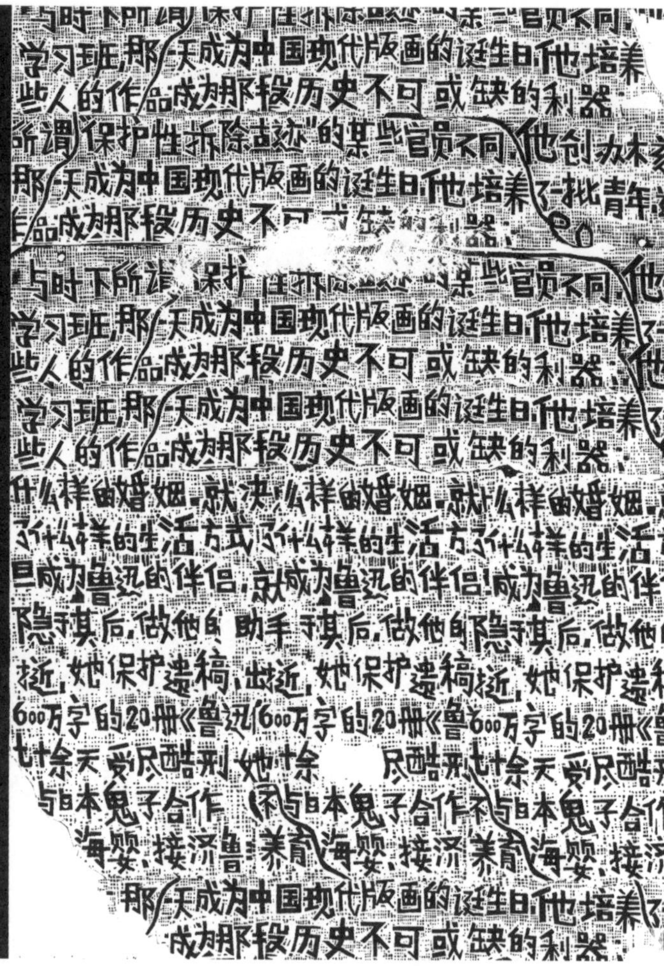
学习班，那一天成为中国现代版画的诞生日，他培养
些人的作品成为那段历史不可或缺的利器
所谓"保护性拆除古迹"的某些官员不同，他创办木刻
那一天成为中国现代版画的诞生日，他培养了一批青年
什么样的婚姻，就决什么样的婚姻，就什么样的婚姻
旦成为鲁迅的伴侣，就成为鲁迅的伴侣，成为鲁迅的伴侣
她保护遗稿，出逝，她保护遗稿，逝，她保护遗稿
600万字的20册《鲁迅600万字的20册《鲁600万字的20册《鲁
与日本鬼子合作，不与日本鬼子合作，不与日本鬼子合作
海婴，接济鲁，养育海婴，接济养育海婴，接济
成为那段历史不可或缺的利器

3.
Zen Mountain and Sacred Water

The supple rice paper. The aged ink. Ink entwining with the brush, the brush following the ink, all harmonised by water; dryness longs for moisture, giving birth to profound paintings. Chinese rice paper, brushes and ink are all made from extraordinarily unique materials, undergoing indescribable transformations upon meeting water, displaying a myriad of forms.

Without long-term practice and adaptation, it's not easy to master the ink-and-wash technique. Let's talk about water: too much of it and the ink runs wild, immediately staining all the white spaces, catching you off guard; too little and the brush won't move smoothly, resulting in a dryness and lack of charm. And here's the strange part: the appearance of a piece when it is completely dry can be vastly different from when it is wet. Chinese ink-wash art is like magic – mysterious and ever-changing, gentle and nourishing. Fortunately, a woodcut artist has a natural sensitivity to materials and a strong control over techniques. I love chaos, haze, vastness, mistiness, illusion and grandeur. Compared to woodcut art, my coloured ink-wash paintings do not seek realism or beauty, discarding form and narrative. Just like birds chirping, it doesn't matter what they're singing, as long as it sounds good. Shedding worldly appearances, boundless like heaven and earth, right and wrong become ambiguous; there is nothing, yet everything, with just freewheeling imagination encompassing all. The outcome is unpredictable, only to be encountered but not sought after. With the oldest tools – brushes, ink, rice paper – new images expand.

I painstakingly created the Zen Mountain and Sacred Water series with coloured ink, layering dyes, shading and texturing, again and again, layer upon layer, like a visual diary. The colours mottled, the ink overlapped – the effect looked like an electrocardiogram – sometimes even tearing the rice paper. Over time, I have stepped beyond where traditional coloured-ink painting stops. Tearing up the paintings (previously only done to unsatisfactory works) became a form of 're-destruction' for works about to be completed. In this series, I create artworks through the actions of tearing, collage and recombination. Tearing becomes another brushstroke or technique, allowing me to touch the pulse of history that survives in the present. By completing a transformation through repairs and patches, unexpected effects are created. Process is transformed into result, the accidental into the inevitable, hiding into revelation, and shame into openness; transparency, interlacing, fragmentation and agility are achieved. The allure of the centuries-old 'zen mountain and sacred water' is removed, restoring it to 'remnant mountains and leftover water'.* It questions whether, in today's post-industrial civilisation, in the tide of consumerism, there is still 'nature' under the sky. The nature that God bestowed upon us, once untouched by humanity, has long been torn apart by the lonely sound of paper-tearing, remaining only within humanity's grand expectations. Although works of the Zen Mountain and Sacred Water series take on different forms, they share a common pursuit: the exploration of the social significance of visual art, which is also in line with the pursuit of the Private Thinker woodcut series.

---

* 'Zen mountain and sacred water (禅山圣水)' and 'remnant mountains and leftover water (残山剩水)' are pronounced very similarly in Chinese.

——*Zen Mountain and Sacred Water*

Ink Wash

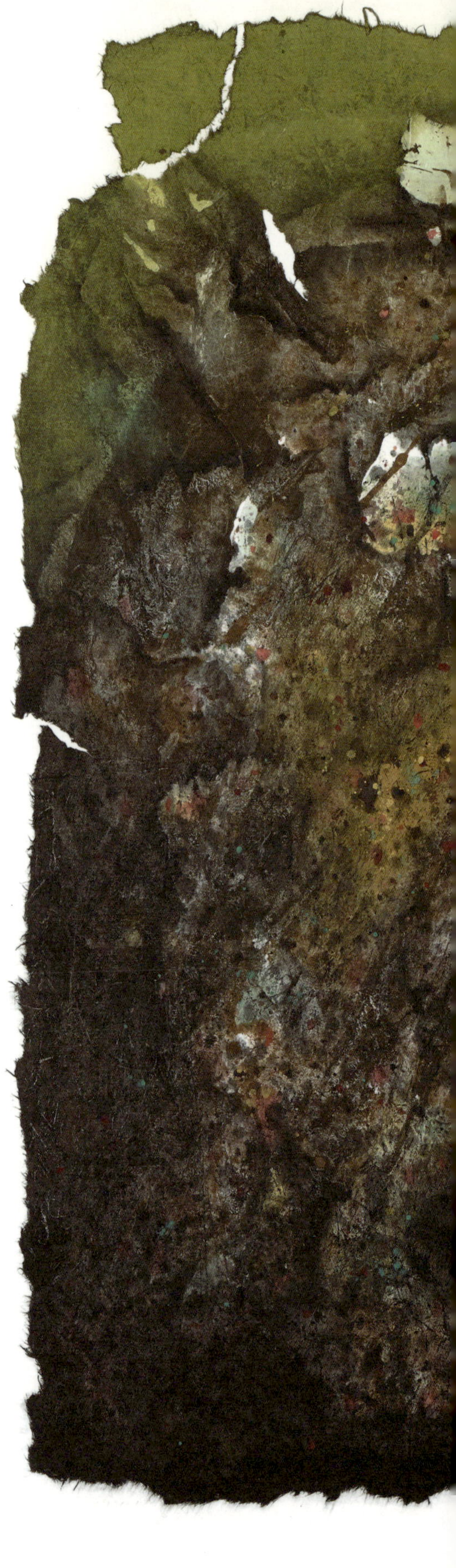

96cm × 190cm 2017

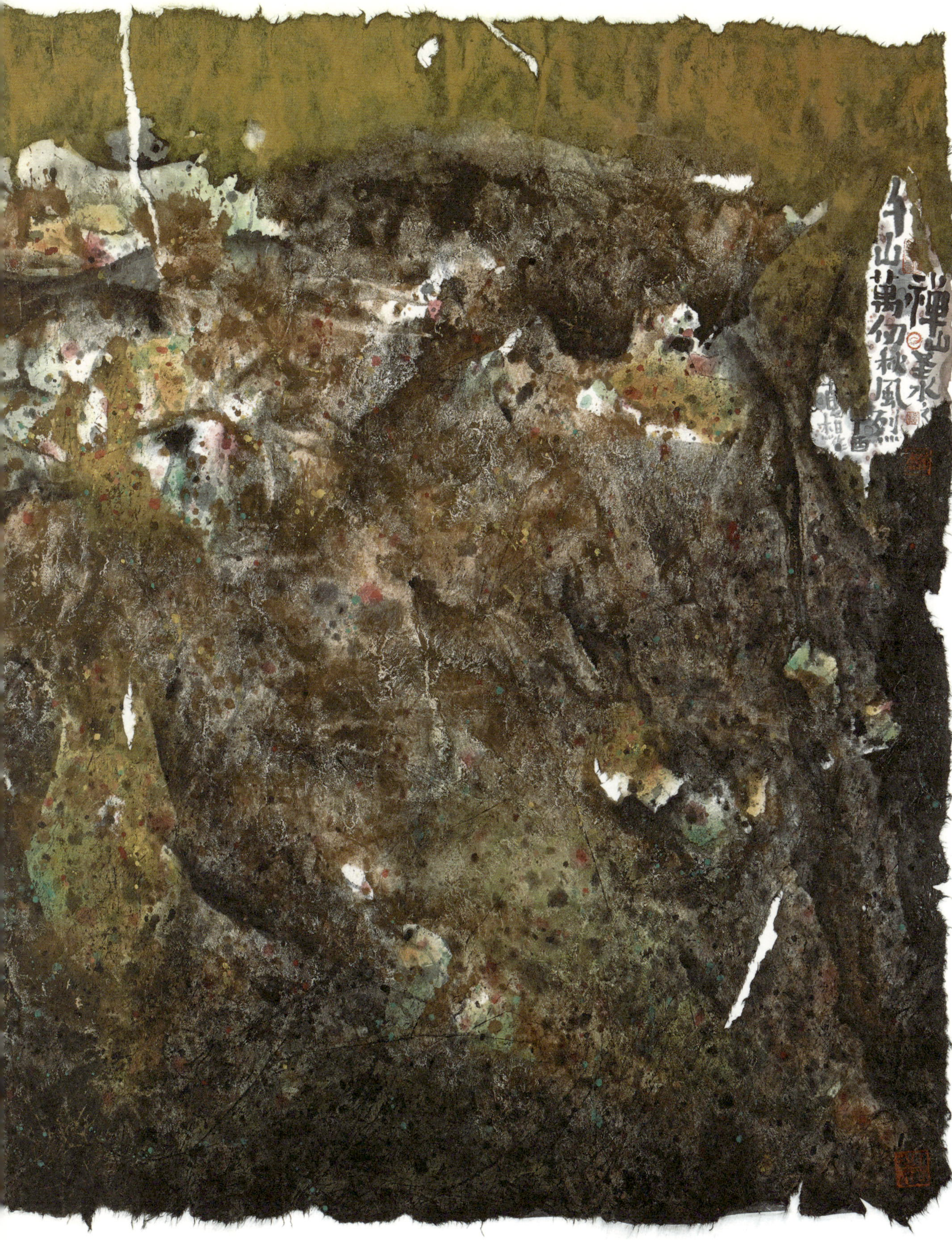
禪山善水
千山萬仞秋風烈
丁酉

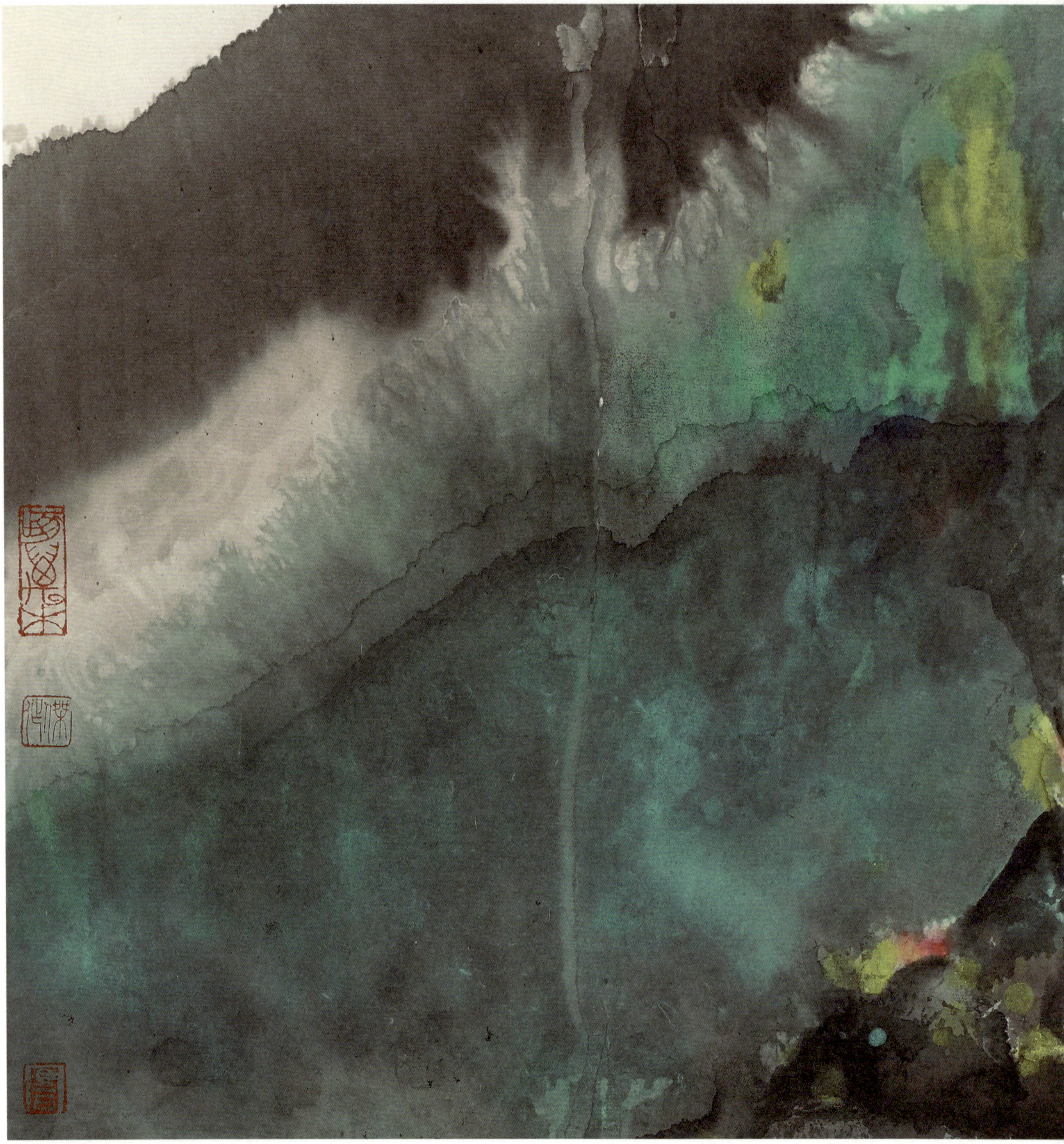

34cm × 139cm　2017

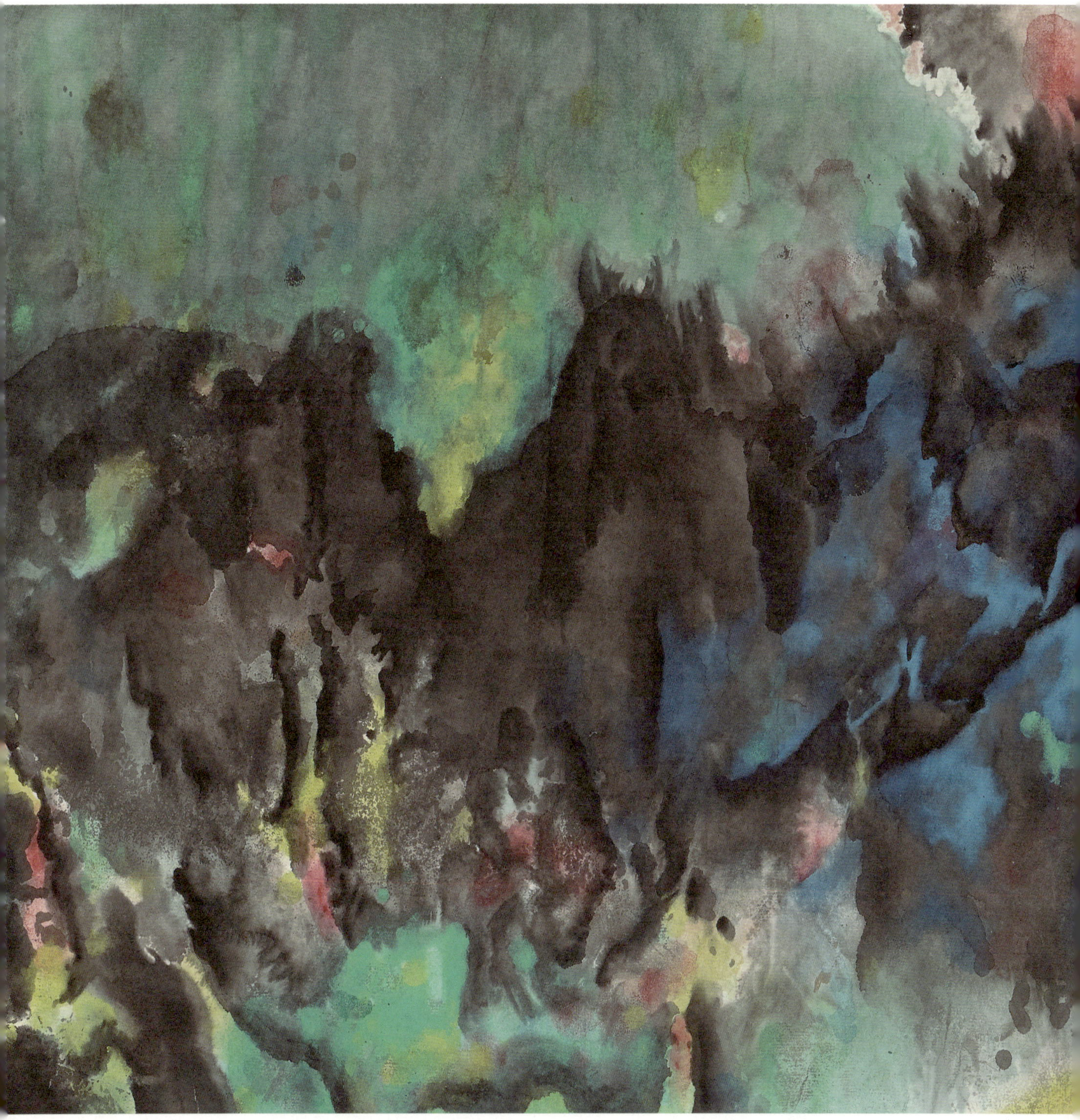

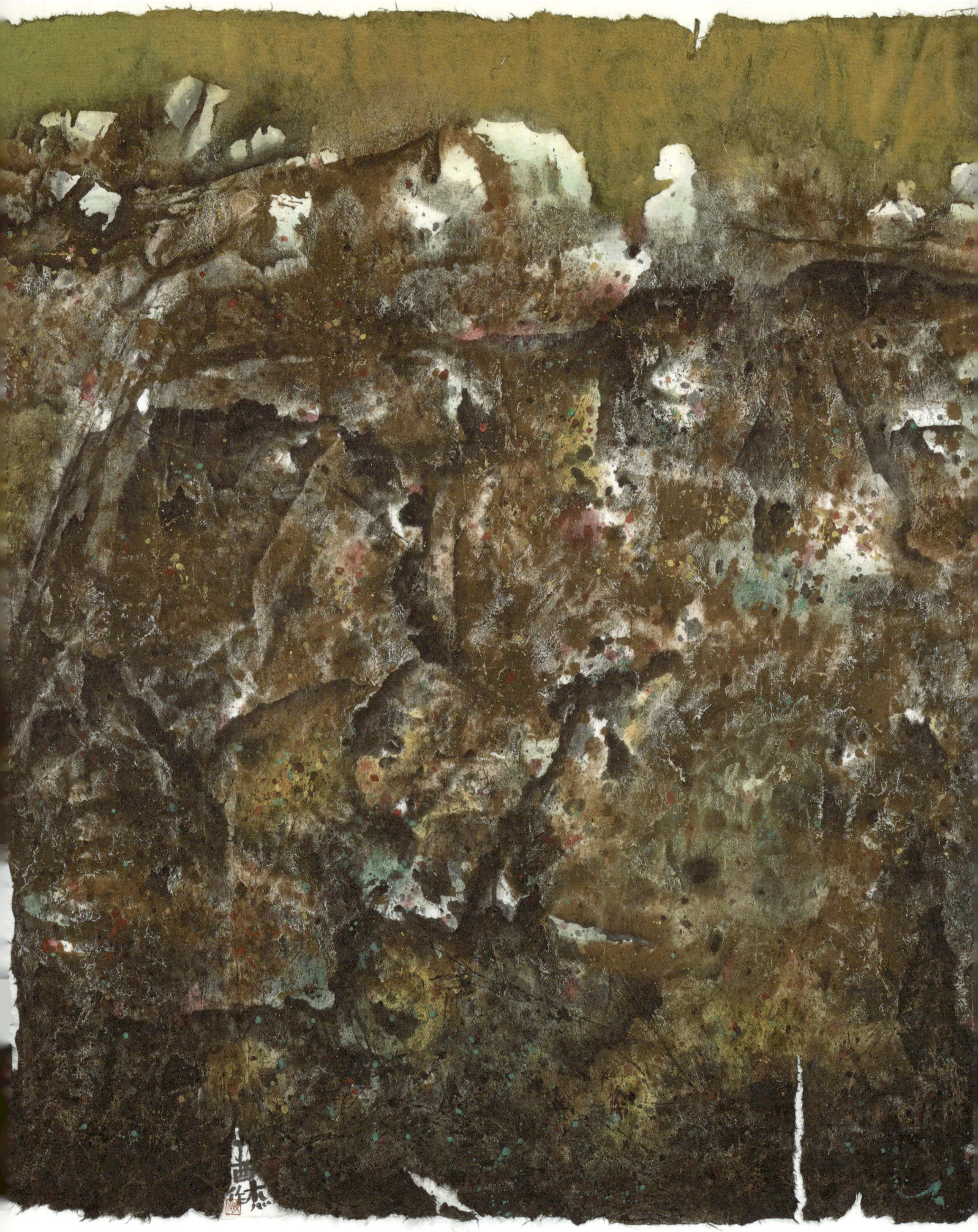

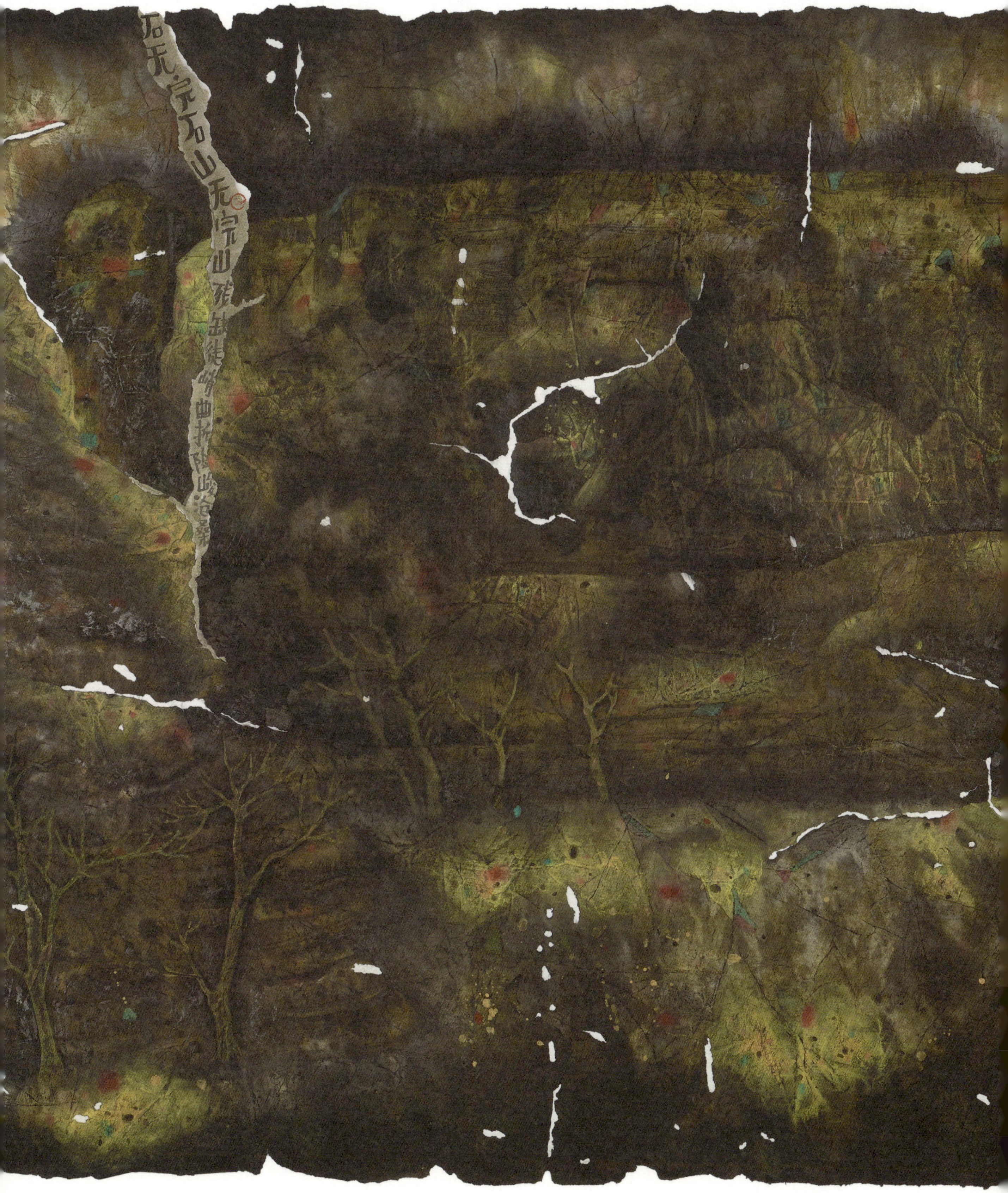

94cm × 176cm　2017

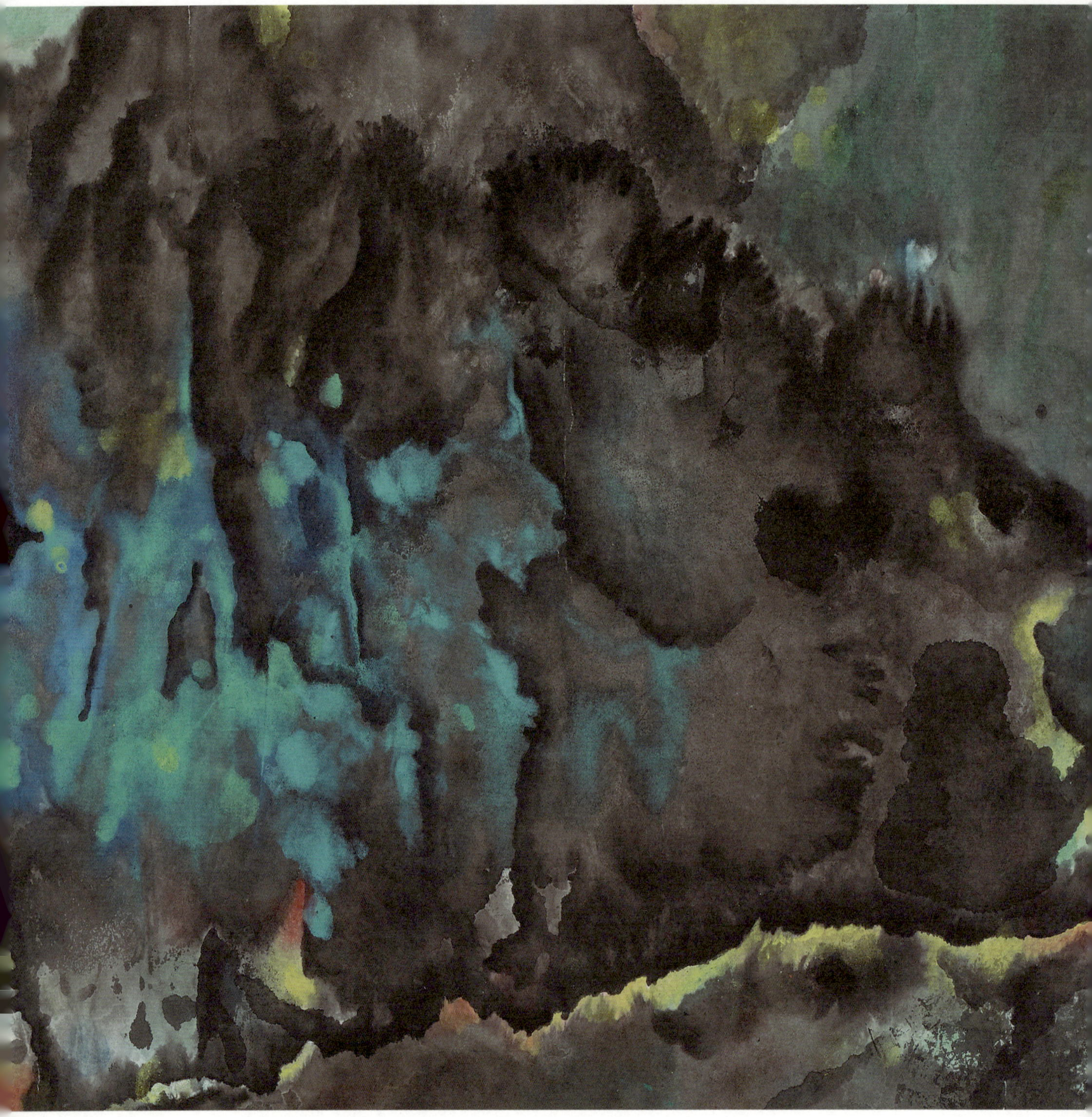

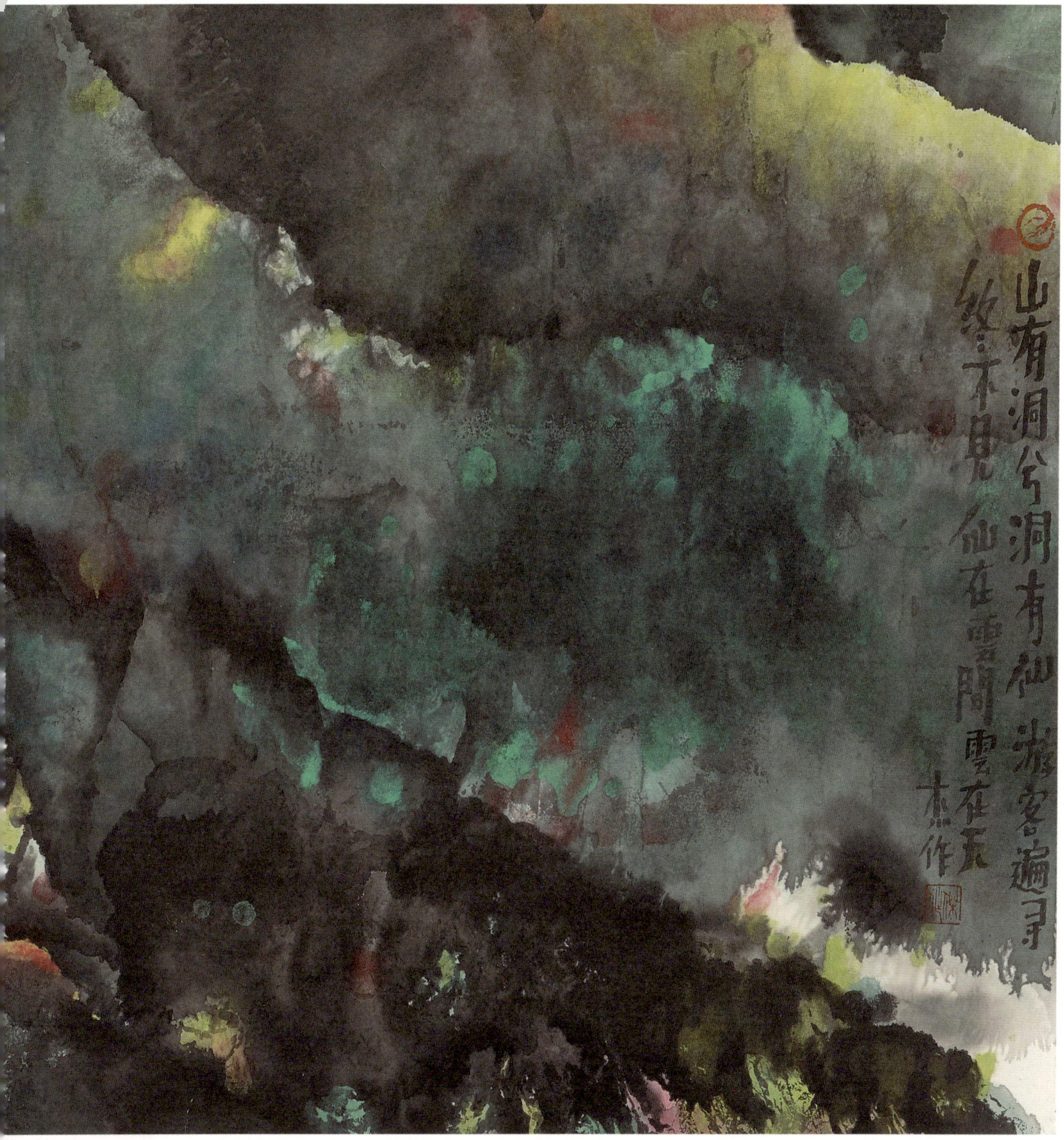
山有洞兮洞有仙游客遍尋
終不見仙在雲間雲在天
杰作

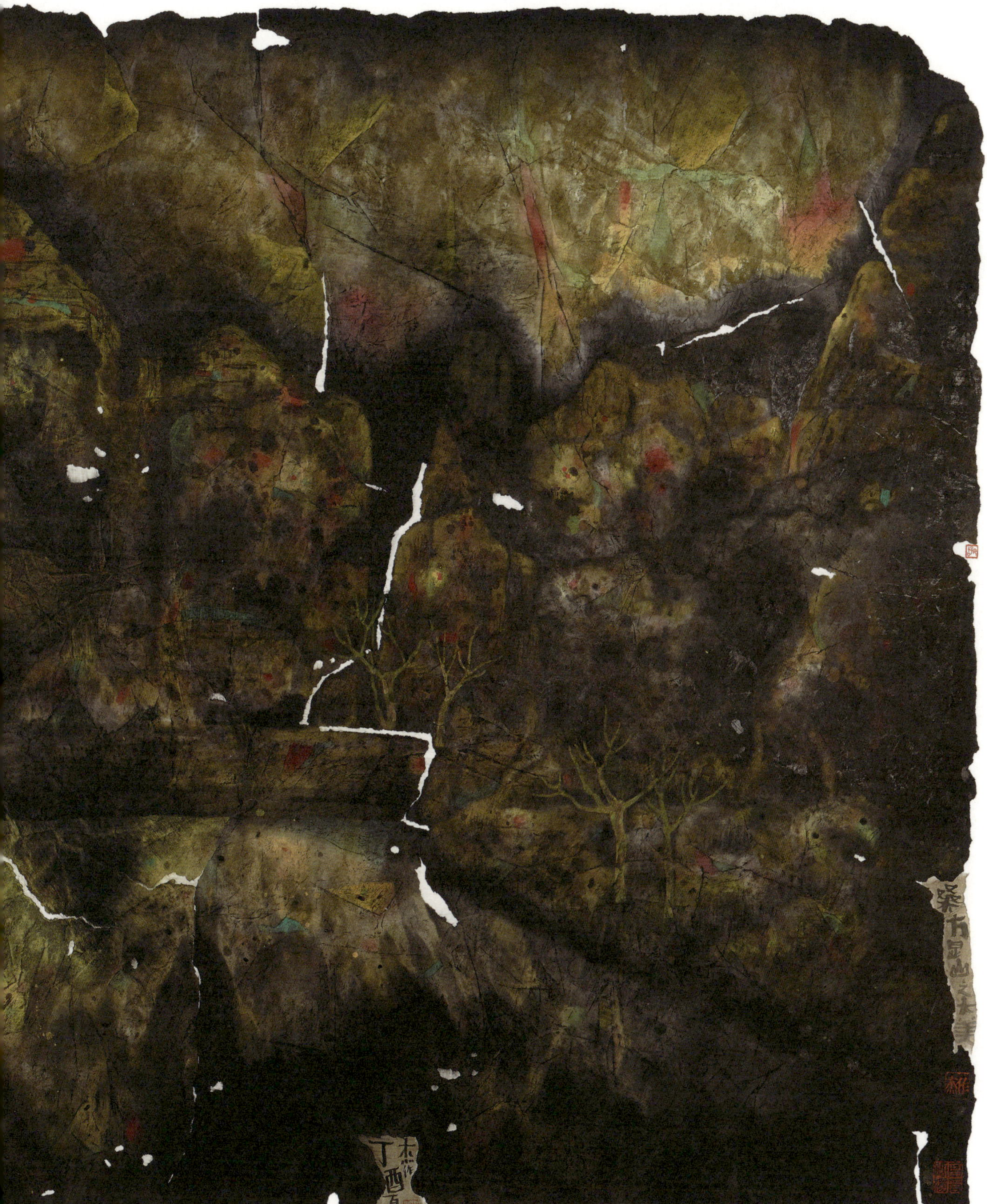

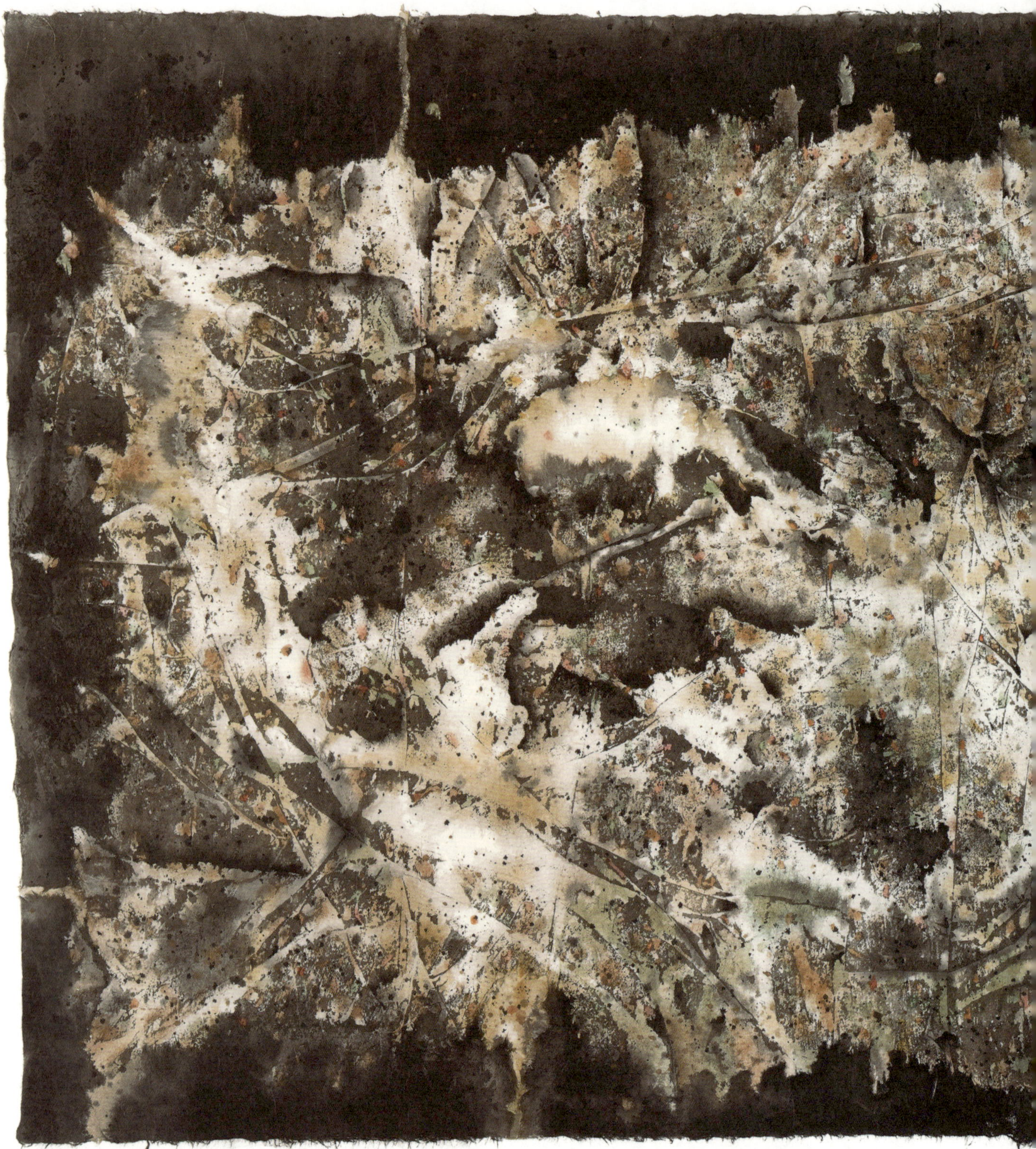

77cm × 147cm 2019

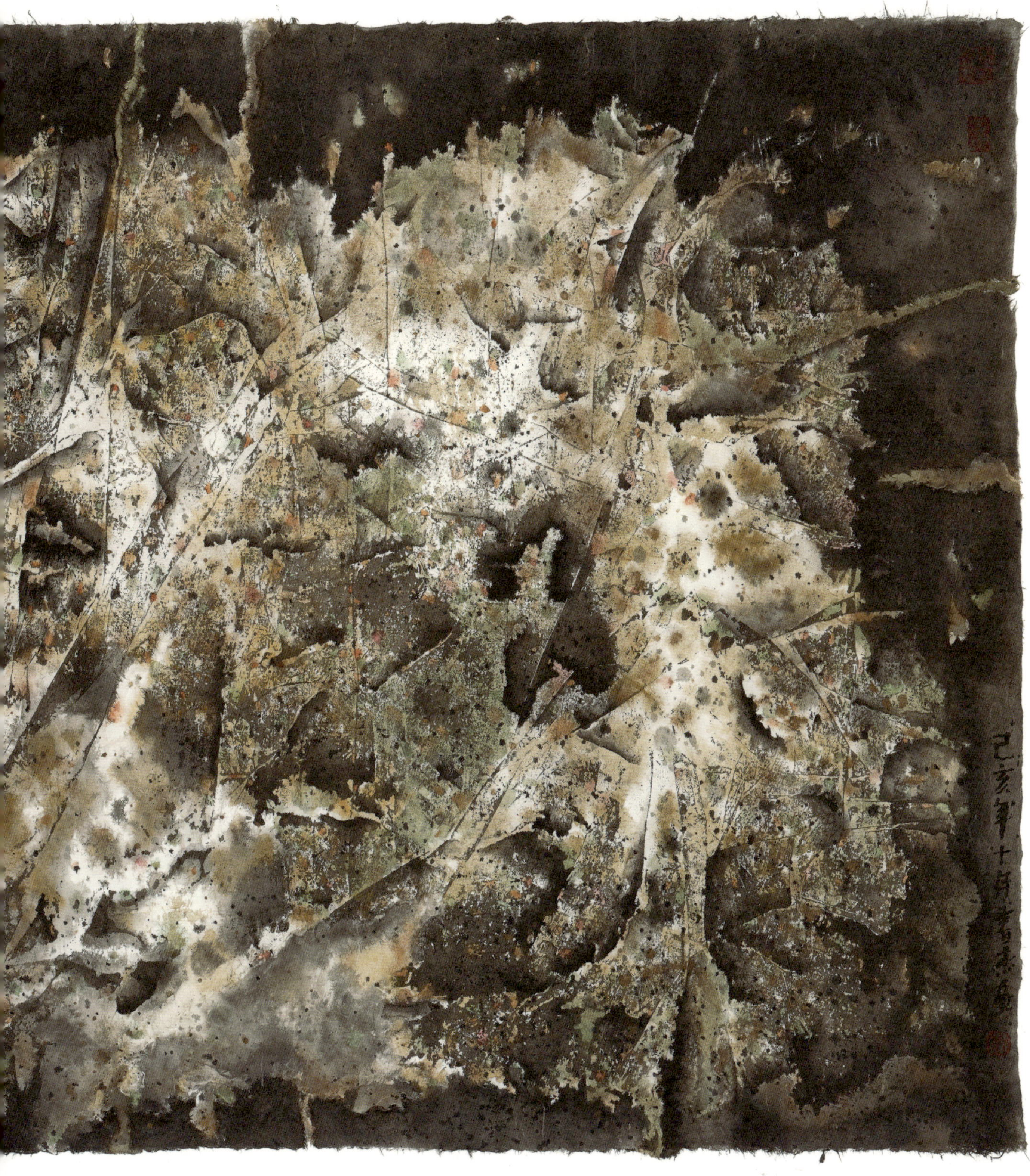
己亥年十月

77.5cm × 147cm 2019

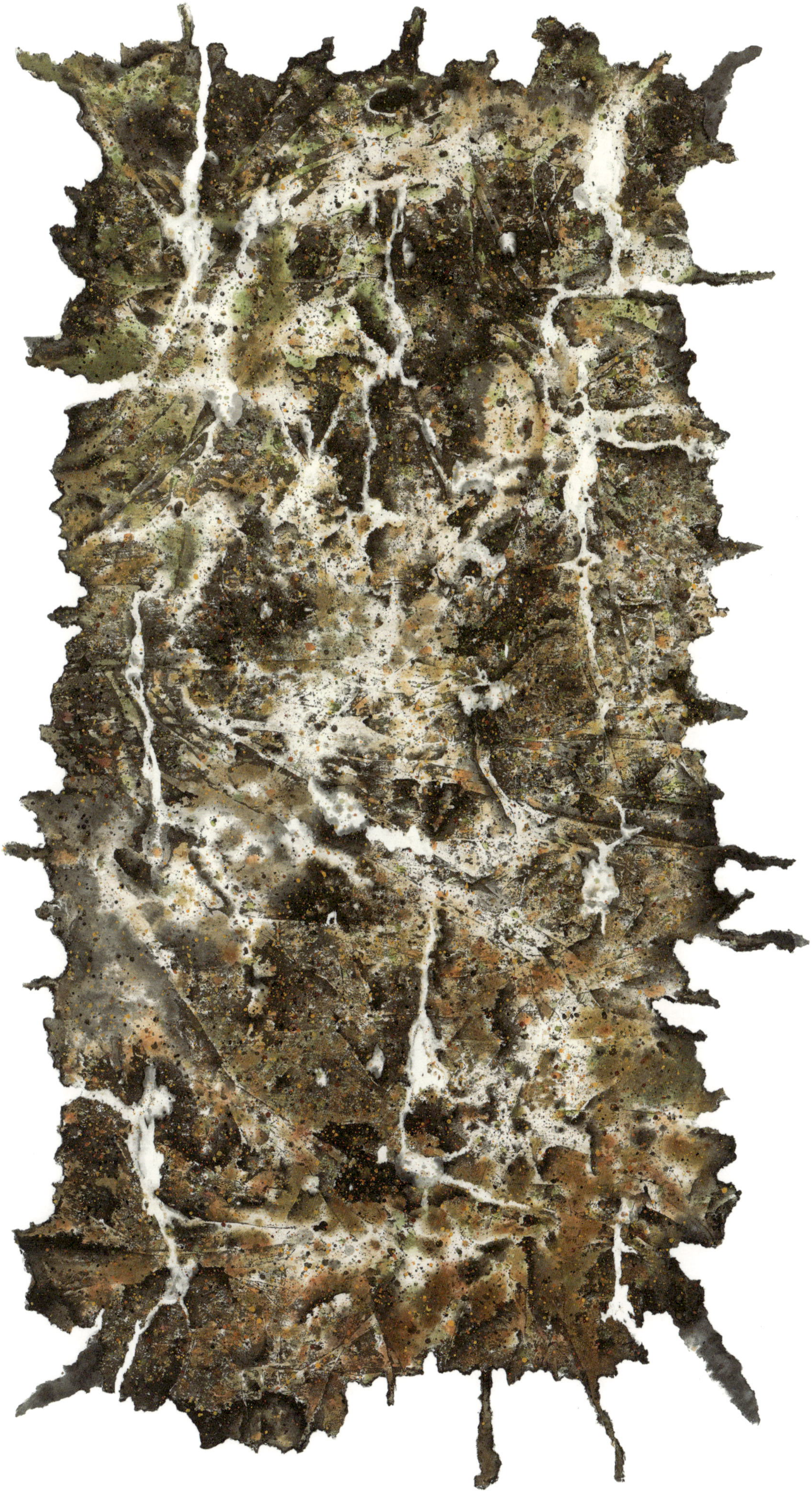

67cm × 76cm　2019

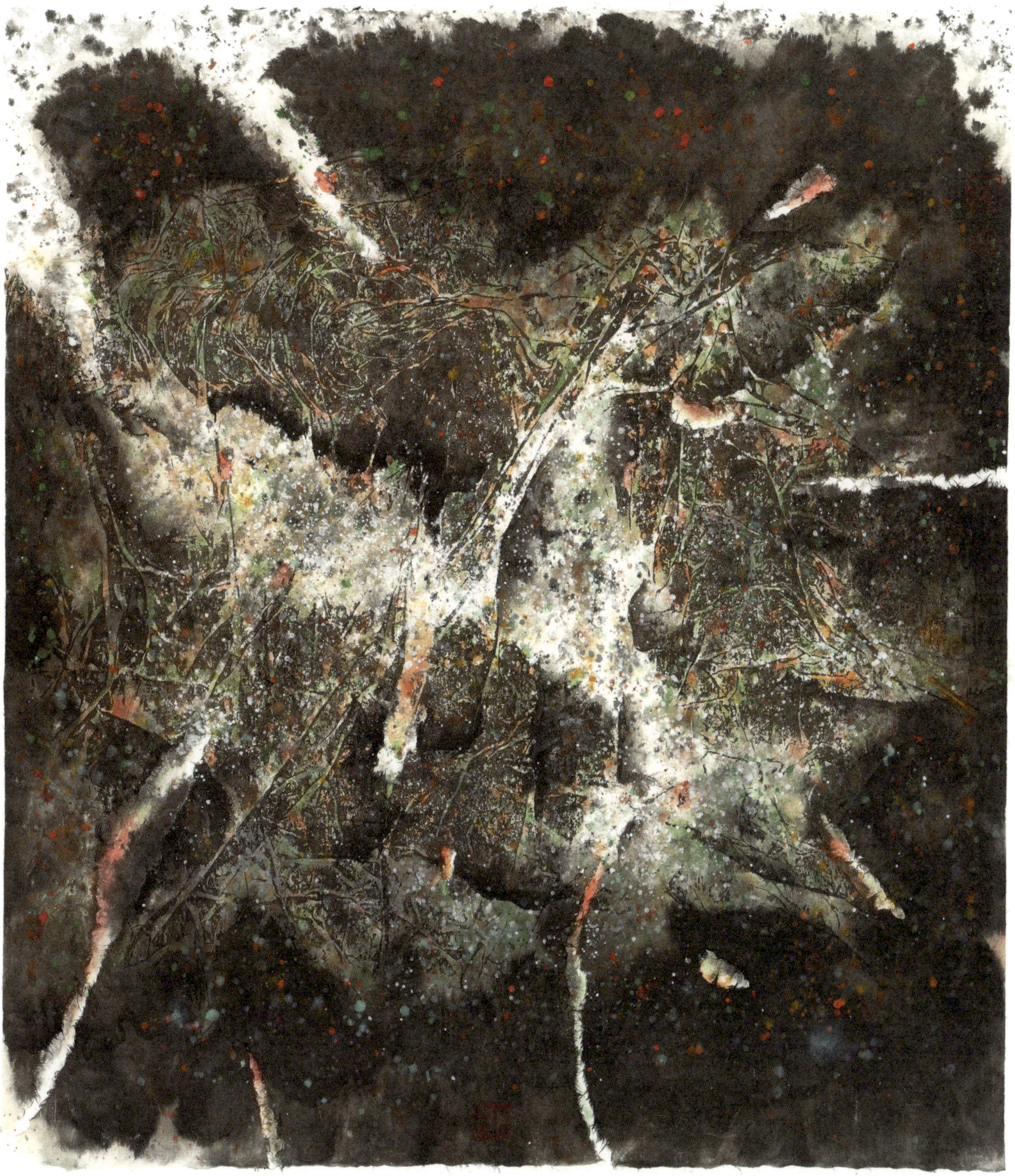

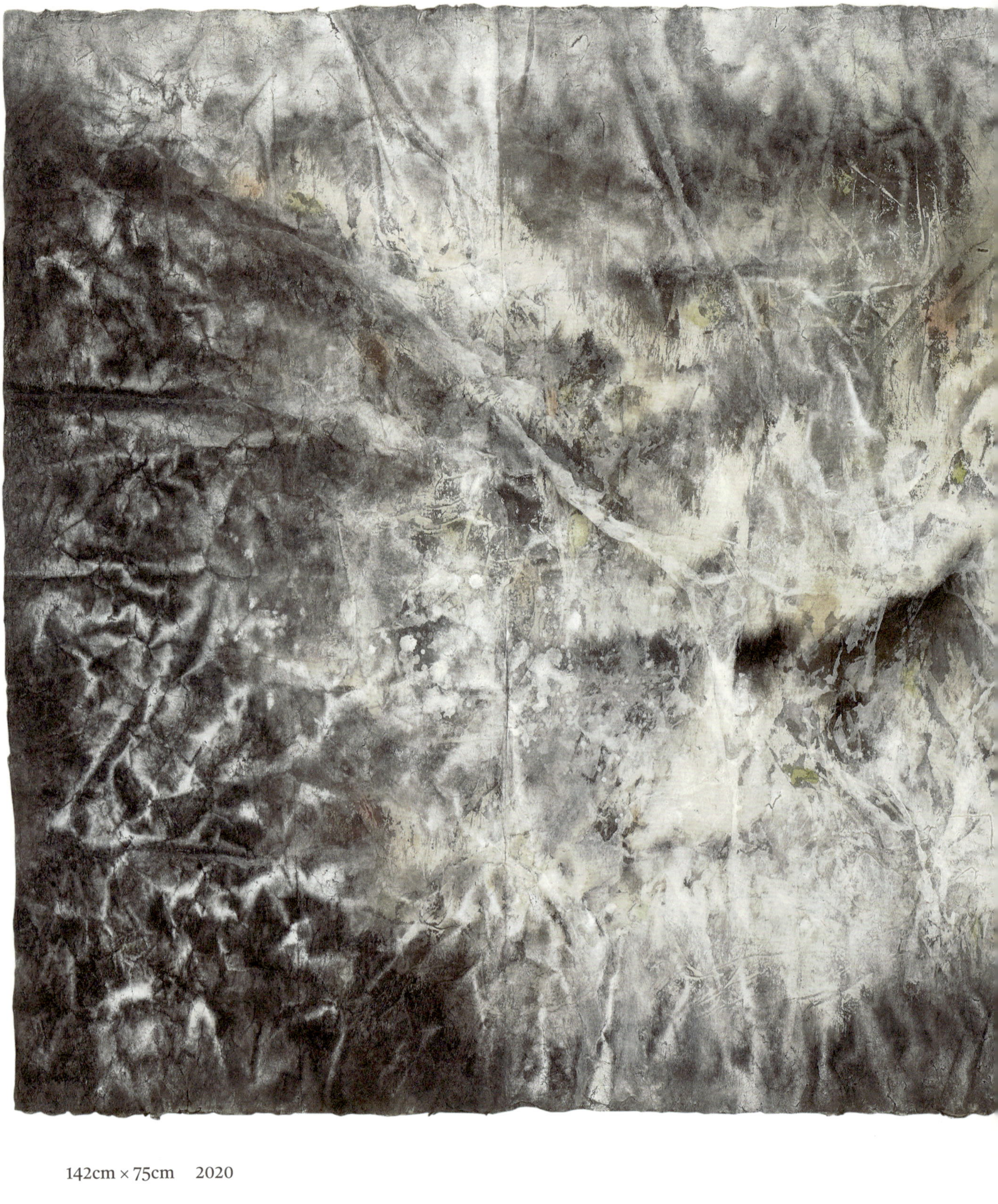

142cm × 75cm 2020

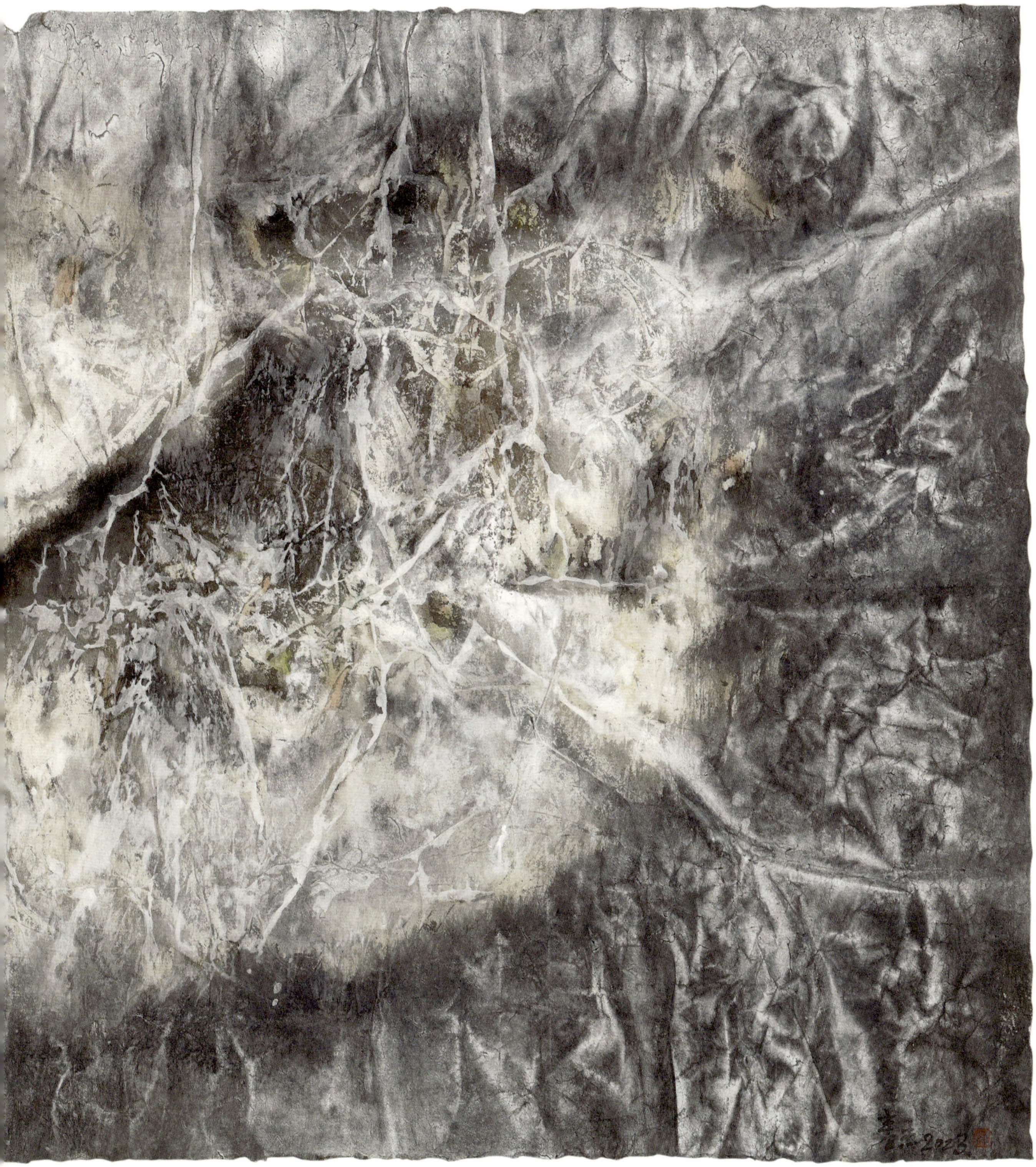

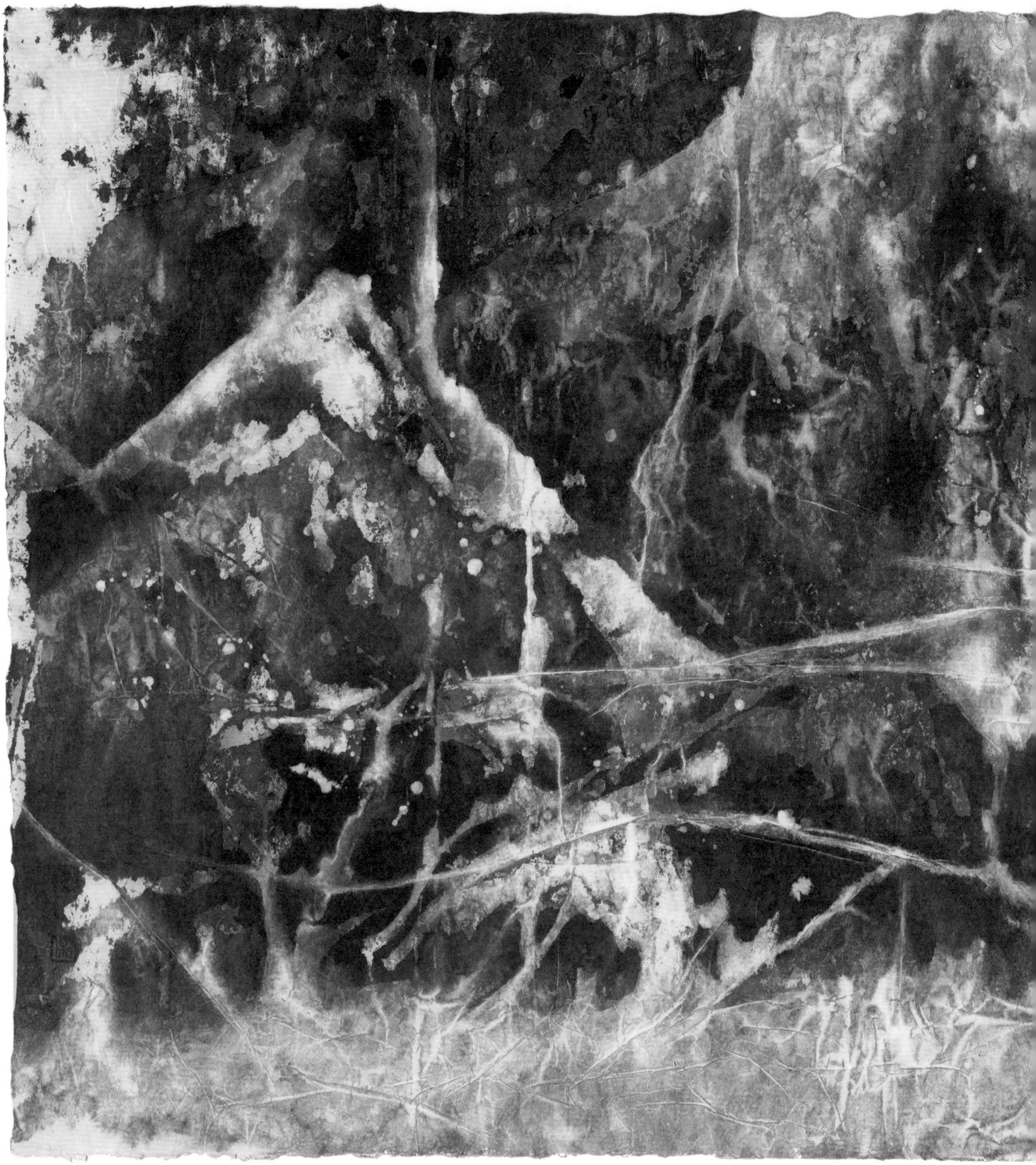

142cm × 75cm　2020

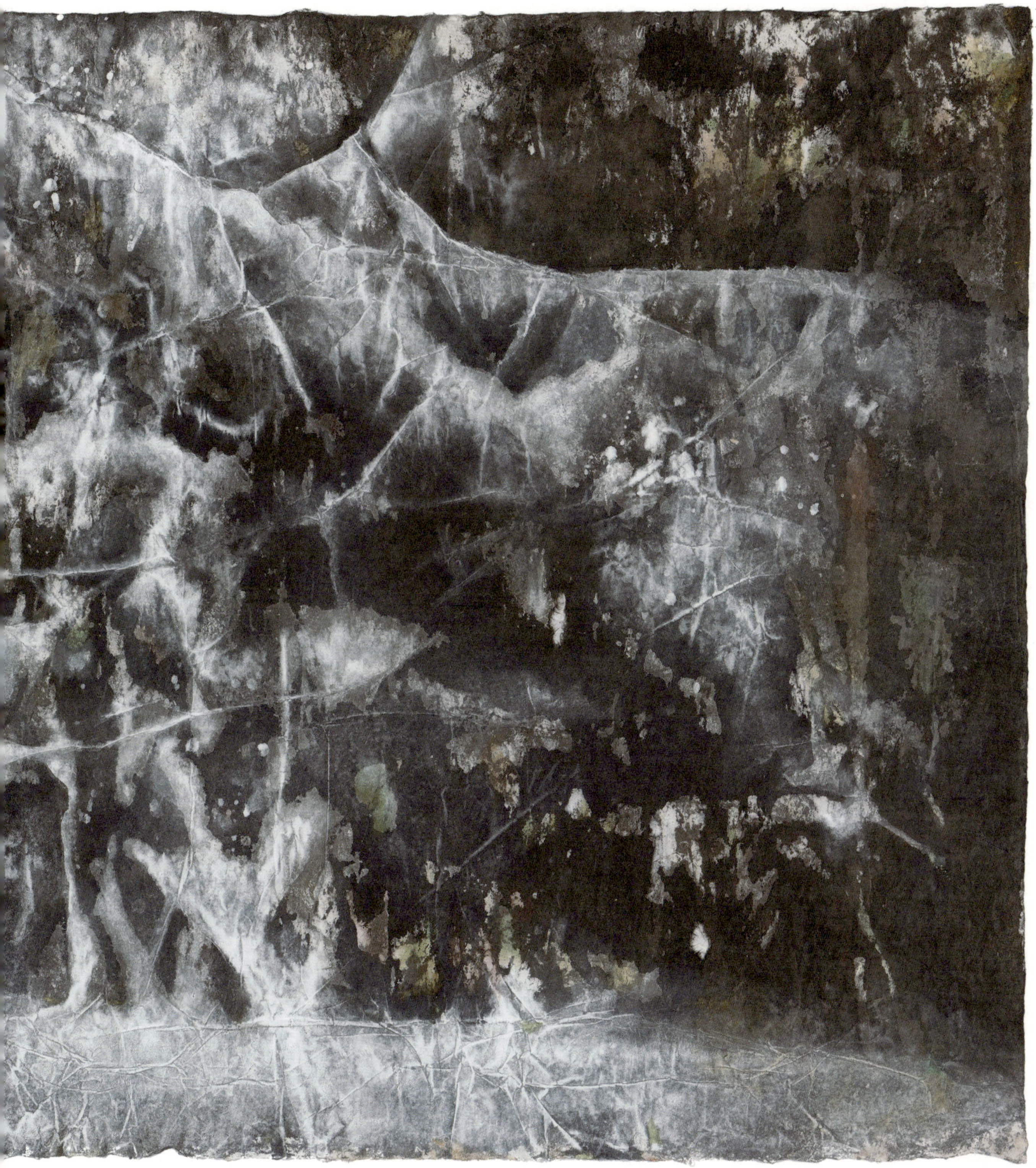

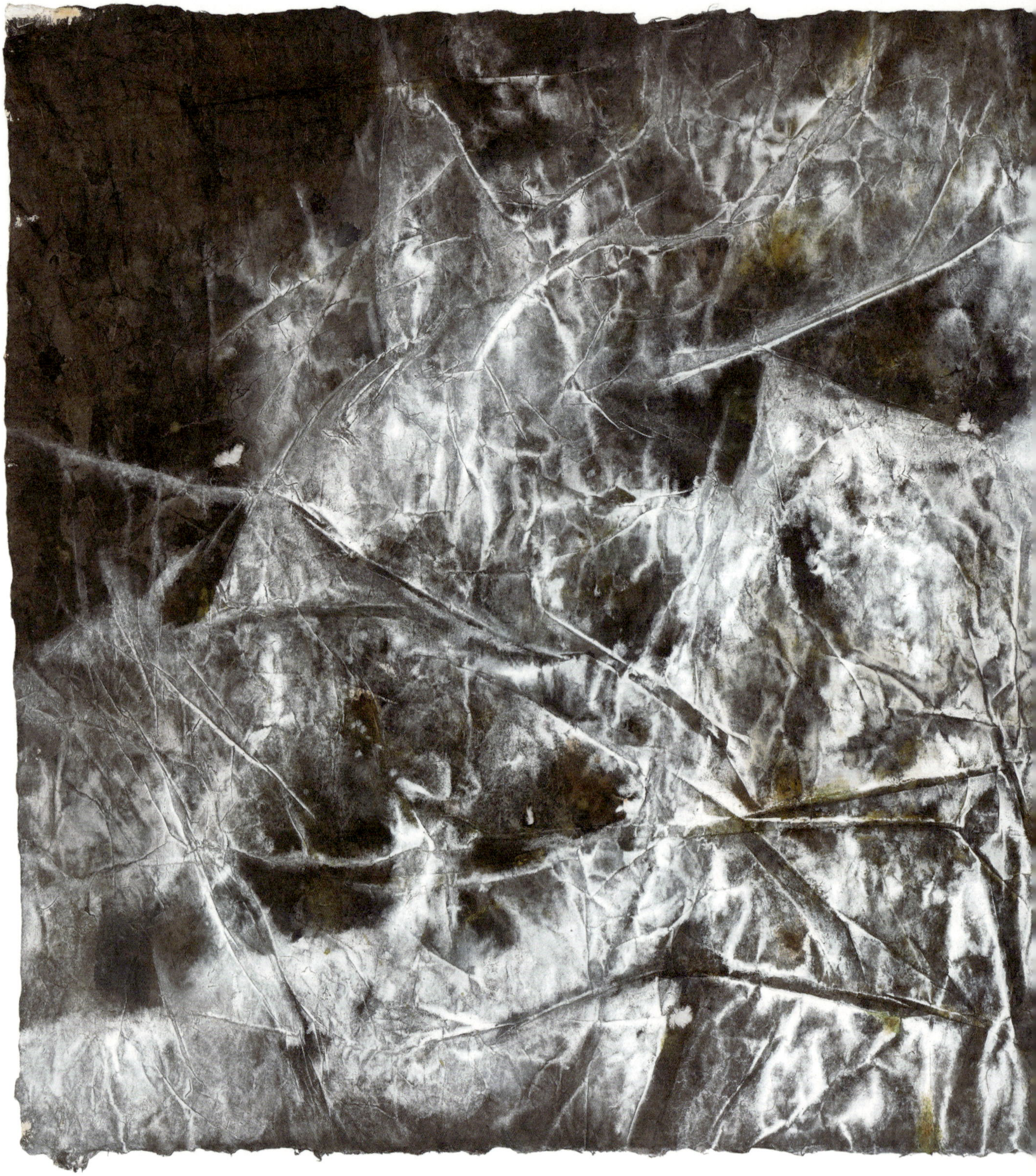

142cm × 75cm 2020

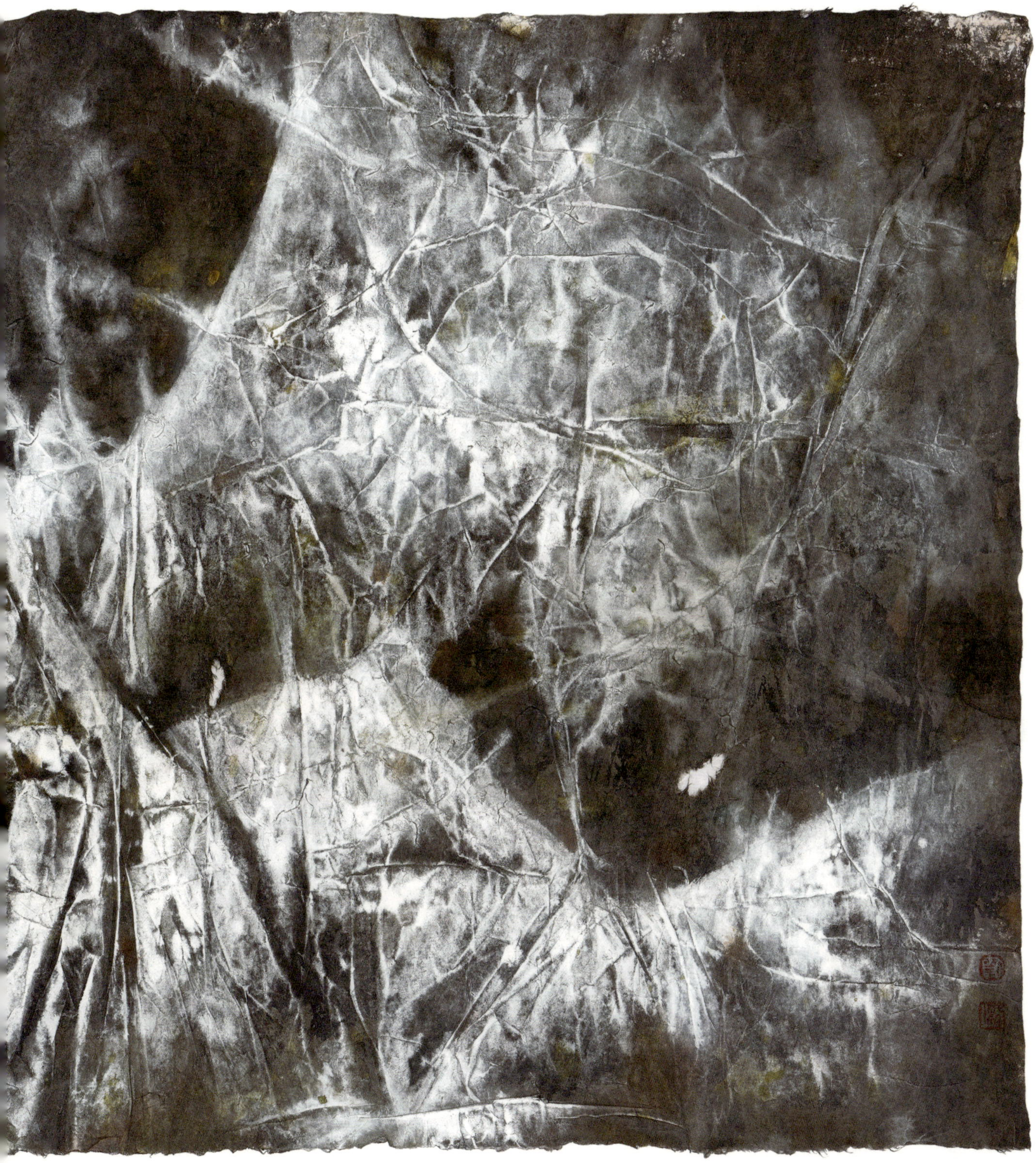

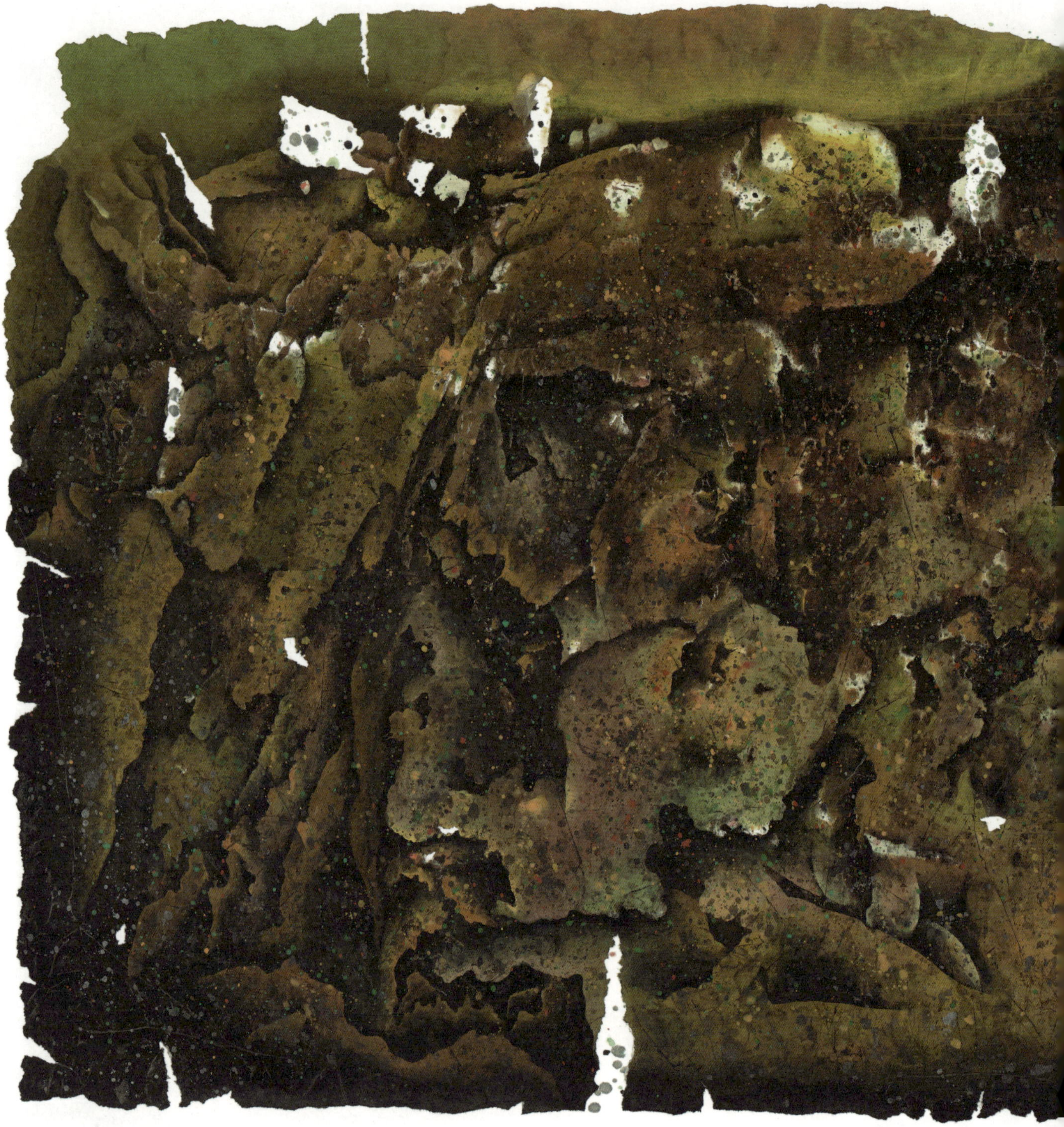

186cm × 97cm　2018

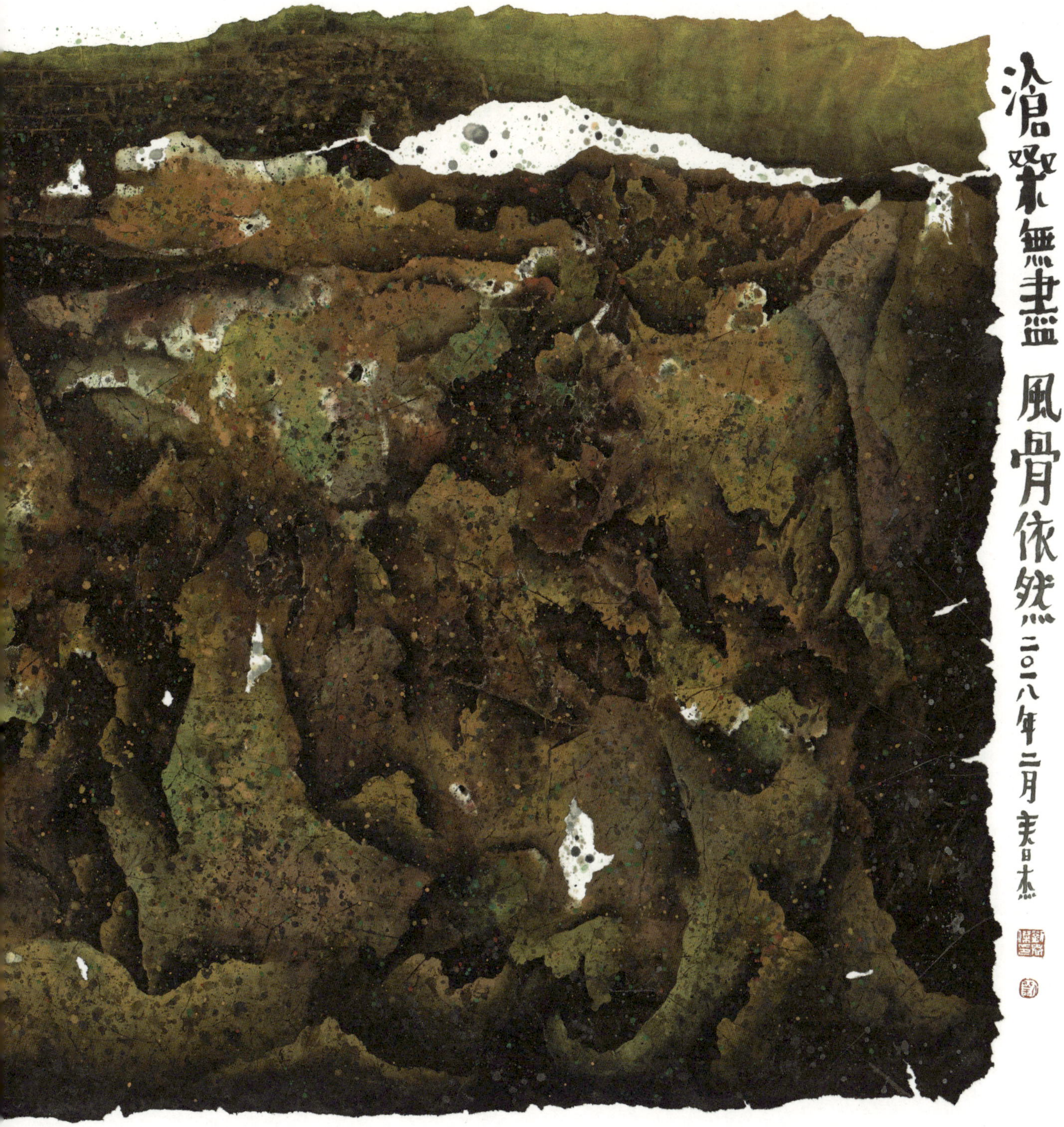
滄桑無盡 風骨依然 二〇一八年二月 春杰

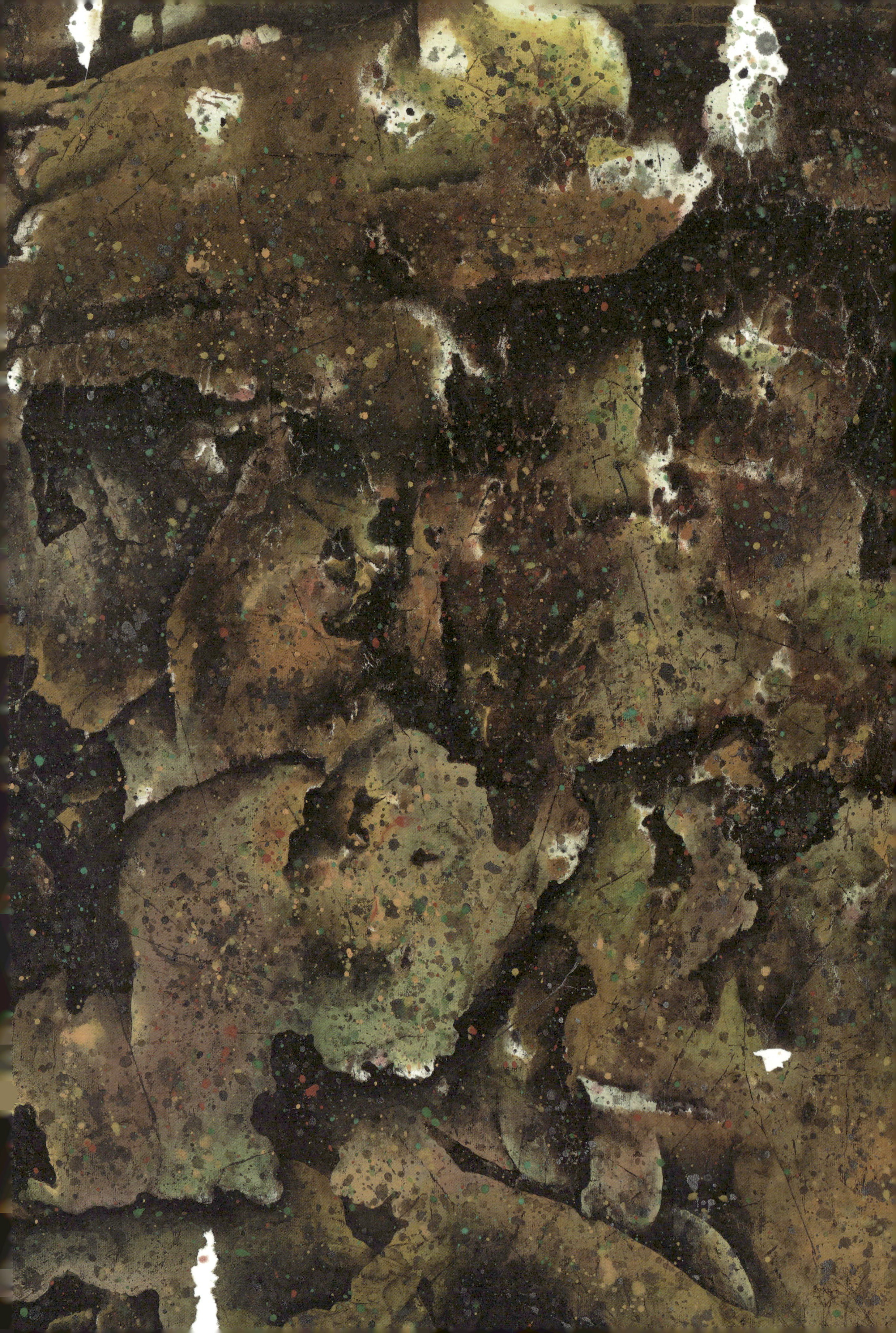

4.
Going Spatial: Installations

———*Keep Flooding the Screen*

Keep Flooding the Screen is composed of 365 acrylic boxes containing issues of the *People's Daily* from the 1960s, 1970s and 1980s, as well as a few other old newspapers. In each box, the topmost issue is printed with a woodcut portrait of Lu Xun, occasionally overlaid with my self-portraits or other works. During the printing process, the woodcut plates were not fixed, allowing for random combinations and colours with multiple layers of printing. After the blueprint design, workers were hired to assemble the boxes, which were then installed on a grey base. The artwork was displayed in the courtyard of the Prince Gong's Mansion in Suzhou Museum, like a tomb of Lu Xun, creating a historical resonance. Each of the 365 pieces corresponds to one day of the year, symbolising Lu Xun's continual presence in the media. Indeed, for over 80 years since Lu Xun's passing, his legacy continues to be recognised and discussed.

During the rainy season, the curator suggested moving the installation indoors after the opening ceremony. However, I insisted on letting these 'monuments' endure the wind and rain, just as Lu Xun himself had weathered the hardships in life. Battered by wind and rain, exposed to the sunlight, buried by falling leaves, most of the acrylic boxes came unglued, some fell apart. Old newspapers became mouldy, yellowed and torn, and Lu Xun's portrait deformed, looking pitiful. The kind-hearted golden osmanthus and magnolia trees scattered petals upon the lonely Lu Xun, covering him with 'gold and jade'. During the exhibition, numerous viewers gathered around him, visited him and memorialised him; the massive amount of newspaper information overlapped with him, some covered, some blurry, some very clear. Undoubtedly, these works underwent changes, becoming vicissitudinous, highlighting a locality. *Keep Flooding the Screen* was born on the exhibition spot, not in the studio.

After three months of being exhibited, the acrylic boxes and their bases became unusable. I dried the old newspapers and carefully stored them in a box. Occasionally, I would open the box and take a look. They were no longer smooth, but rather wrinkled; they no longer shouted. Sometimes they seemed to whisper, 'Let me out, I'm still here, I have something to say'.

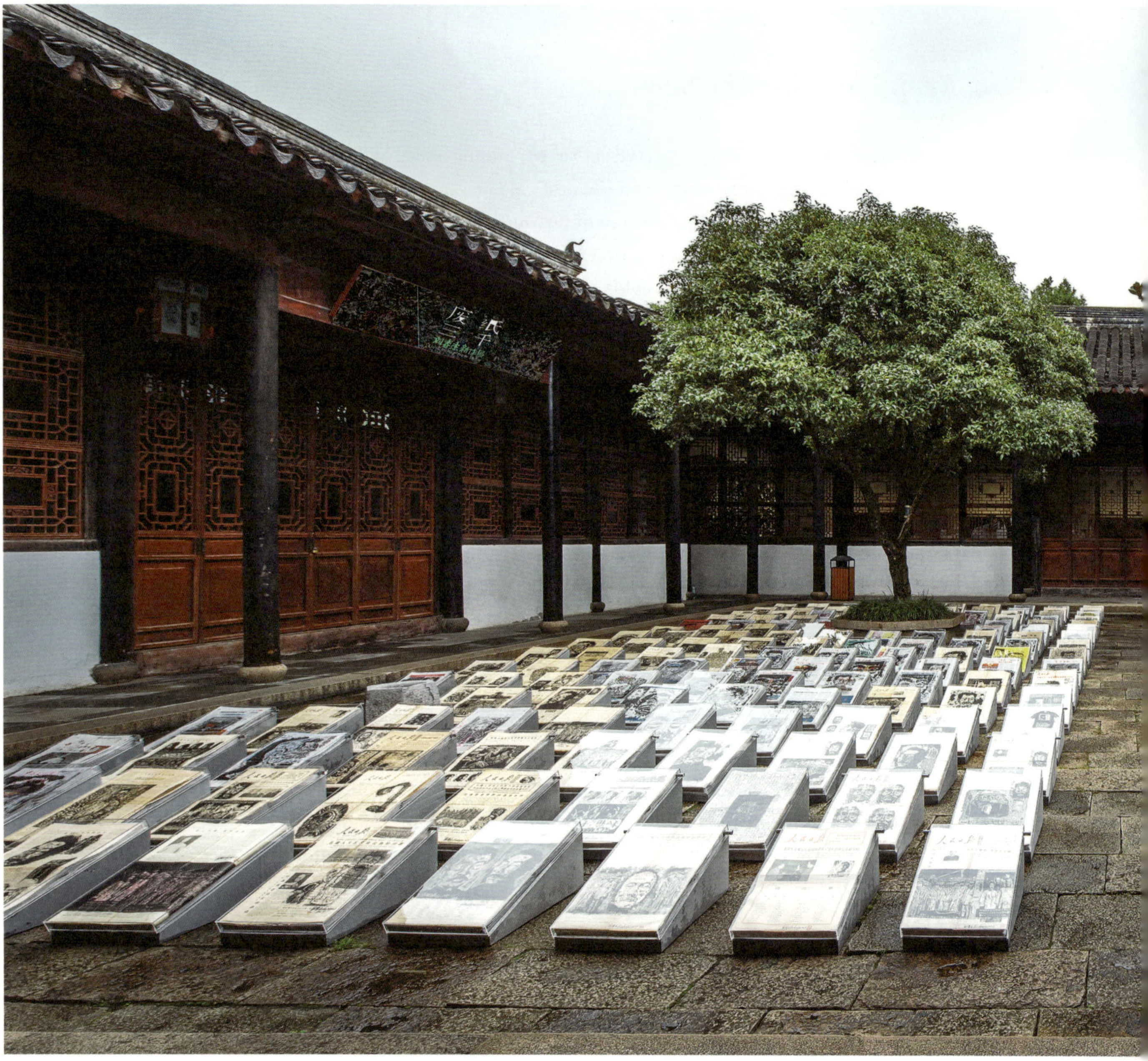

Keep Flooding the Screen 41.2cm × 58cm × 32cm Woodcut, Acrylic and Polystyrene 2017

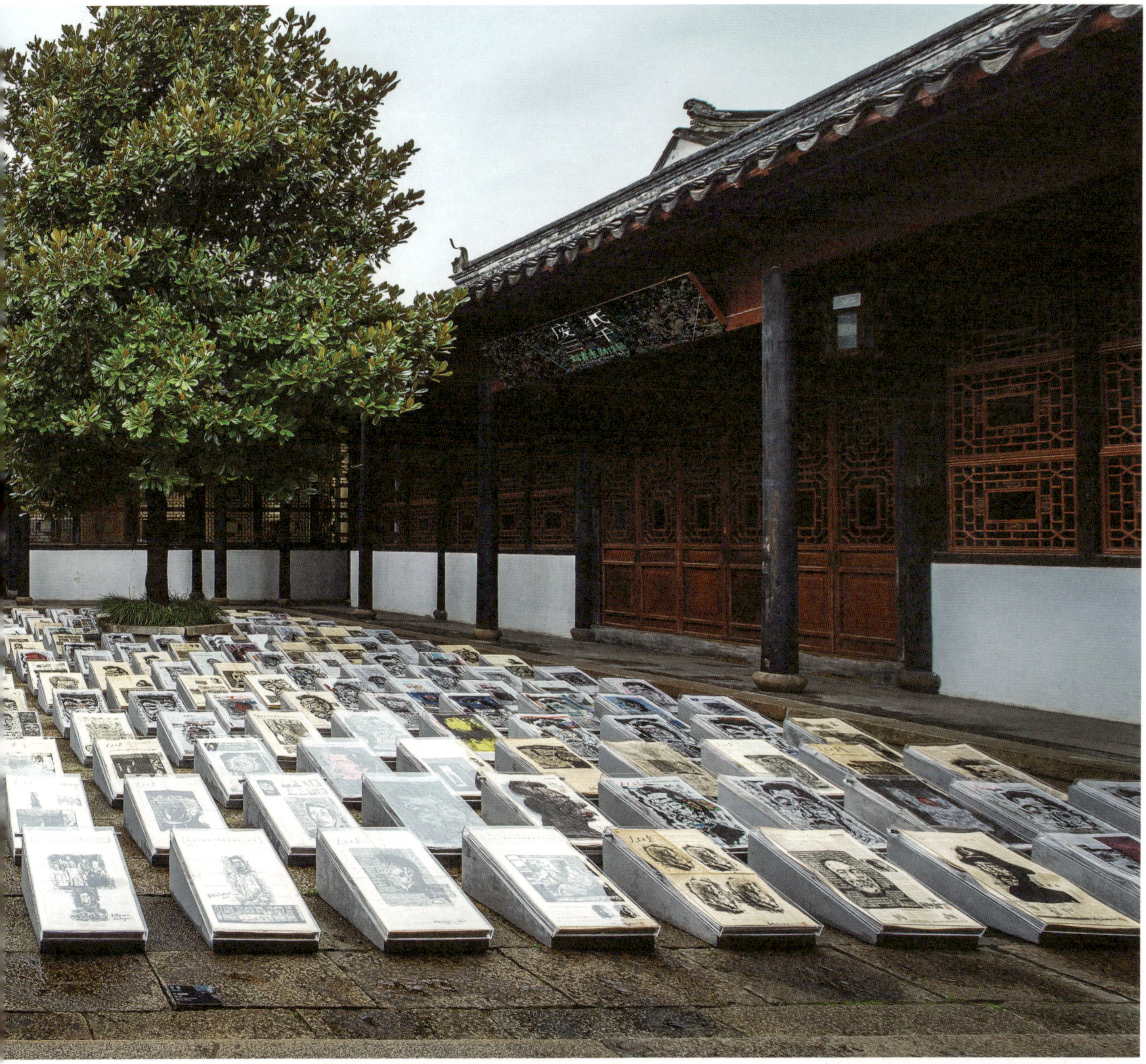
废纸三千

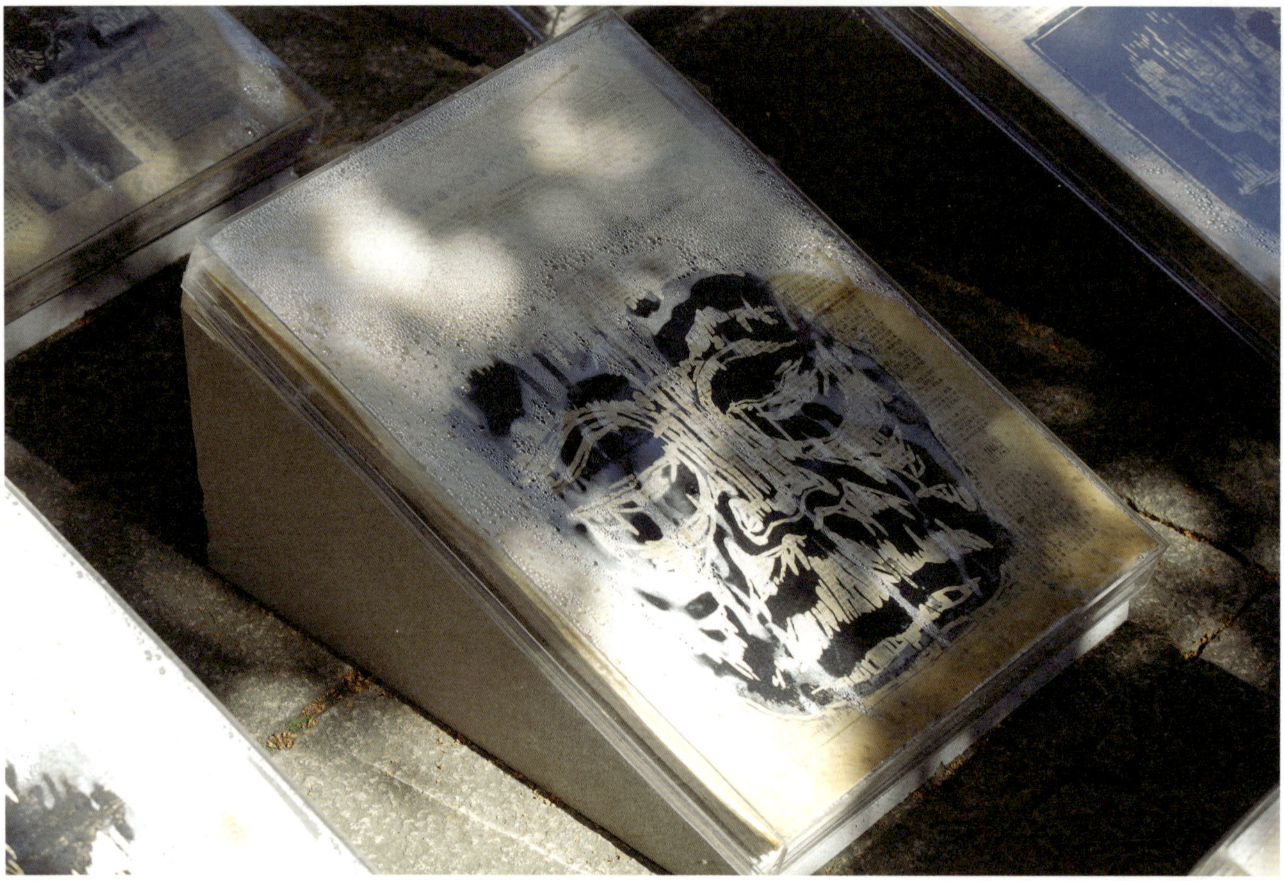

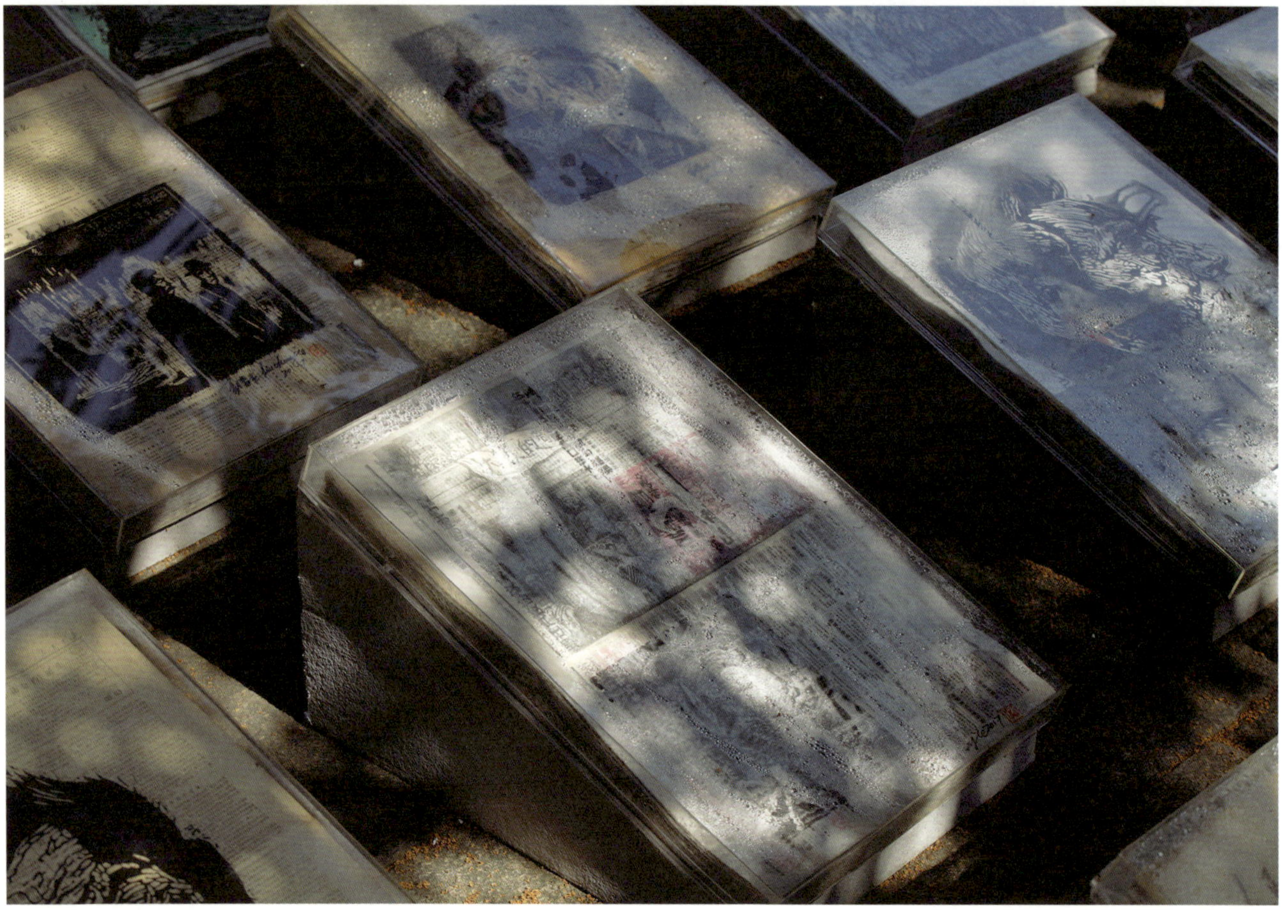

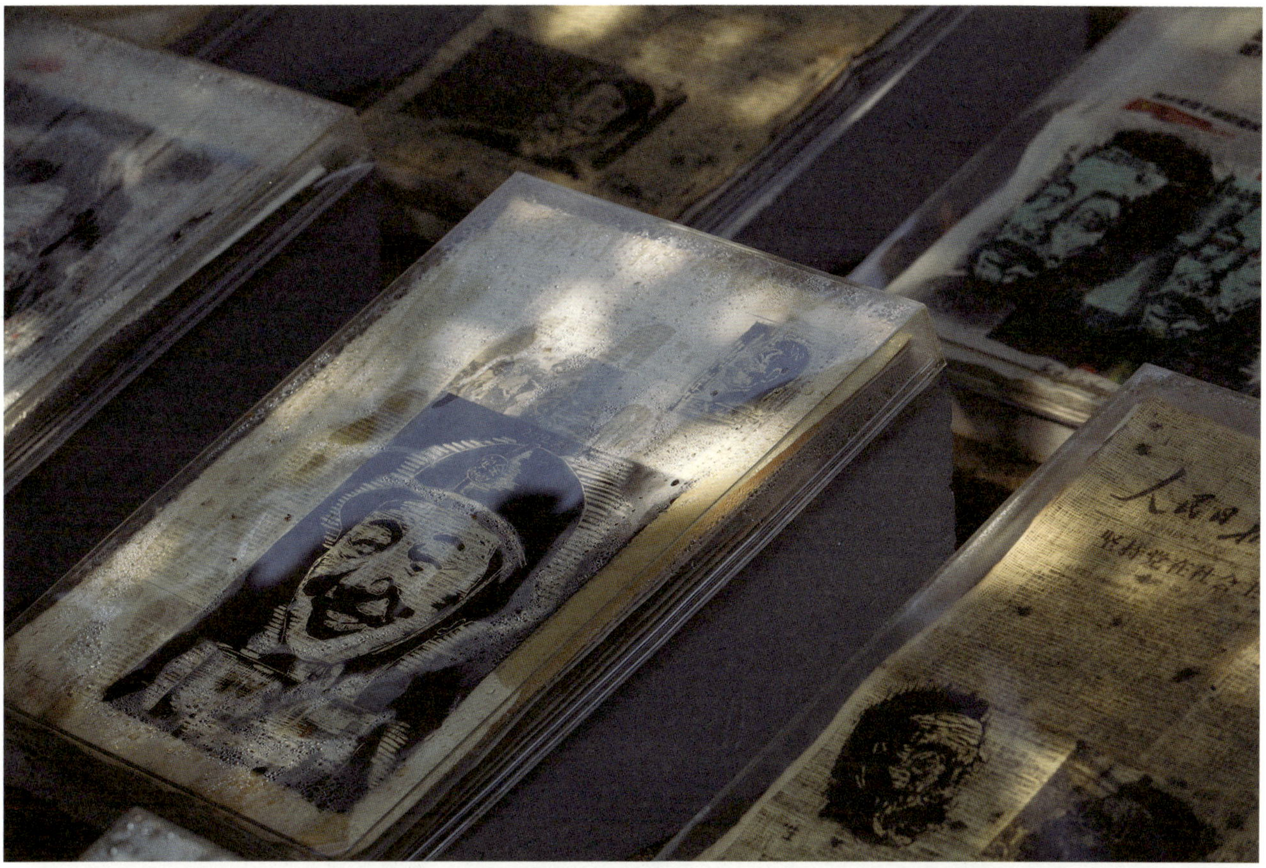

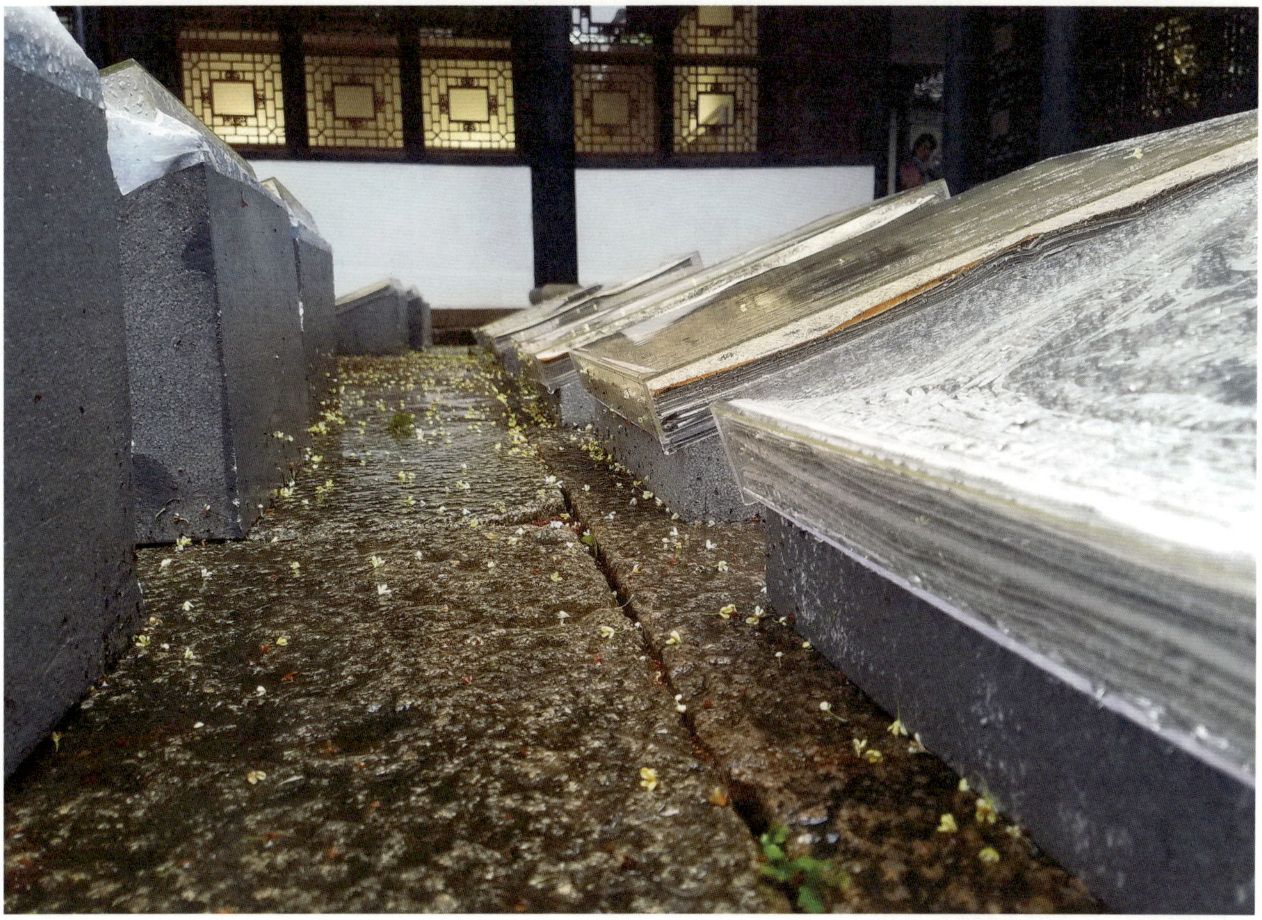

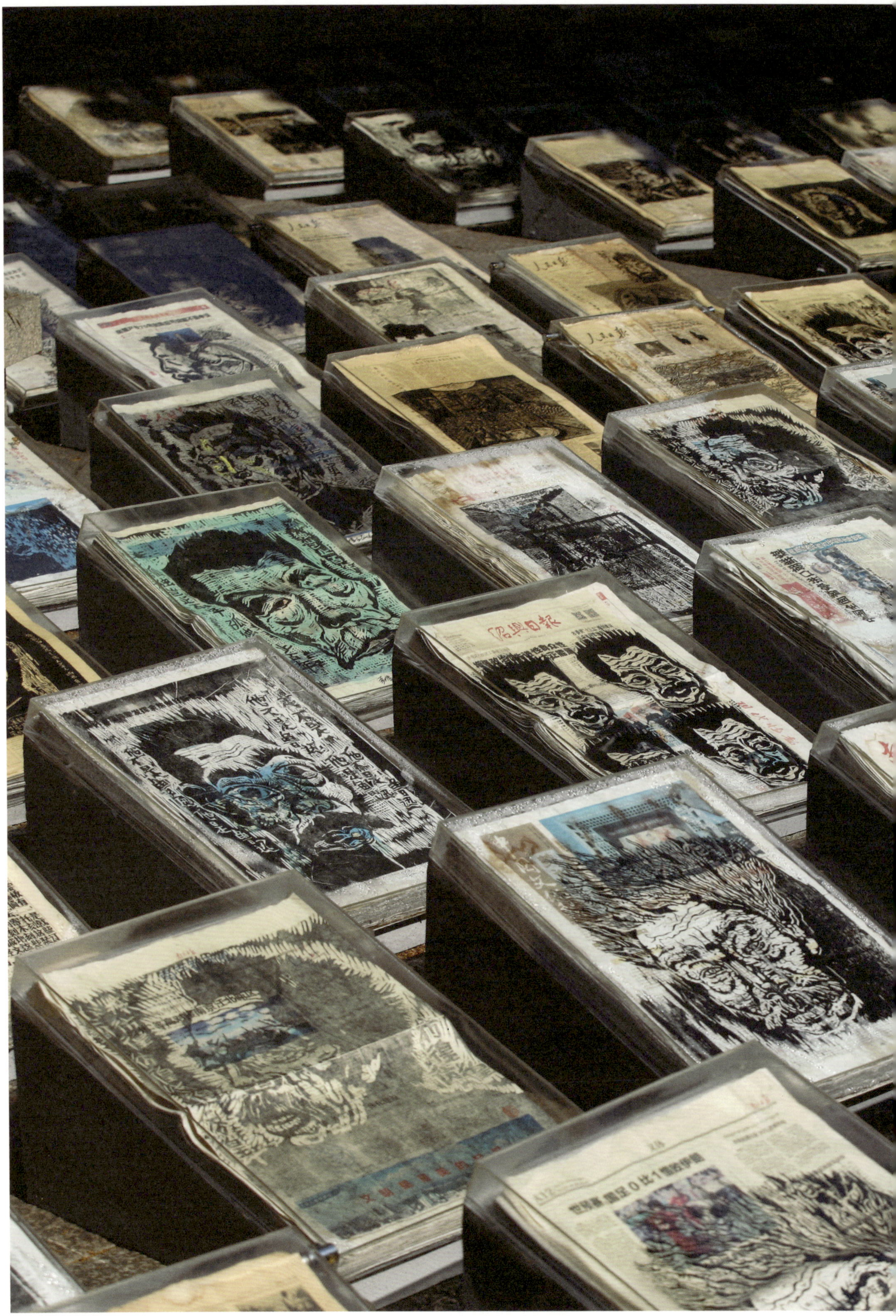

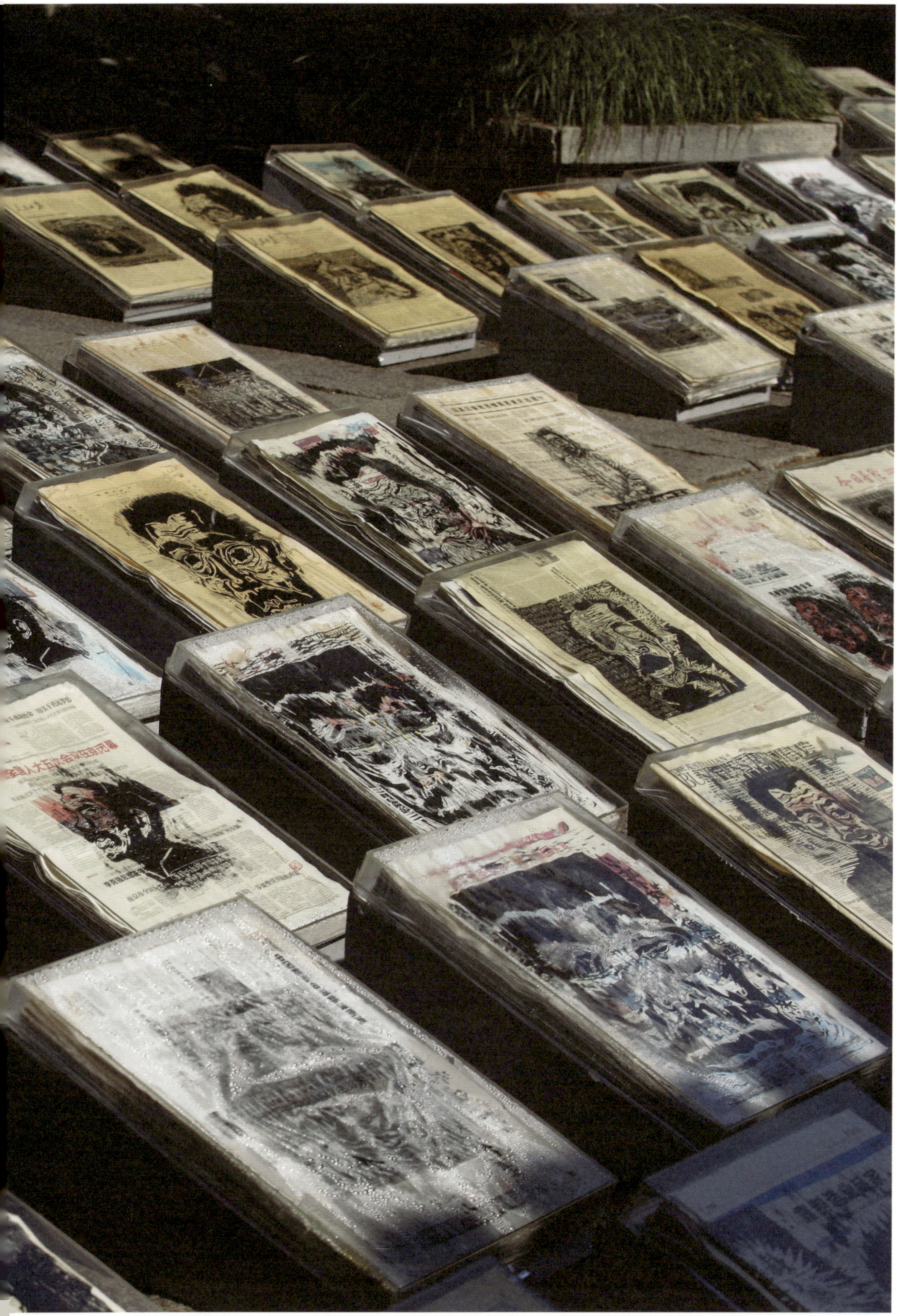

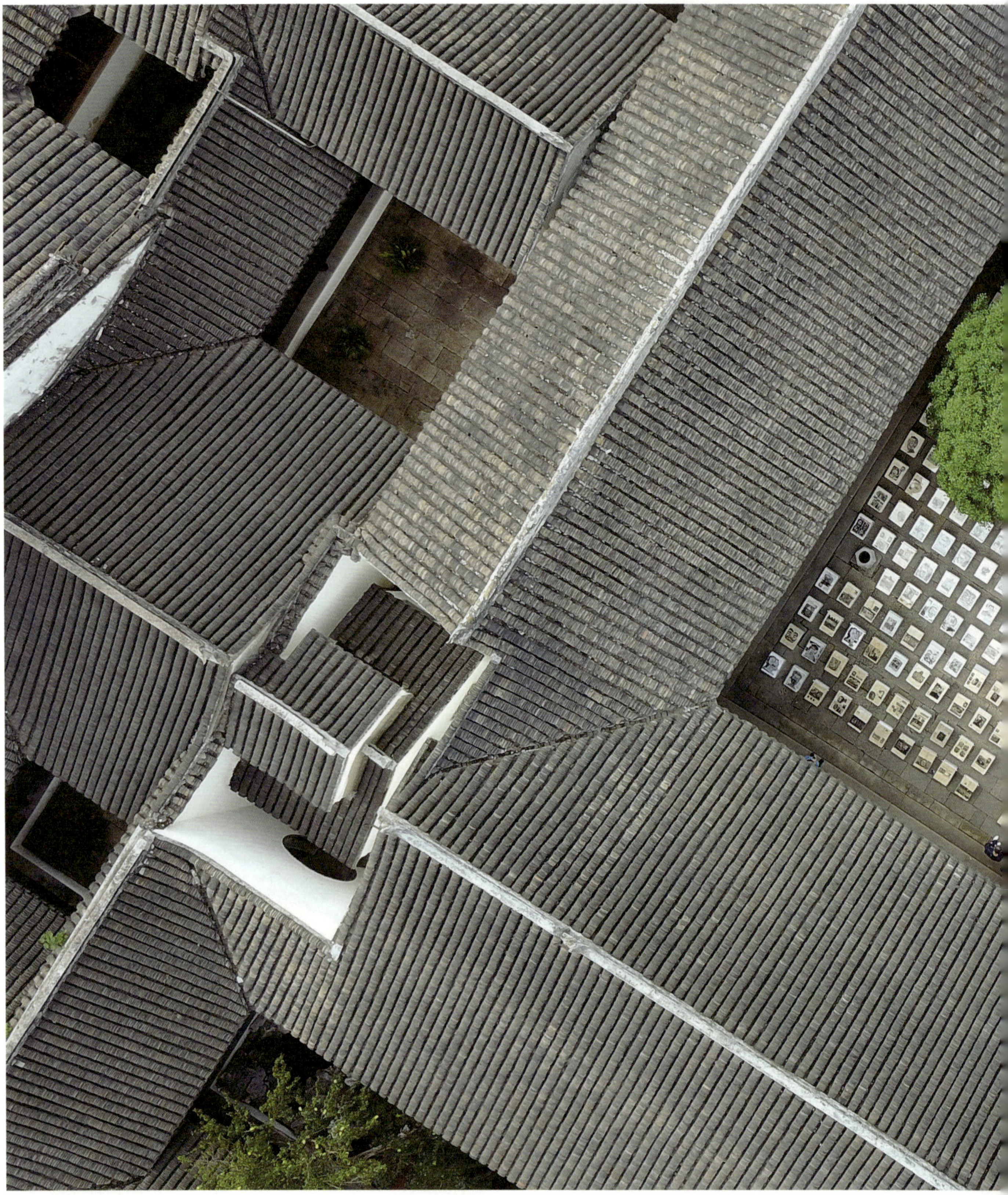

Overhead view

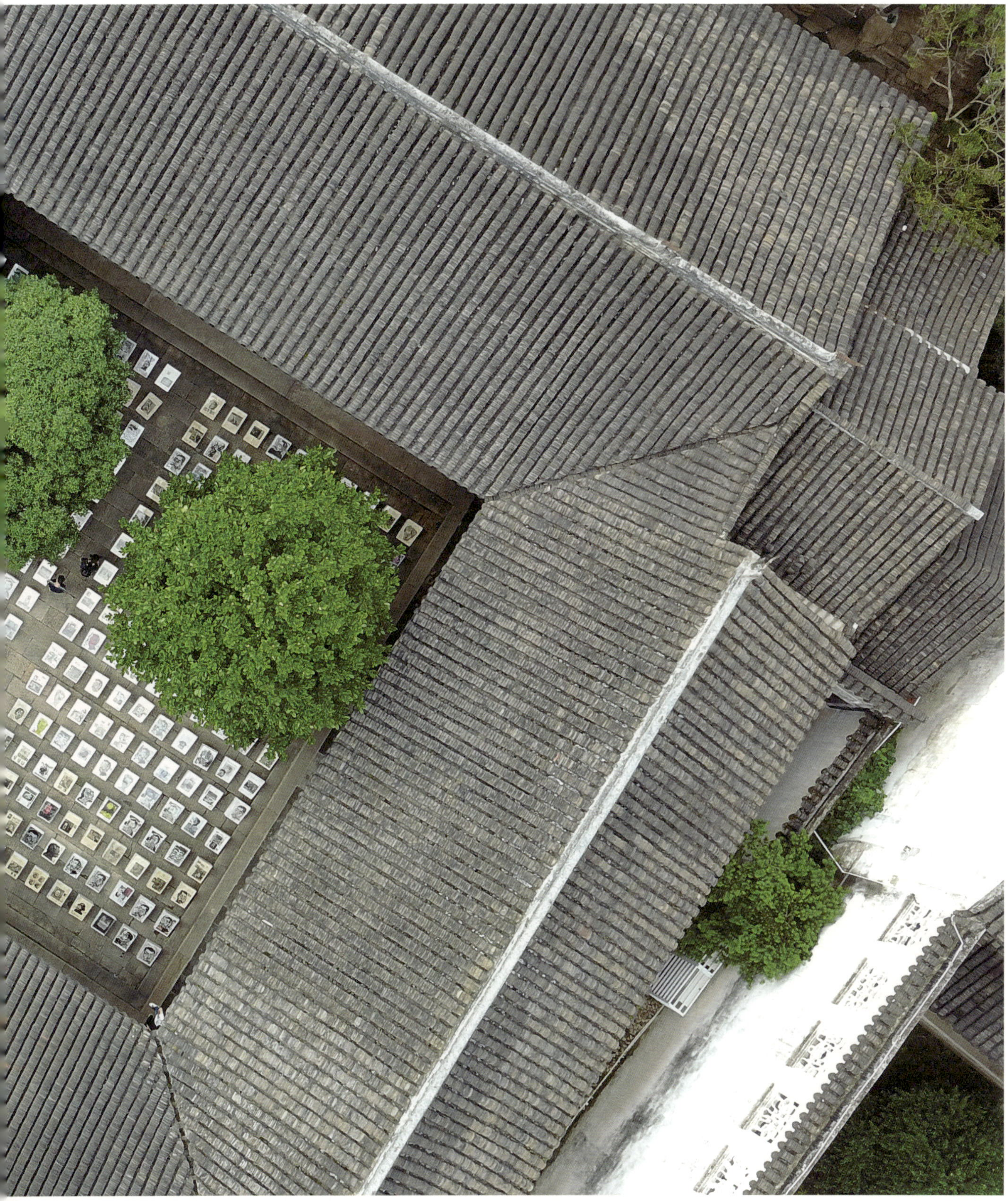

——*Three Thousand Scraps of Paper*

I have a habit of seeing nothing as real waste in my studio. All the discarded materials and failed works are kept, waiting for the right moment and inspiration. Who knows, one day they might become another new piece.

When I grew weary of woodcut, I delved into ink painting, exploring the rhythms between brush and rice paper, water and ink. Because it was an exploration, there were a large number of failed works. I tore these paintings into shreds and put them in cardboard boxes. Over time, there were over a dozen boxes of scrap paper in the studio – quite a sight! As the materials accumulated, the basic idea of an installation work took shape, and the process naturally evolved. I hoped the artwork could leave the studio and engage with public spaces, interacting with the audience. It was not just an extension of physical space but also an infinite extension of personal imagination.

These paintings featured humans, flowers, birds, fish and insects, as well as torn and discarded woodcut works. Because they were torn, the images were incomplete, fragmented and irregular. After being combined, pasted and suspended, and after being presented to viewers, they sometimes appeared strange, abrupt and intriguing, prompting contemplation. Moreover, all artists have discarded works and have experienced the process of 'three thousand scraps of paper'. This is therefore also a tribute to every hardworking artist. Thus, I named this series Three Thousand Scraps of Paper.

Transforming material substances into visual expressions, I found that the dry and withered scraps of paper suddenly gained a vibrant meaning. Occasionally creating triptychs – a natural monument form – with the discarded raw materials became a tribute to human effort and manual labour. In front of this artwork was a toilet painted gold and surrounded by scattered paper, conveying a sense of tragic power. I used to flush away my too-embarrassing-to-show works until one day the toilet got clogged. The most convenient solution turned out to be piling up the scrap paper and then thinking about how to use it. This helpless method unexpectedly became a way to gather materials, truly a blessing in disguise. The toilet represented an absent presence, a metaphor of the 'three thousand scraps of paper' that disappeared with the water flow. Meanwhile, the audience could see scraps of paper scattered on the walls and floor, blossoming like flowers, compensating for the long-standing absence of that which has always been discarded, now appearing in the spotlight as ready-made material. The paper served as the material but, at the same time, became the artwork itself, blurring the lines between waste art and art, trash and treasure.

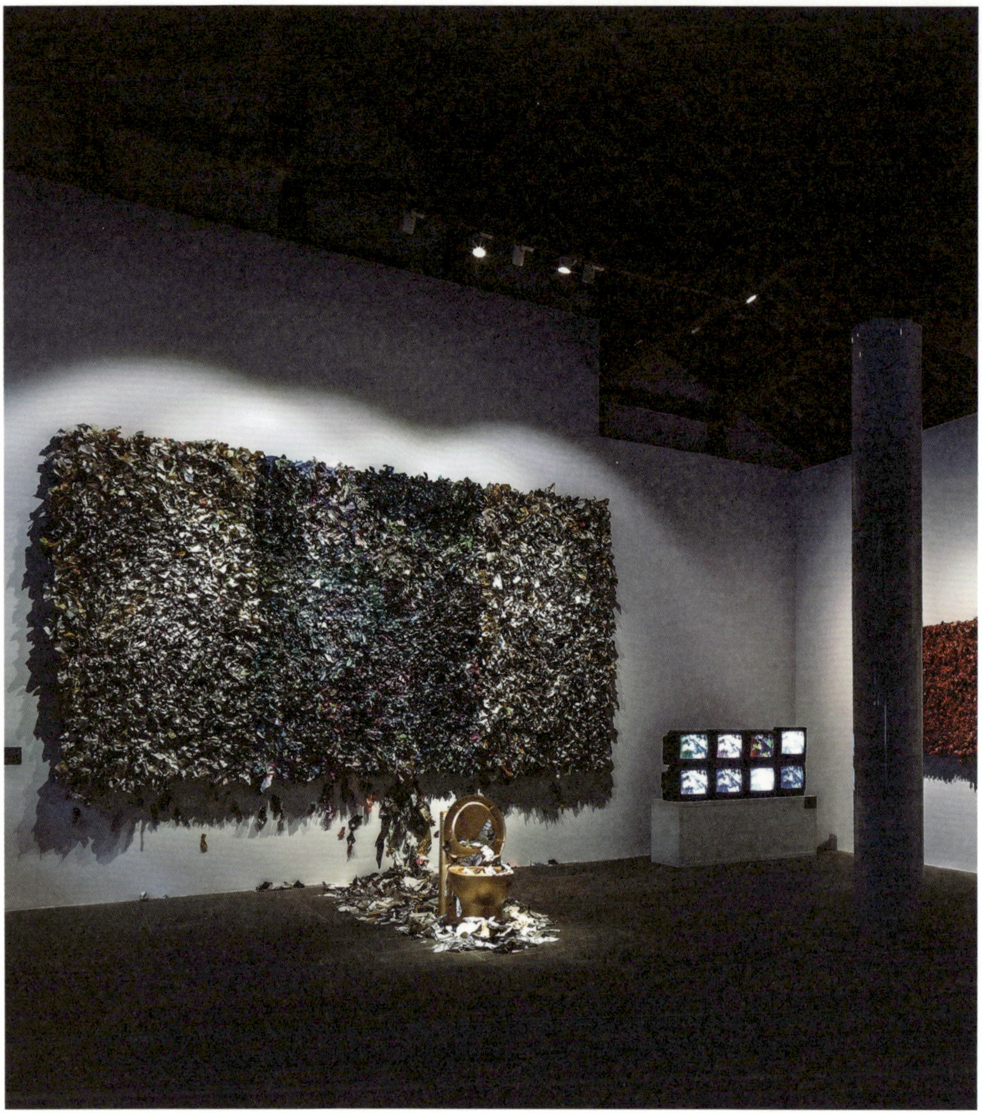

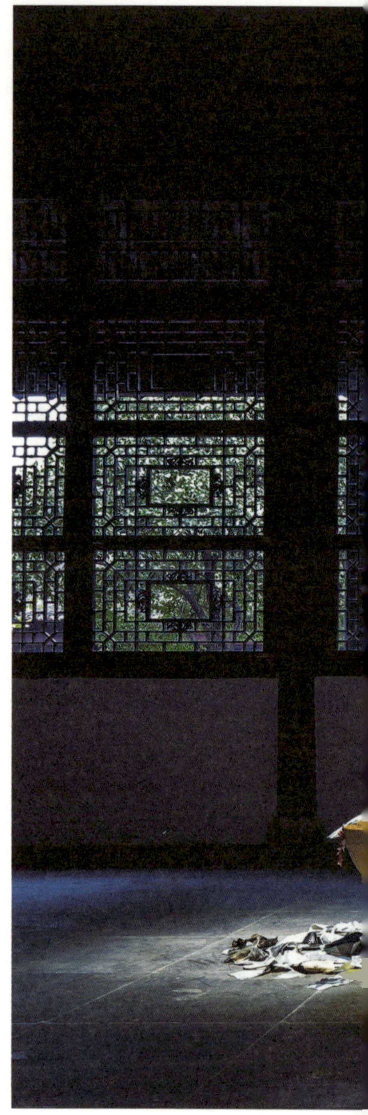

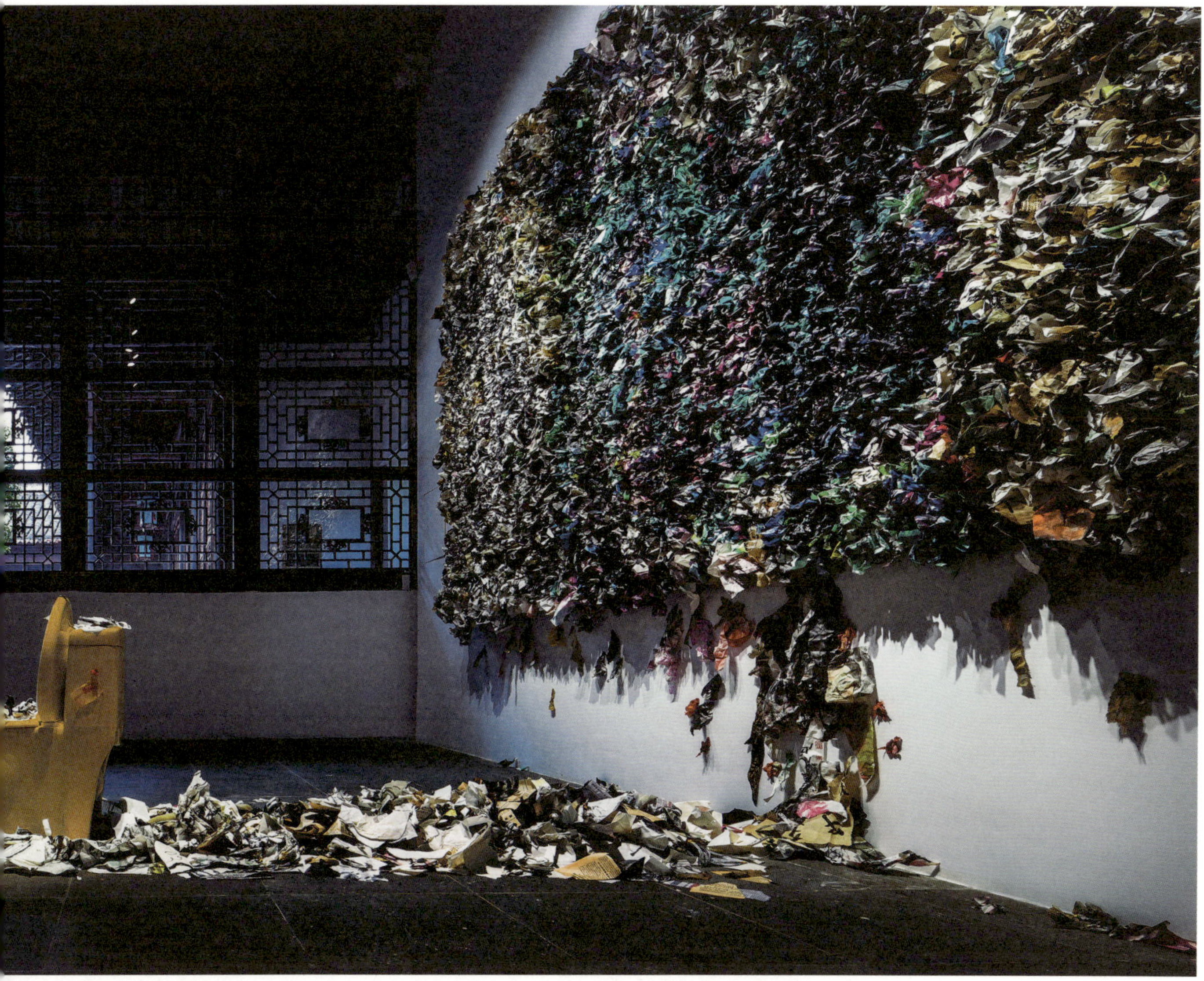

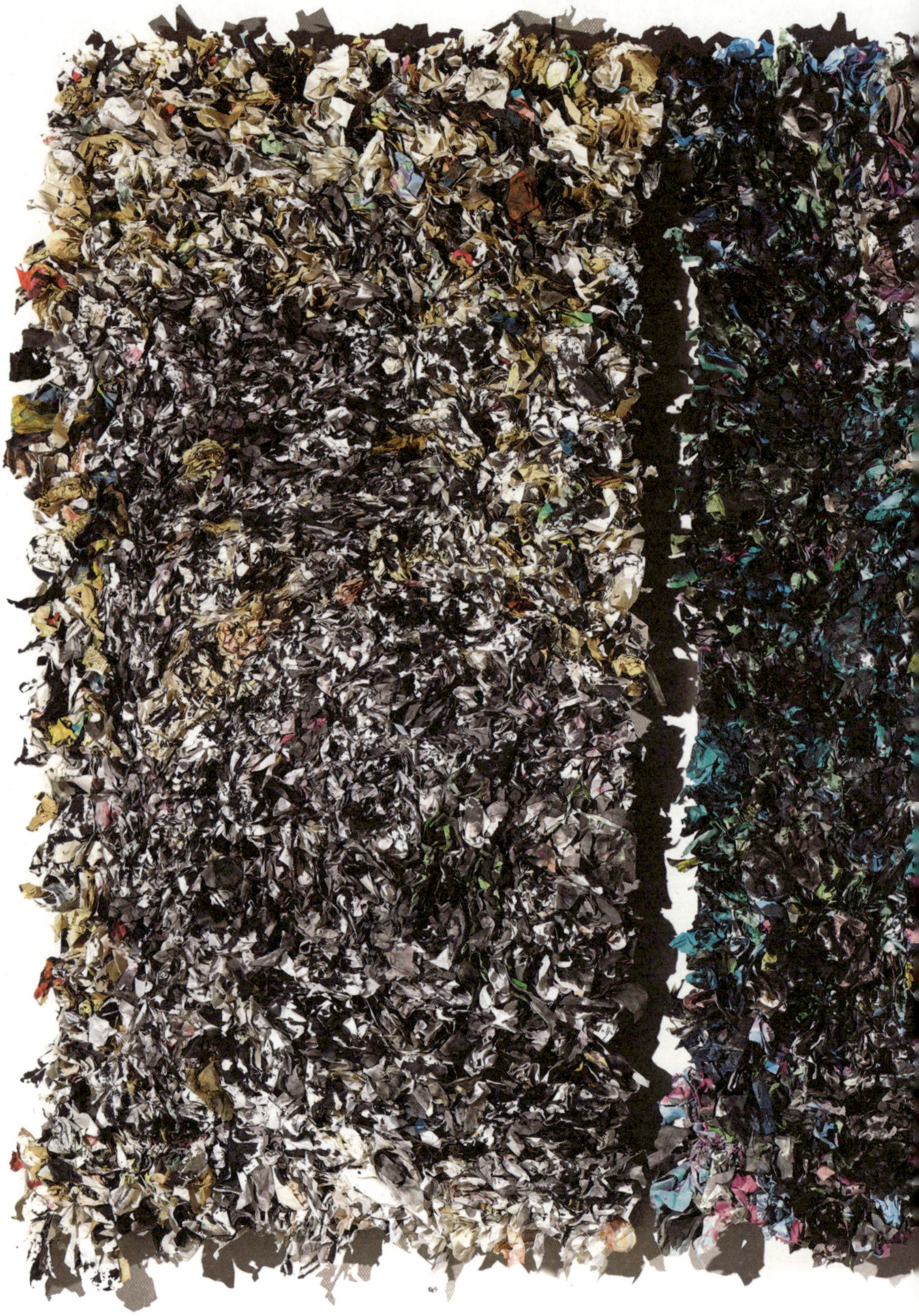

244cm × 424cm 2017

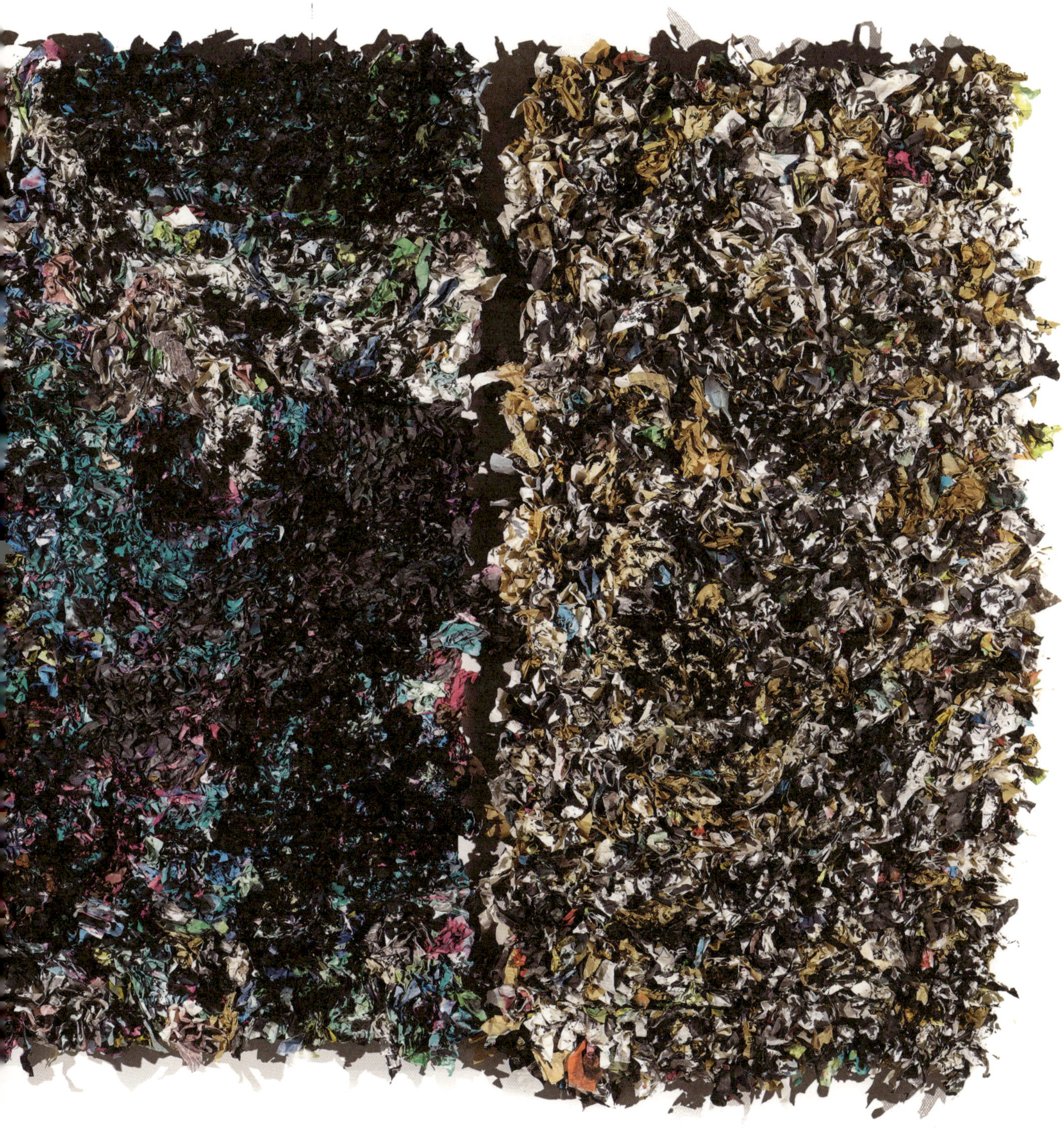

115cm × 206cm 2017

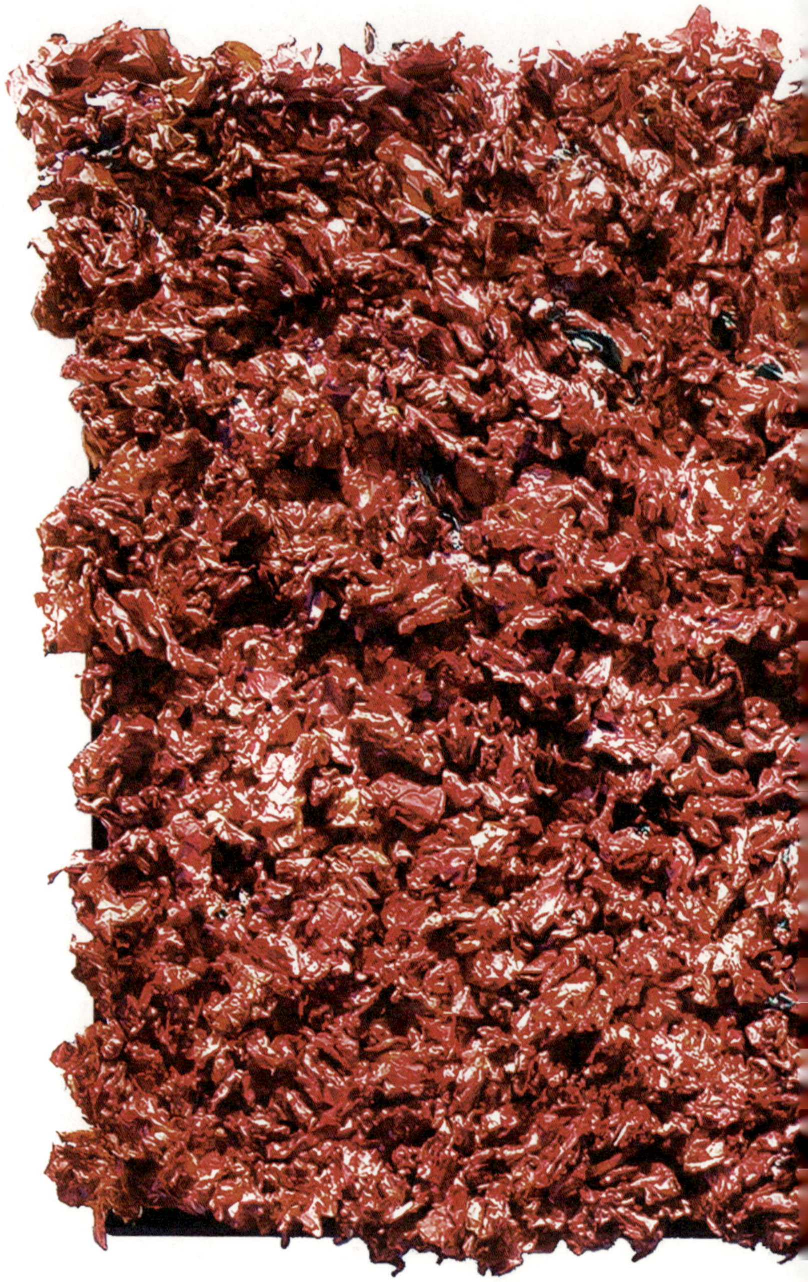

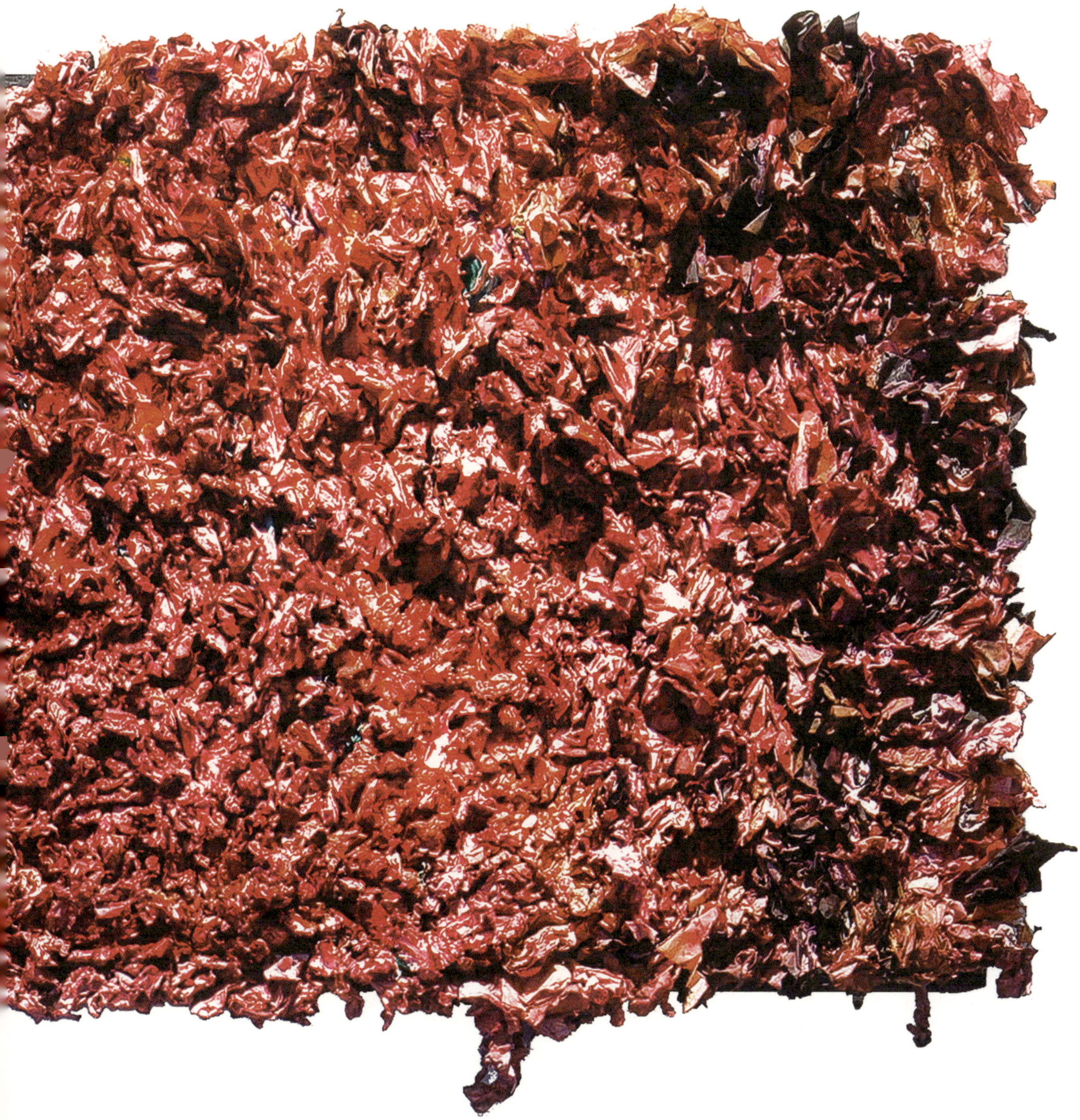

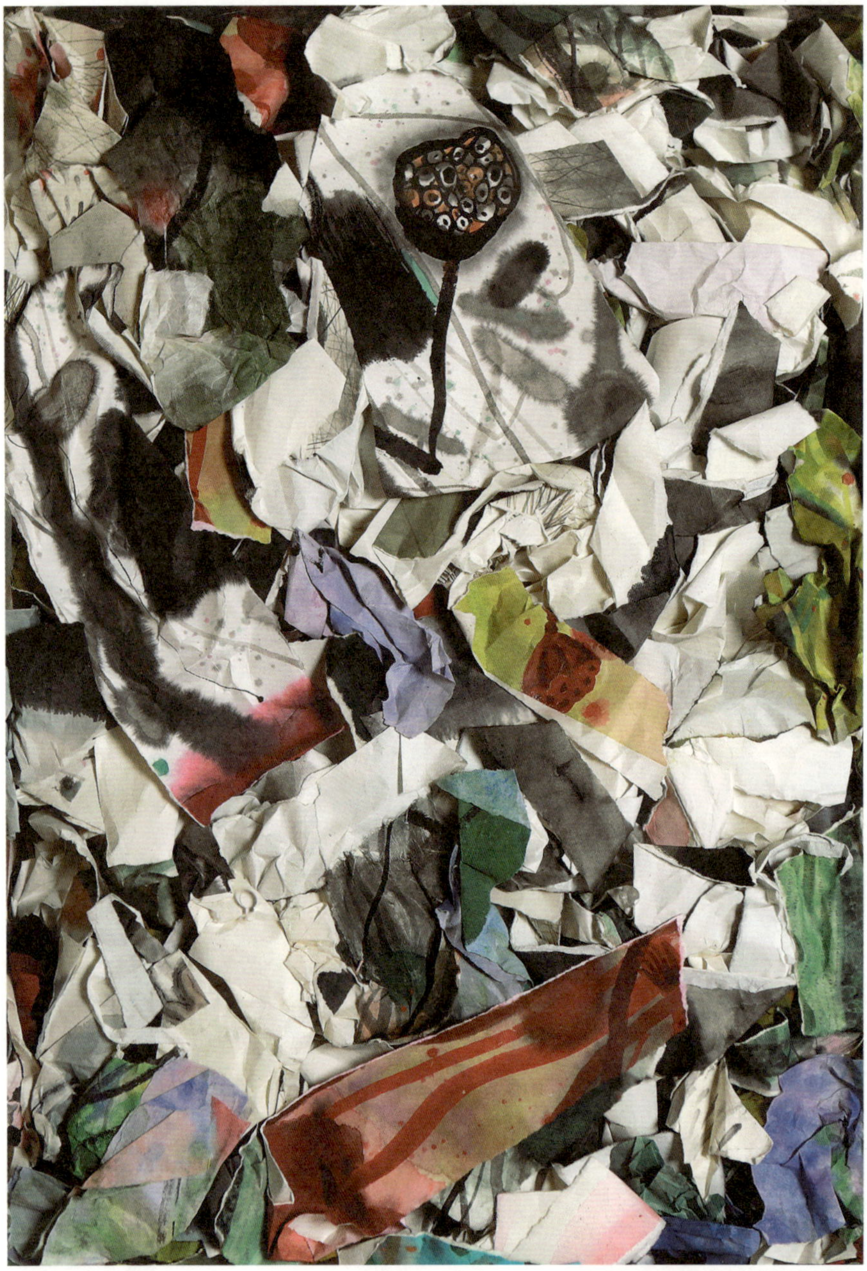

118cm × 48 × 48cm 2021

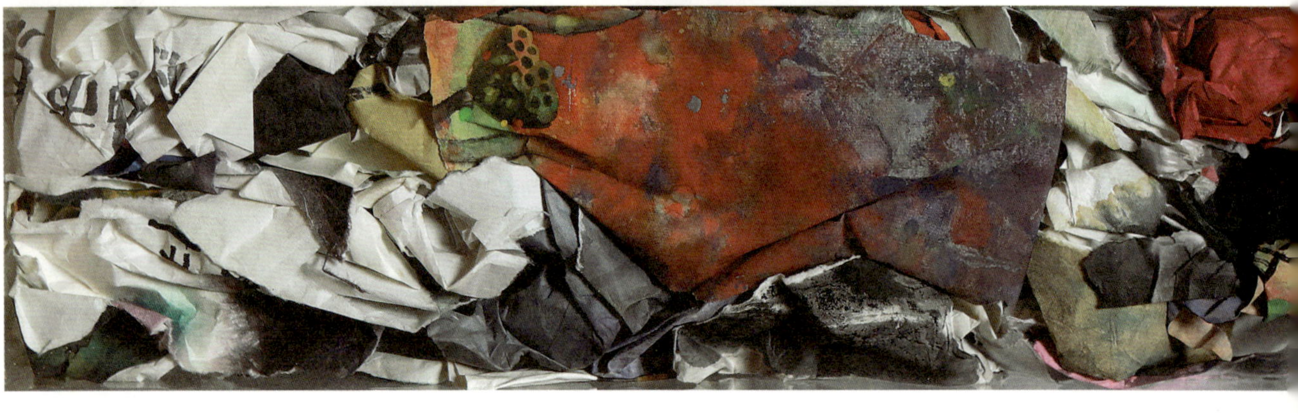

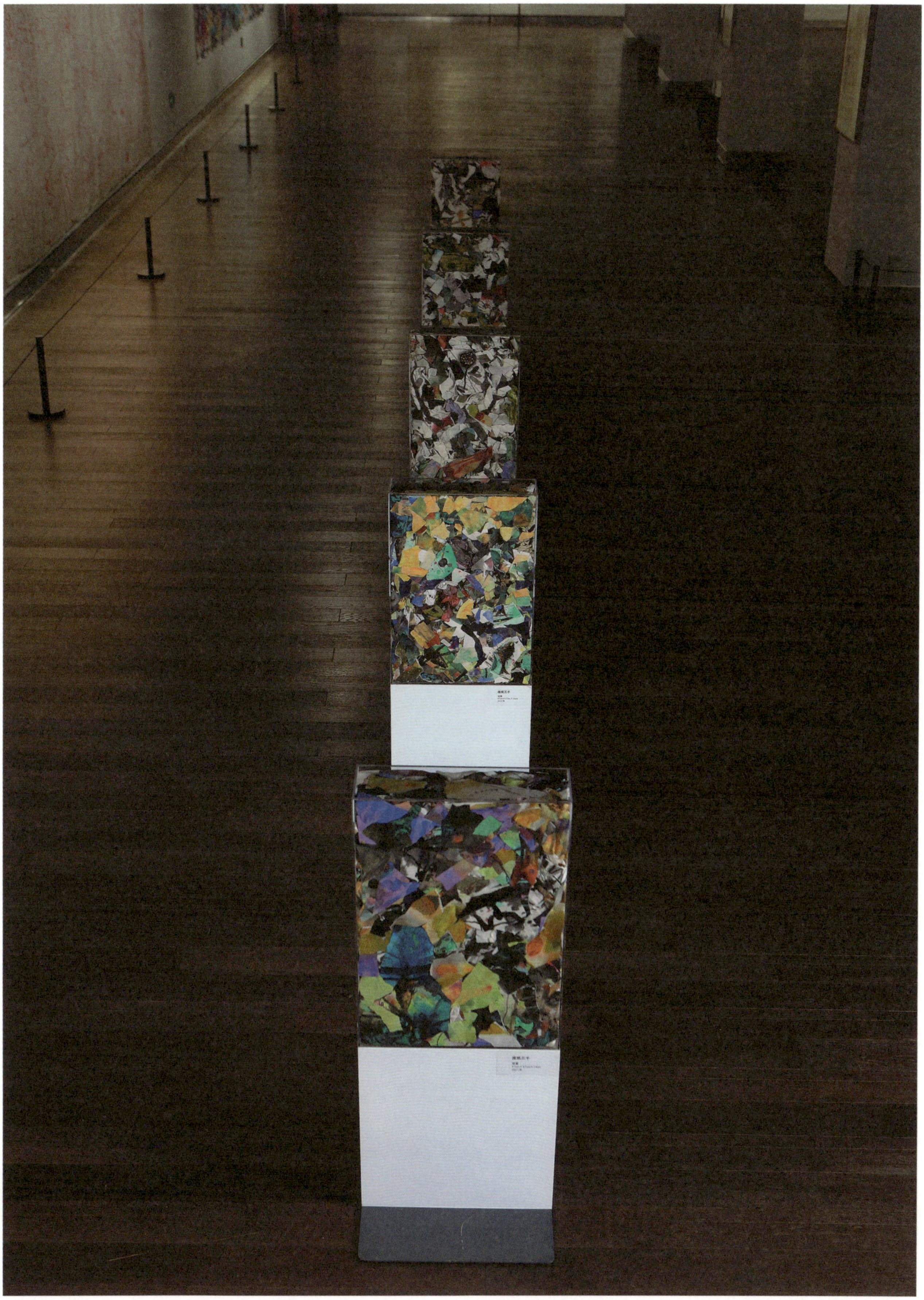

———*Arrays*

Old Newspapers, Ink, Acrylic and Composite Materials 2007—2023

How to restore the 365 pieces of *Keep Flooding the Screen*? If I were to hire a framer to mount them, the images would undoubtedly become too flat, losing the creases and seams of the worn-out newspapers, losing the texture of time. If I were to use paper strips to paste on the back of the works, I could not only preserve the words and images on the newspapers but also restore them to be old, keeping the bumps and creases, the expressions of time.

Cutting paper, brushing paste, carefully repairing. Some newspapers were too broken, so I pasted dozens of paper strips, crisscrossing and overlapping like gauze on wounded skin, shimmering with a sense of care. During the process, I would sometimes be attracted to the content of newspapers from decades ago, feeling sadness, heaviness, or giving a hearty laugh. Repairing them felt like repairing myself, an action of self-healing. The unevenness and yellowing of these old newspapers emitted the scent of bygone years. Opening the wrinkles, smoothing the gaps, occasionally cutting a headline from a then newly released news article, pasting a flower or fish, or a celebrity photo, or random labels from packets of disinfectant wipes, recording the darkest moments when people wrestled with viruses. All the patches repair wounds, repair an era full of scars, interspersed with voices conversing with the world, preserving expressions of the times.

While black-and-white works remained a significant portion of the whole, I transformed the rest into colourful, thick, mysterious, solemn pieces, prompting them to split off into new artworks. I aimed for fluctuation and temperature change across the entire set. Old newspapers were overlaid with my woodcut 'grid language', with some more directly overlaid with oil paint on the surface, adding colours to the previous black-and-white woodcuts. Then titles, symbols, dots, lines, surfaces, road signs, geometric shapes and more were pasted onto the surface, making the works lively, light-hearted and funny. After transformation, *Keep Flooding the Screen* from five years ago became the later *Arrays*.

Arrays contains a series of works presented in double-sided acrylic frames, increasing a sense of space. Viewers can see the ubiquitous 'grid' on the front, and the large amount of information from the old newspapers on the back of the works, including residual colours and traces of hand printing. The frames are arranged irregularly, hanging high and low, with infrared rays and shadows to create confusion and abruptness, enhancing a sense of disorientation, like arrays in Taoism. The red light fills the space between works, falling on the faces and bodies of the viewers, inviting them to experience the tension, oppression and confusion more deeply, to seek the source of light. Following the light, the viewers step into the next exhibition hall, shiny and spacious, a free and bright world.

As long as life exists, hope remains; where there is hope, we can continue our private thinking.

Old newspapers grow older, new newspapers will become old newspapers in the same way that news will inevitably become old news. However, eroded things will eventually be reborn. Using old newspapers for art is not simply a matter of material choice; it is using the vastness of eras as a canvas, painting personal interpretations of the world, dancing with the past, implanting reflection, infusing care, and provoking the rebirth of art. No matter how diverse the form, the essence is only conceptual.

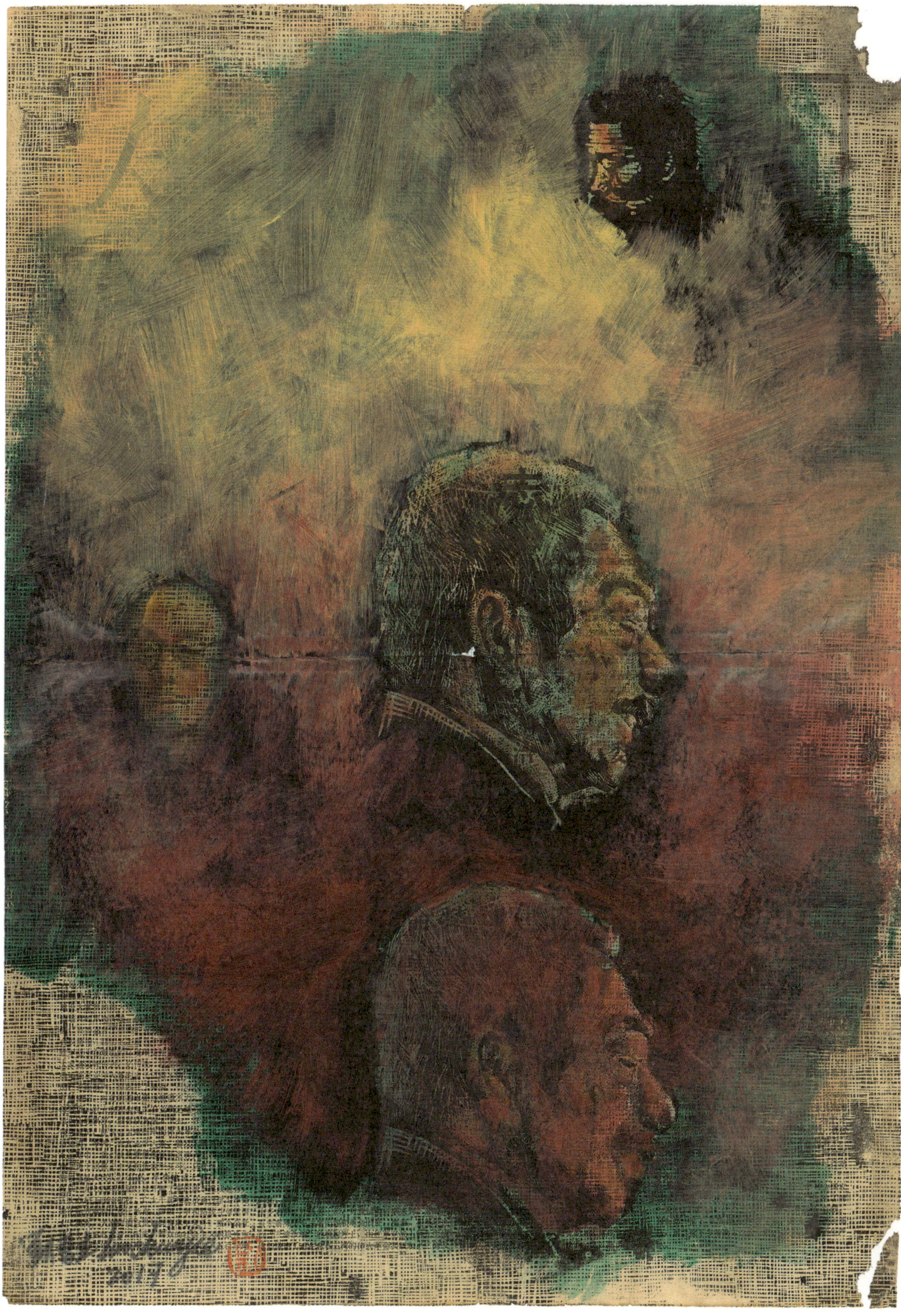

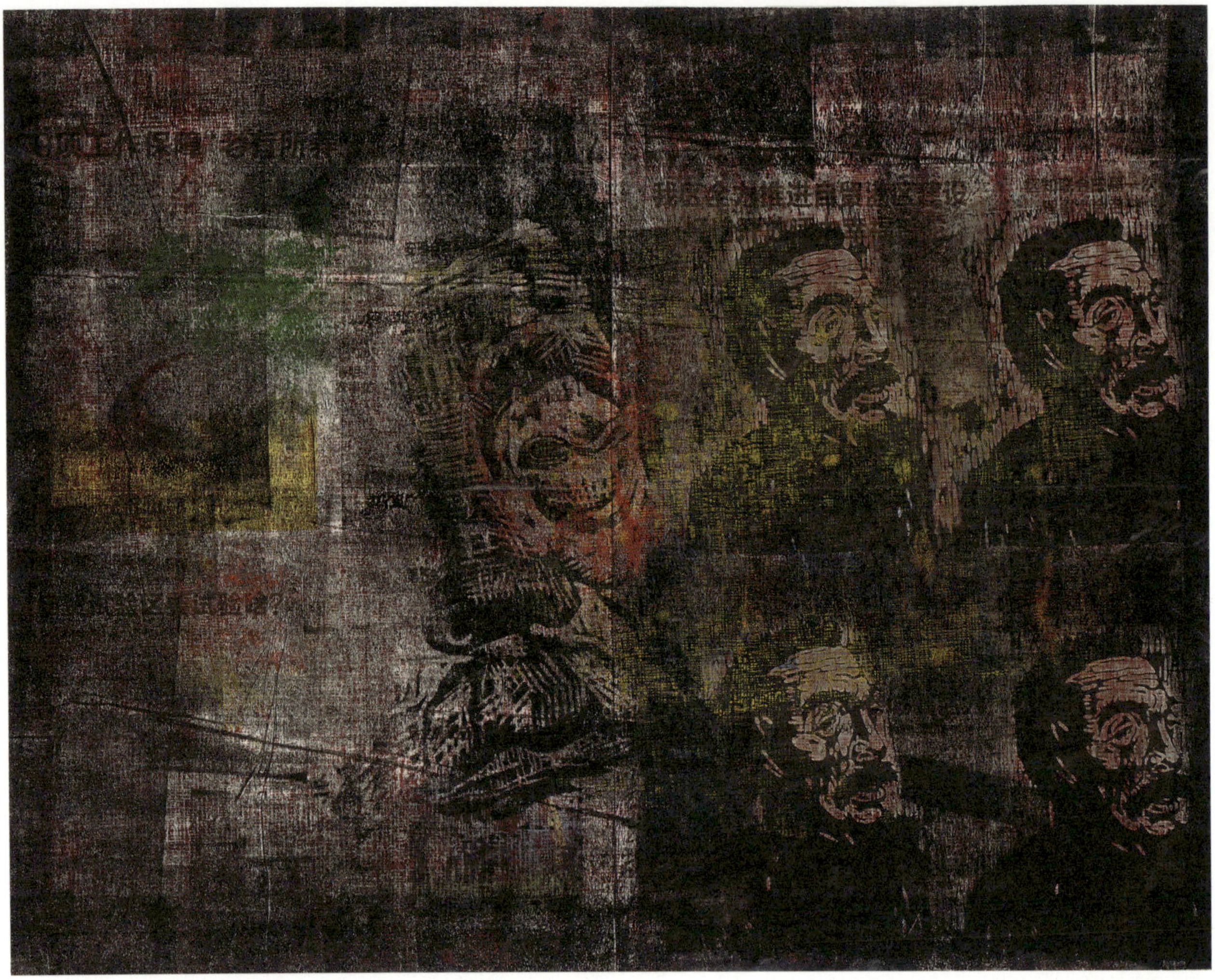

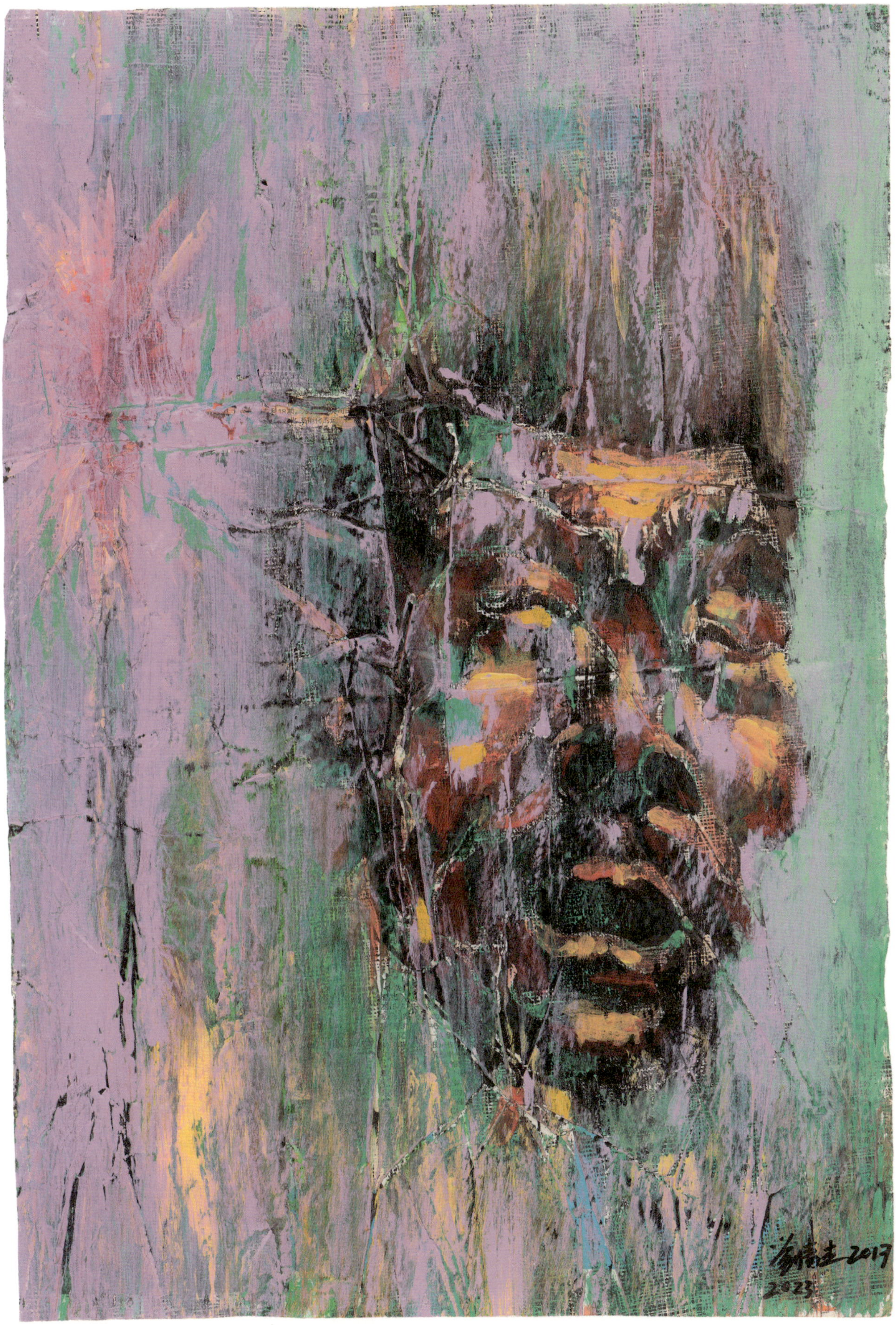

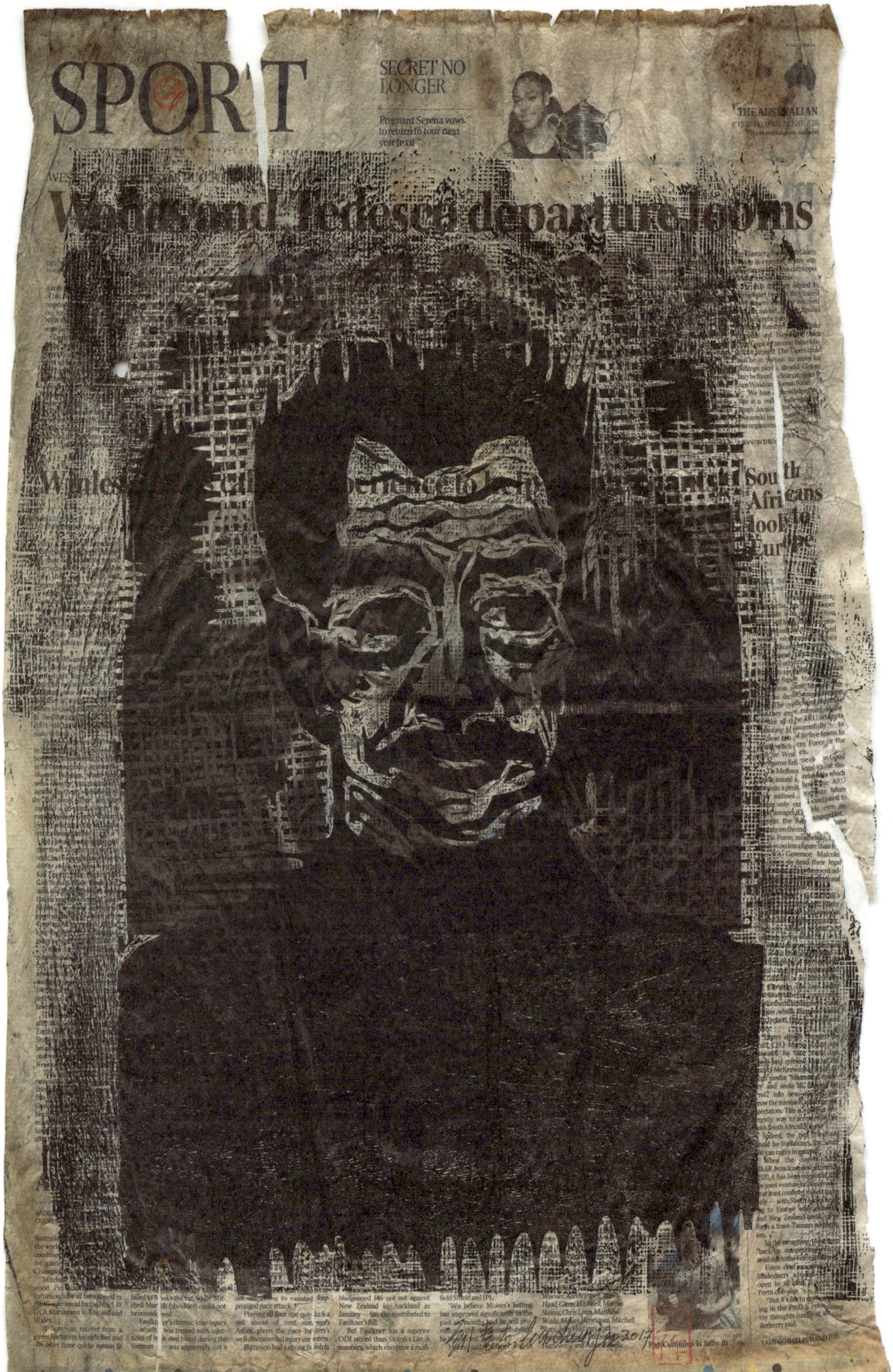
SPORT
SECRET NO LONGER
Pregnant Serena vows to return to tour next year [p33]
THE AUSTRALIAN
departure looms

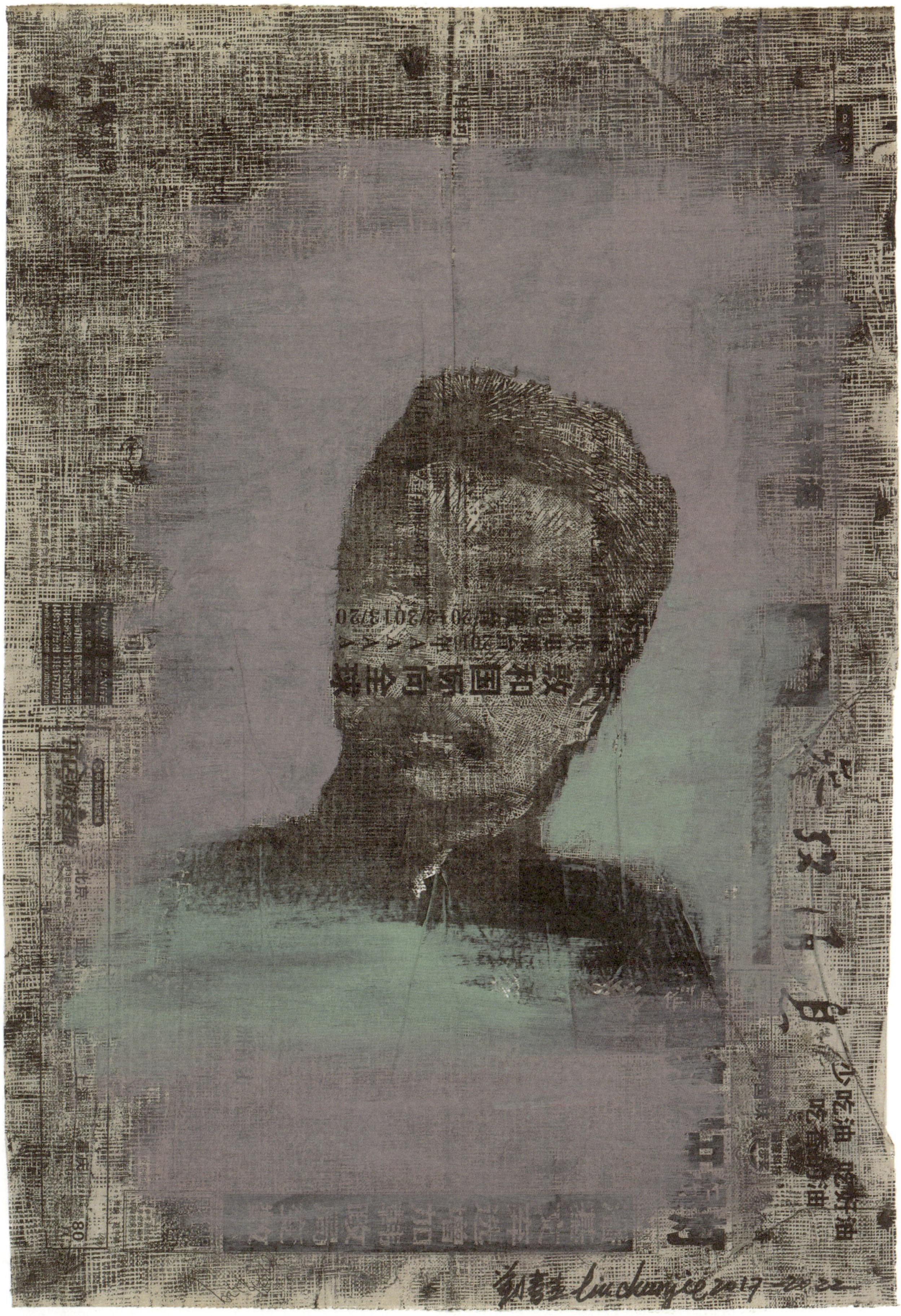

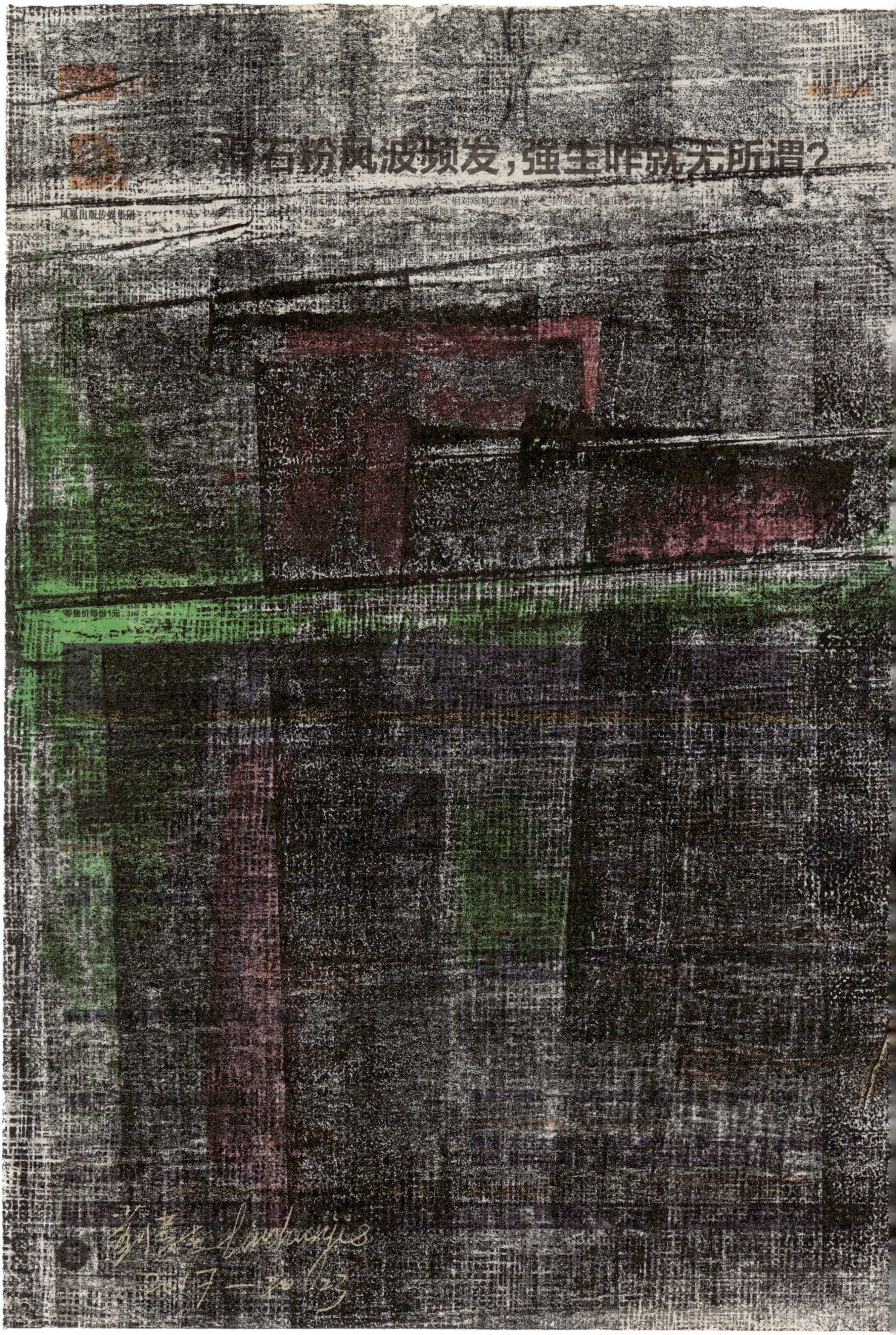
滑石粉风波频发，强生咋就无所谓？

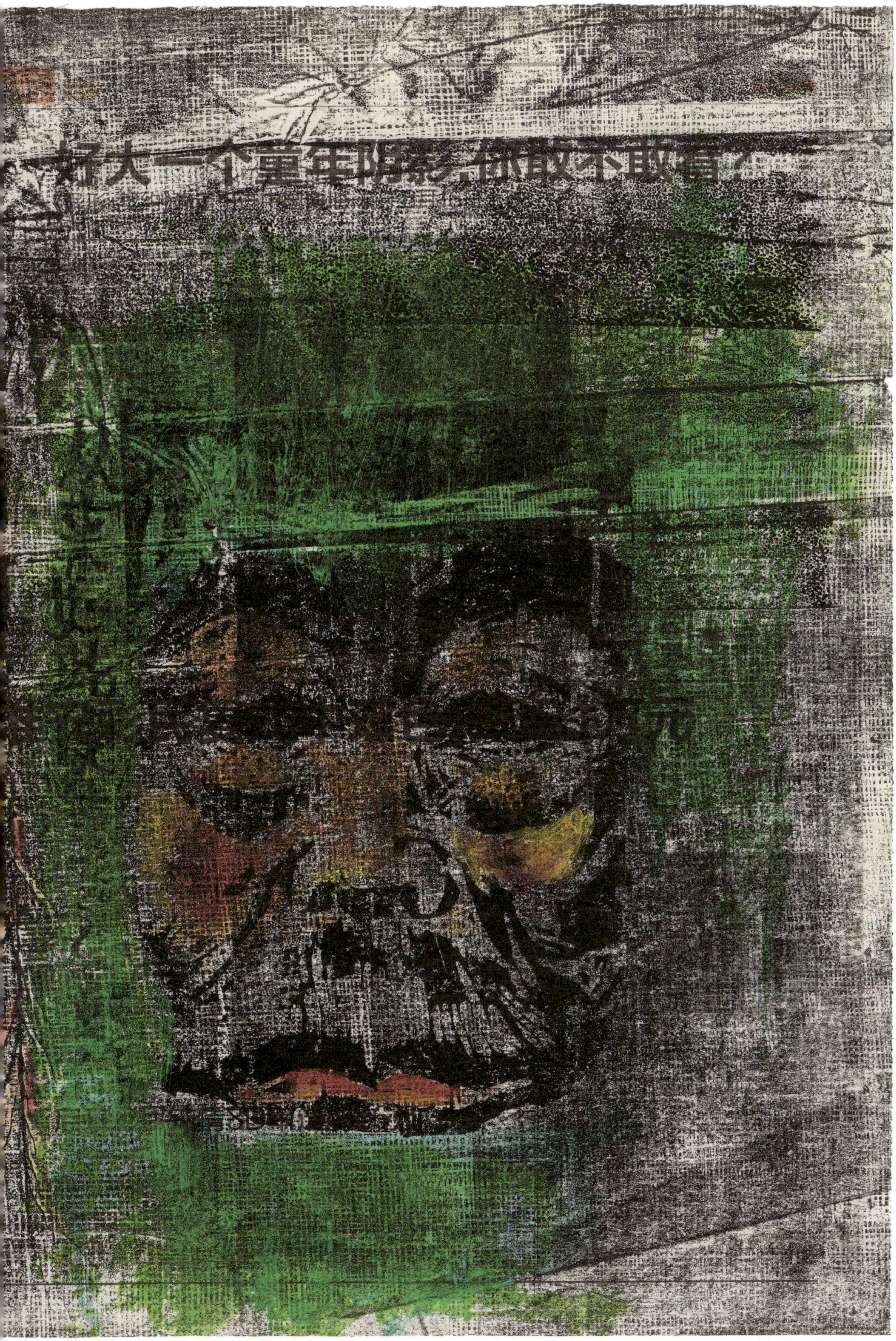
好大一个童年阴影,你敢不敢看?

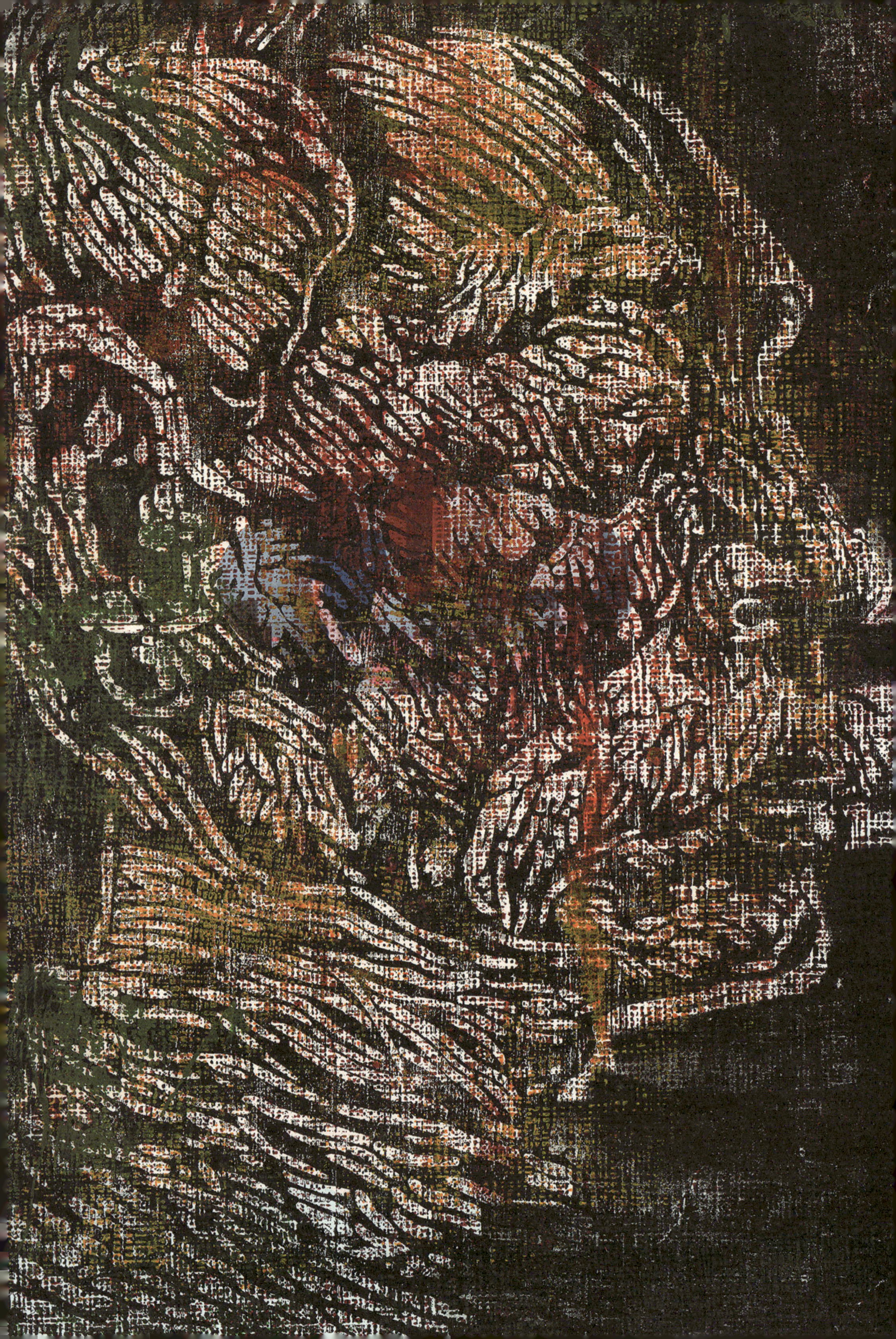

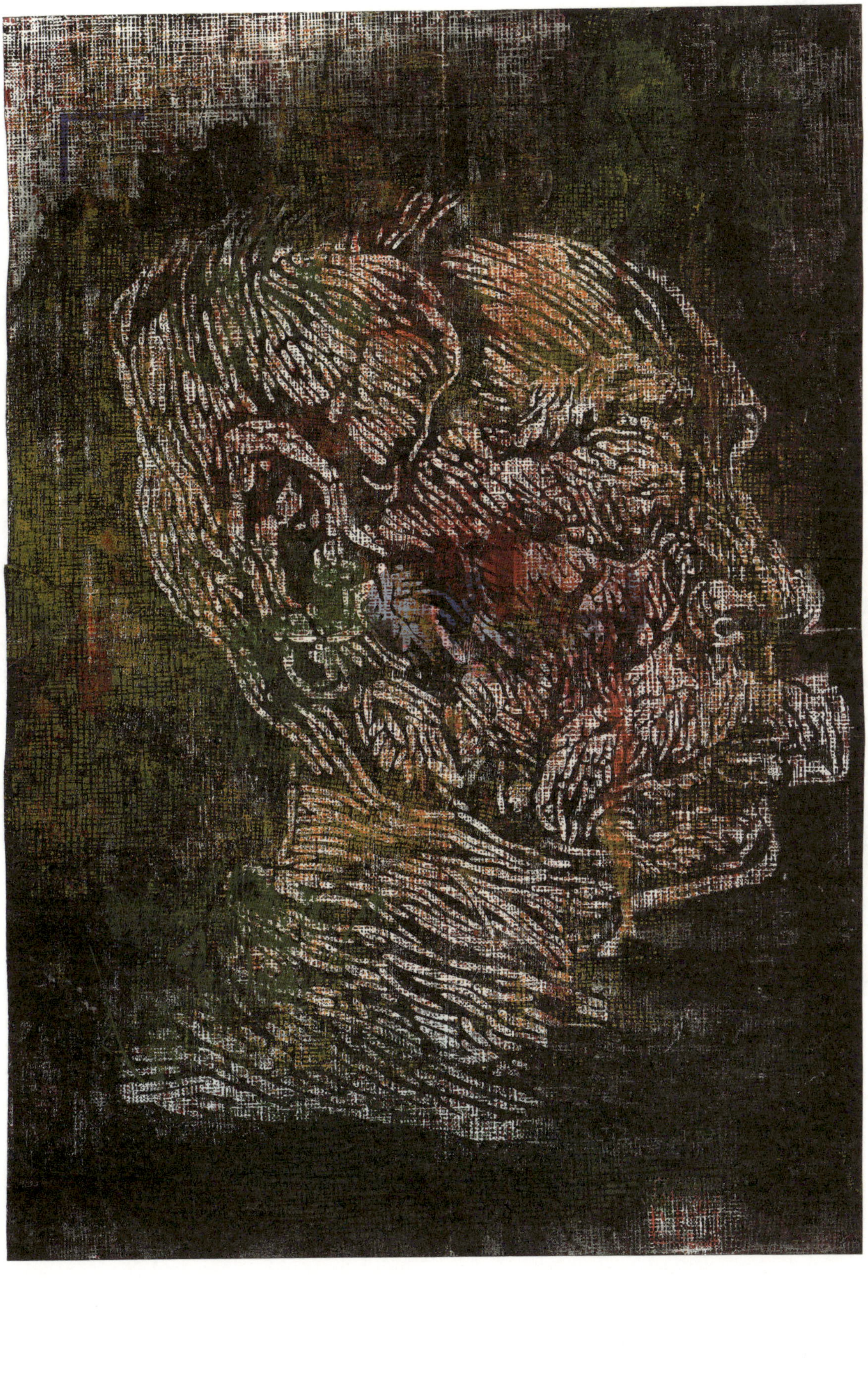

Installation Site

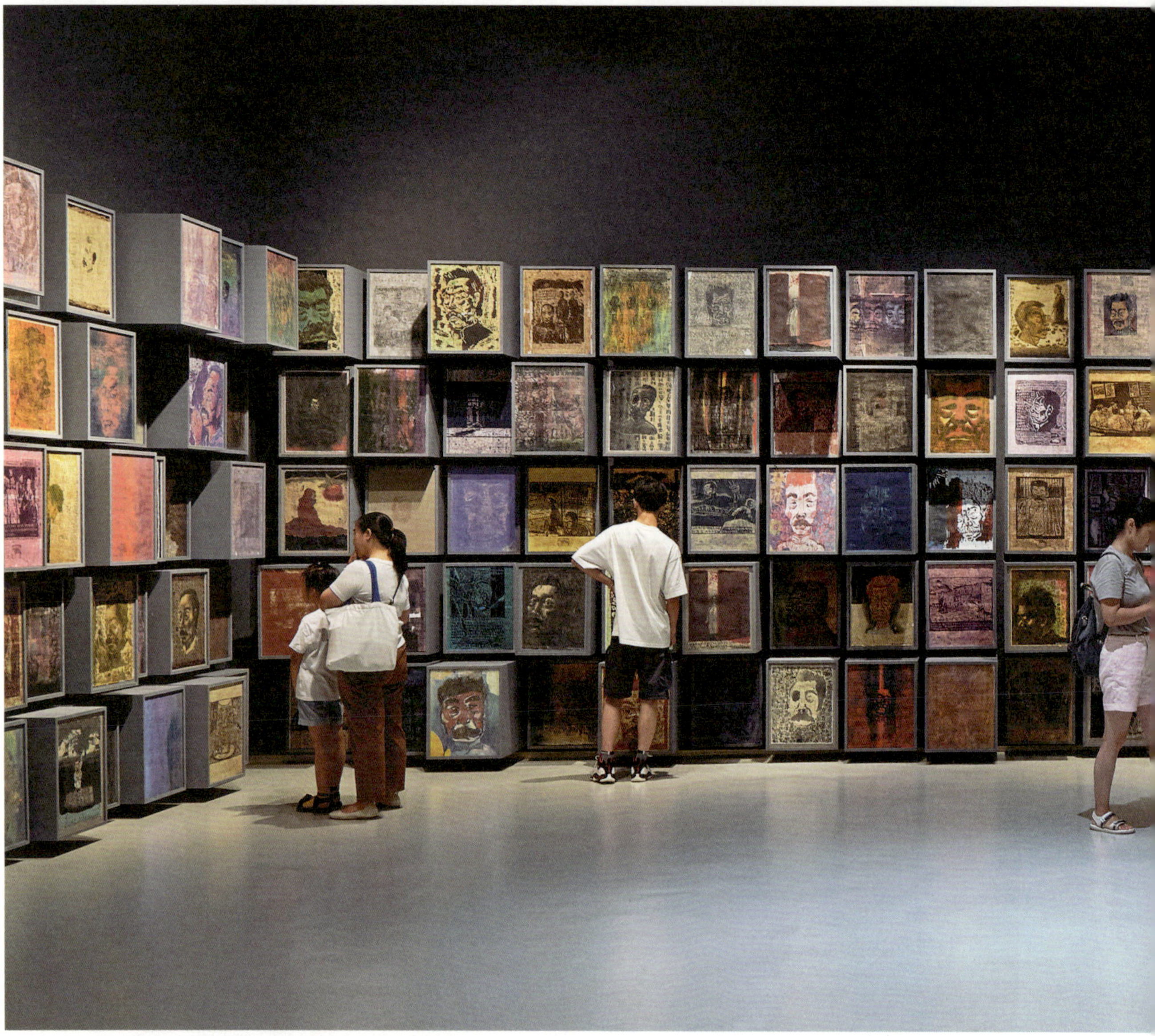

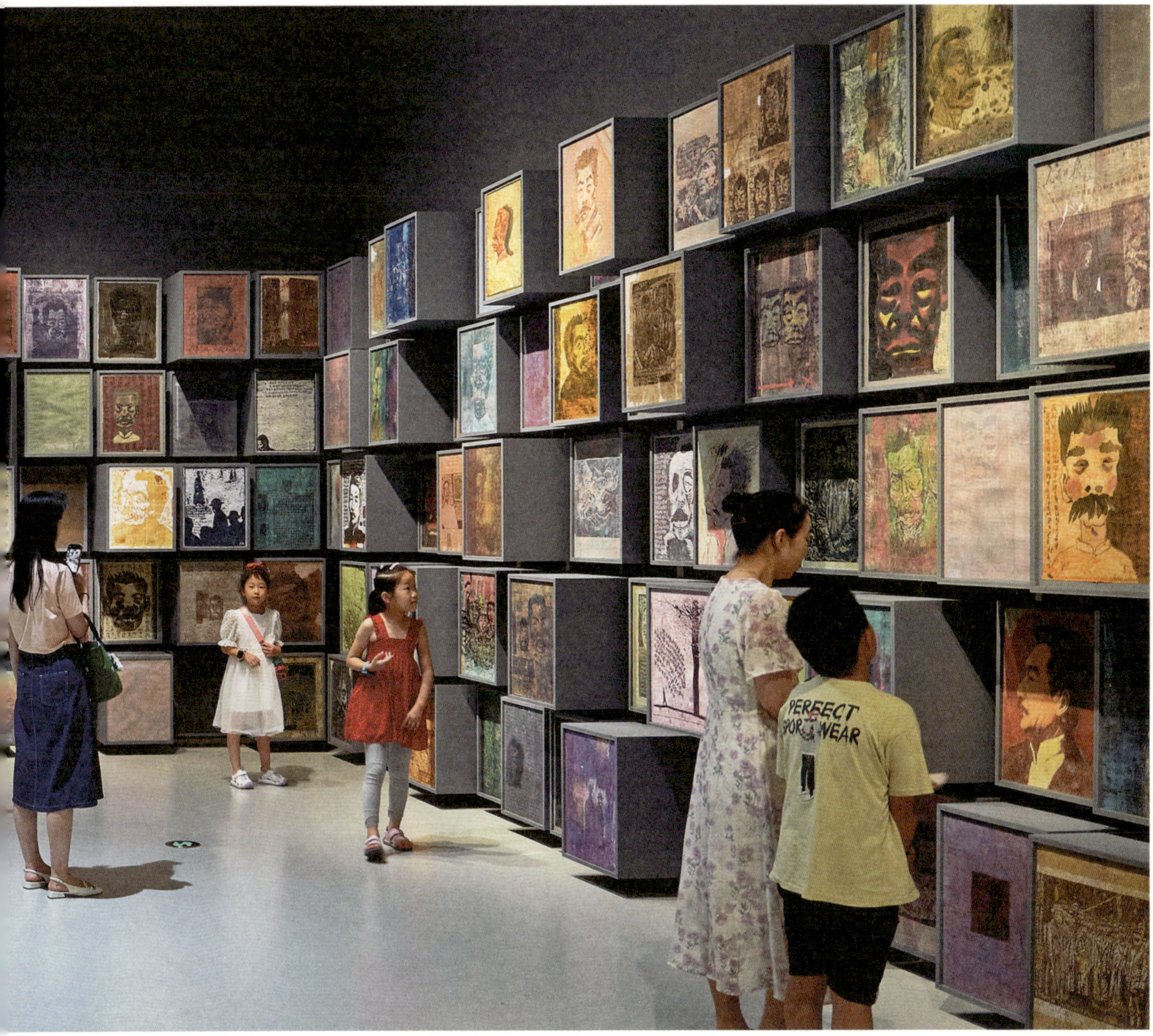
PERFECT

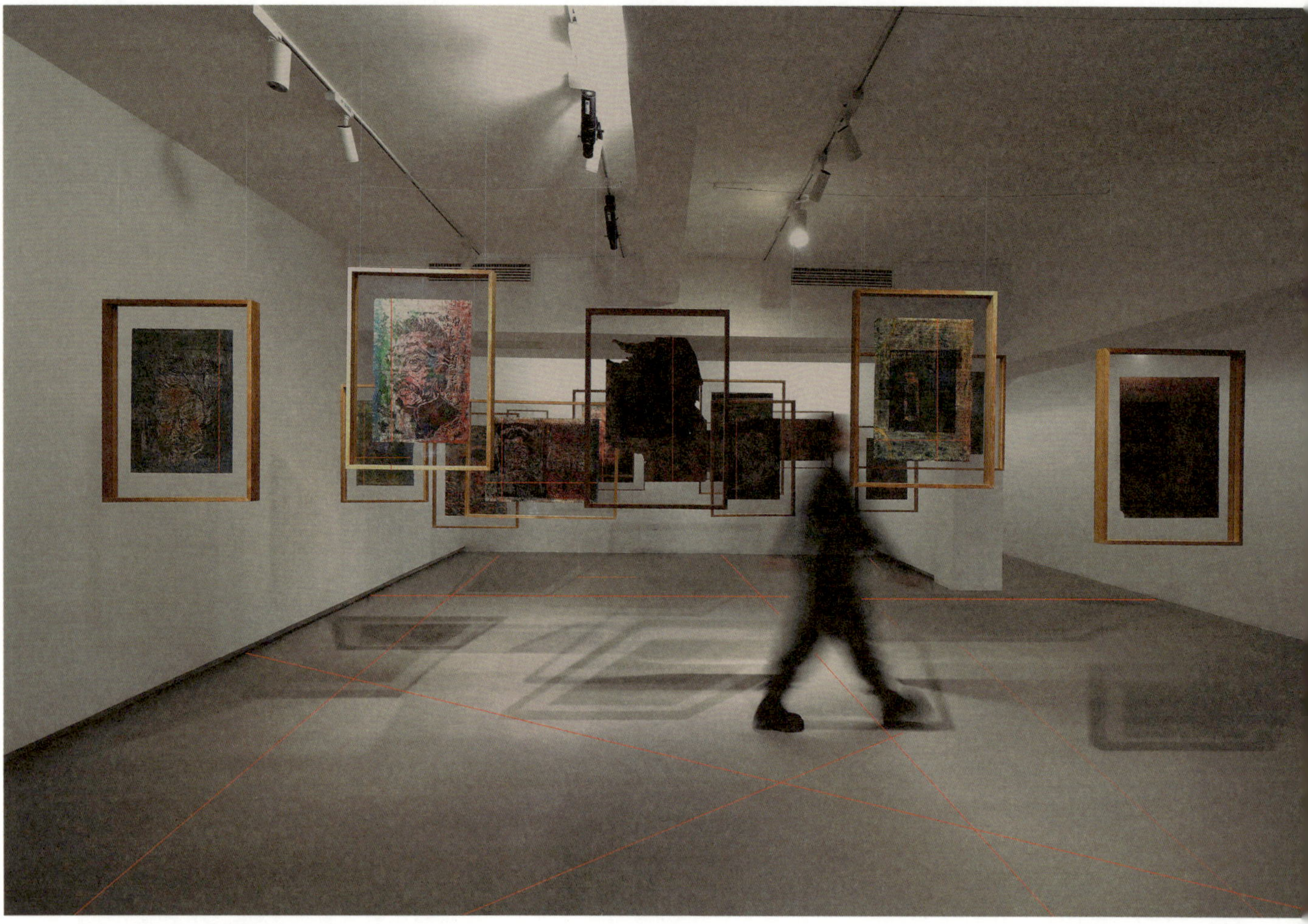

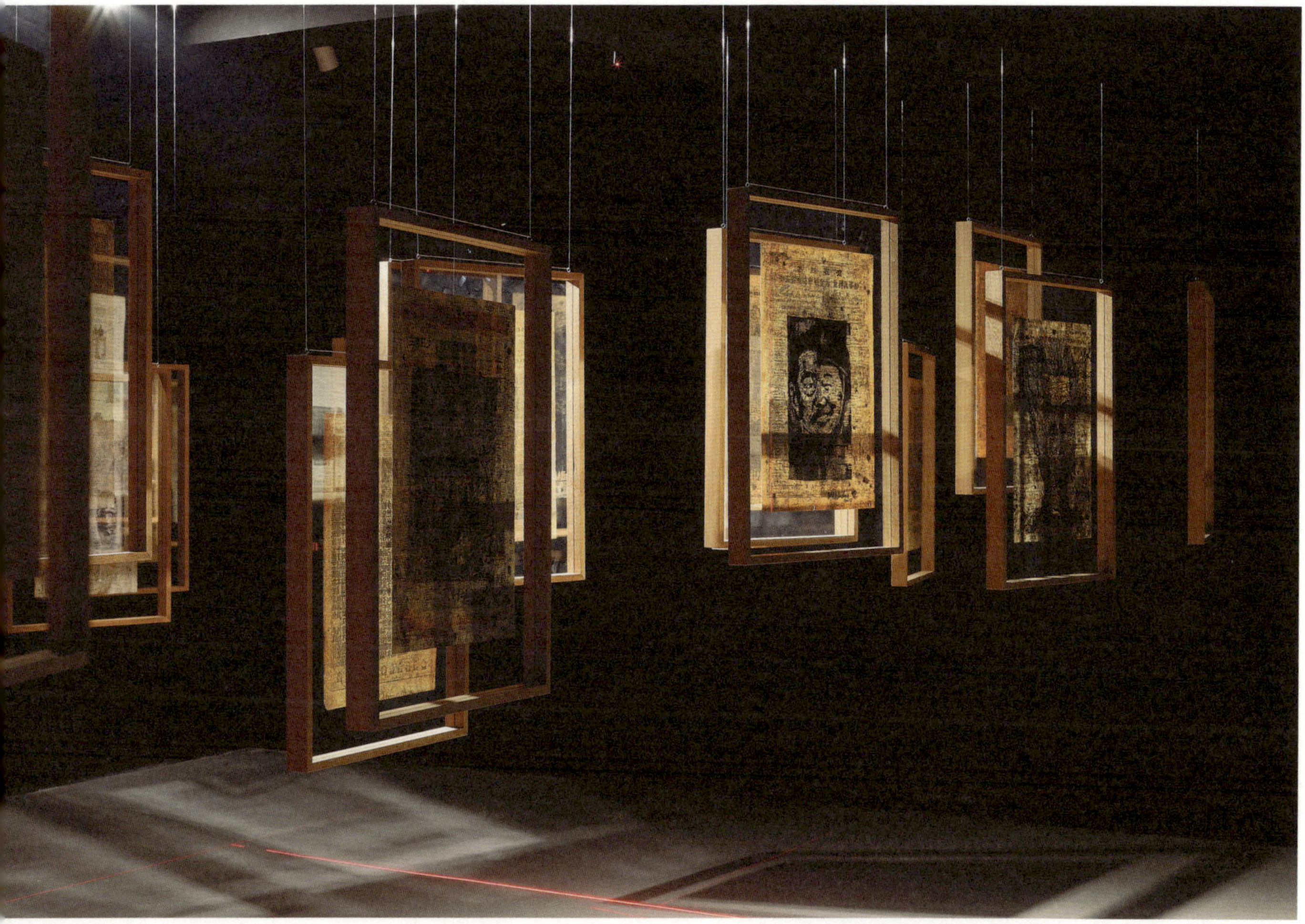

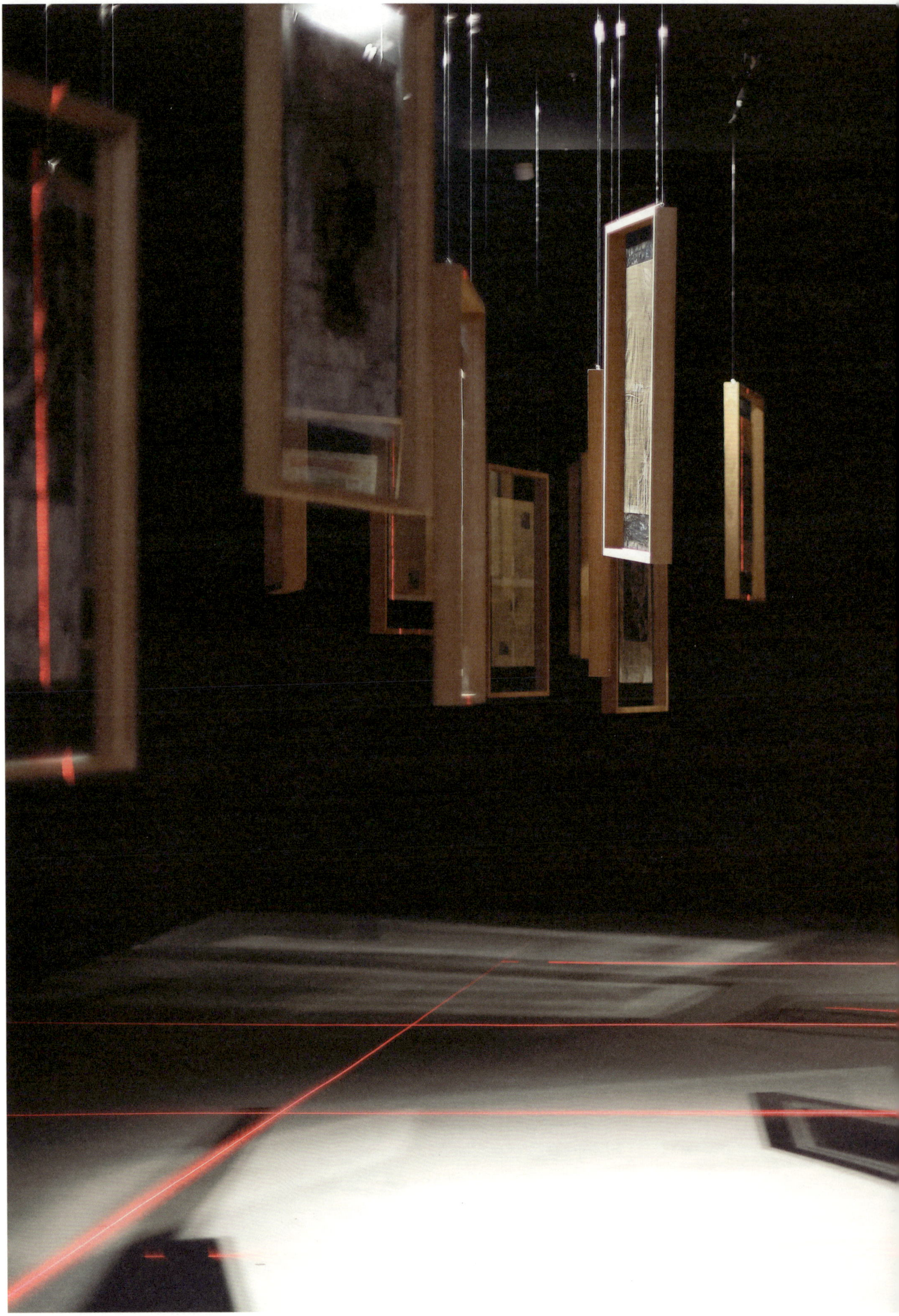

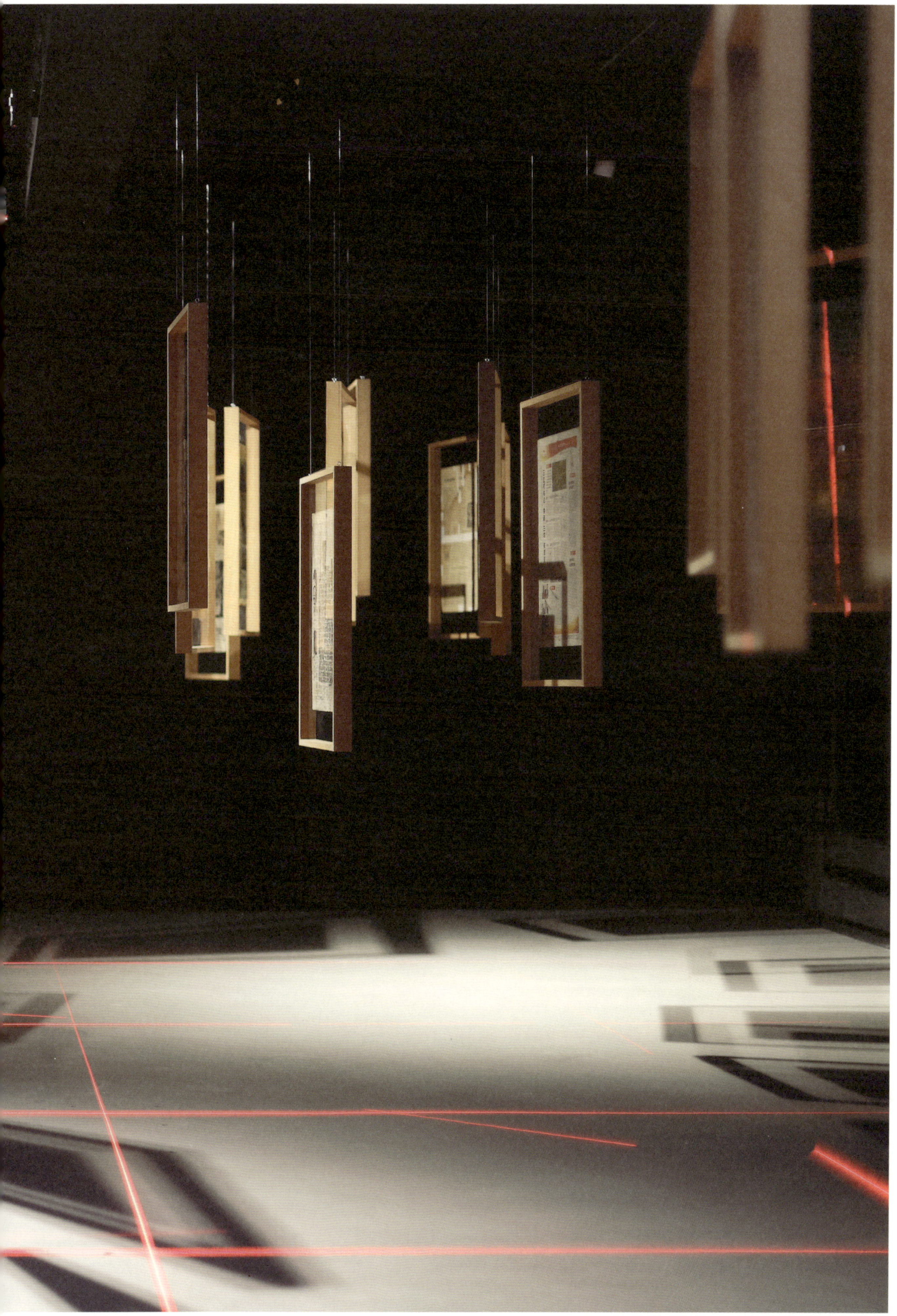

The Creative Process Using Old Newspapers

1. Preparing to Restore Old Newspapers

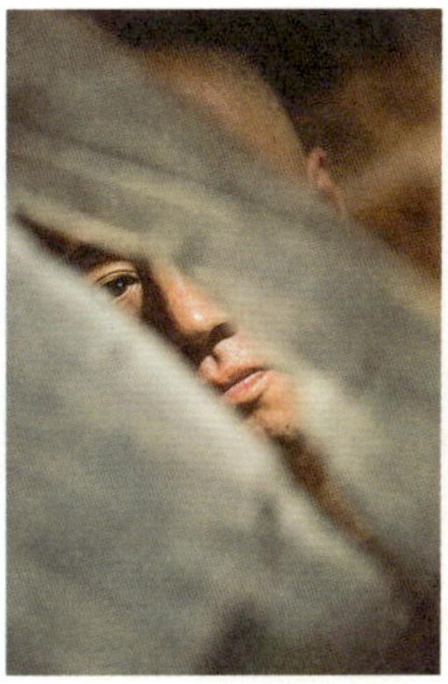

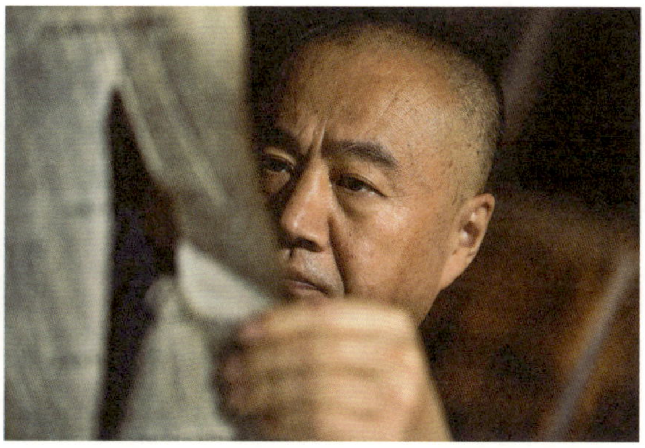

2. Restoring Old Newspapers

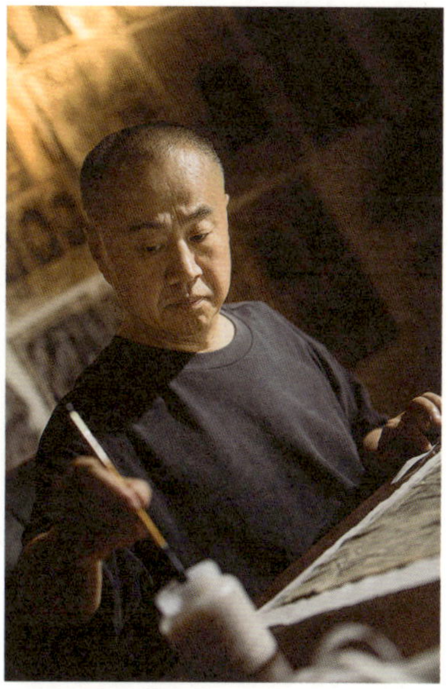

3. Paste and Repair

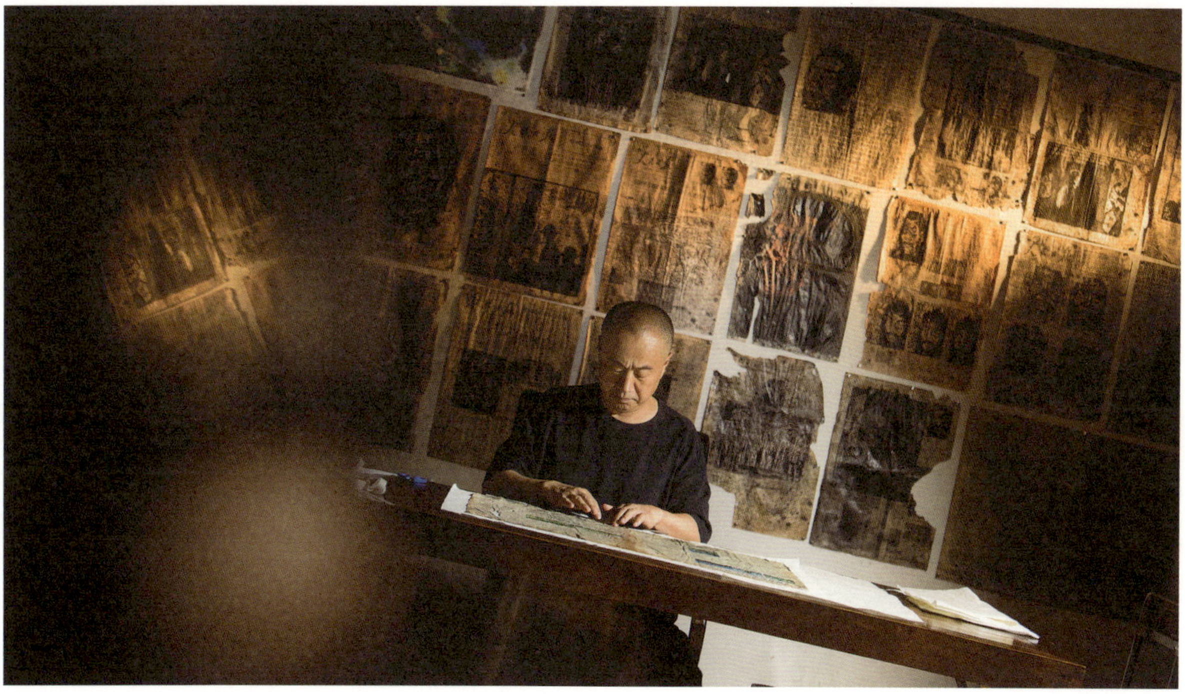

4. Preparation Before Rubbing (Printing)

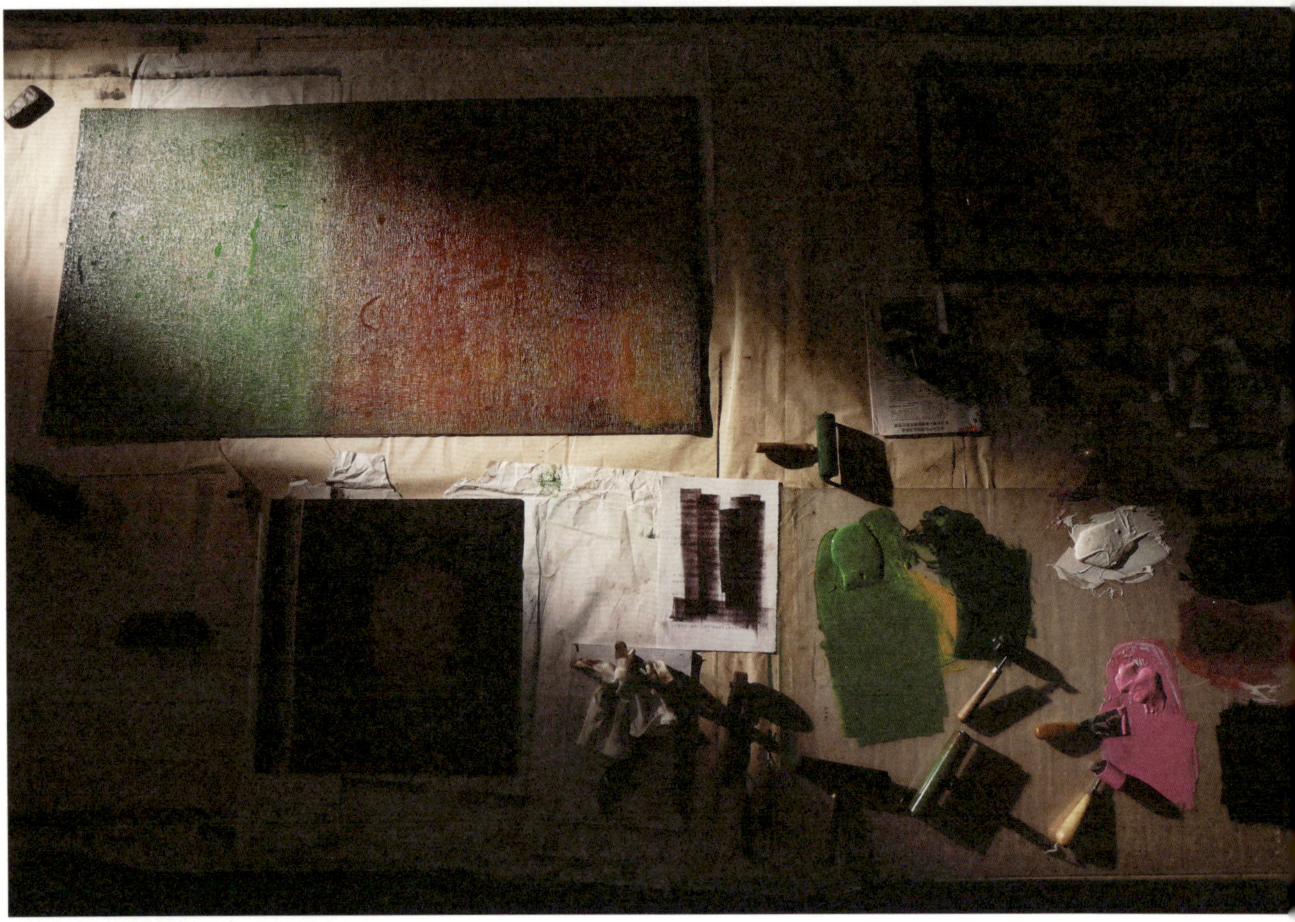

5. Wiping the Woodcut Plate

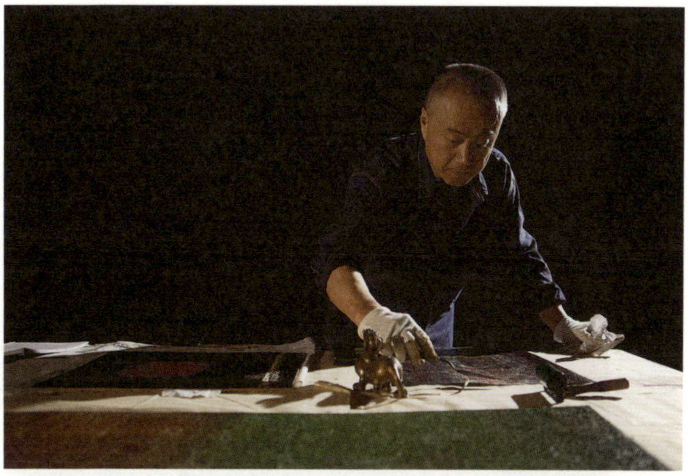

6. Rolling Ink

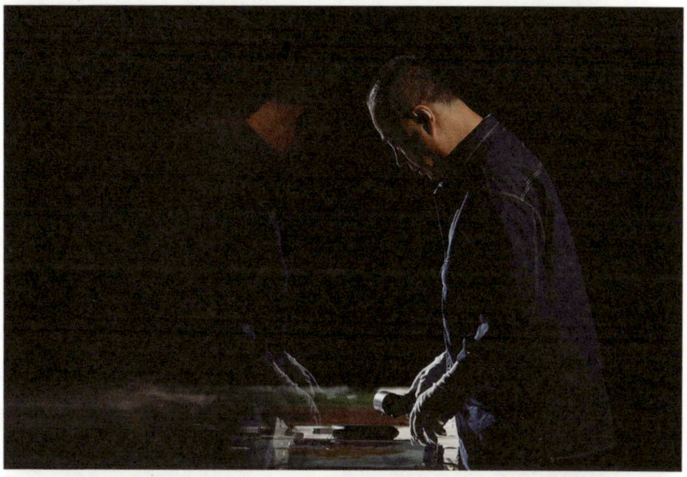

7. Rubbing (Printing)

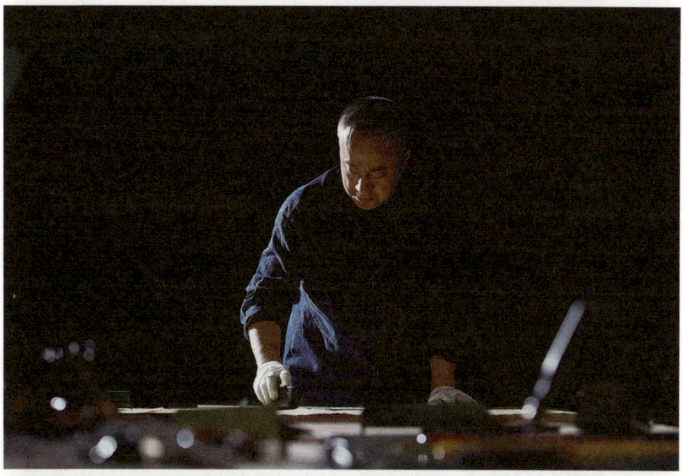

8. Pressing

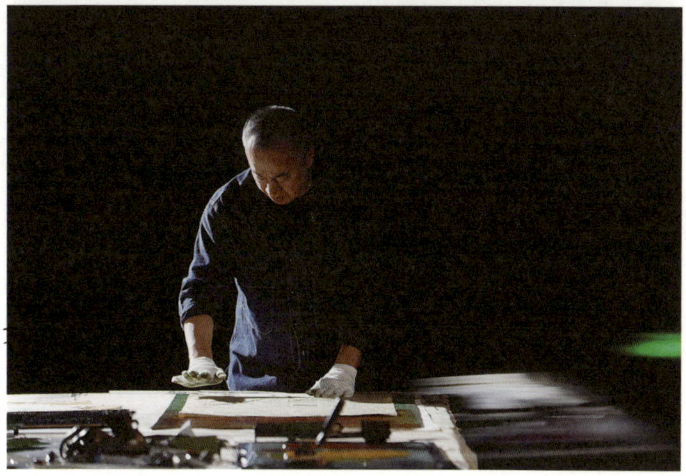

9. Lifting the Artwork

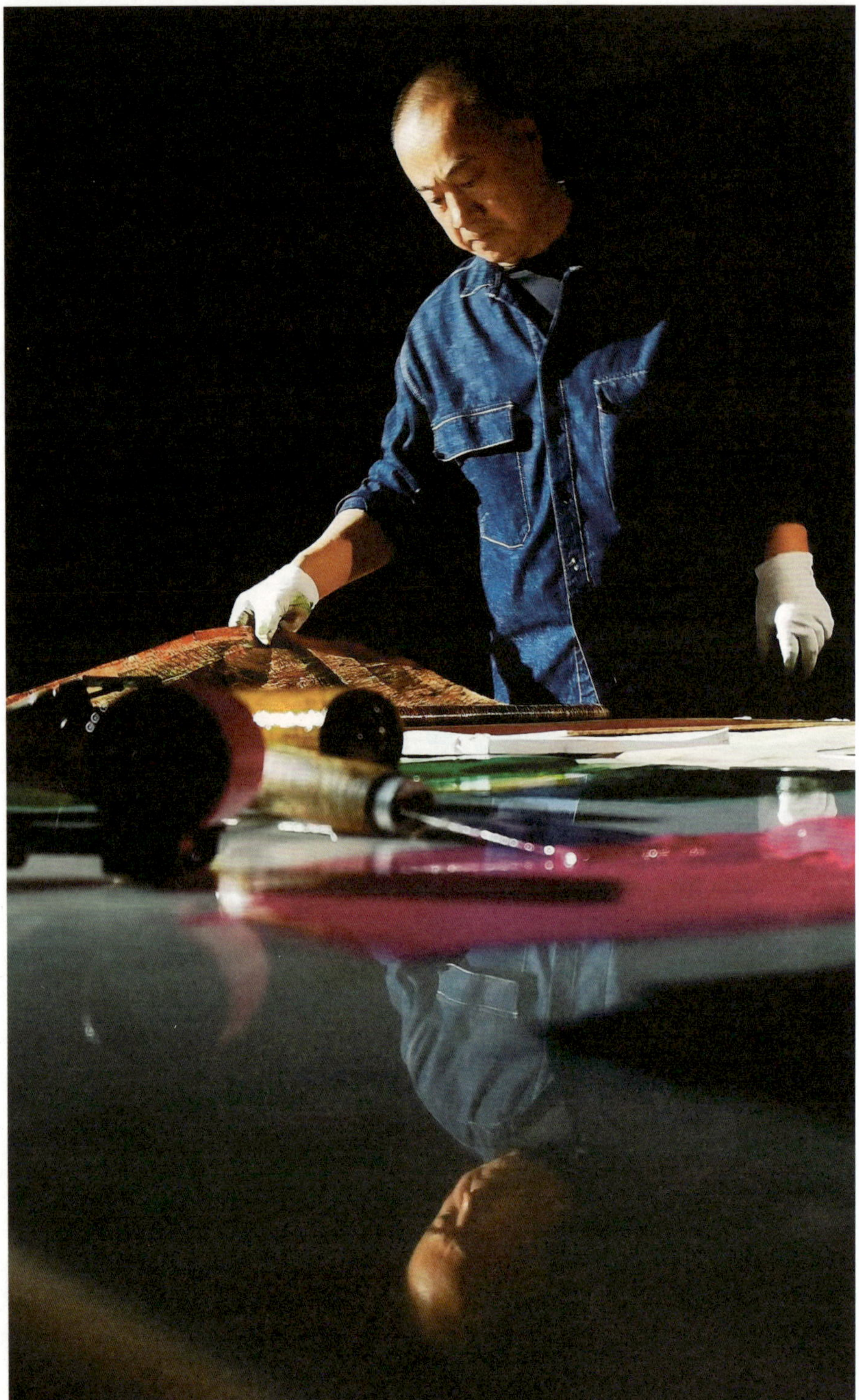

10. Comparing the Artwork to the Original Version

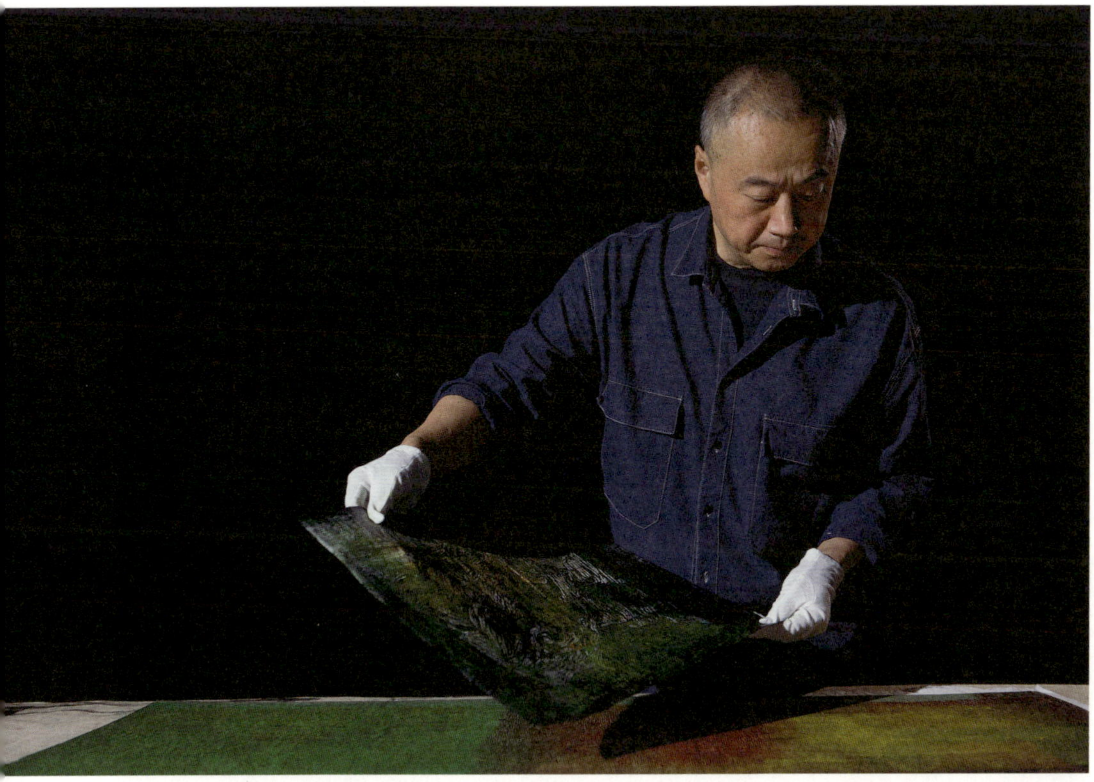

11. Complete

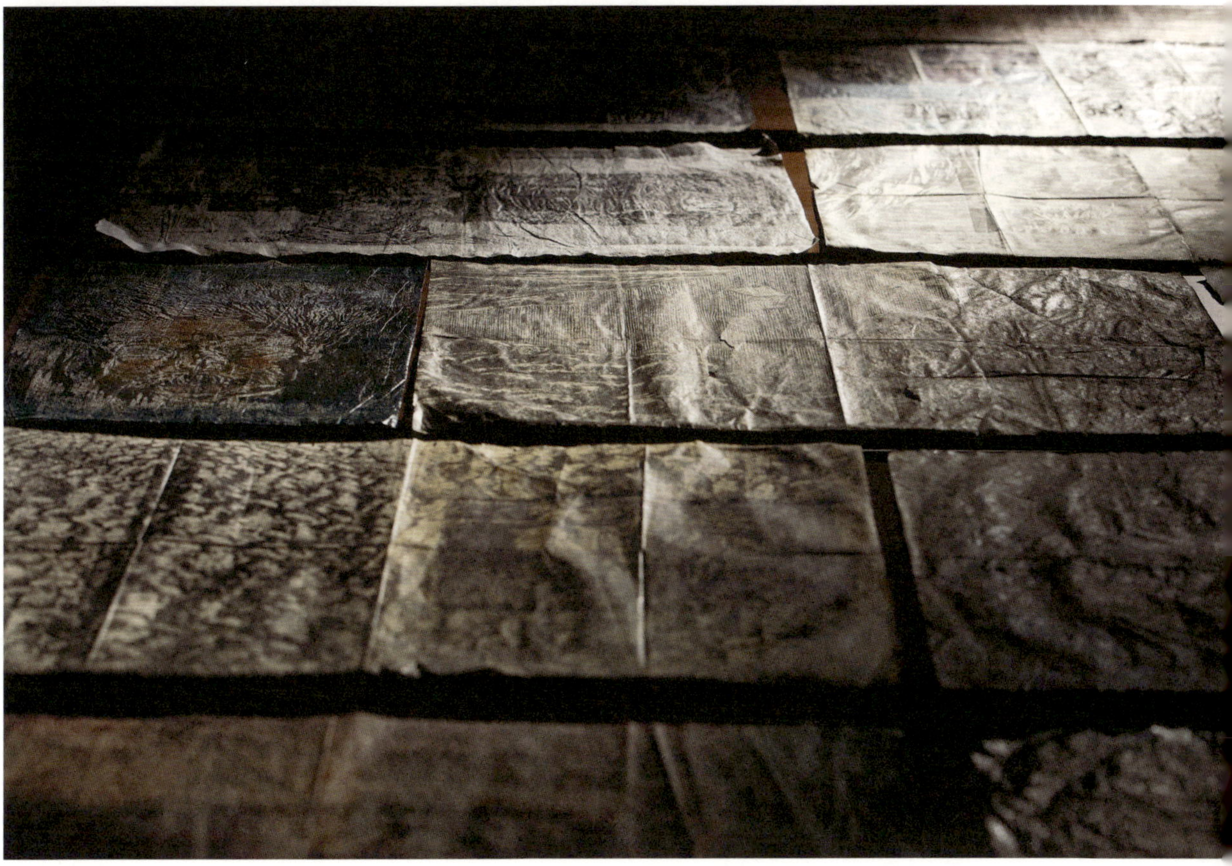

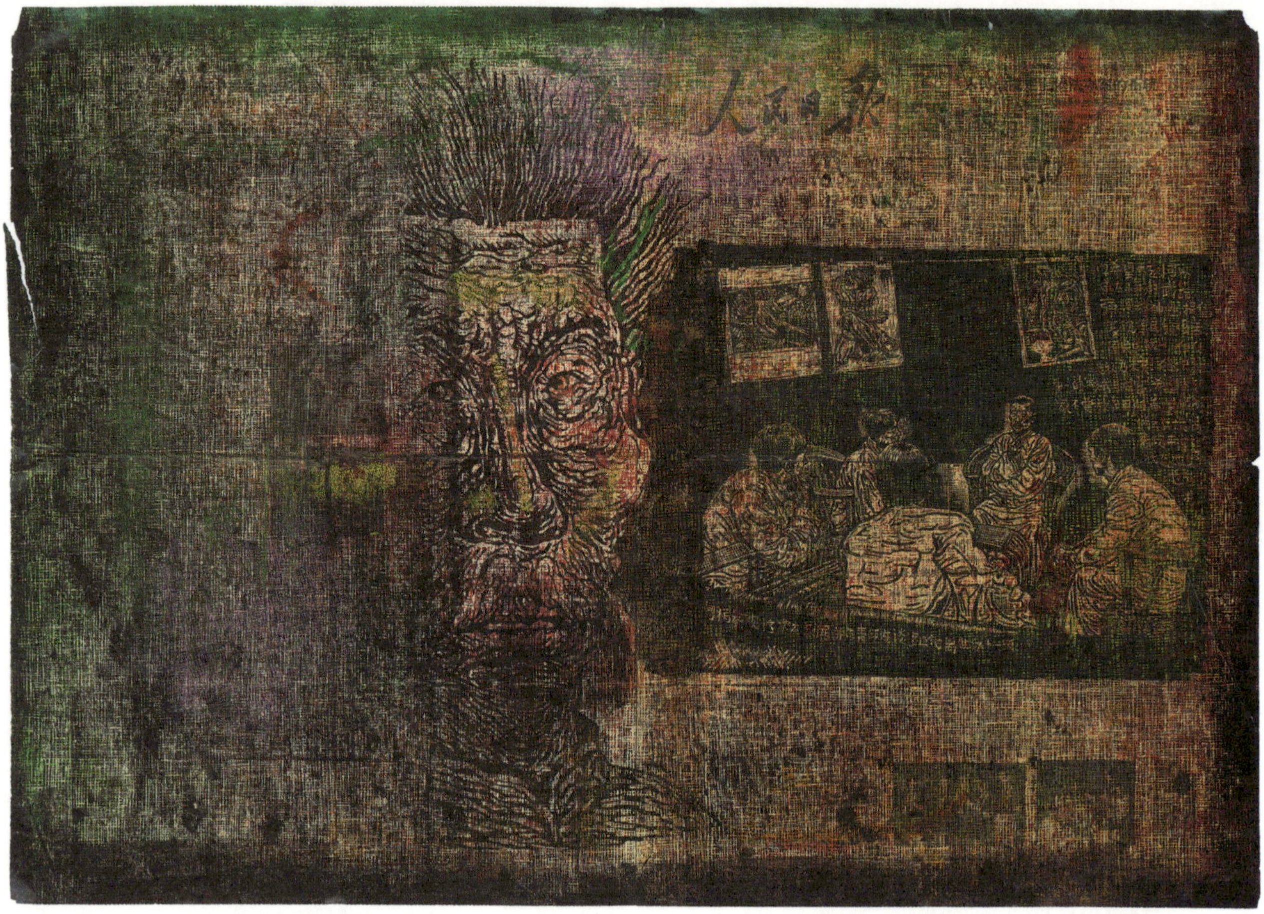

5.
Beyond Recognition

In 2023, as the pandemic came to an end, life gradually returned to normal. I began to deal with the most severely sticky and unrepairable parts of the old newspapers that were exhibited outdoors at the Suzhou Museum in 2017, which had been soaked by rain. After more than five years, they had become overlapping, glued and broken layers, but as a result, they also became heavy in a good way, substantial, even resembling small reliefs.

I had a sudden inspiration to give them a third transformation, a phoenix-like rebirth, by applying colourful acrylic paint. The woodcut image of Lu Xun printed on the old newspapers gradually became obscured and dissolved, and I added glue to fix the broken parts. As a result, the newspapers became thicker and sturdier, and under the refraction of light, they even emitted a metallic lustre. I named them Hot Wind, much like the light and warmth emitted by Lu Xun for us. It no longer matters whether they are woodcuts, paintings or installations. Whether it is the deconstruction of the image elements or the use of the three-dimensional form that emerged due to the stickiness, everything happened as it was meant to.
Life is humorous enough to be dealt with humour, and it seems that all my works have a hidden humour and jest. Sun Zhouxing, Professor of Philosophy at Zhejiang University, wrote: 'Jest is a highly complex action and posture, as well as a method of self-protection. Liu Chunjie has this posture, which is philosophical, artistic and individual. If Liu Chunjie

is a warrior, then the knife and brush are his spears. His artistic incisions are very precise, touching on the spiritual vein linking Nietzsche and Lu Xun.' (*Objects of Nothingness - Liu Chunjie's Art on Lu Xun*, 2022)

Hot Wind transformed from Keep Flooding the Screen, but because it was created on old newspapers, the size was limited. During the exhibition, some suggested enlarging the works. However, the batch of over 300 old newspapers had been used multiple times, becoming very fragile, and I didn't want to change them anymore. I therefore used traditional Chinese rice paper, which led to the creation of the Semblance of Nothingness series of composite paintings.

Rice paper is different from newspaper; it can be much larger in size and has strong water-absorbing properties. My previous experience with coloured-ink creation played its part here. During the experimental process, chaos and cracks appeared on the paper, evoking a sense of history and heaviness. I gradually used larger sizes of rice paper, slowly mastering the ability to control the colours of the ink, striving for strong contrasts between ink and paint, and seeking to preserve the sense of power in the zigzagging lines. I would spray water to create undulating textures on the damp rice paper, aiming for a crisscrossing texture after the paper dried. And in some works, Chinese characters were incorporated, intertwined with ink and paint. The texture generated after folding also disrupted the integrity of the characters. Unlike traditional Chinese paintings that must be mounted flat after completion, these works are sturdy and heavy, resembling mottled rocks and soil, even having a metallic glow, resembling ruins and broken walls. This effect is radically different from the one that rice paper works have presented over thousands of years.

———*Hot Wind Series*

54cm × 34cm   Woodcut, Old Newspapers and Composite Materials   2023

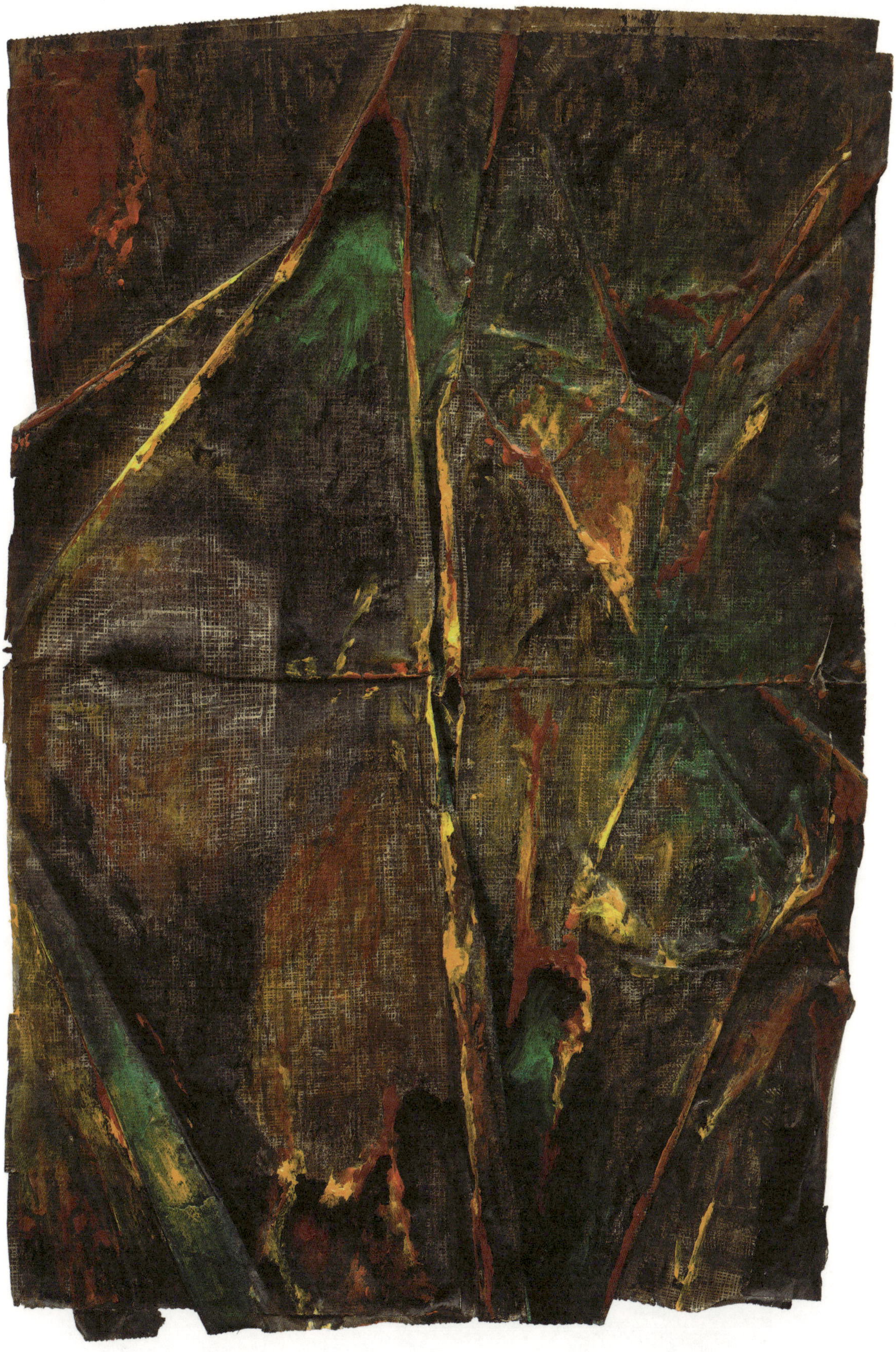

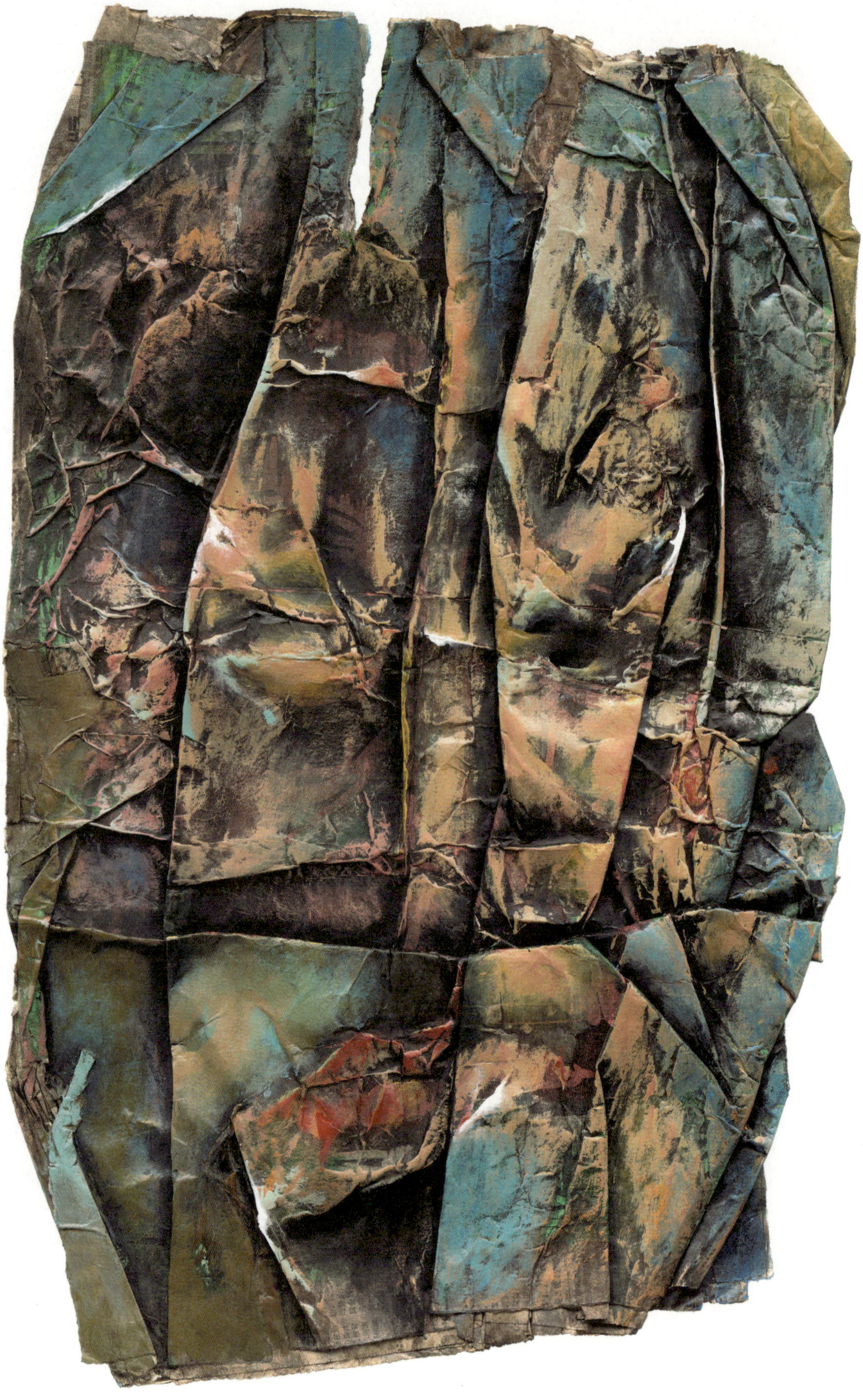

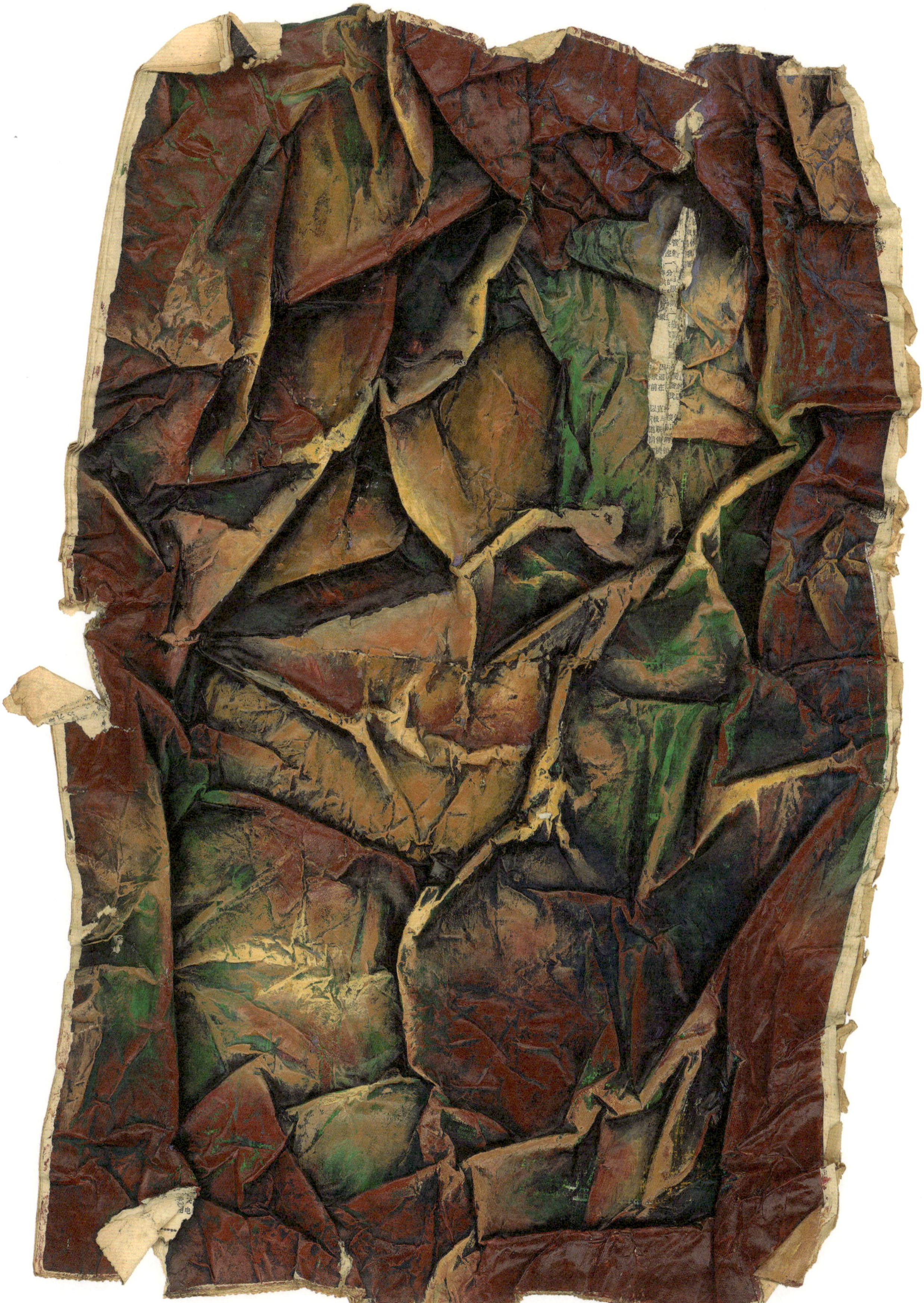

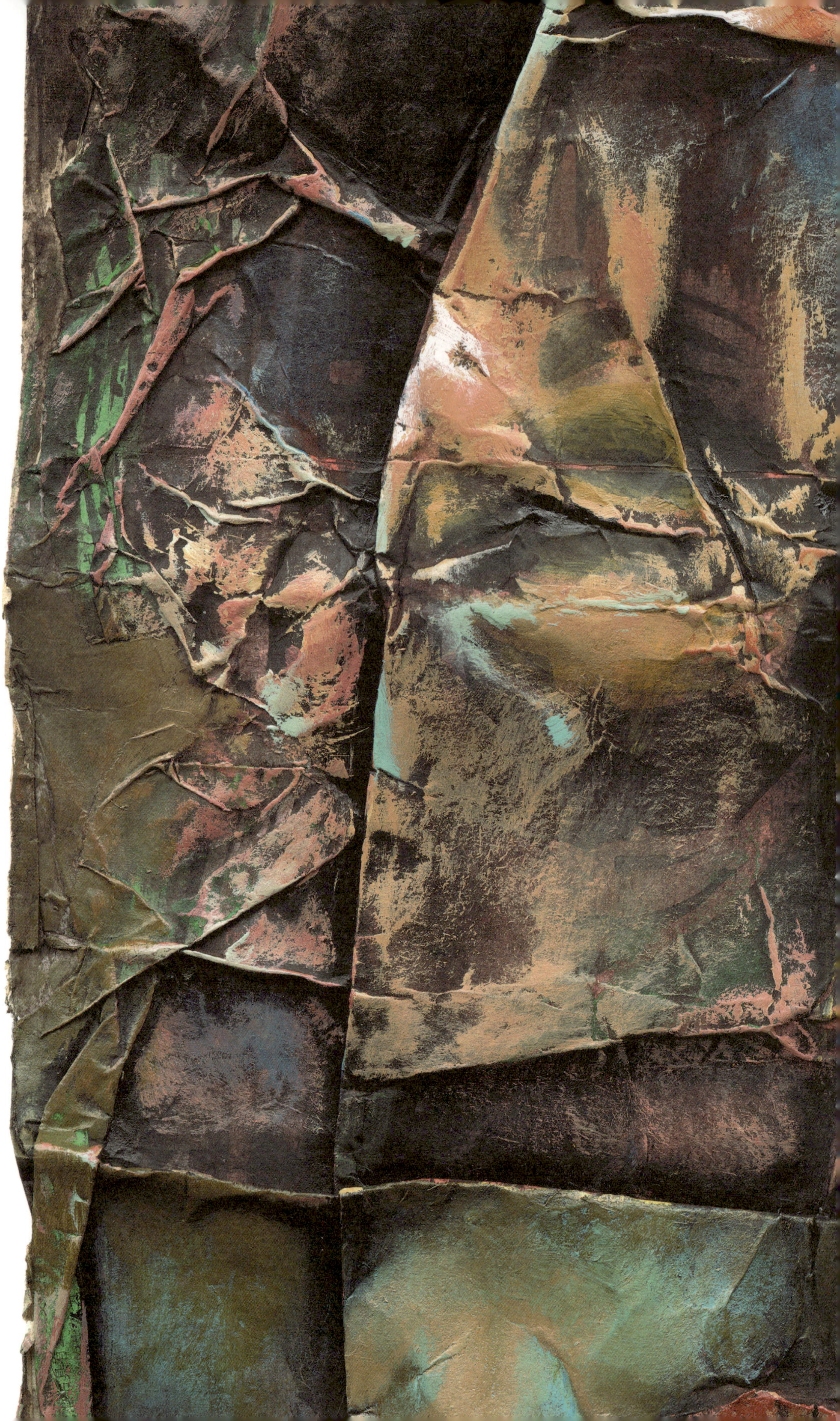

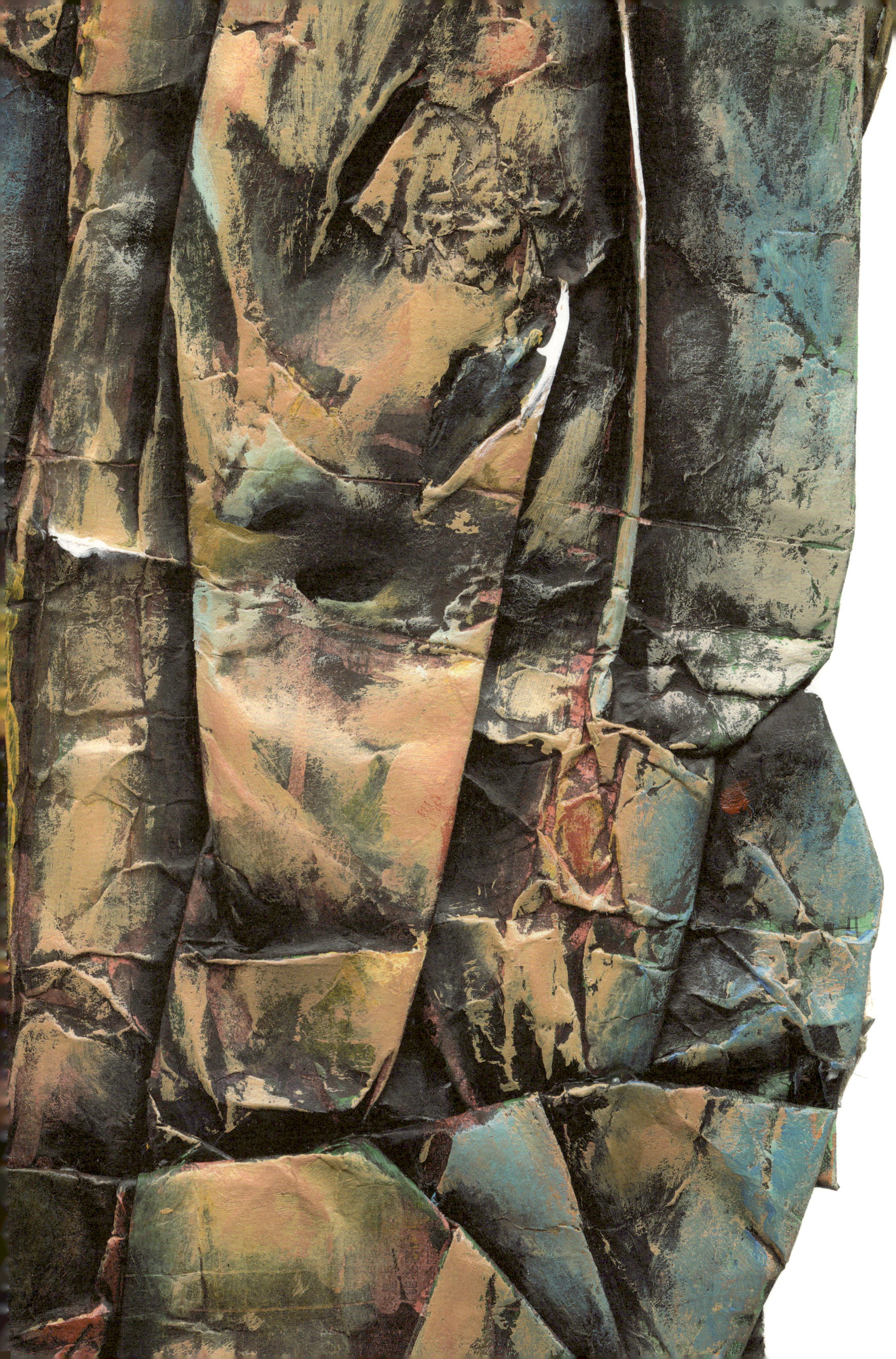

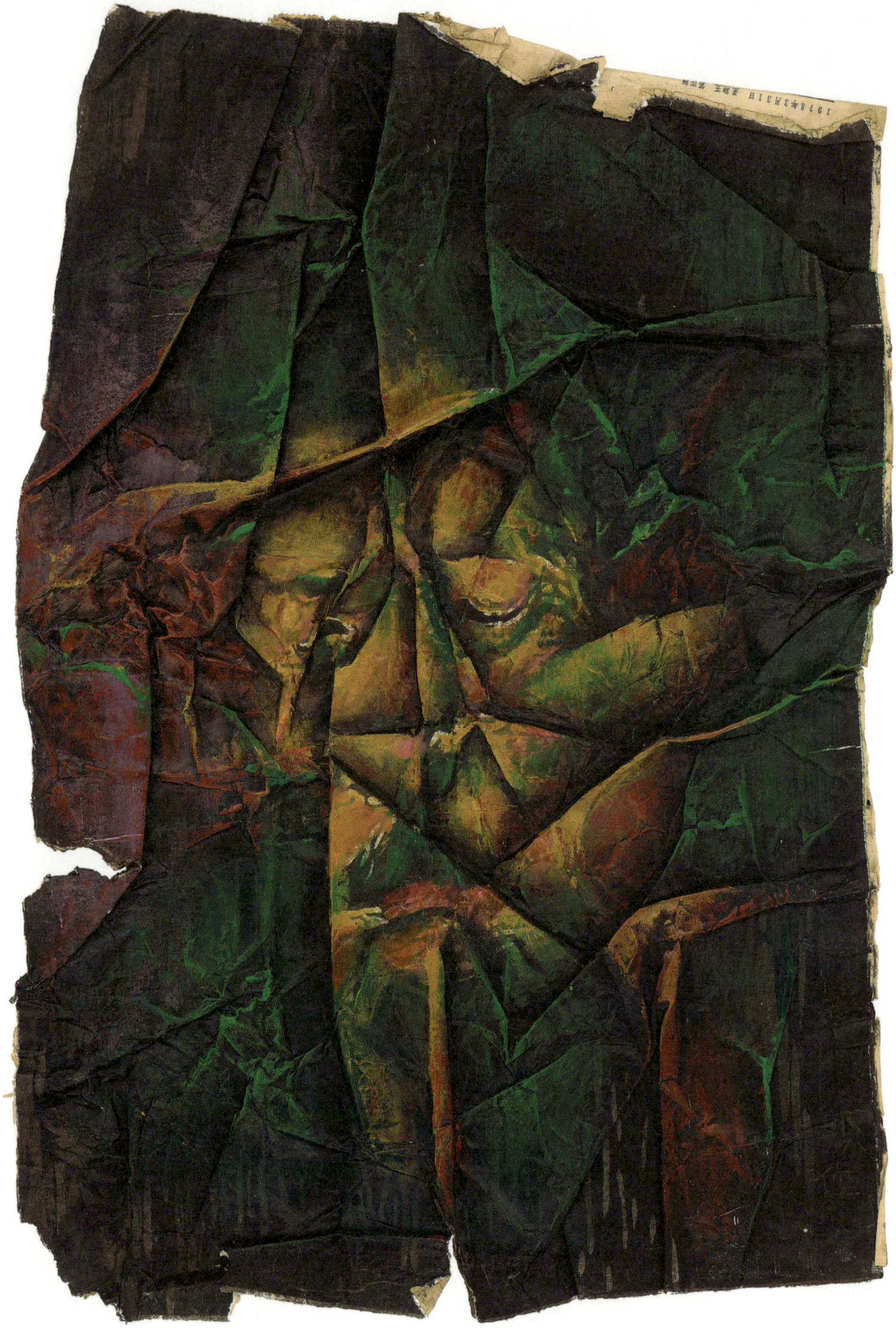

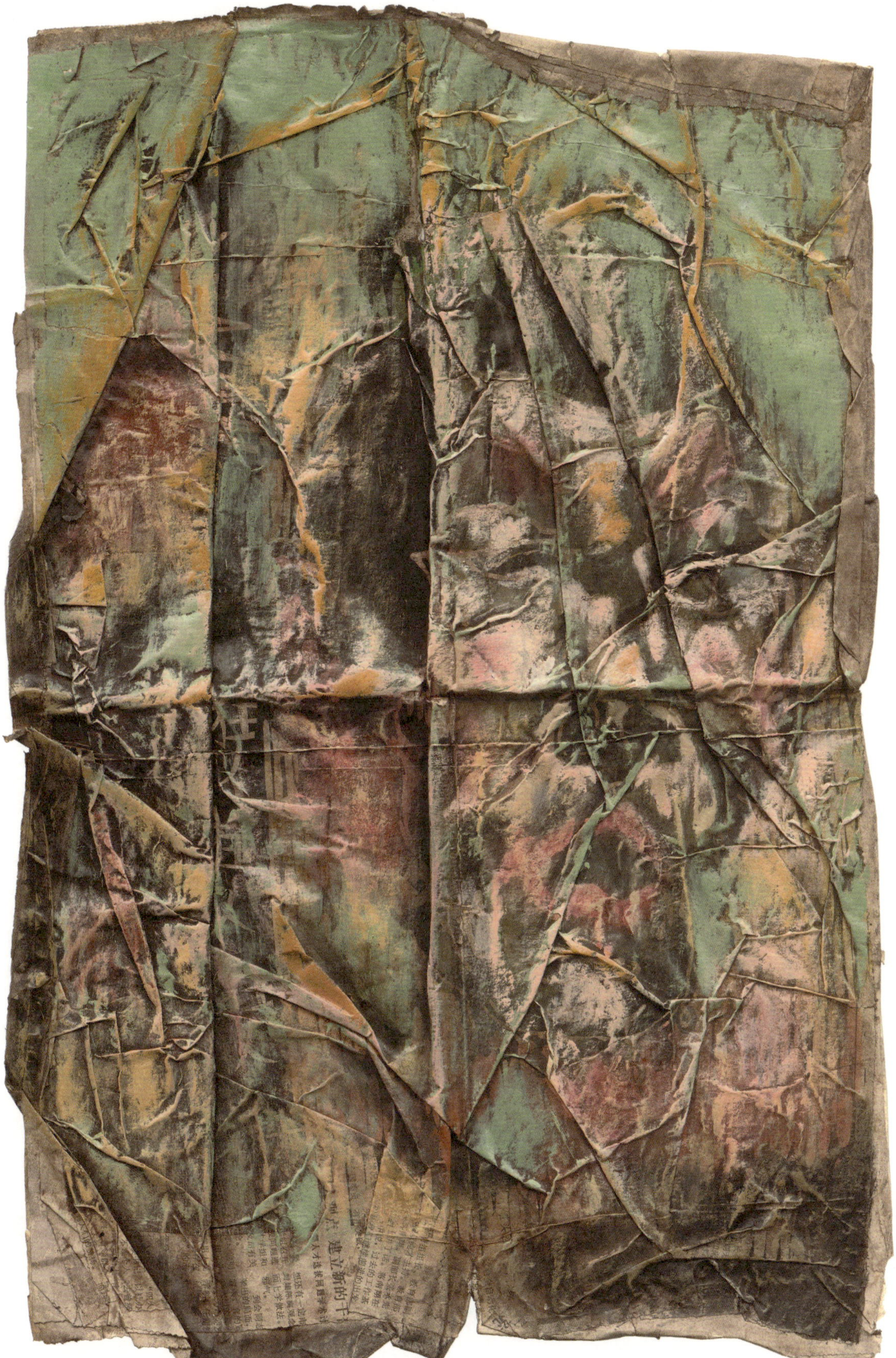

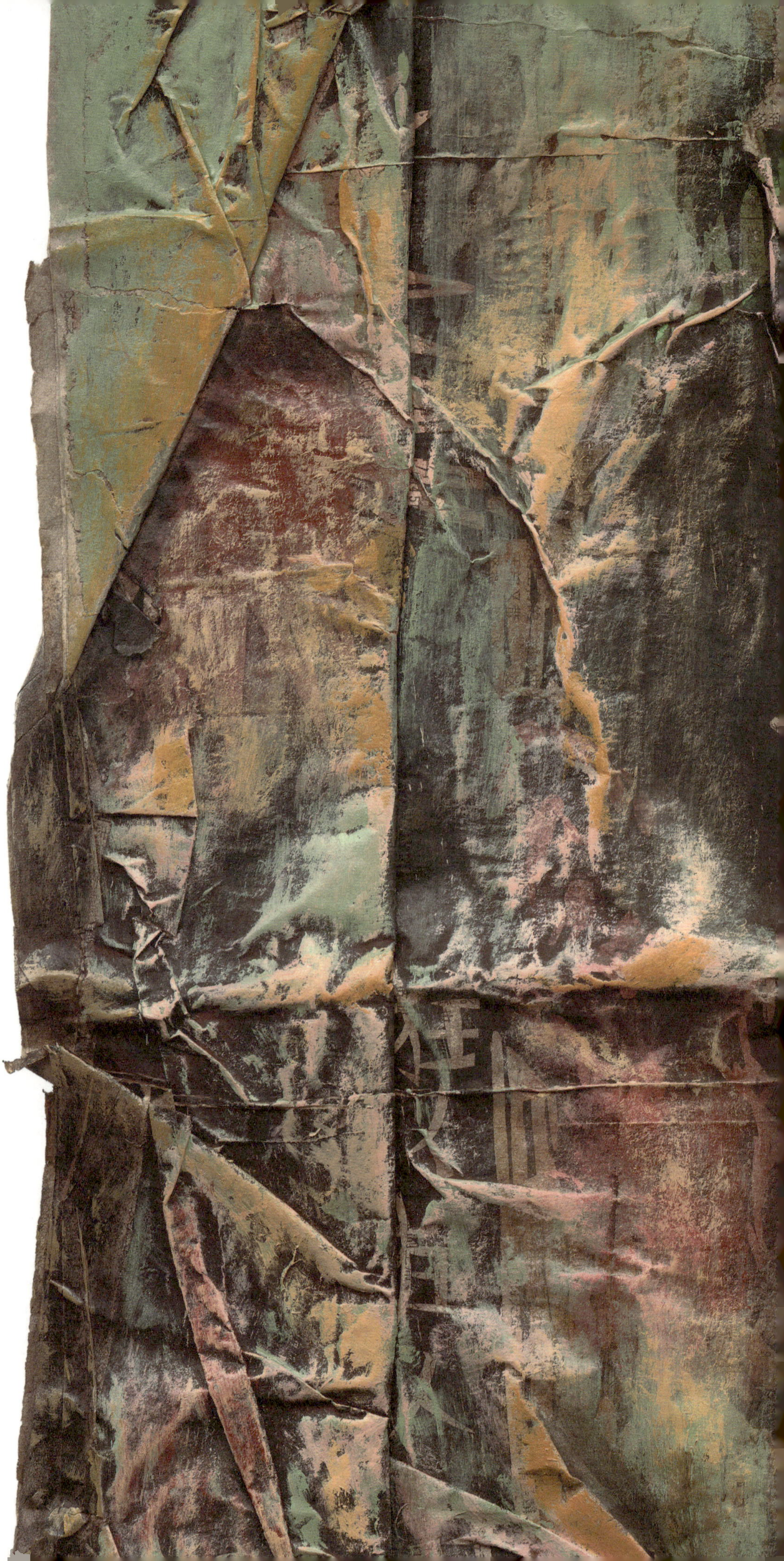

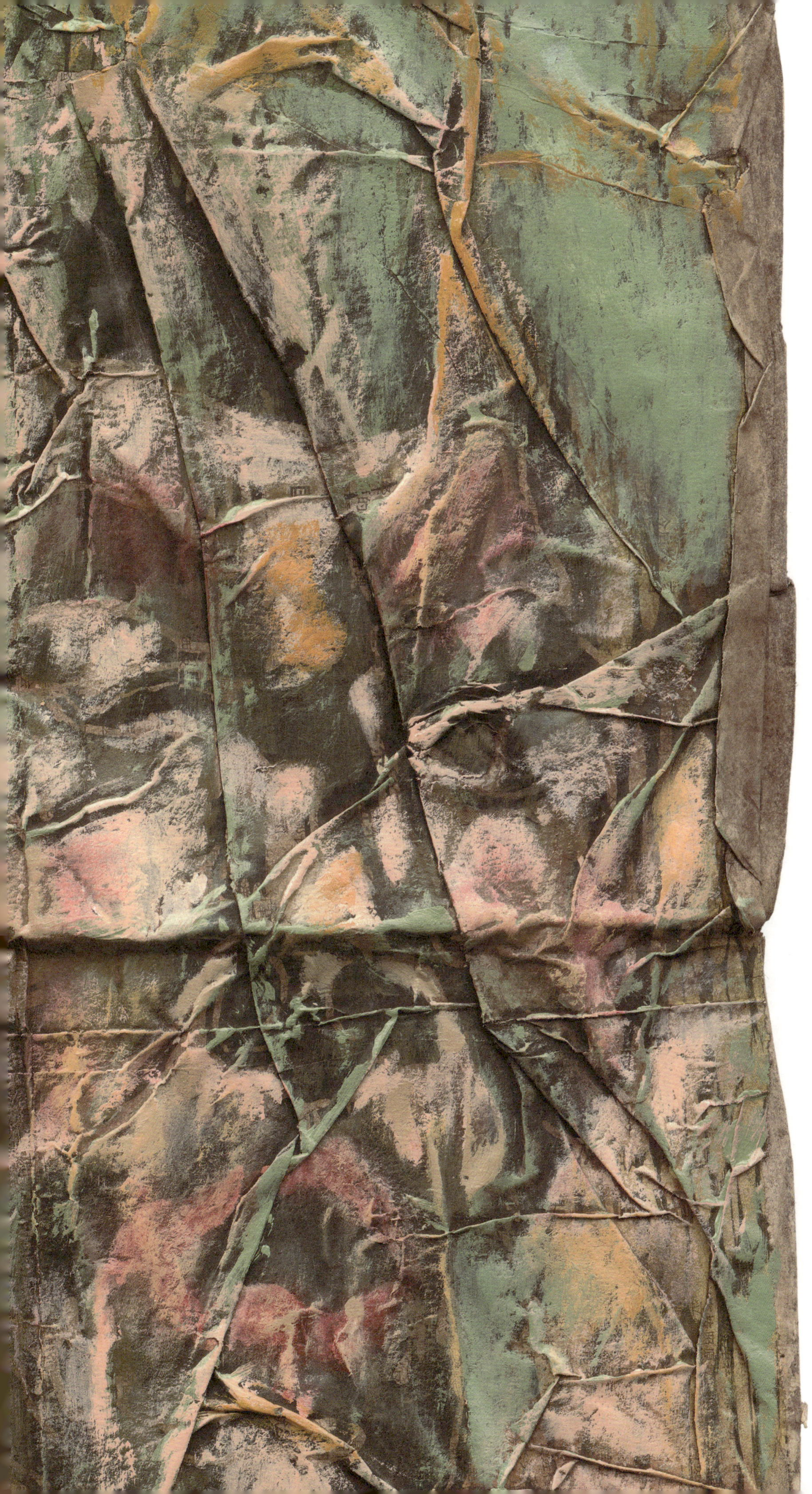

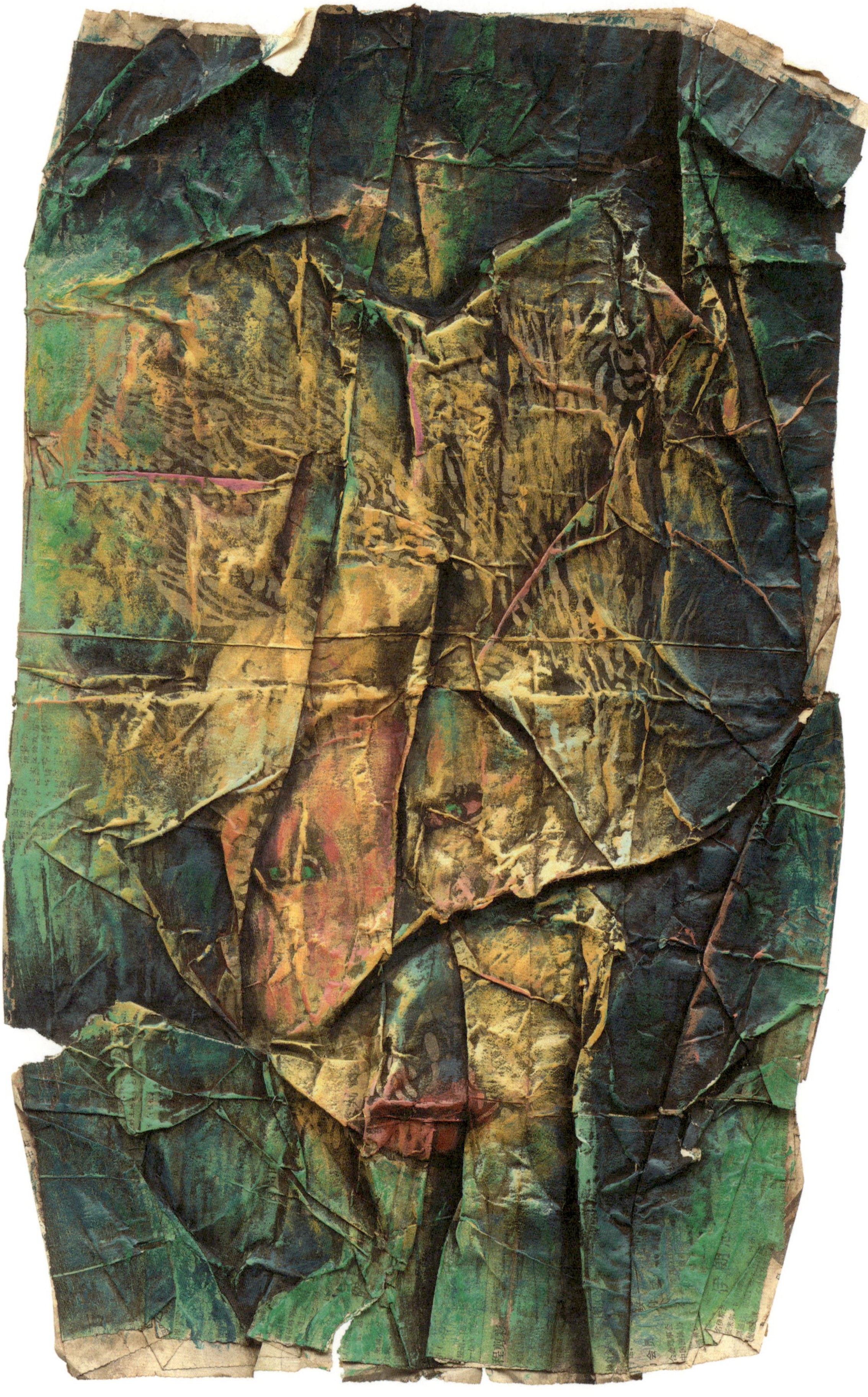

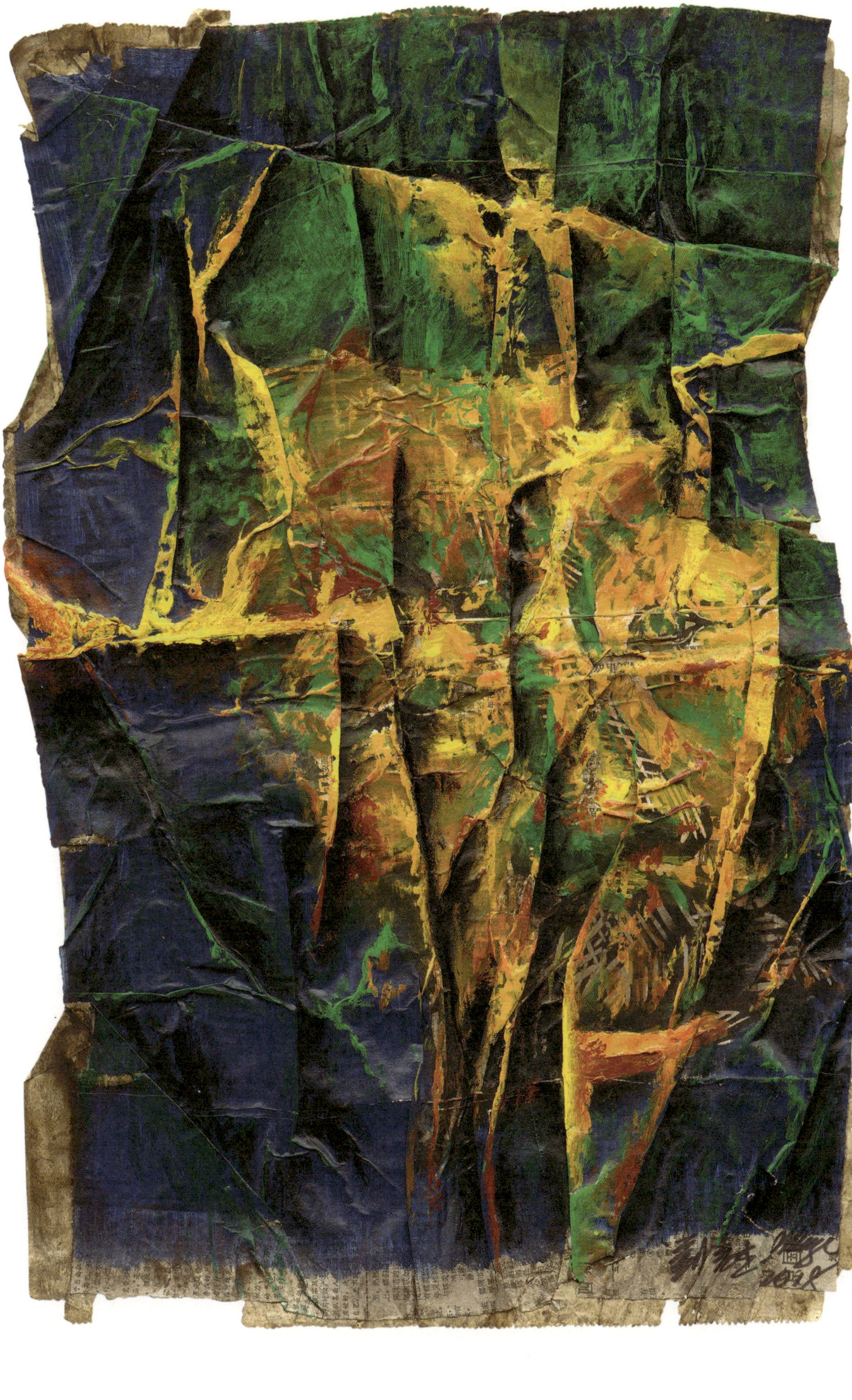

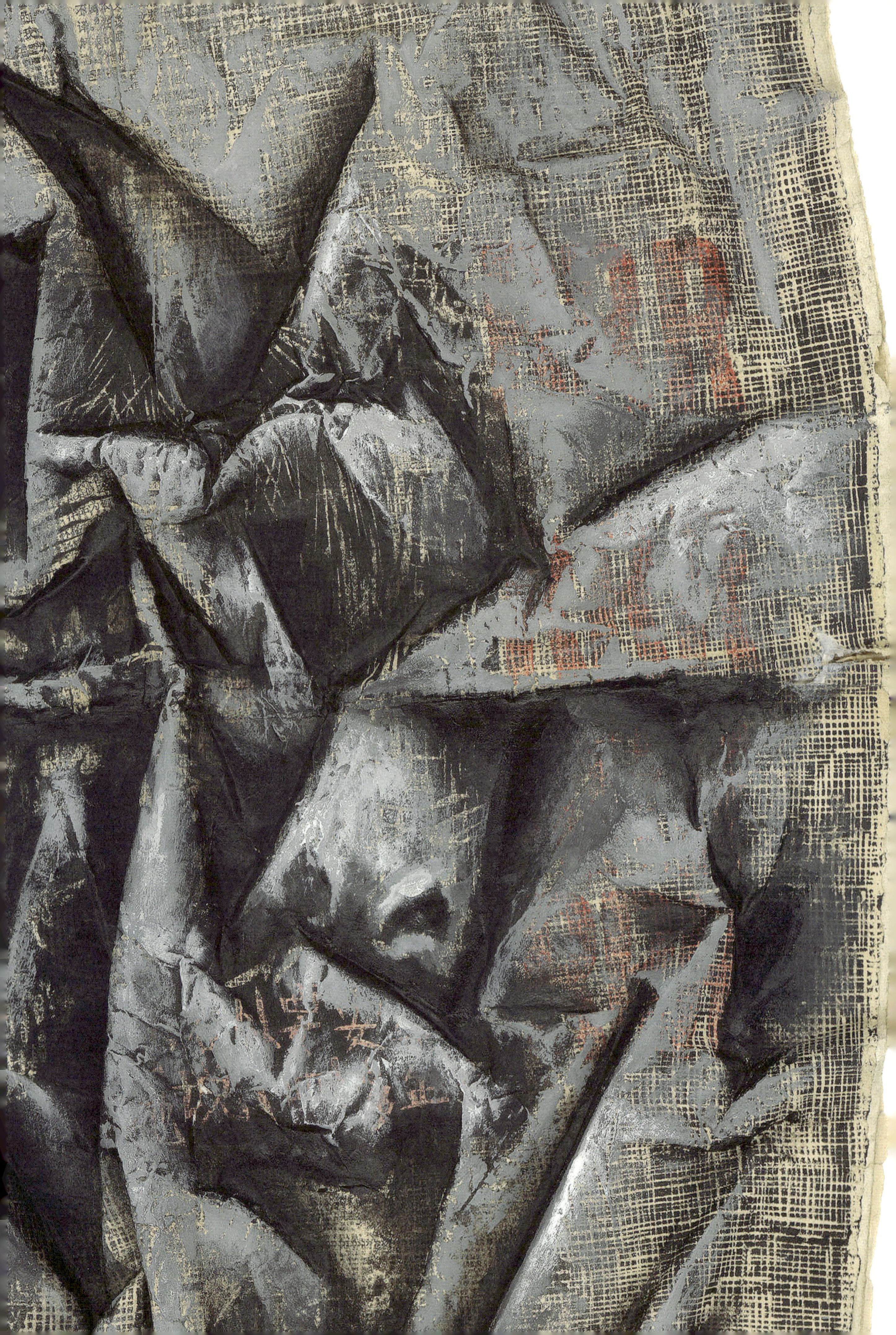

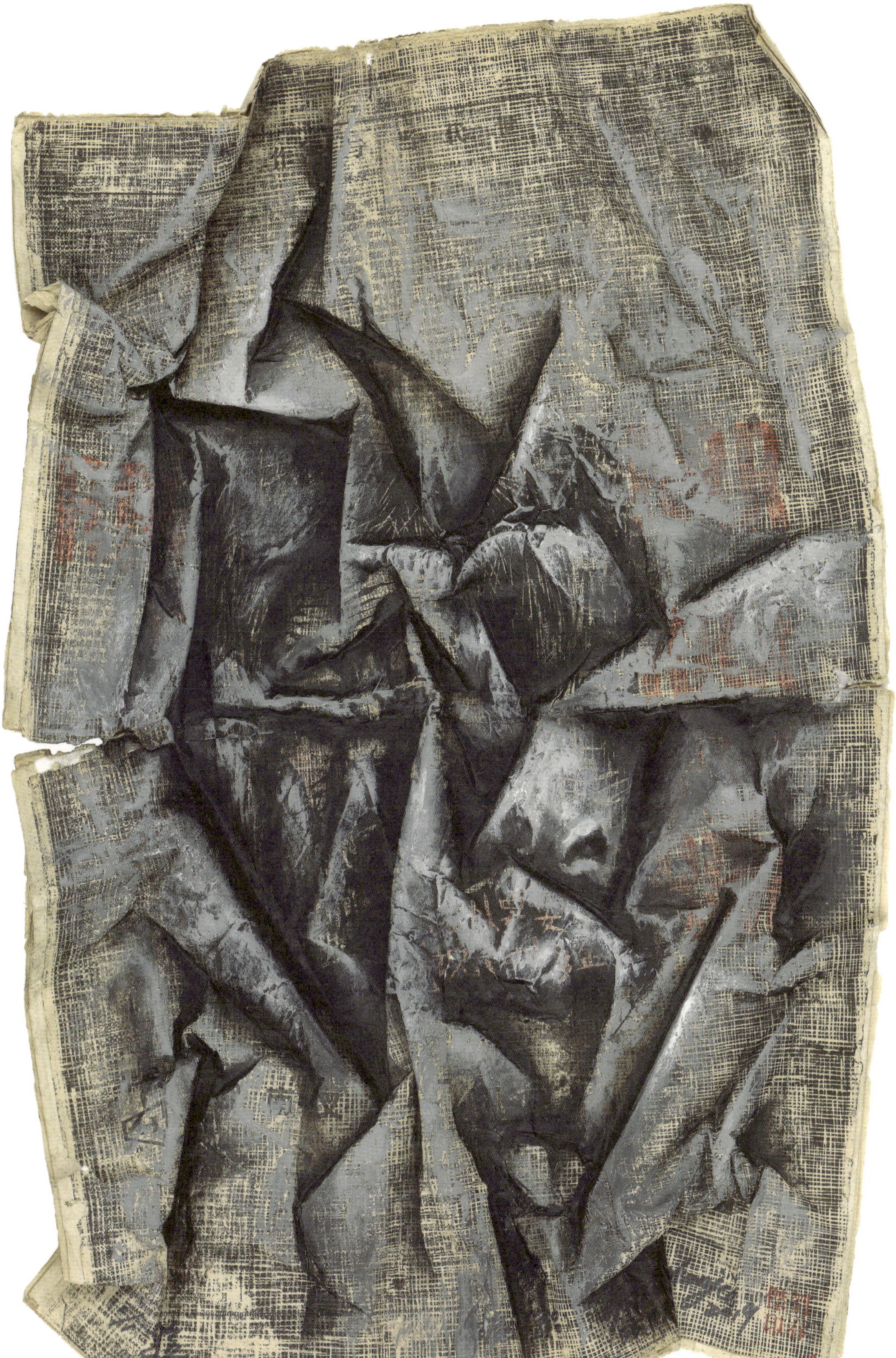

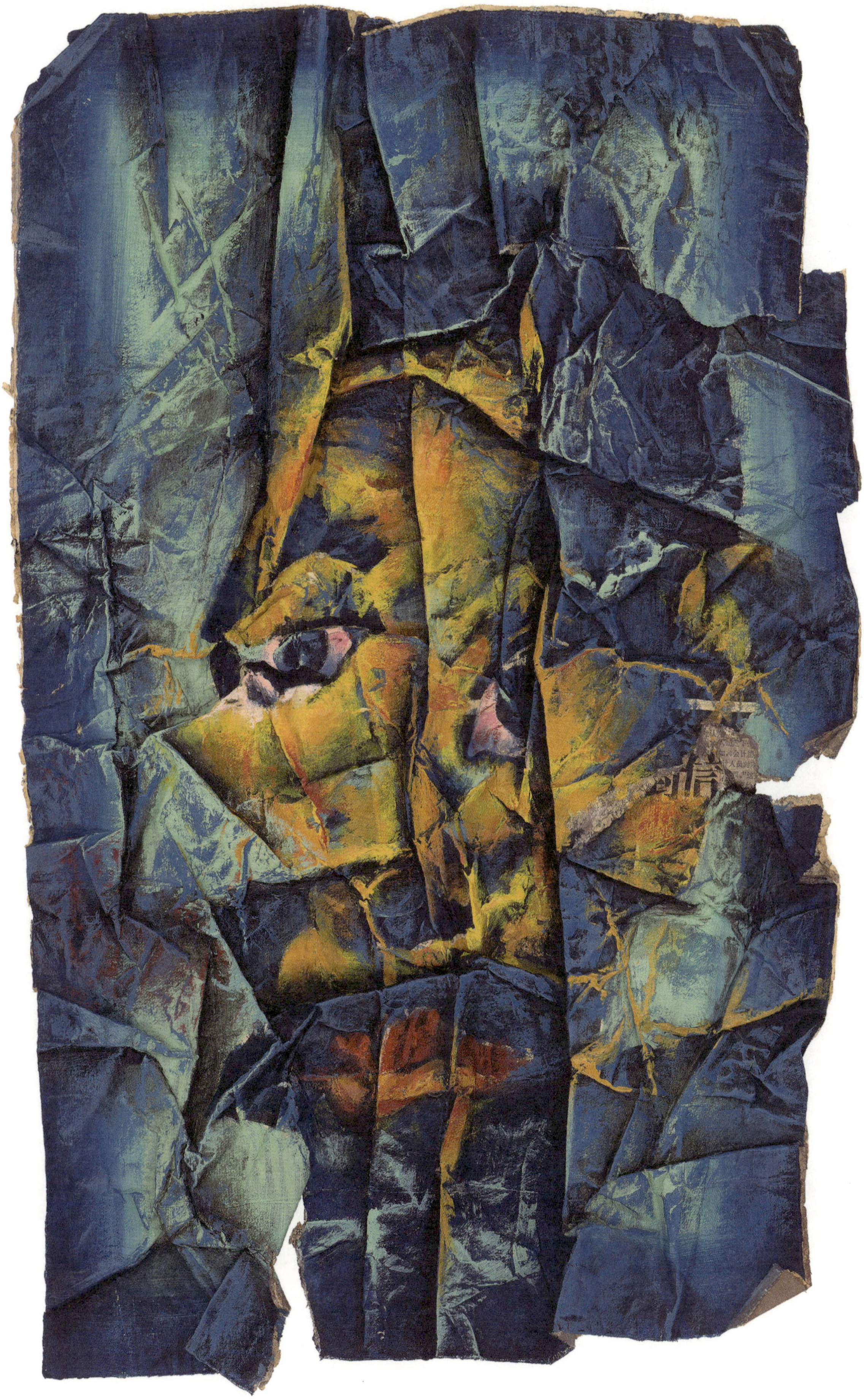

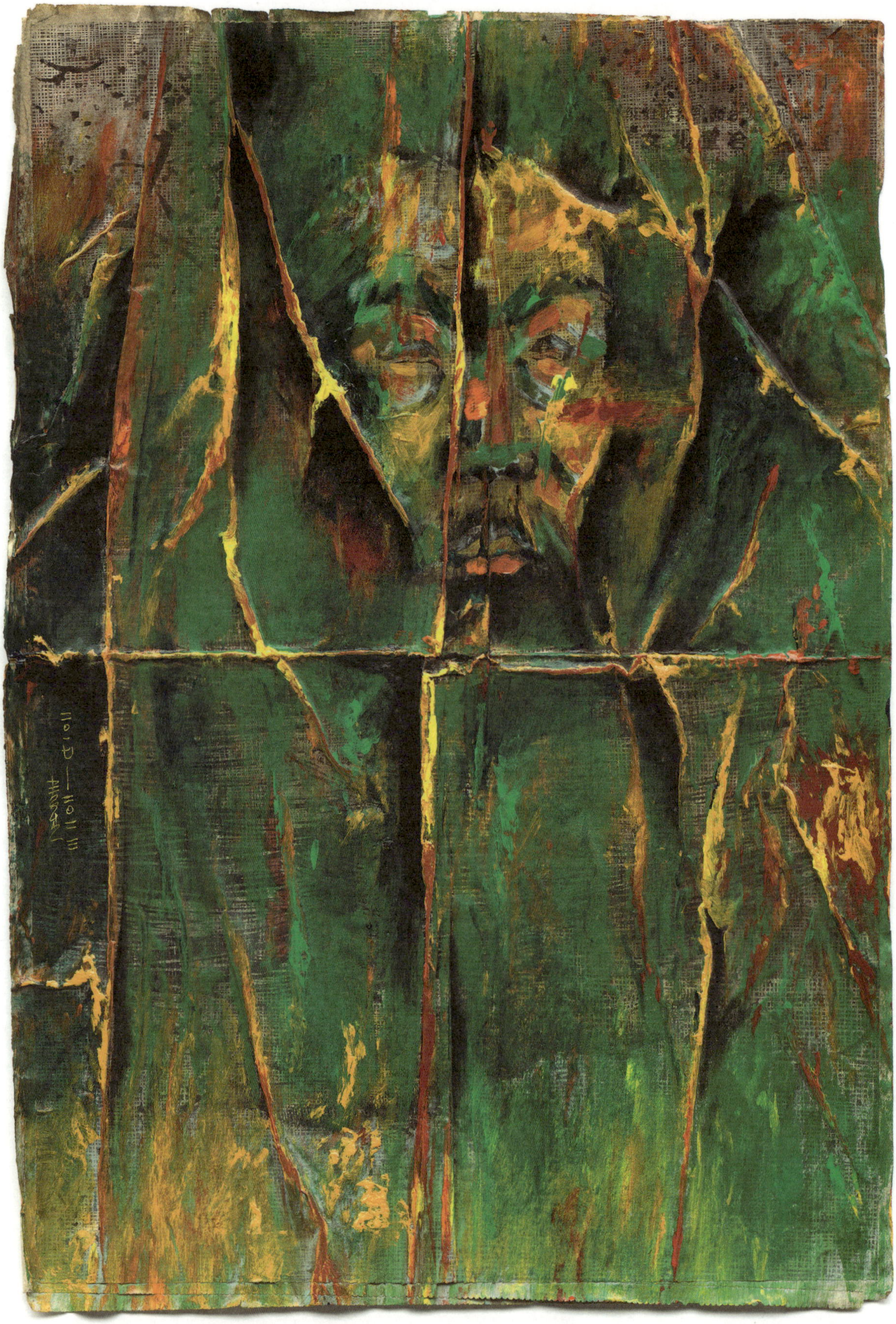

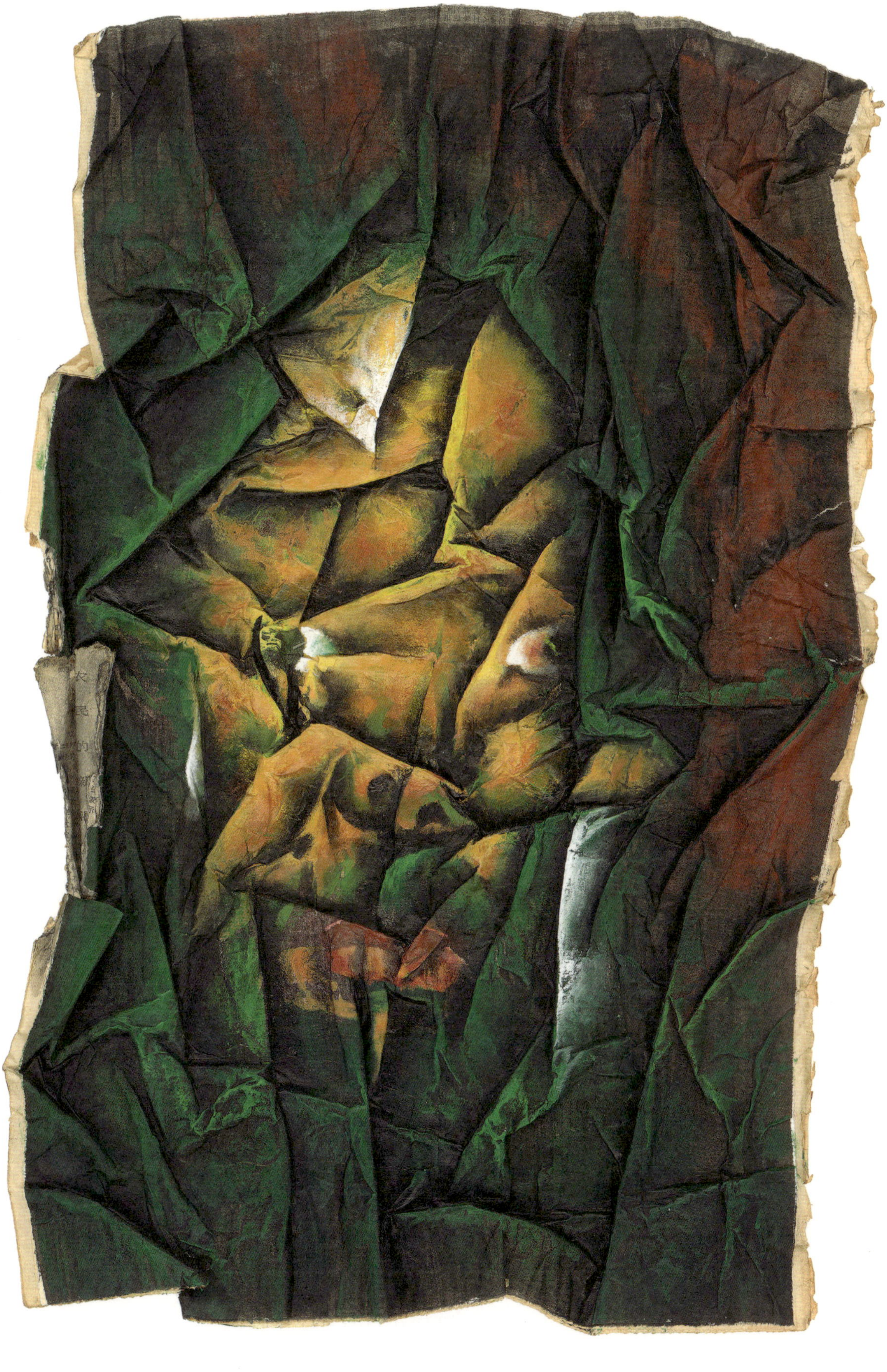

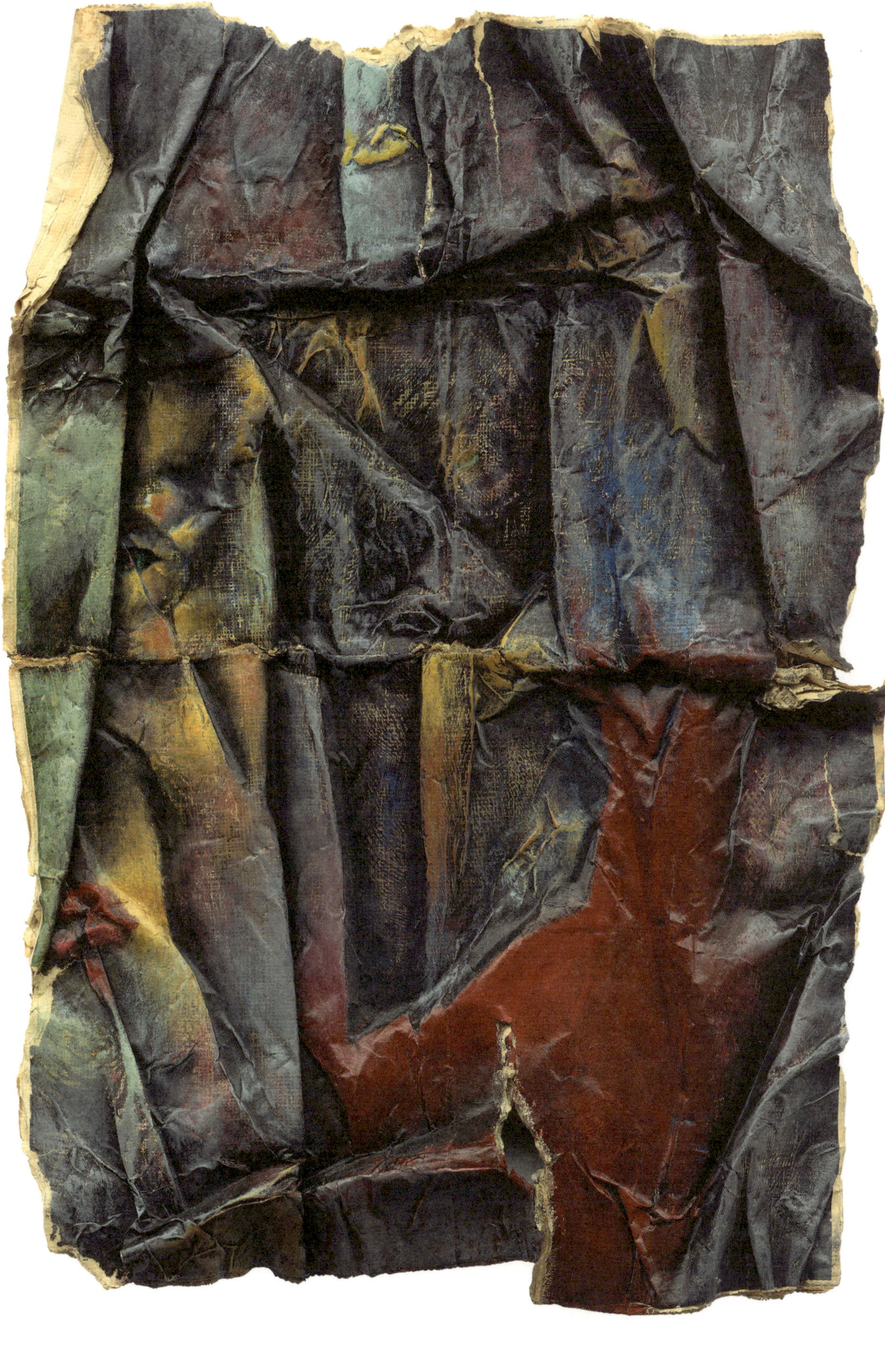

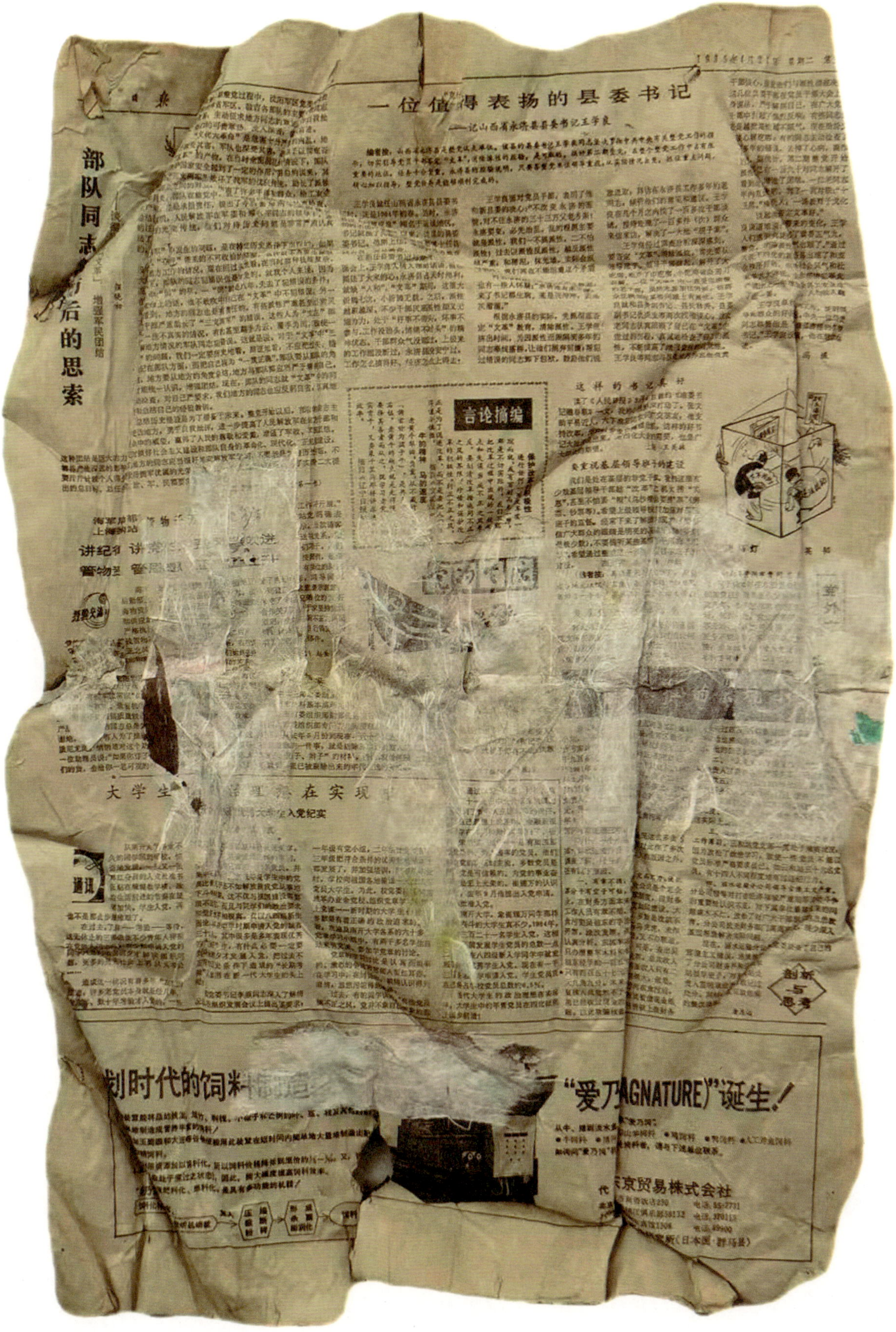

一位值得表扬的县委书记

——记山西省永济县县委书记王学良

部队同志

后的思索

言论摘编

大学生　　　　在实现

入党纪实

划时代的饲料

“爱乃(AGNATURE)”诞生！

东京贸易株式会社

——*Semblance of Nothingness* Series

Rice Paper, Ink, Chinese Painting Pigments and Composite Materials
2023—2024

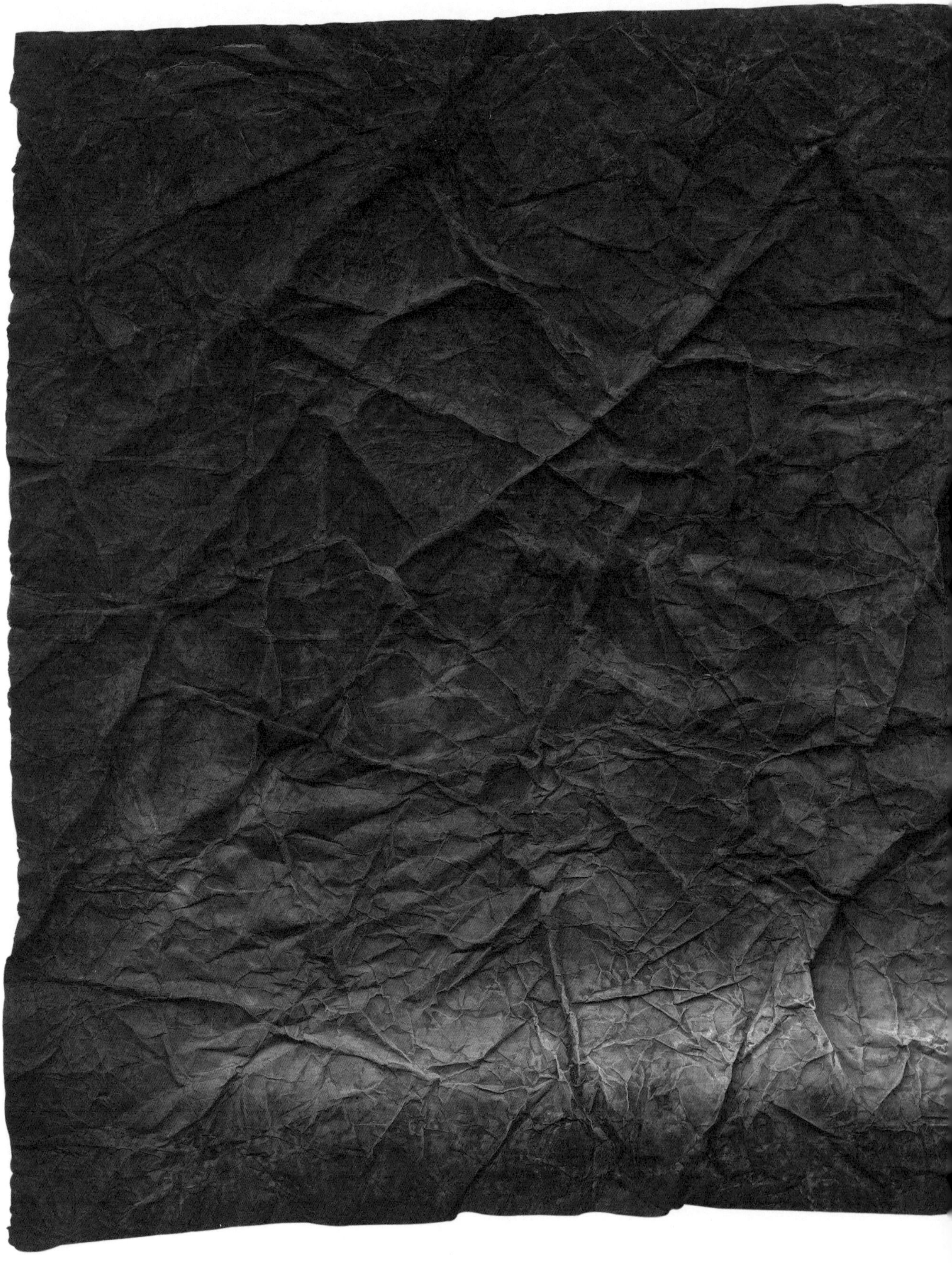

With Light 232cm × 140cm 2023

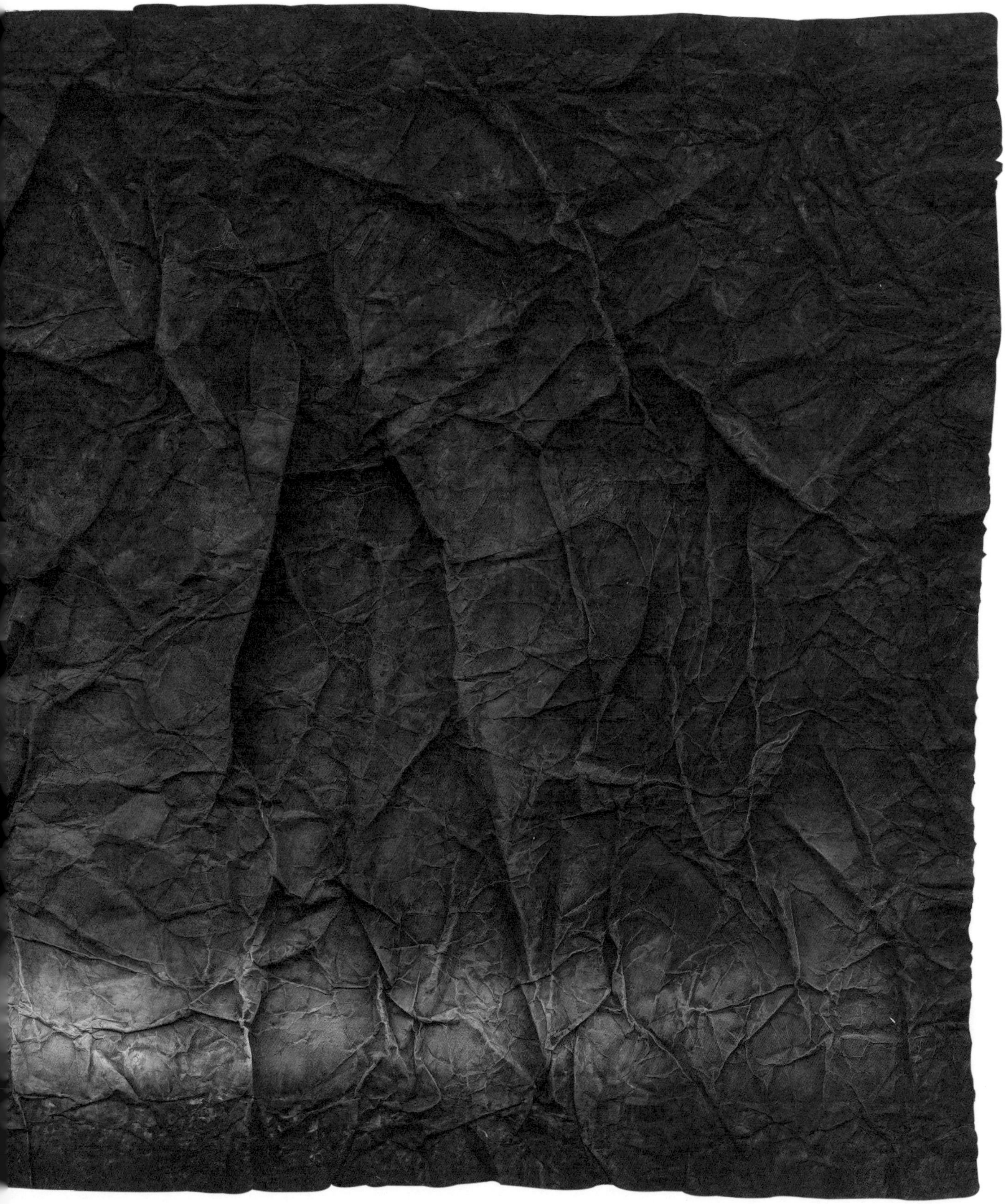

Great Wilderness 143cm × 226cm 2023

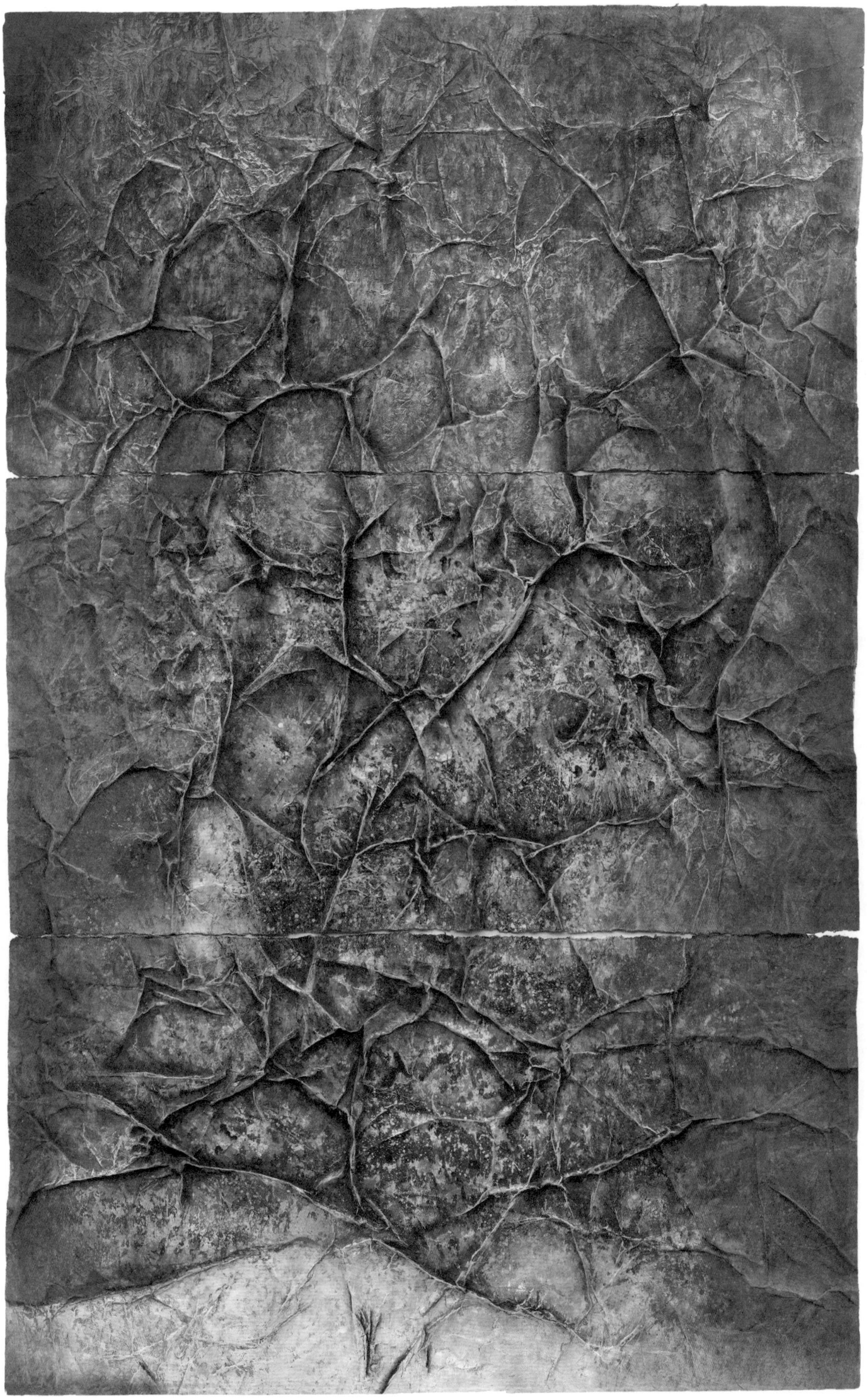

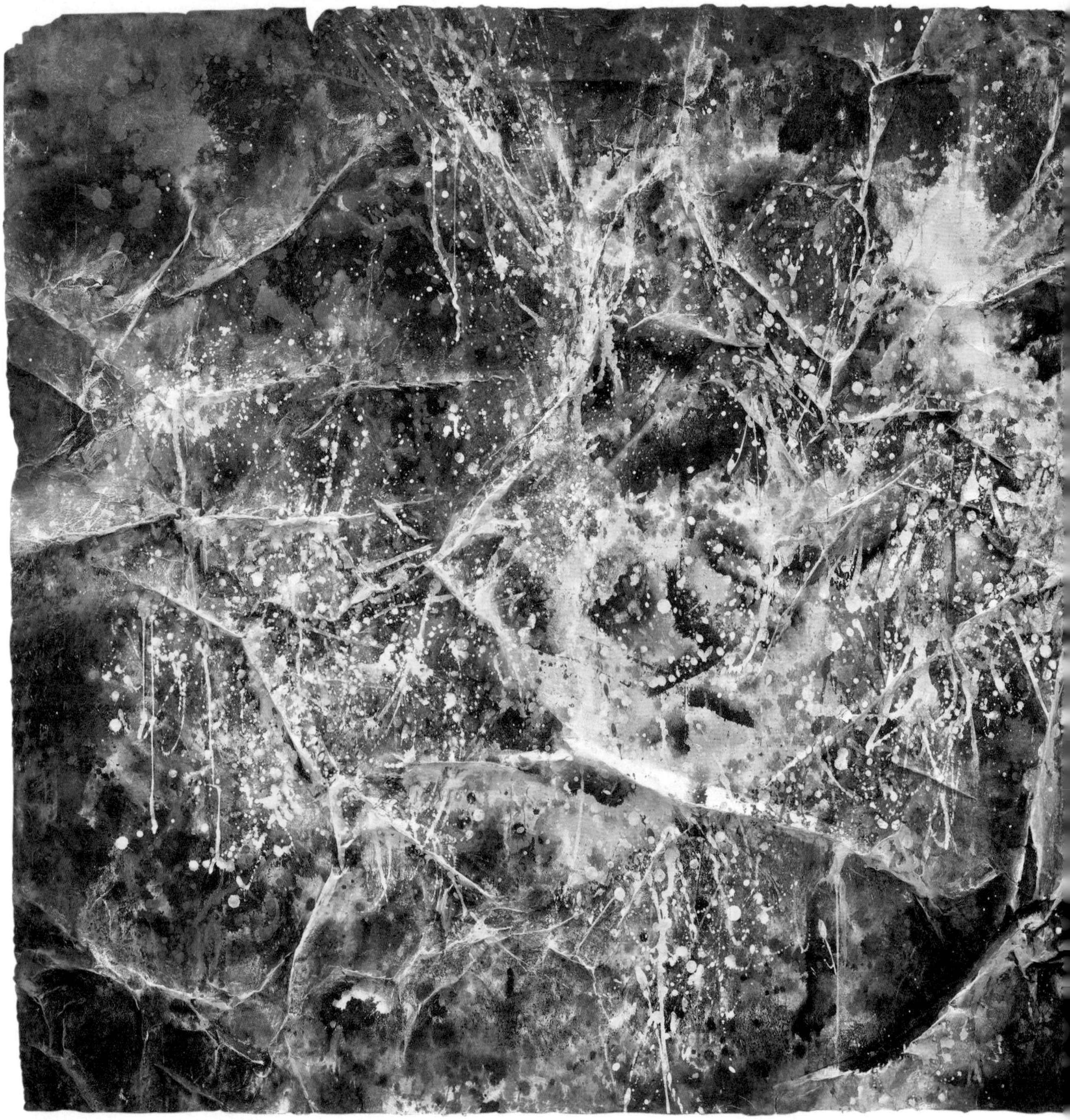

Breath 120cm × 241cm 2024

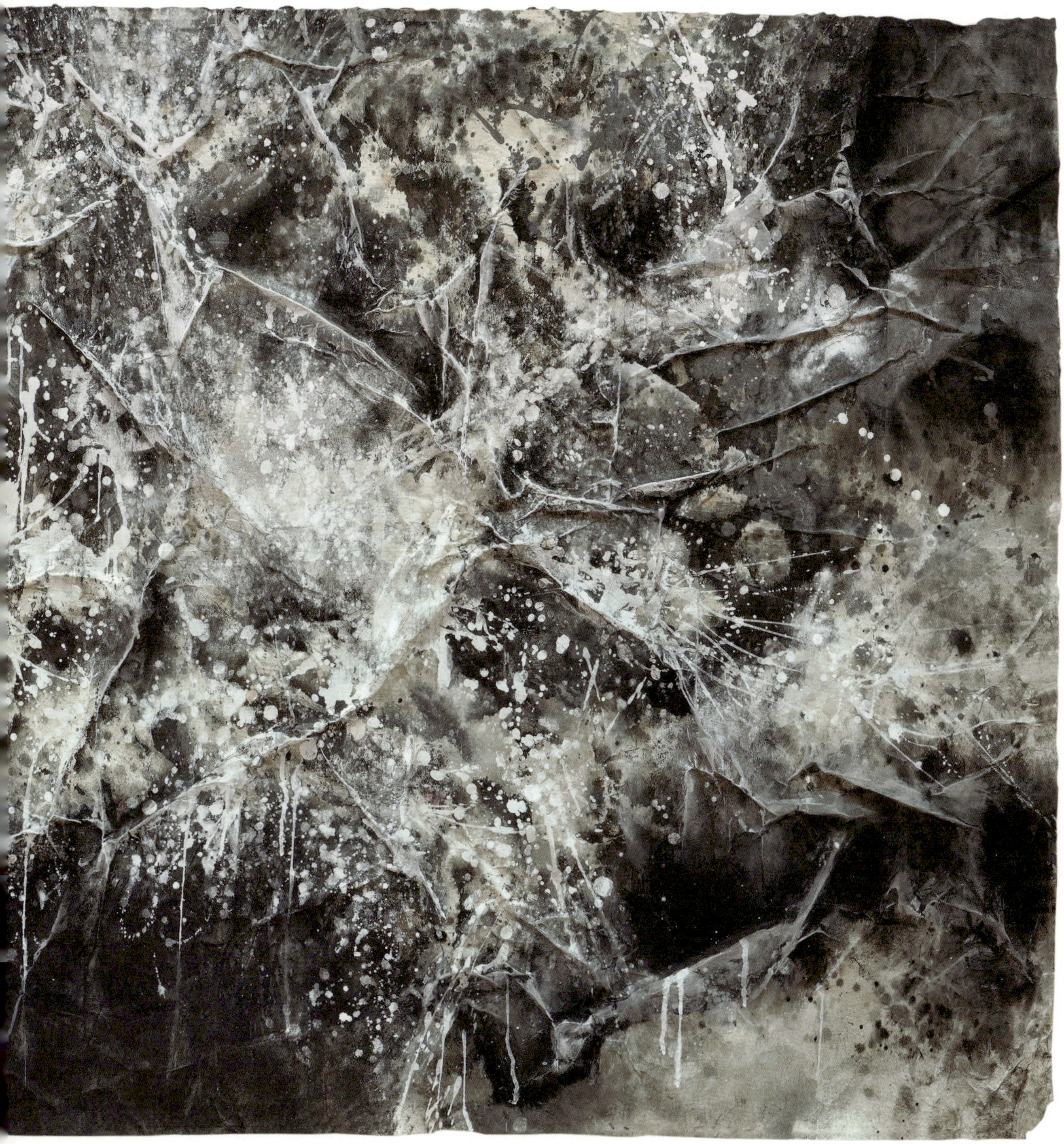

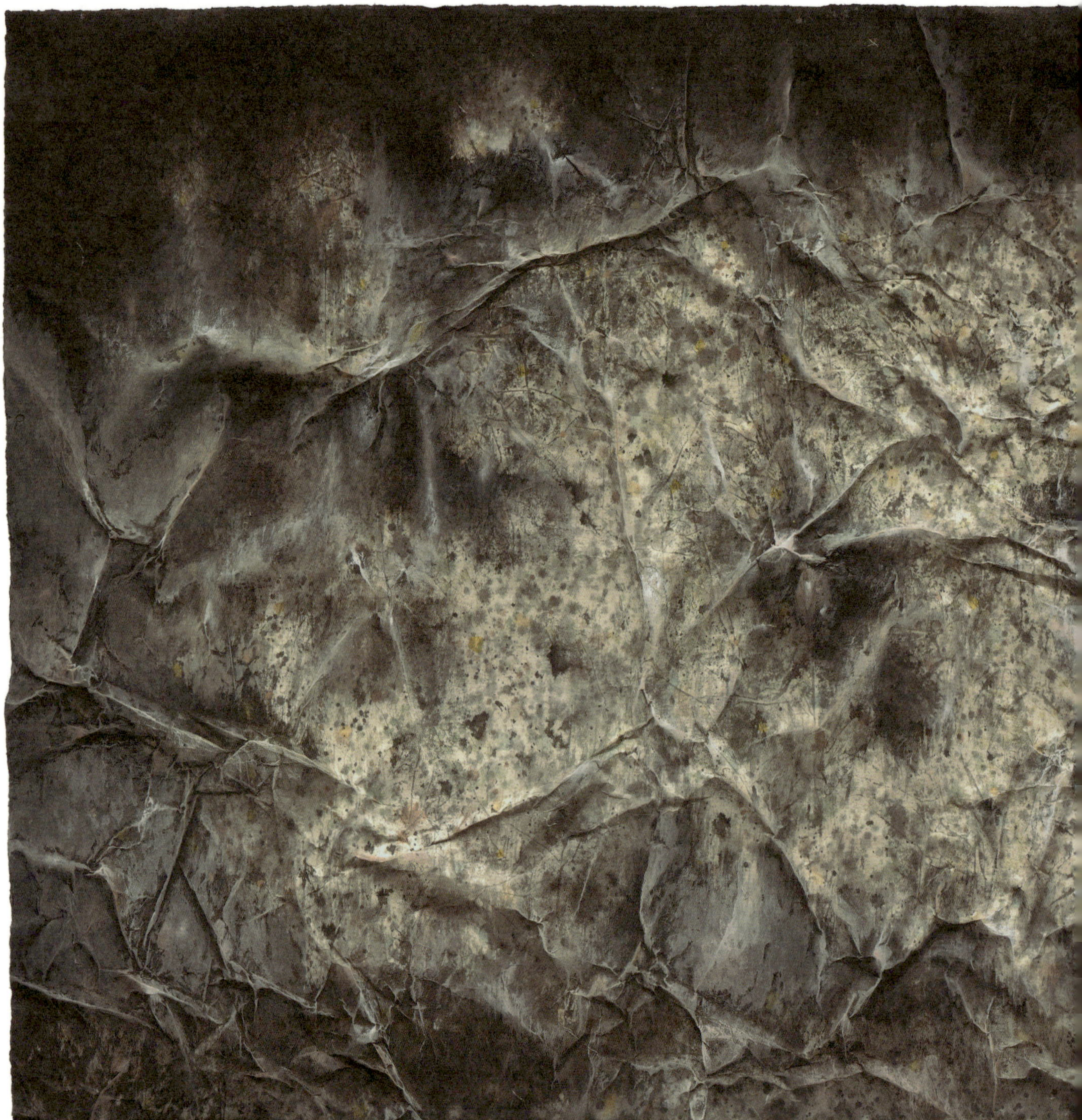

Vast Desolation 122cm × 235cm 2024

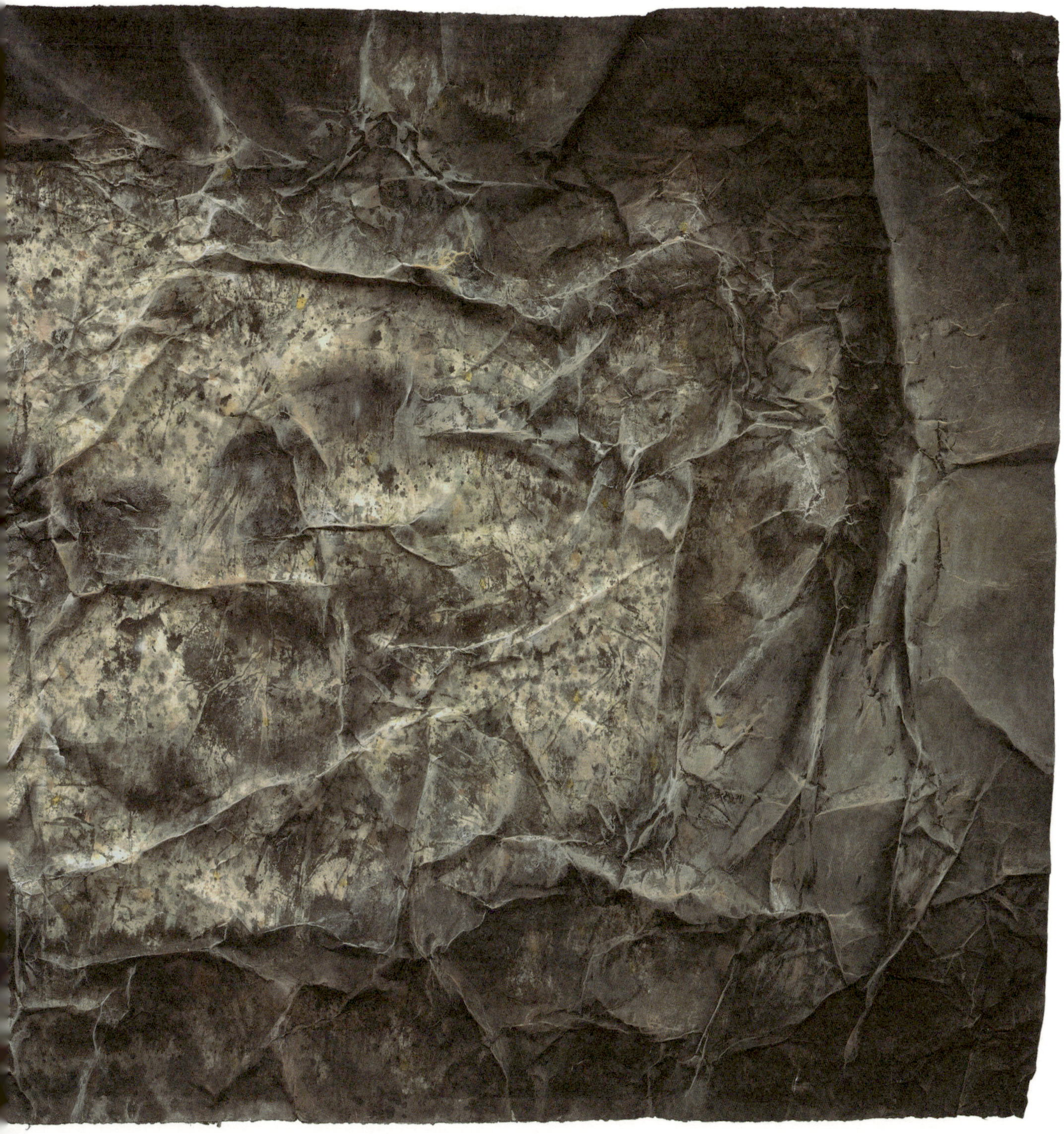

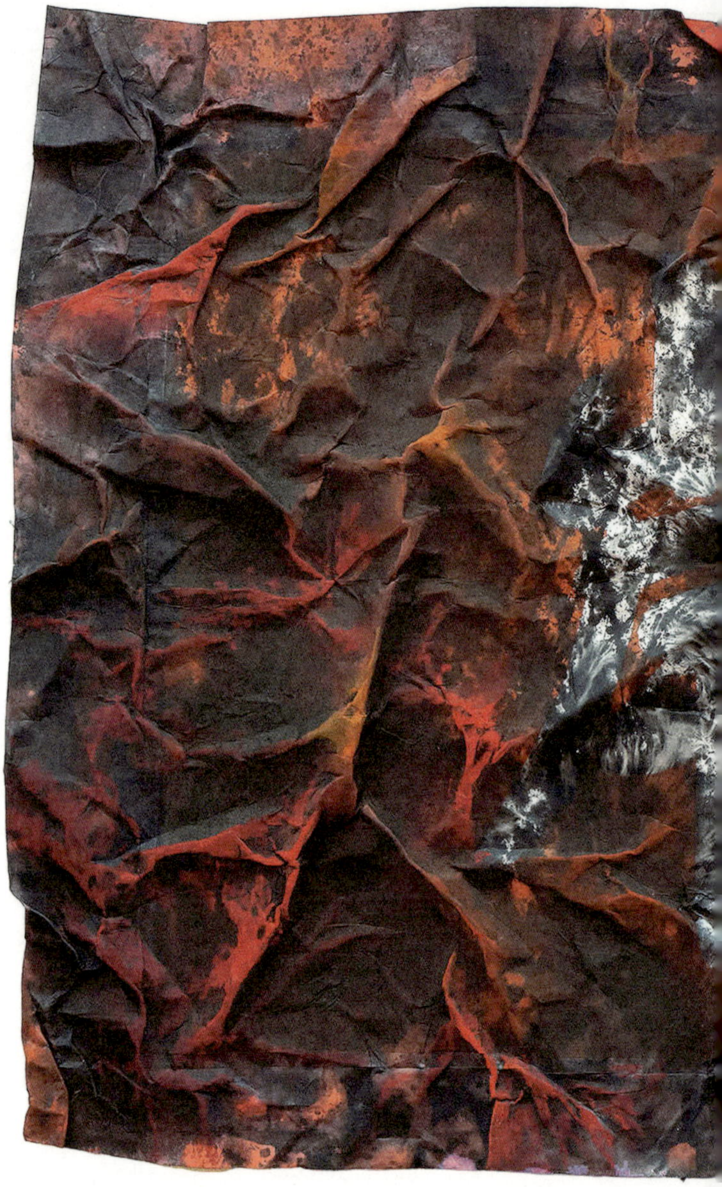

Enlightened Shore 83cm × 153cm 2024

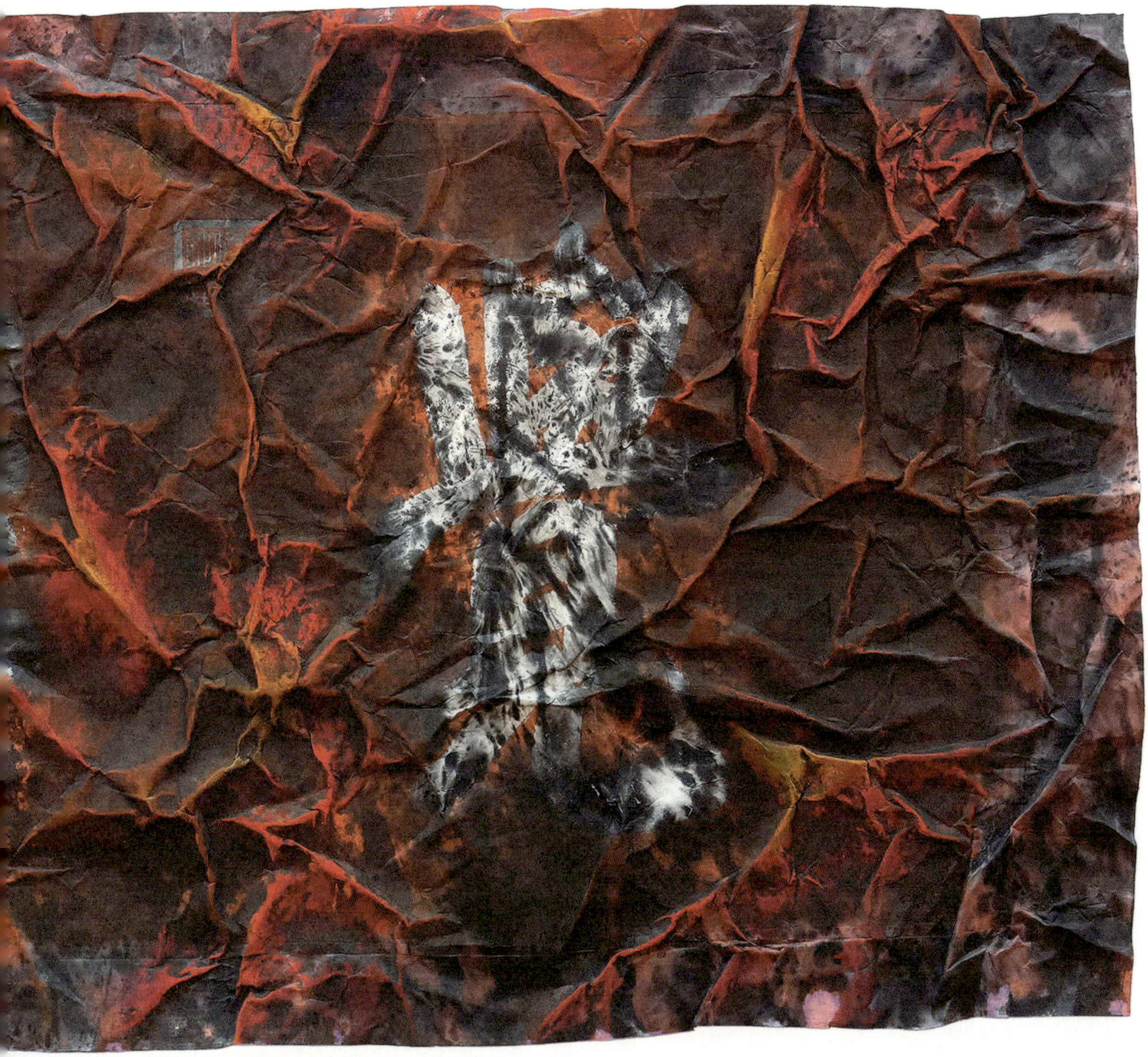

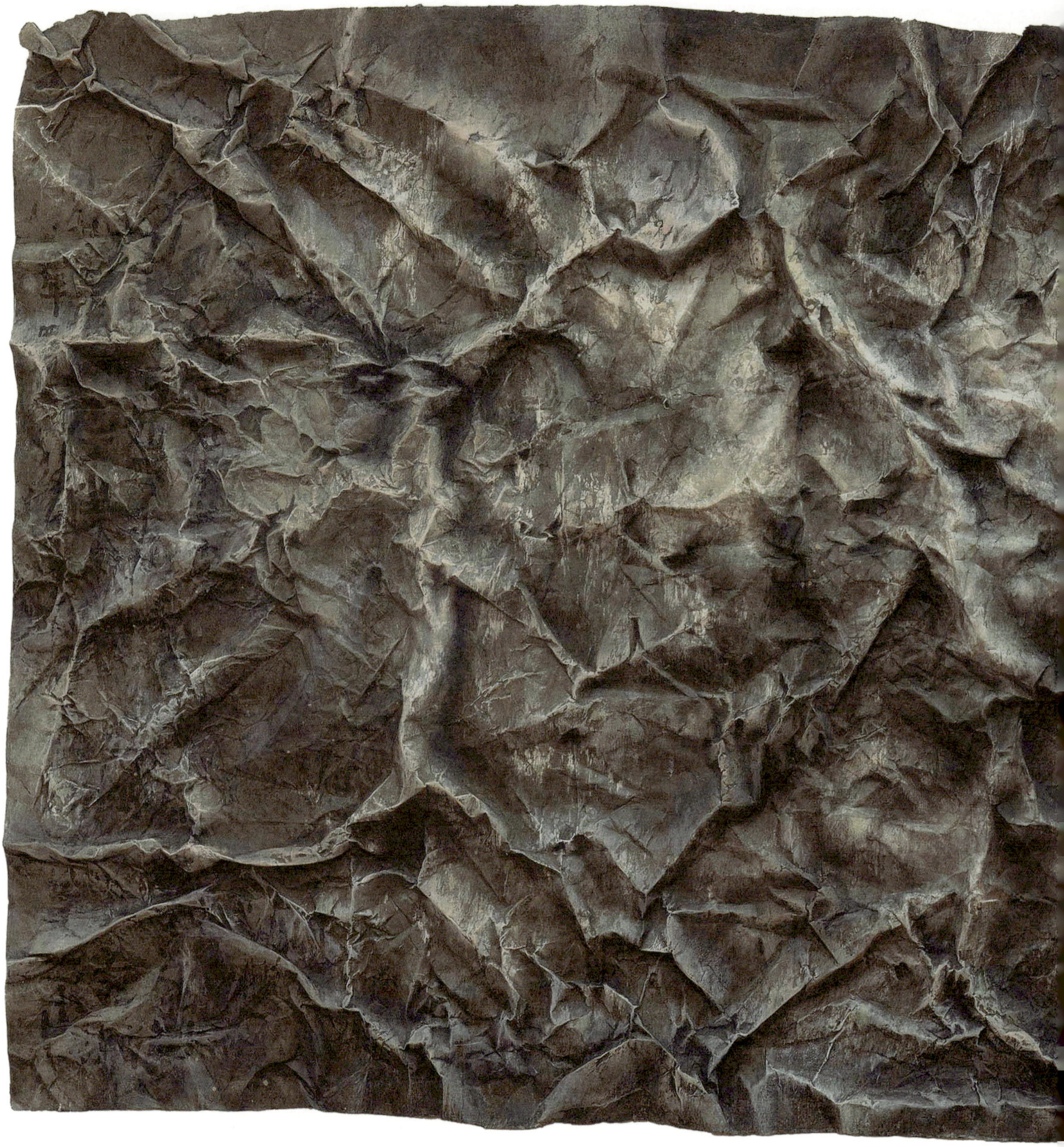

Like Water 113cm × 229cm 2024

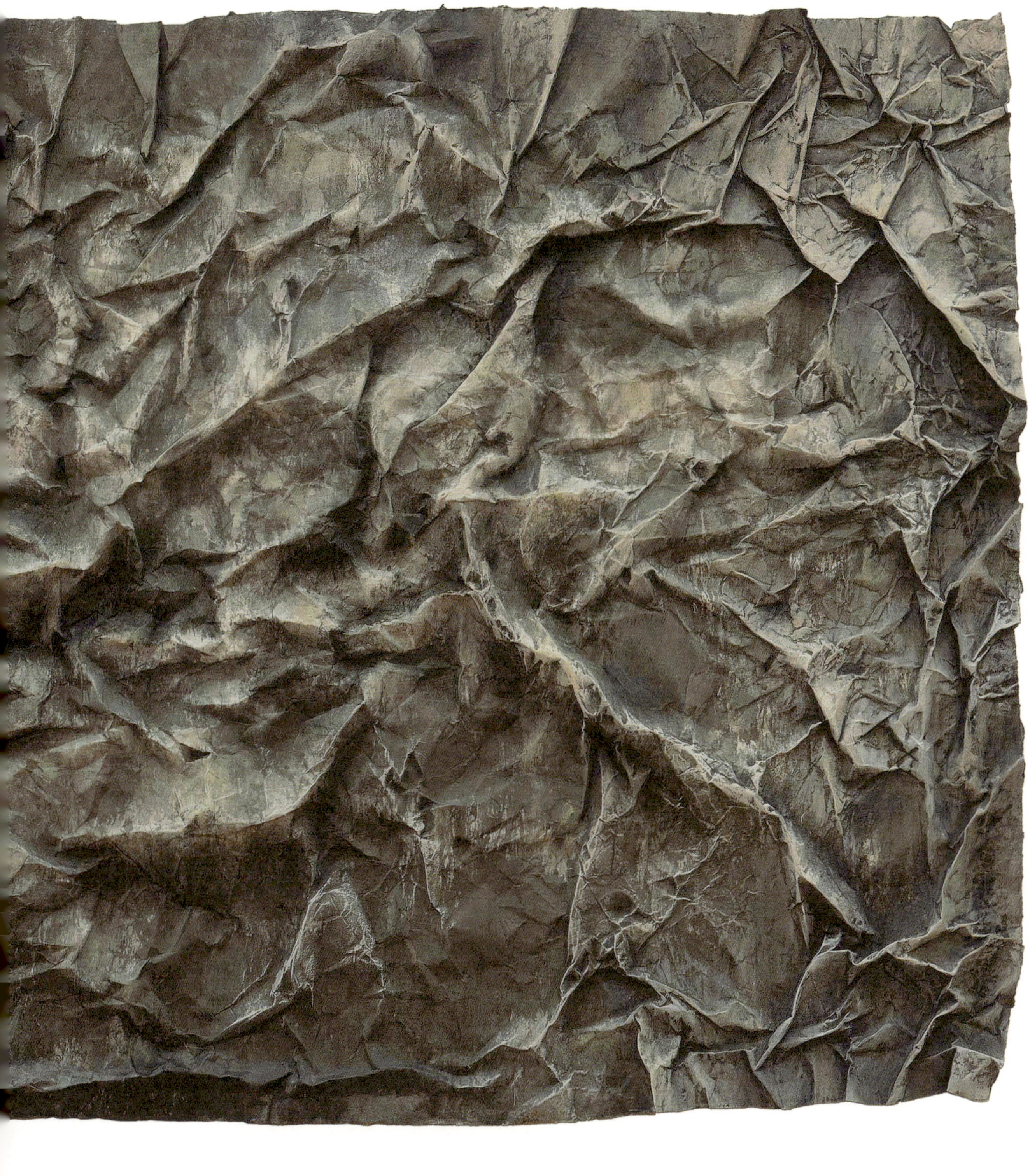

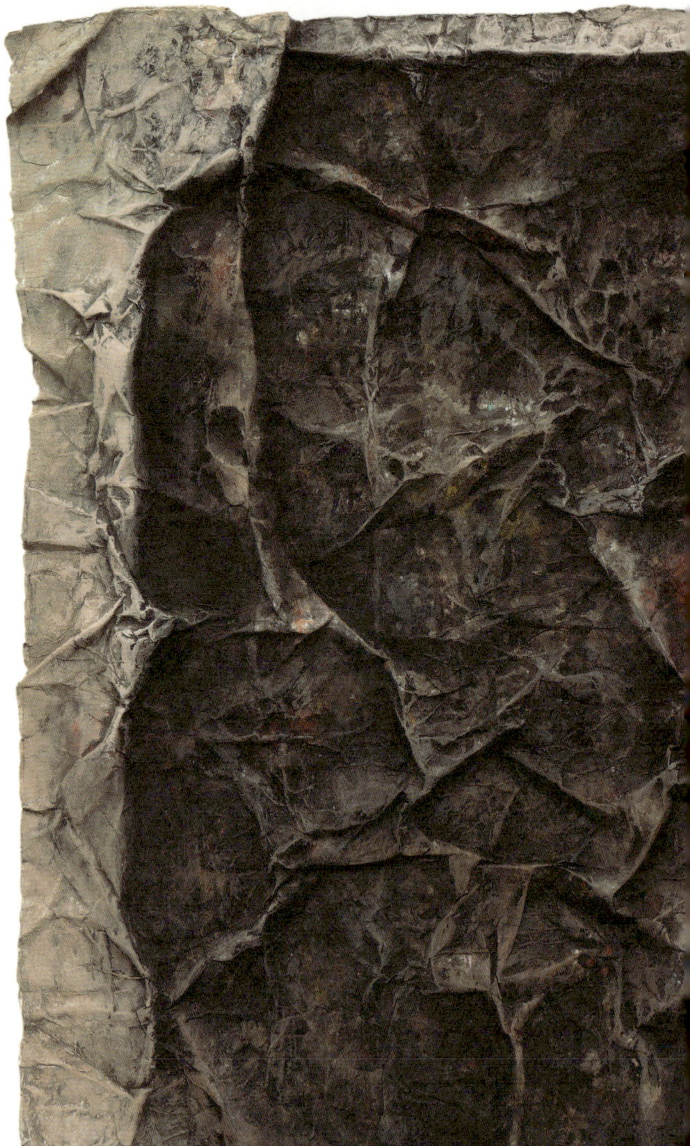

Dust 74cm × 126cm 2023

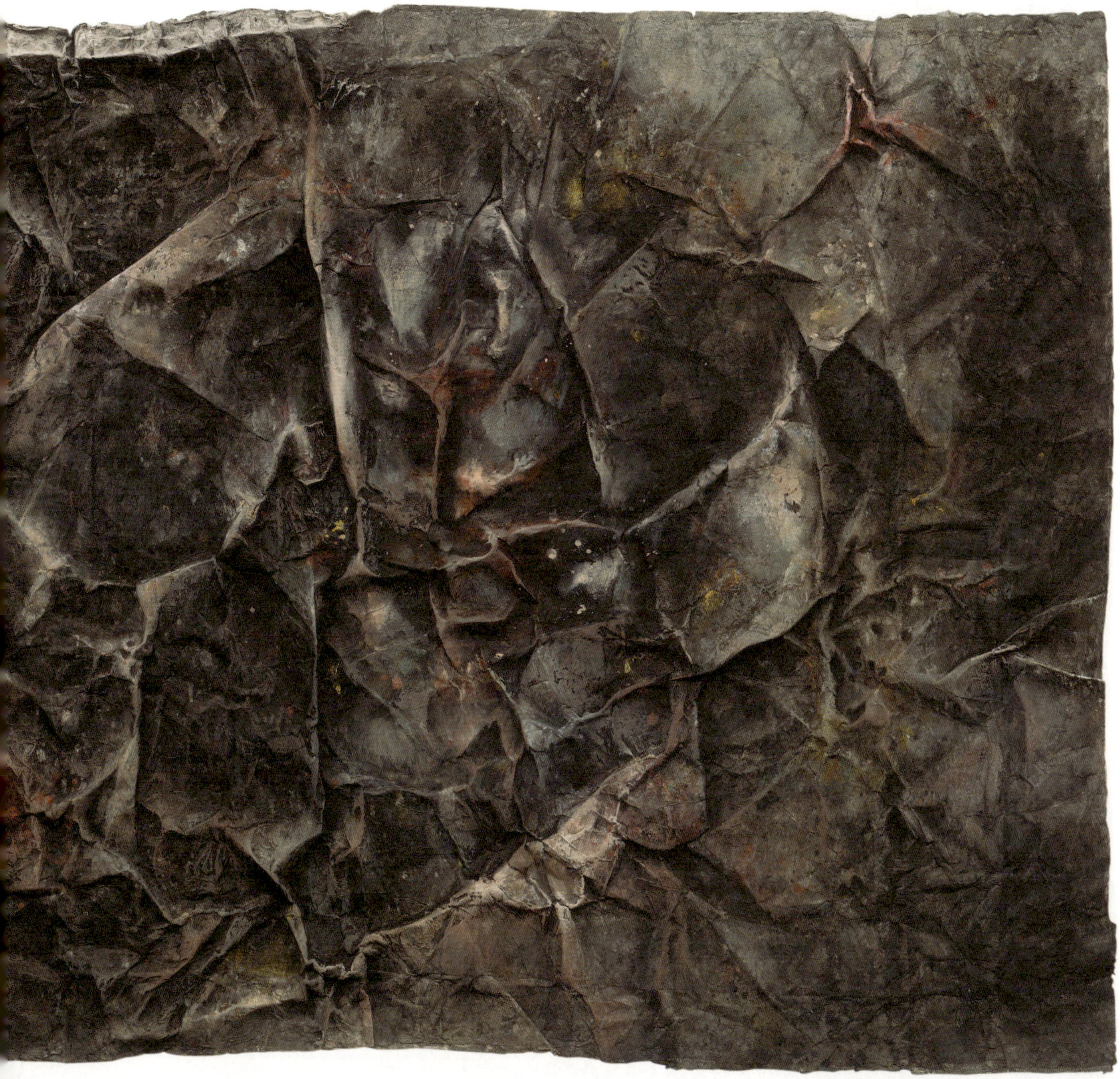

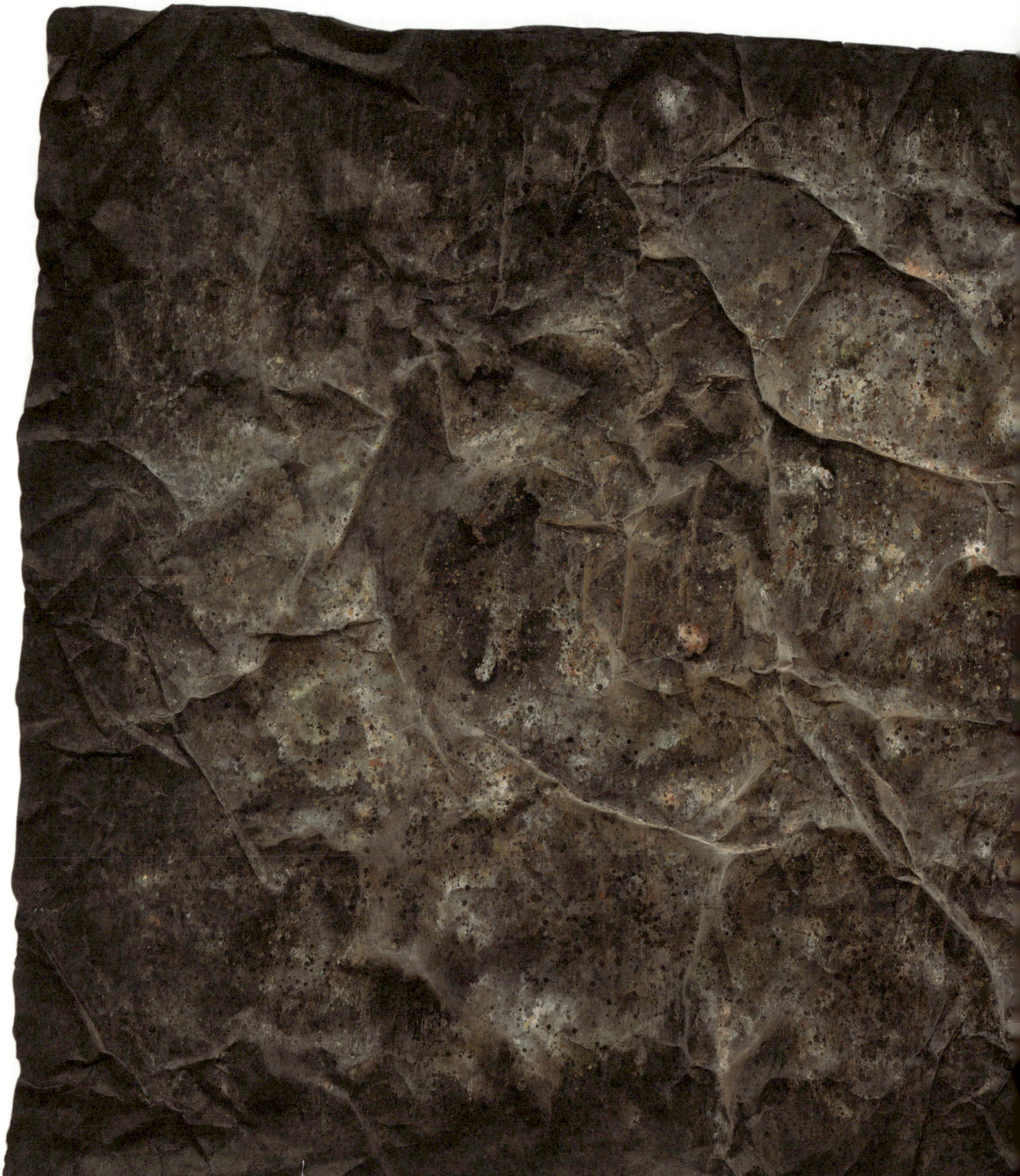

Beginning of All 120cm × 216cm 2023

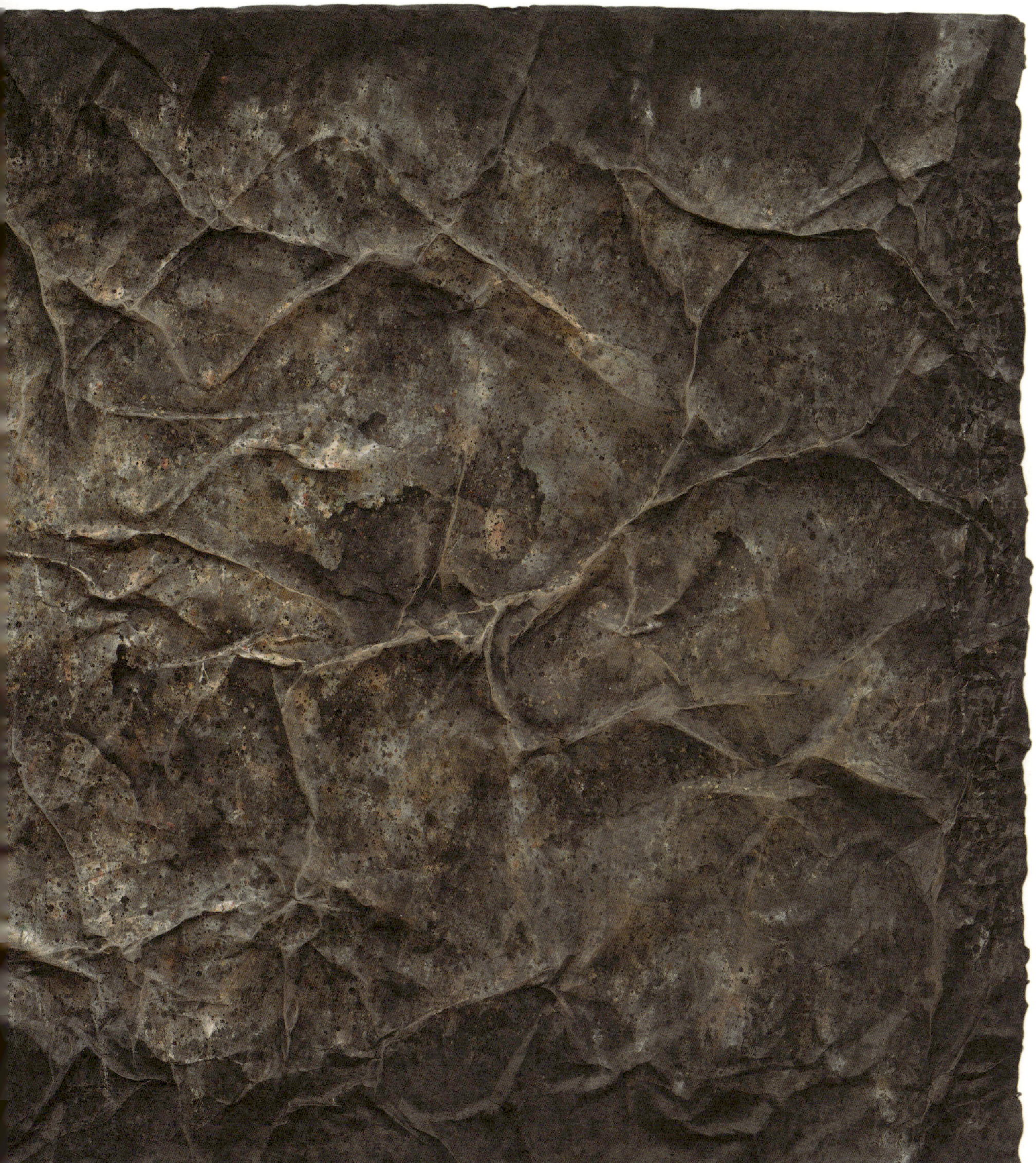

Flowing Wind 65cm × 75cm 2023

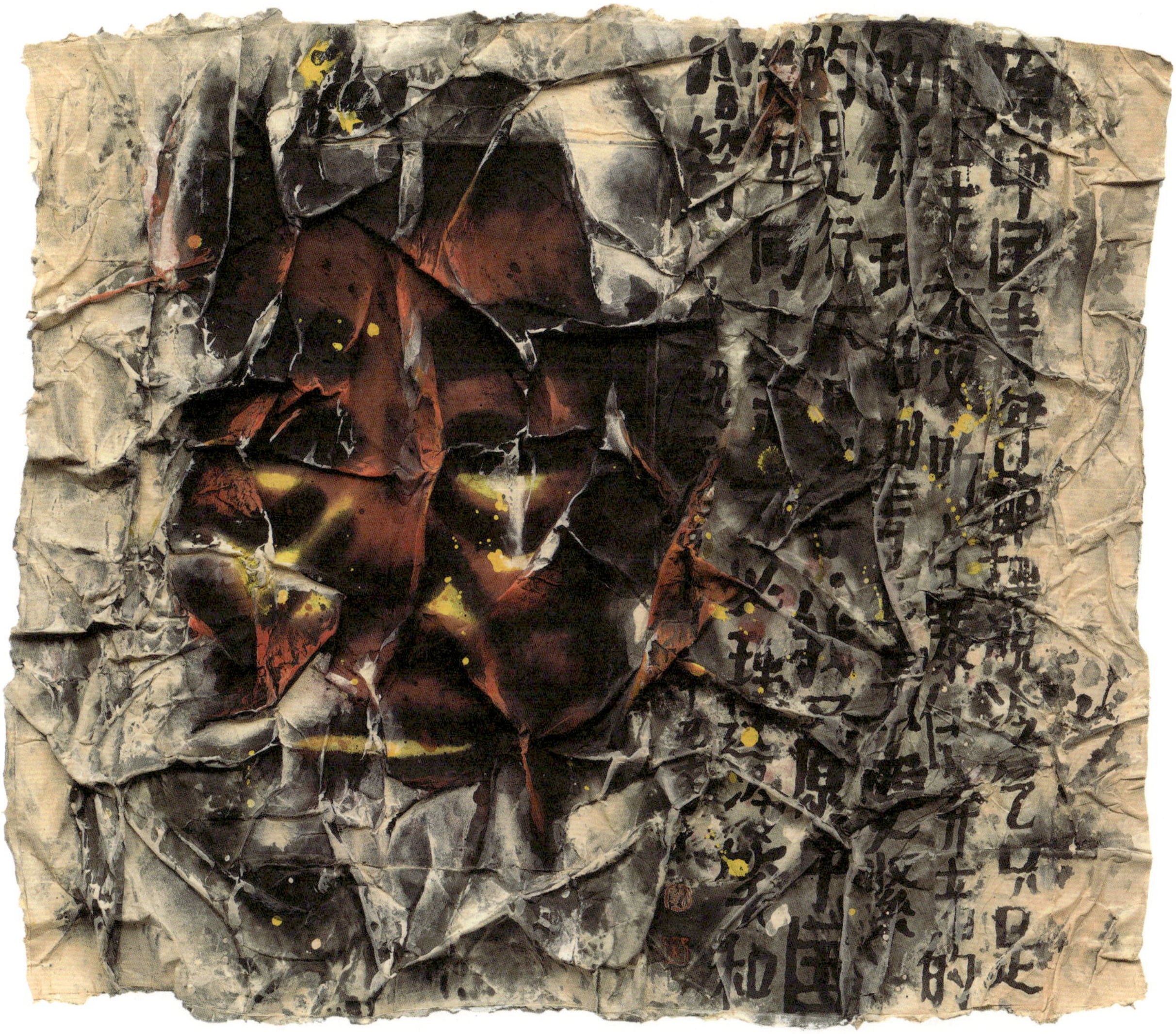

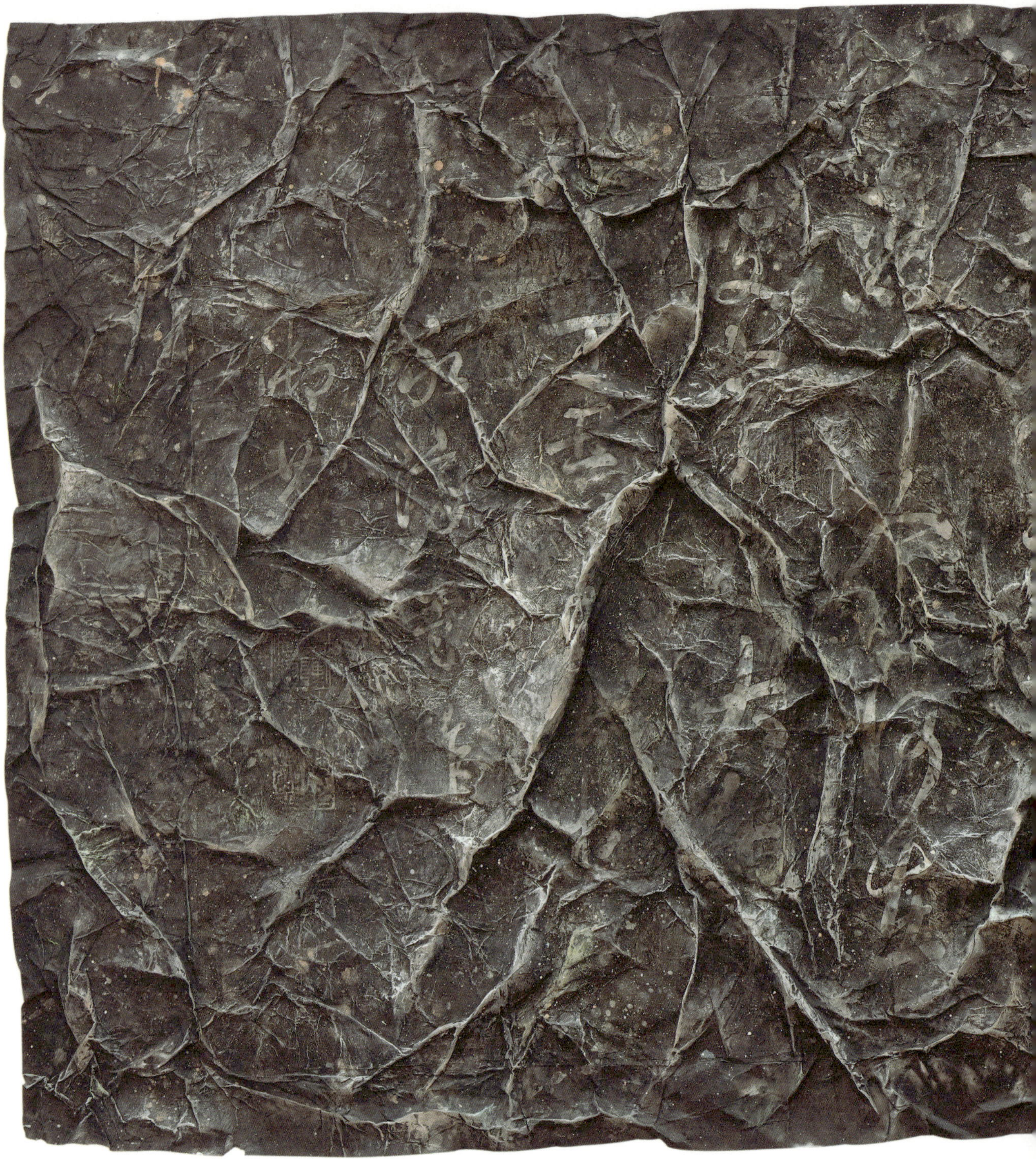

Traces Left 108cm × 218cm 2024

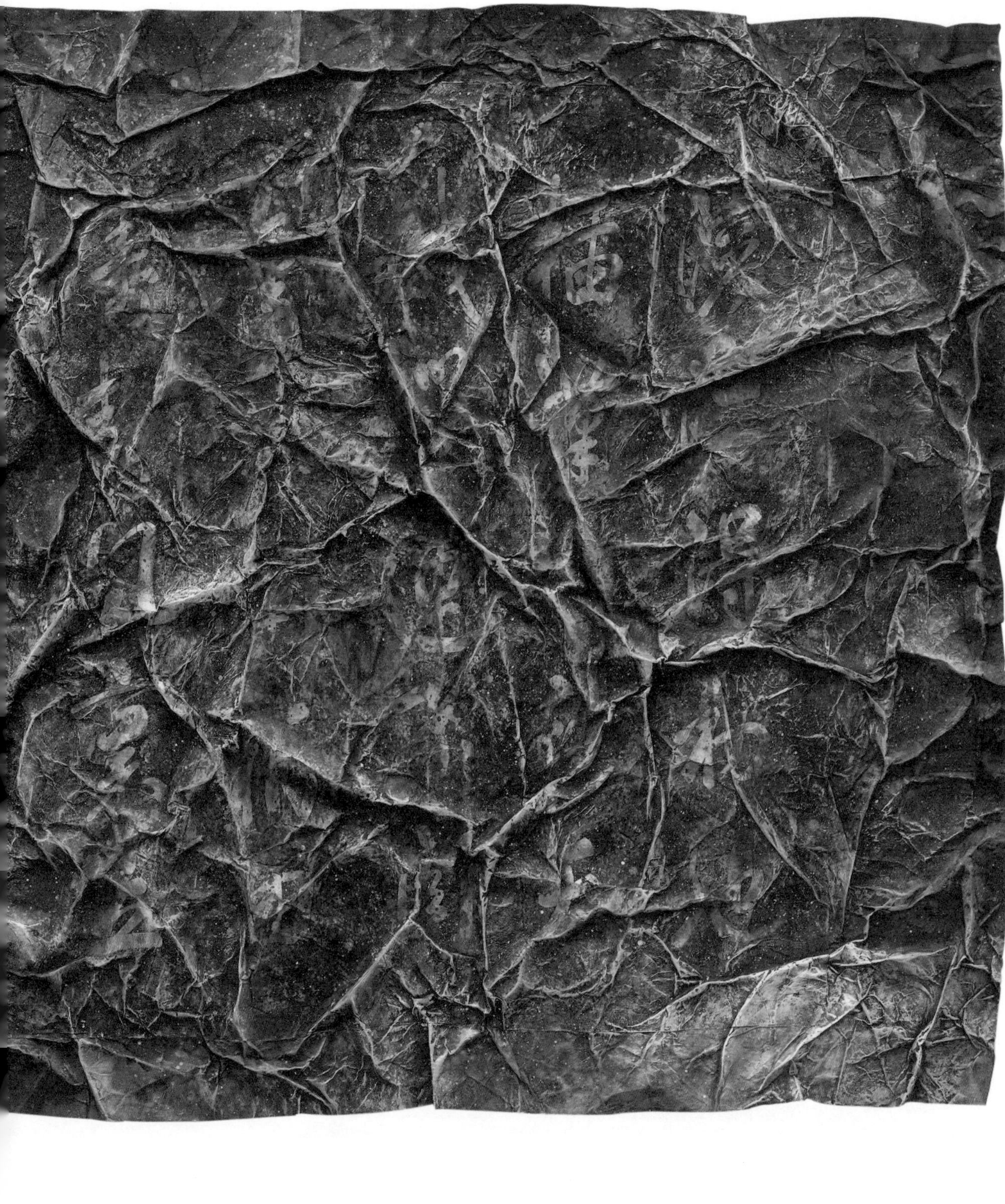

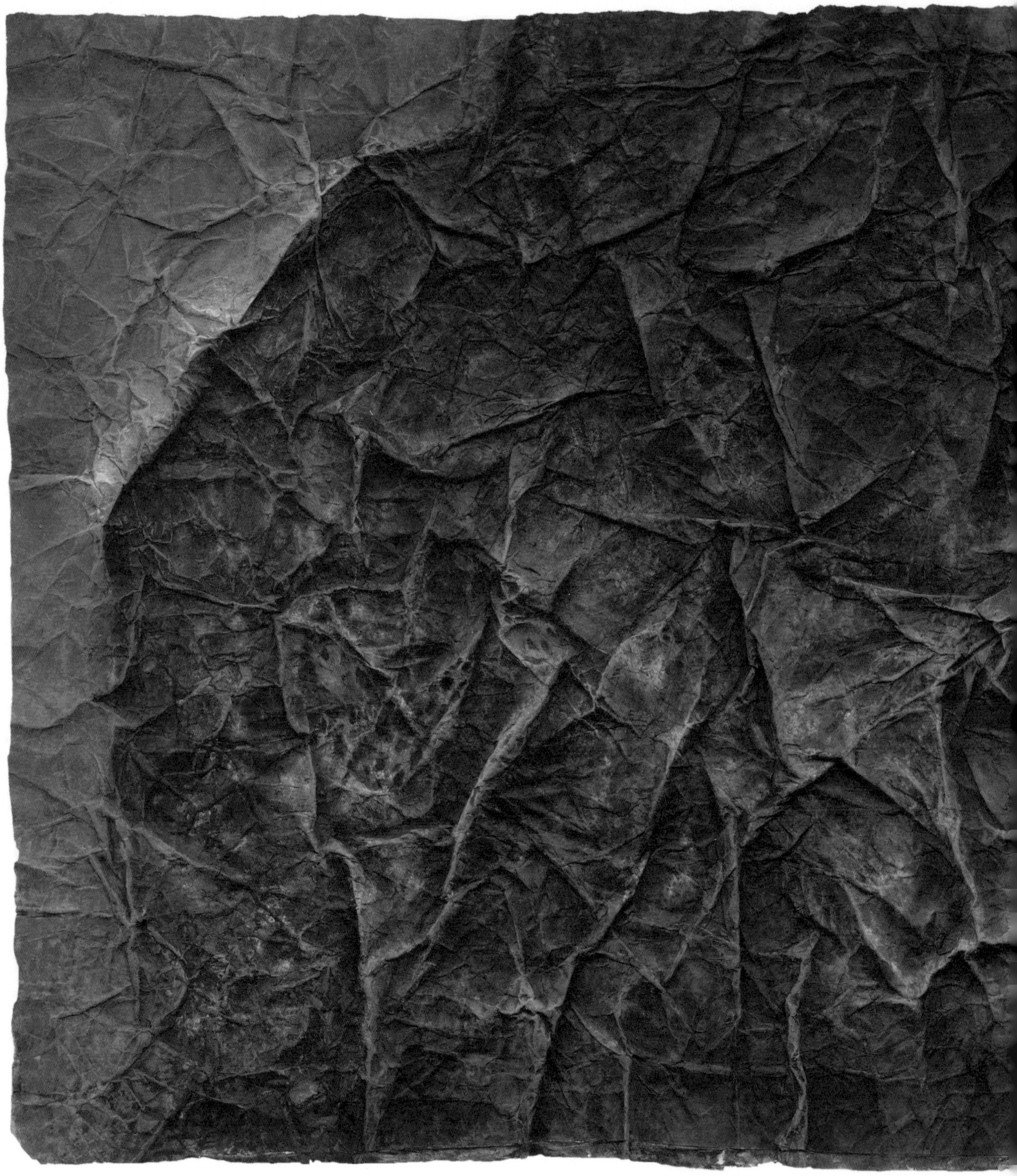

Sacred Valley 112cm × 195cm 2024

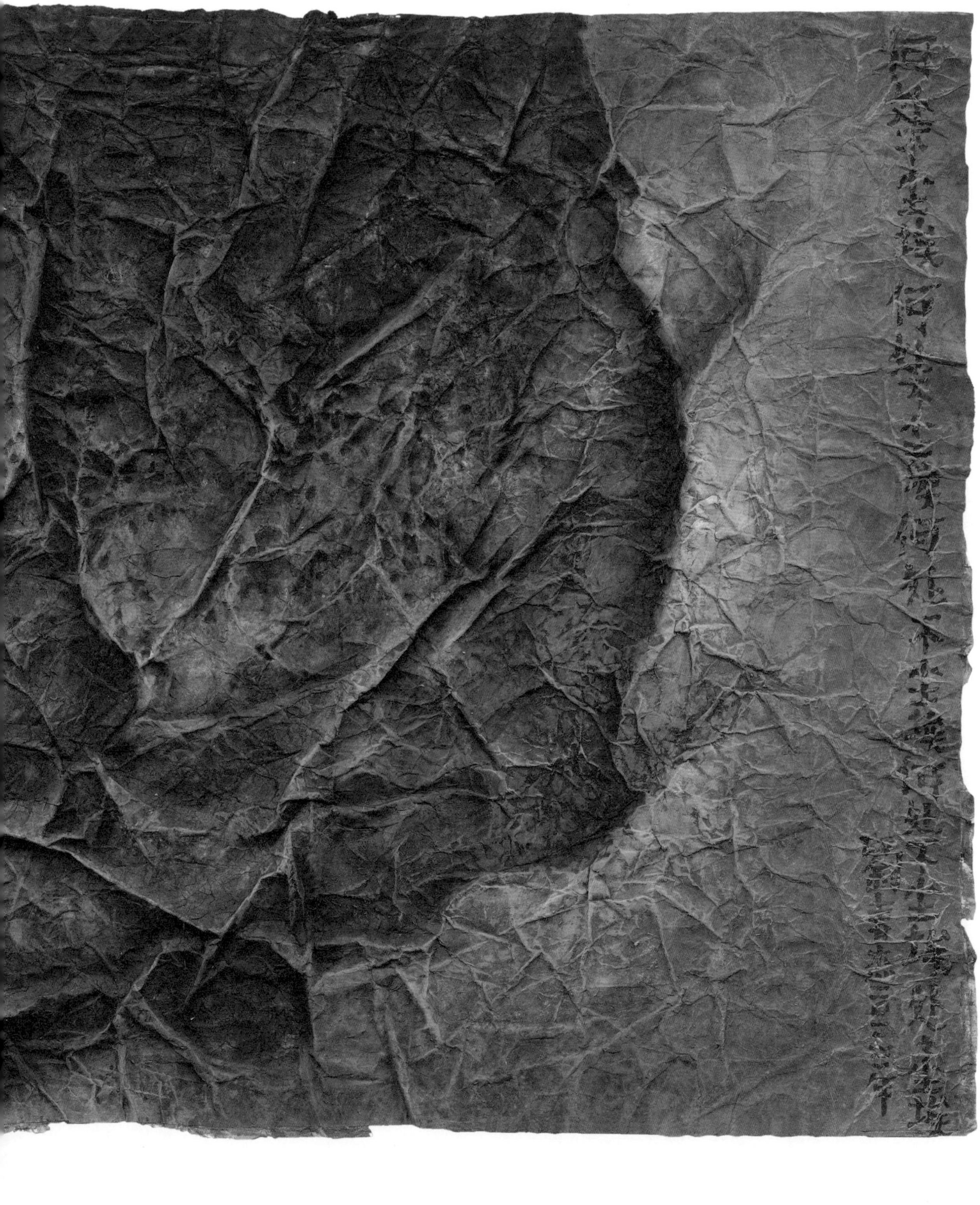

Life Unfolds 76cm × 140cm 2023

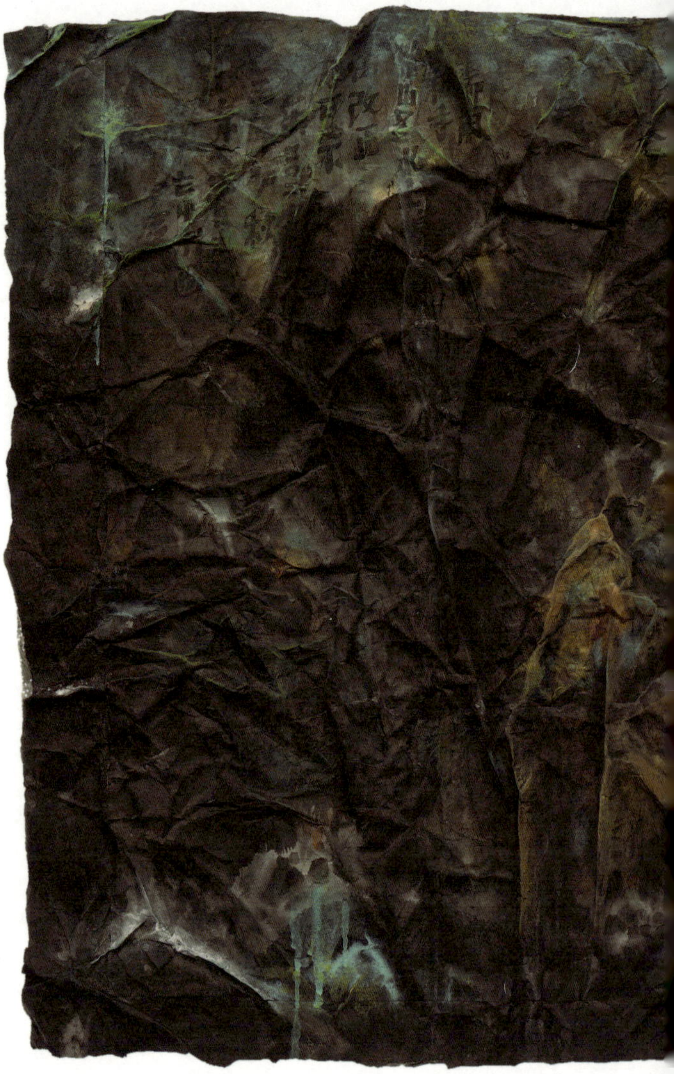

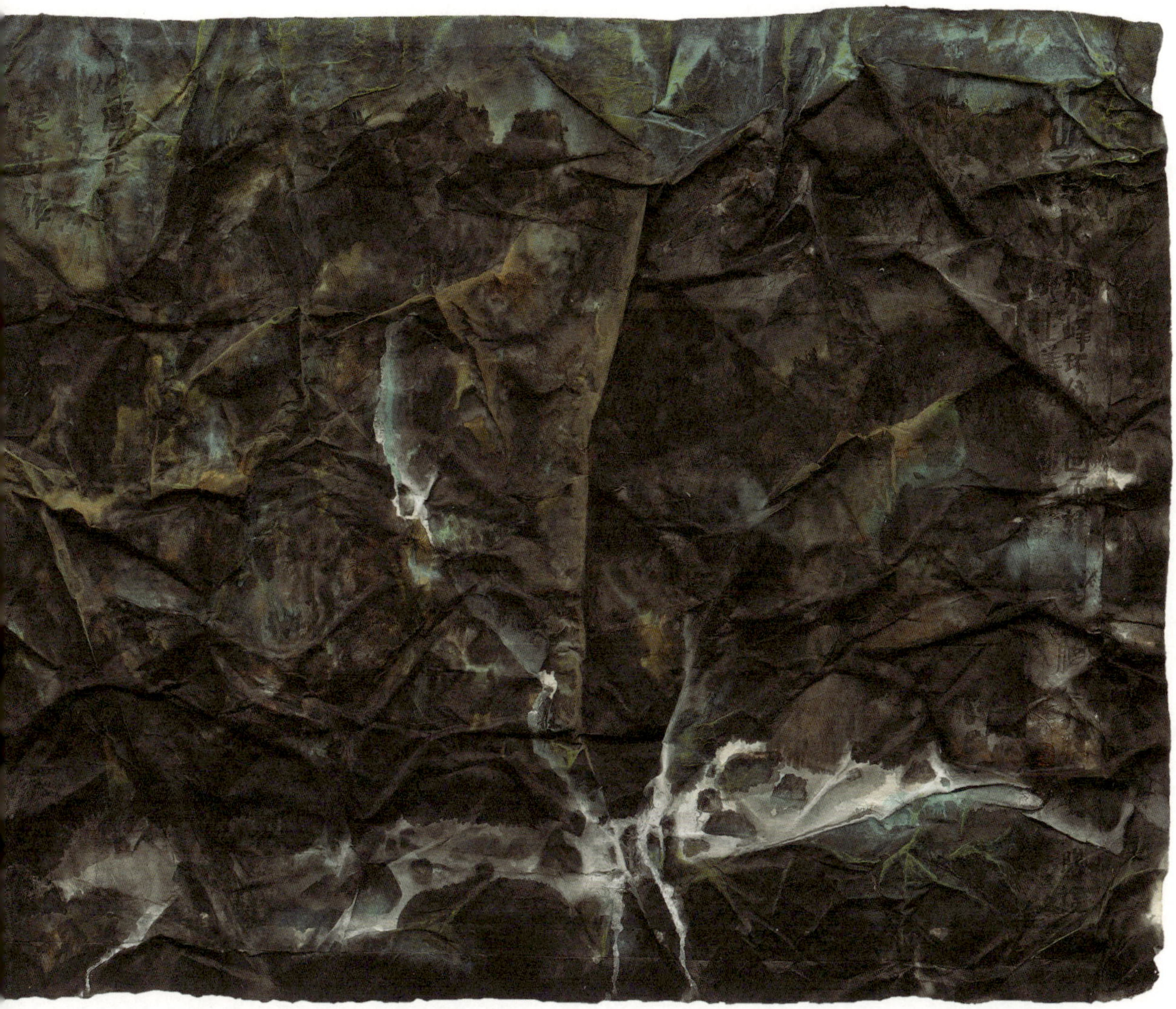

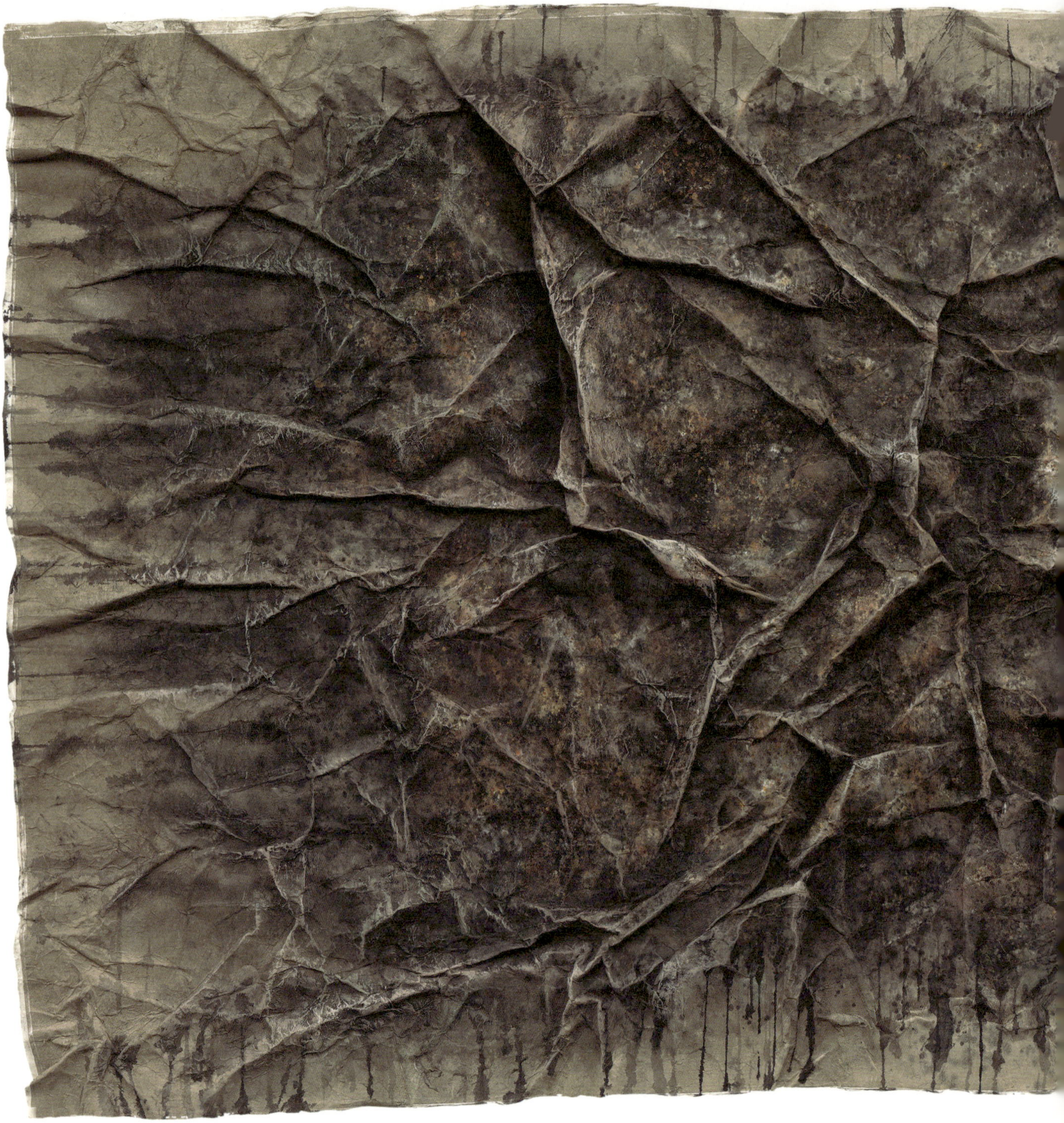

Sky Sign 120cm × 249cm 2023

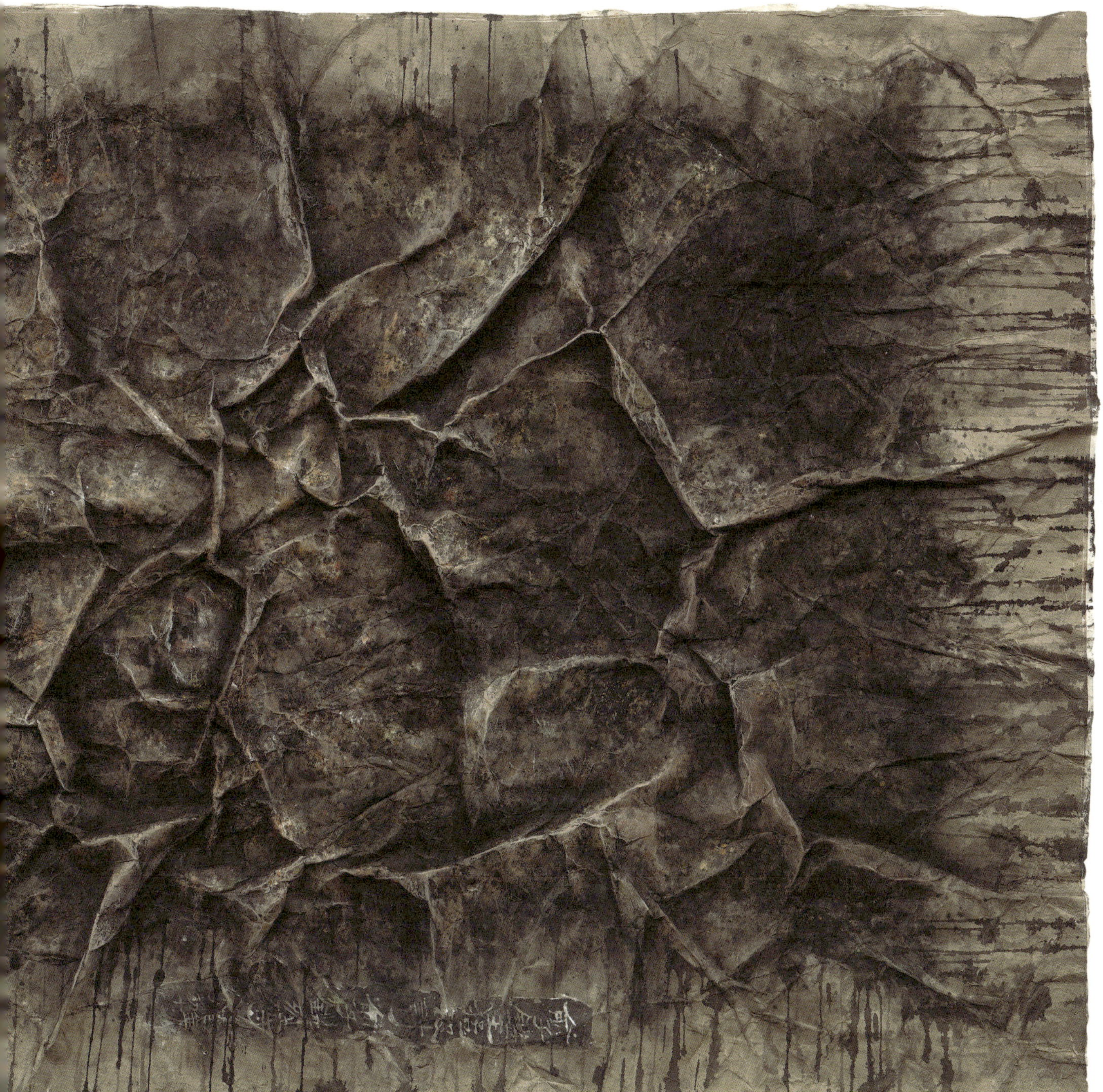

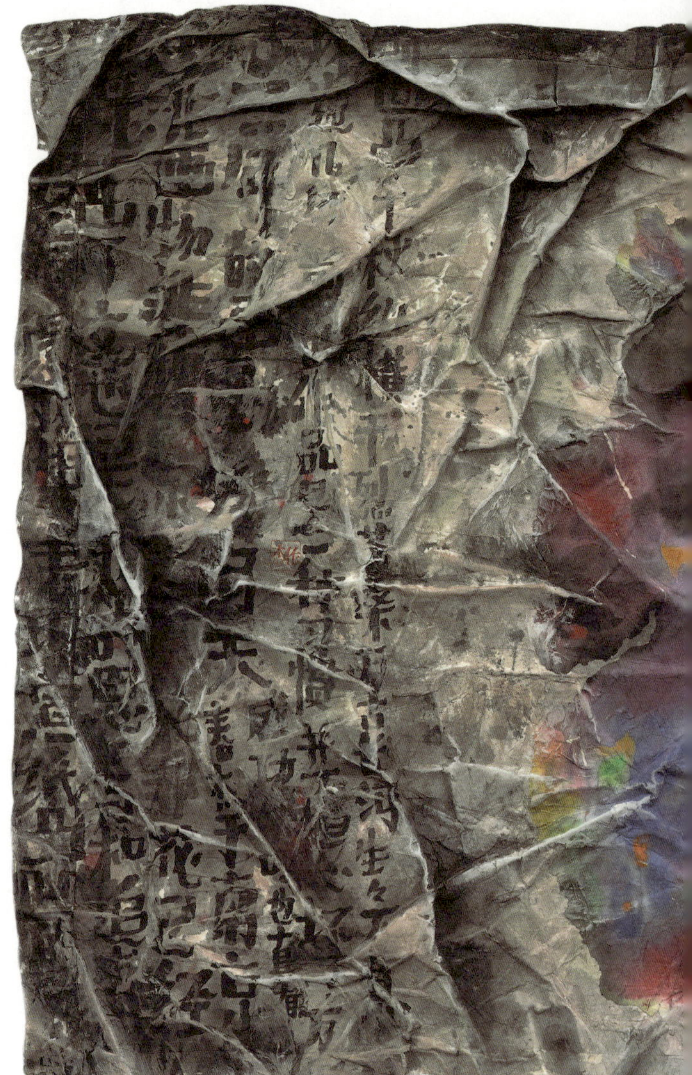

Nature's Choice 72cm × 136cm 2023

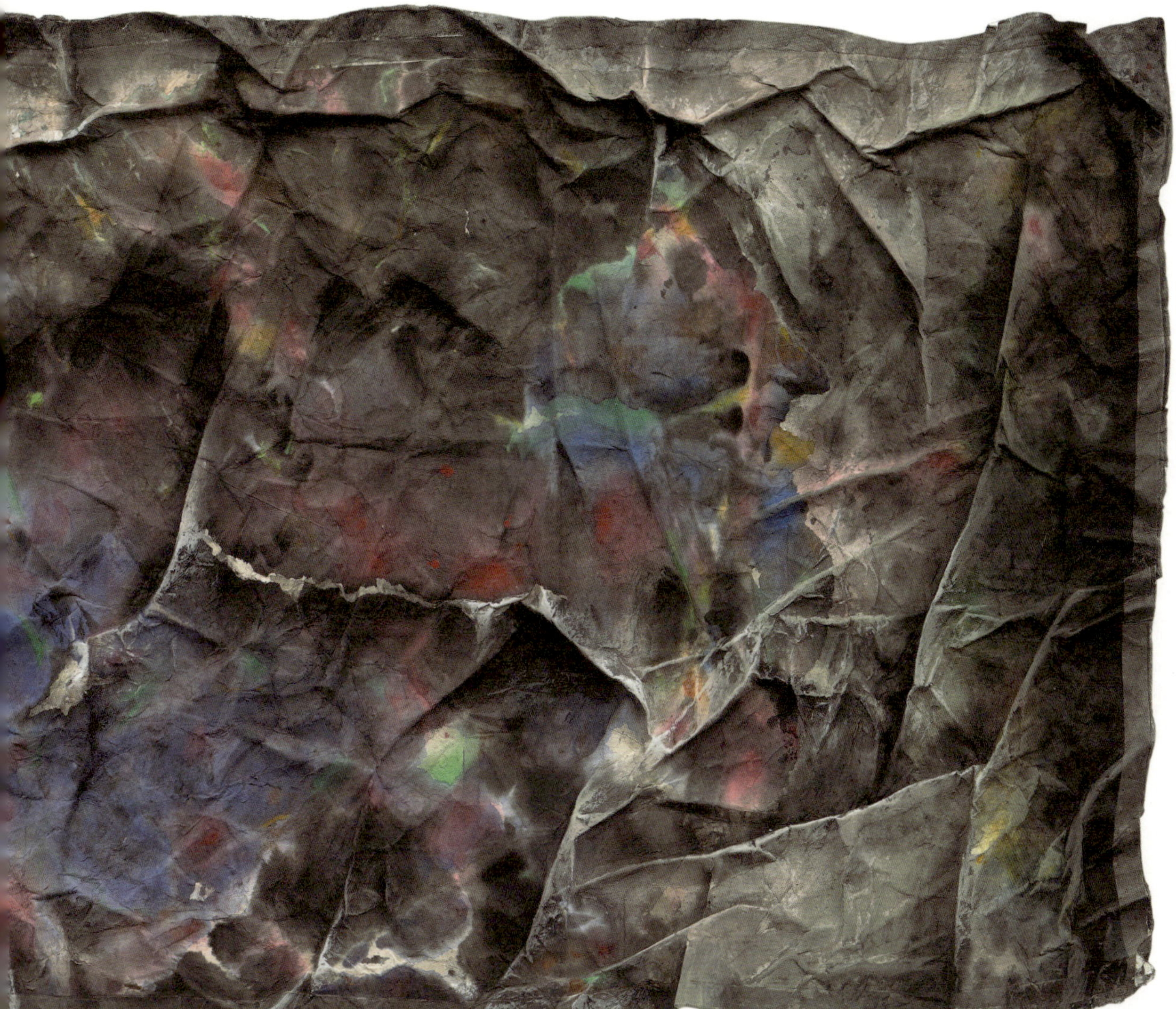

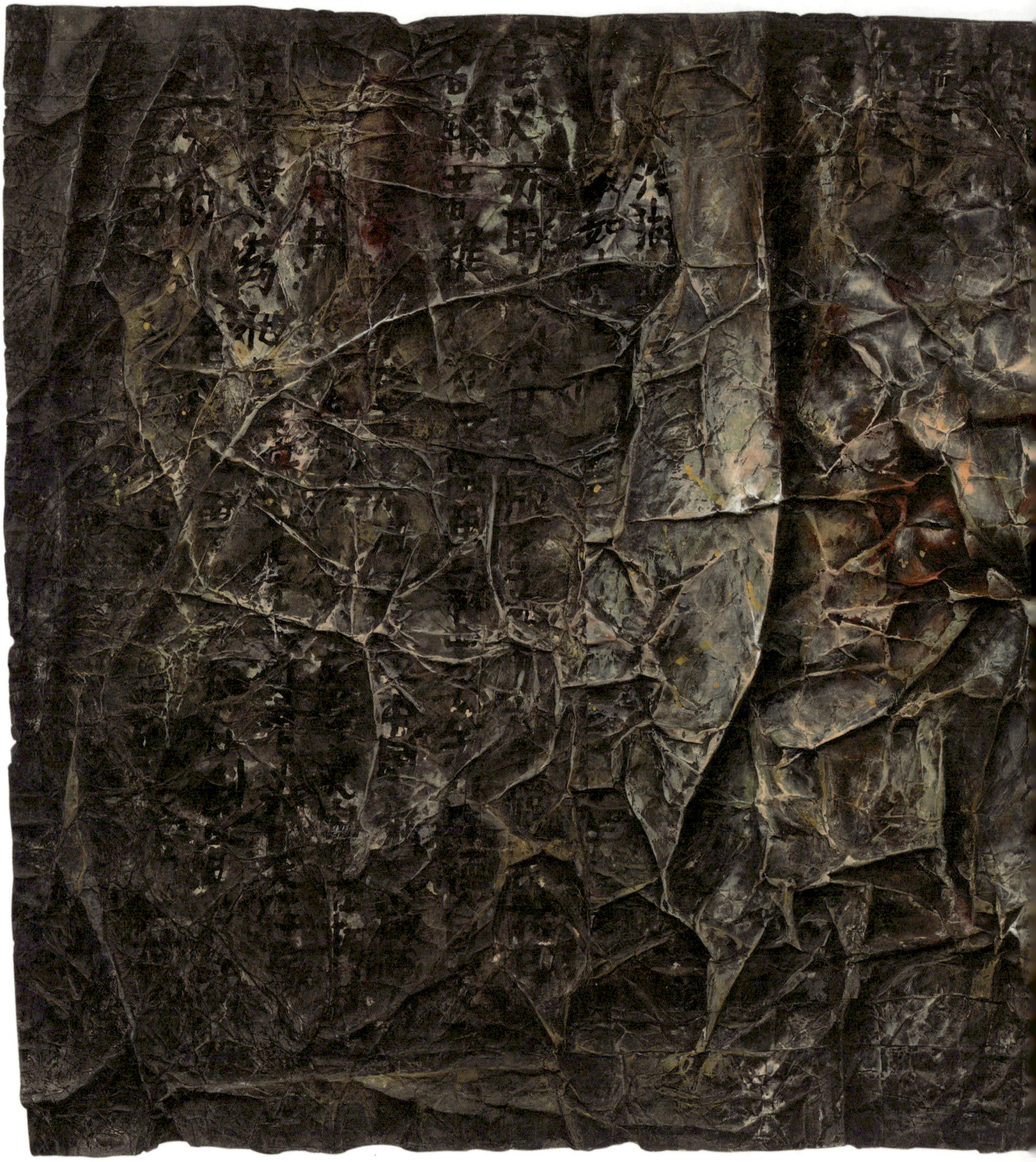

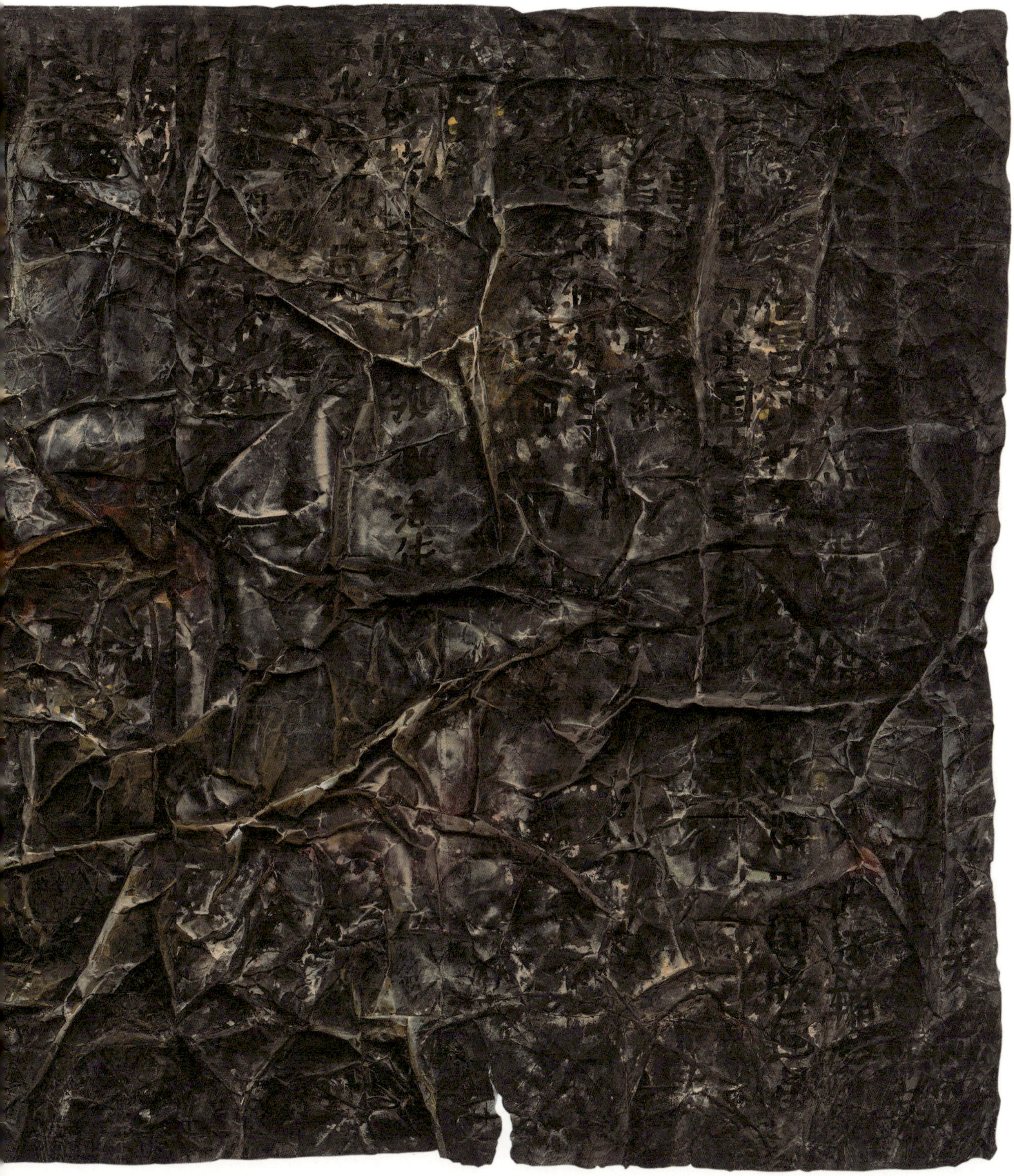

Carrying the Path 128cm × 238cm 2023

Qianlong 249.5cm × 150.5cm 2024

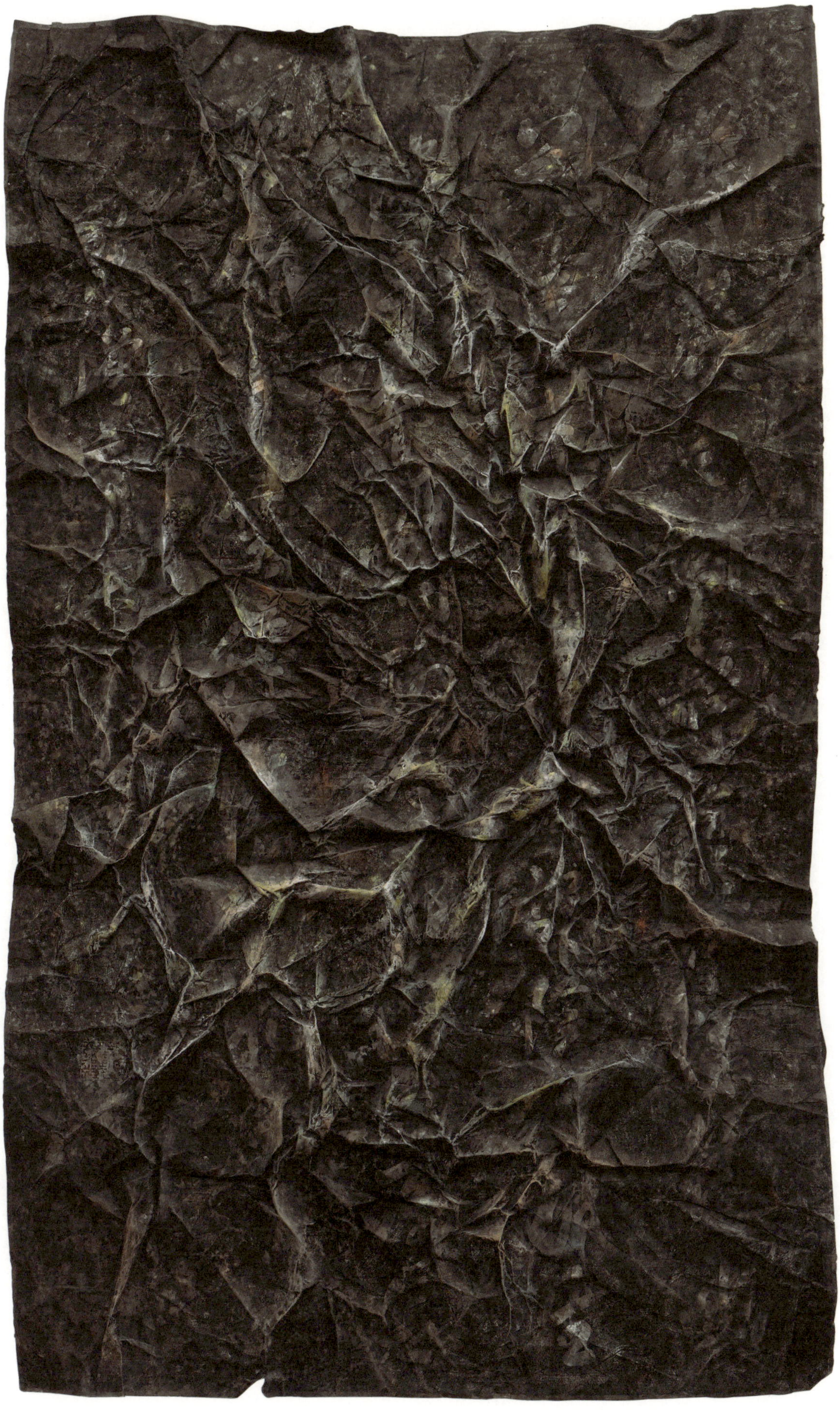

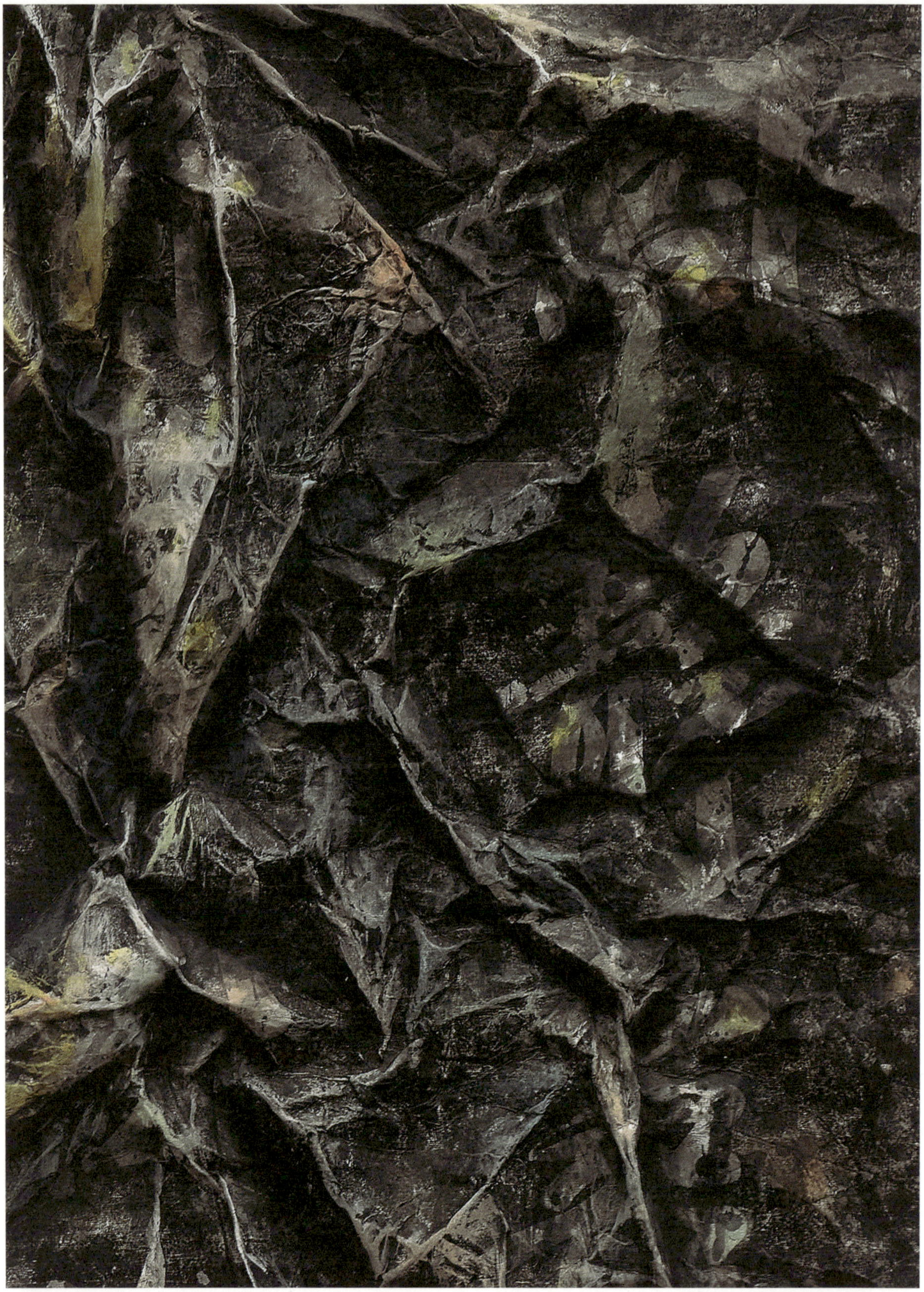

Details of *Qianlong*

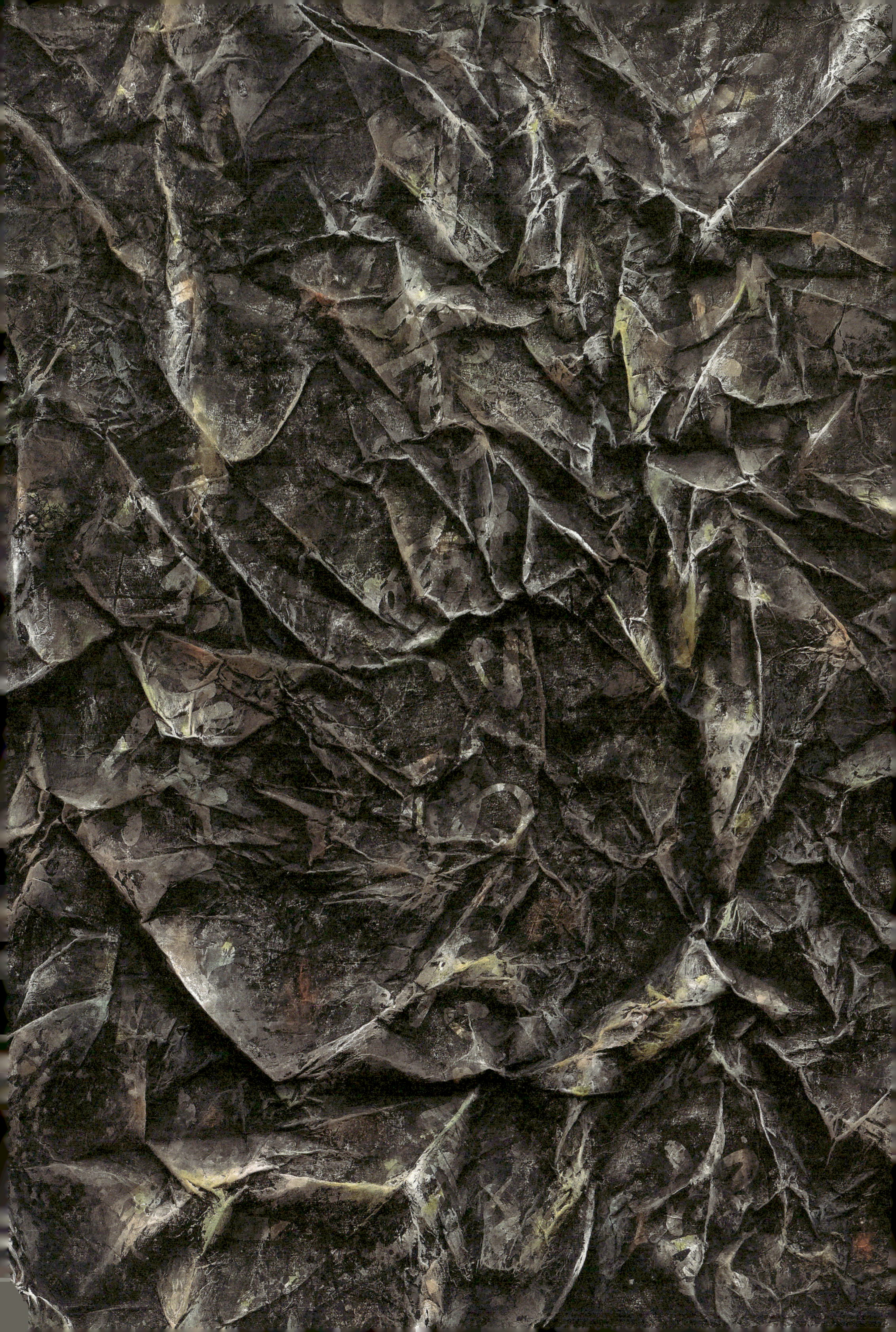

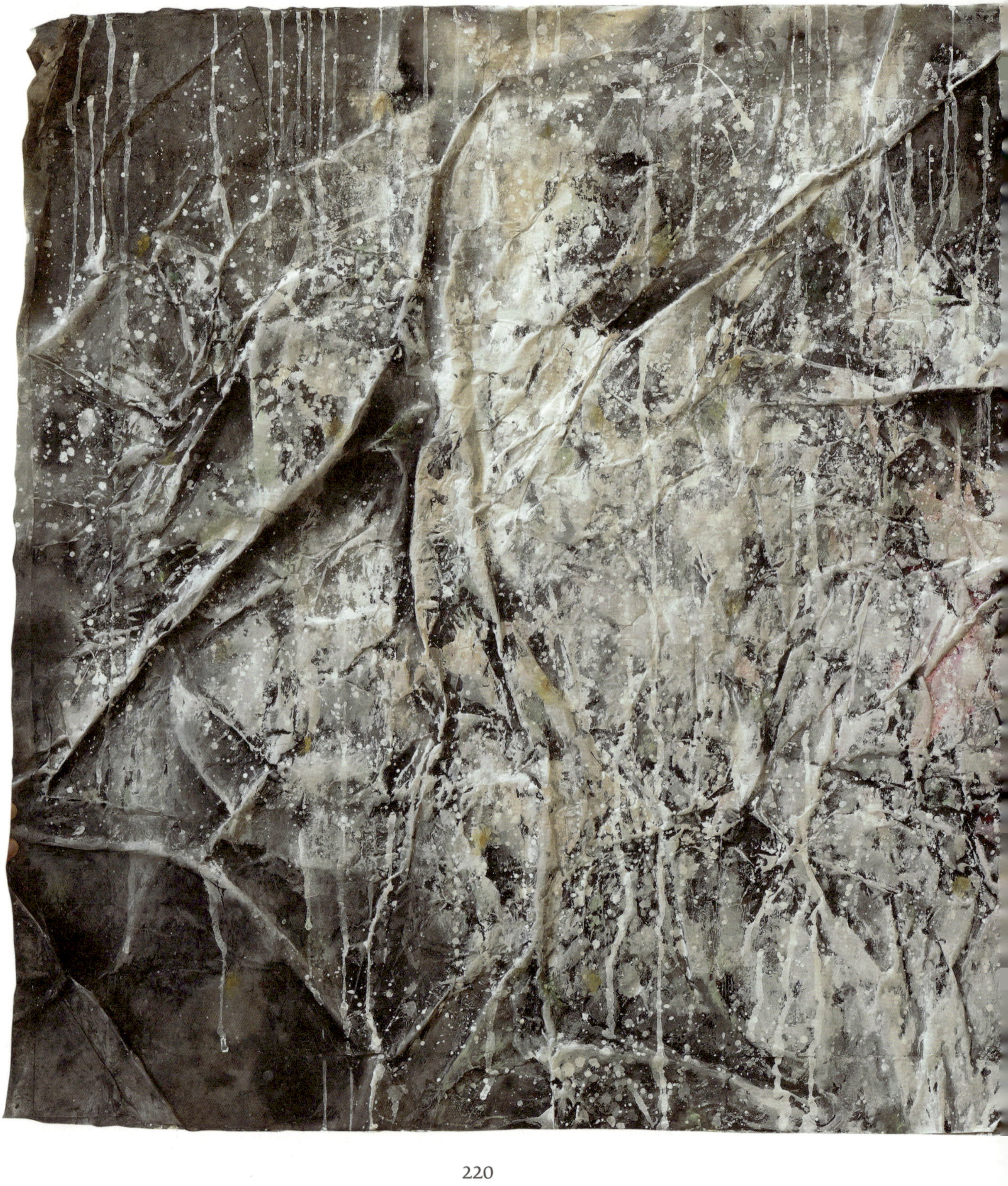

Like Ice 128cm × 238cm 2023

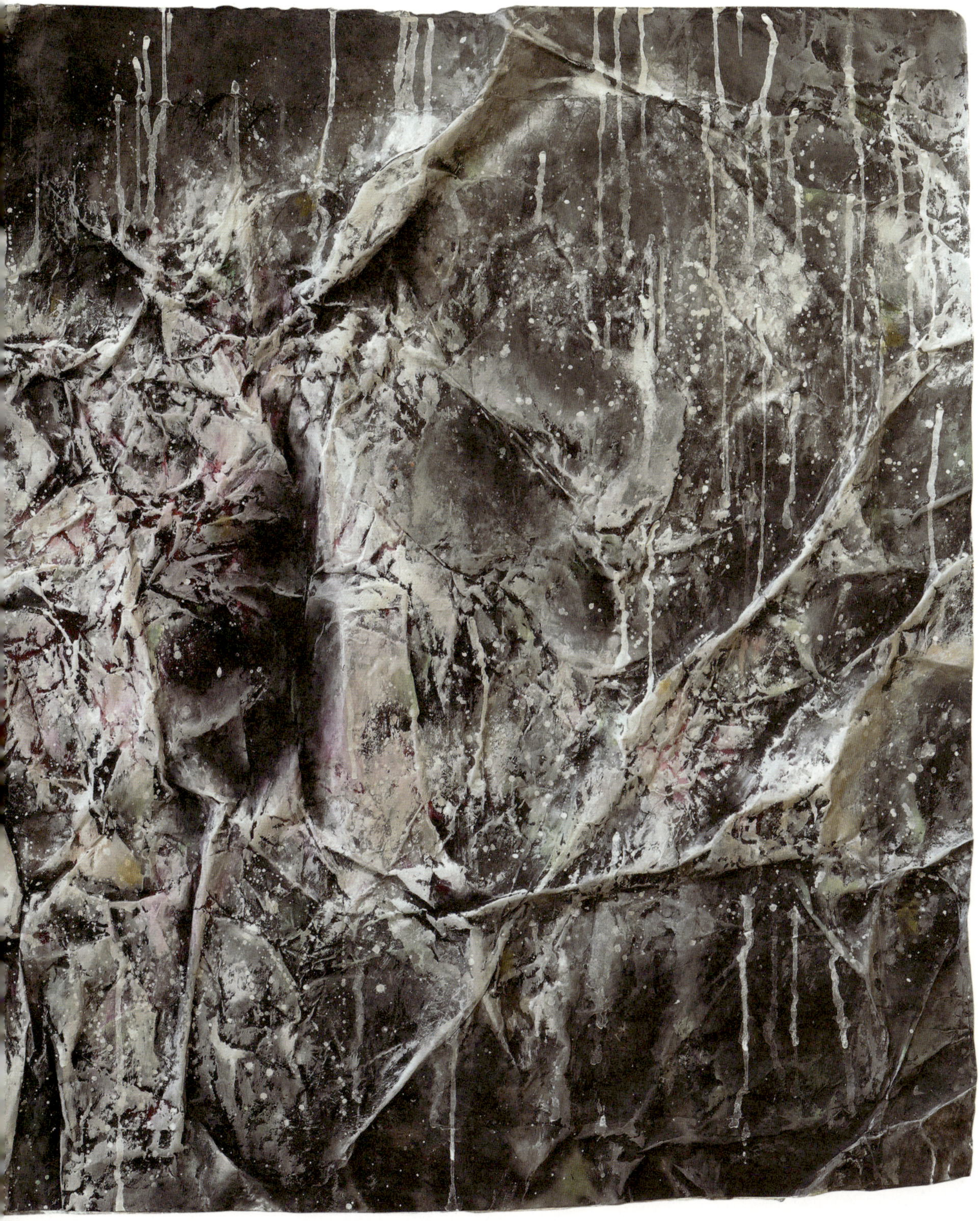

Some say these paintings resemble the cultural traces of wars and disasters; some say they evoke a feeling of the beginning of the universe, of ancient times. Others say they evoke a sense of chaos and vastness, of cosmic primordiality... I am delighted to achieve such effects. Nowhere is 'dust-free' – isn't it true? Great men, the mortal and the immortal, all come into the world naked and depart naked; all things in the world, steel and concrete, aeroplanes and cannons, ultimately return to dust.

As fate would have it, I found myself revising the manuscript for this book during the holidays, returning to the distant Beidahuang to celebrate with my father. I am already a stranger to my hometown, which brings about some doubts: the latest series of works, Nowhere is Dust-Free, once again features the land, much like the fields I was beholding, which were no longer the dark and fertile Beidahuang lands of the past. What about me? The long-haired youth who left decades ago has sailed through countless journeys, returning no longer as a youth.

Making small changes, gathering grains of sand into a tower, working hard; sometimes creating art is as painful as pulling one's own hair in an attempt to fly. It needs constant self-propulsion. Slowly, 40 years have passed, and the dream of being an artist has long been achieved. And now, no matter how much I seek and explore, handcraft and traditional materials are always embraced, the spirit of woodcut unchanged, but both my art and I have long since transformed beyond recognition.

Biography

Exhibitions

2003 - Guangdong Museum of Art
2007 - Shanghai Museum; Wong's Art, Hong Kong; Nanjing Museum; Taiwan Caves Art Center
2008 - Turchin Center for the Visual Arts , United States
2009 - Xi'an Academy of Fine Arts
2010 - Baiyaxuan Art Center, Shanghai
2011 - Shengshi Sky Art Museum, 798 Art Zone, Beijing
2012 - Shanghai Aosai Gallery
2013 - Nanjing Ancient Bank Art Center; ShiJiaZhuang Art Museum
2014 - Hangzhou Kuaiyi Space; Jiangsu Shengde Culture and Art Center; ShiJiaZhuang Art Museum
2015 - Shenzhen Museum of Art; Guancheng Art Museum; Tianjin Art Museum; Liangyou Bookstore Ouduo Space, Qingdao
2016 - Shaoxing Lu Xun Memorial Hall, Zhejiang; Zhoushan Putuo Cultural Essence House, Zhejiang Province; Chinese Children's Art Museum, Xiamen; Beijing Aimer Art Museum
2017 - Suzhou Museum
2018 - Jiangsu Provincial Museum of Fine Arts
2019 – Yi Space Gallery, Nanjing
2021 - Moon Center for Contemporary Art, Changsha, Hunan Province (MCCA)
2022 - Nanjing Yuhua Art Museum; Huai'an City Art Museum; The Arts Bridge Space, Shanghai; Yiguan Art Centre, Nanjing
2023 - Shanghai Haipai Art Museum
2024 - Beijing Fine Art Academy

Awards

China Lu Xun Printmaking Award, Outstanding Works Award at the Fifth Indigo-Prefecture International Printmaking Triennial Exhibition in Japan, Gold Award at the Japan International Printmaking Association, Outstanding Award at the 20th National Printmaking Exhibition, Outstanding Award at the First National Screenprinting Exhibition, China Publishing Government Award, China's Most Beautiful Book Award, Outstanding Award at the Eighth National Book Design Art Exhibition, Jiangsu Province Zijin Cultural Talent, 2018 Nanjing Most Beautiful Book Award, Nanjing City Hundred Top Cultural Talents, Seventh Nanjing Literature and Art Award for Excellent Works, Cambridge University 'Xu Zhimo Art Award'.

Collections

China: National Art Museum of China, Shanghai Museum of Art, Guangdong Museum of Art, Shenzhen Museum of Art, Shenzhen Painting Academy, Guancheng Art Museum, Qingdao Art Museum, China Printmaking Museum, Shijiazhuang Art Museum, Hebei Provincial Museum of Fine Arts, Chinese Children's Art Museum, Suzhou Museum, Heilongjiang Provincial Museum of Fine Arts, Zhejiang Provincial Museum of Fine Arts, Hubei Provincial Museum of Fine Arts, Anhui Provincial Museum of Fine Arts, Jiangsu Provincial Museum of Fine Arts. USA: Art Institute of Chicago, Turchin Center for the Visual Arts. UK: British Museum, British Library, Victoria and Albert Museum, Ashmolean Museum of Art & Archaeology, Kent Print Collection at the University of Kent, St. Ives Gallery in Cornwall. Rest of the world: Muban Educational Trust; Whangārei Art Museum, New Zealand; National Art Gallery, Sri Lanka; Ministry of Culture, Ukraine; Tagore Library at the University of Lucknow, India.

Publications

1. *Private Thinker* (2005) Heilongjiang Fine Arts Publishing House
2. *Private Thoughts* (2008) East China Normal University Press
3. *The Private Thinker: Chinese-English Edition* (2009) East China Normal University Press (second edition)
4. *New Private Thoughts* (2010) Liangyou Bookstore and Huangshan Bookstore Co. Ltd.
5. *Cool Longsibao - a Chinese painter's sketch diary* (2010) East China Normal University Press
6. *Monkey Tickets* (2011) East China Normal University Press
7. *Private Thinker · Liu Yanfei Language* (2012) East China Normal University Press
8. *Dan Qing Ji* (2012) Guangxi Normal University Press
9. *A Decade of Private Thoughts - A Painter's Harvest in a Foreign Land* (2014) Guangxi Normal University Press
10. *Private Thinker·What's My Surname?* (2016) Guangxi Normal University Press
11. *Think about Lu Xun* (2017) East China Normal University Press
12. *His hometown is his foreign land·a Chinese painter's sketch Europe* (2019) Jiangsu Phoenix Fine Arts Publishing House (reprinted edition)

References

Zheng Sun, from *A Decade of Private Thoughts - A Painter's Harvest in a Foreign Land*, Guangxi Normaol University Press, 2014.

Sun Zhouxing, from the Preface of the Exhibition *Objects of Nothingness - Liu Chunjie's Art on Lu Xun*, Yiguan Art Centre, Nanjing, 2022.

© 2025 Liu Chunjie
World copyright reserved

ISBN: 978-1-78884-287-7

Published by ACC Art Books with Guangxi Normal University Press 2025

The right of Liu Chunjie to be identified as author of this work has been asserted by him in accordance with the Copyright, Designs and Patents Act 1988

All rights reserved. No part of this publication may be reproduced, stored in a retrieval system, or transmitted in any form or by any means electronic, mechanical, photocopying, recording or otherwise, without the prior permission of the publisher

A CIP catalogue record for this book is available from the British Library

Editors: Alice Bowden, Ru Jingyu
Designer: Lu Mingjing

EU GPSR Authorised Representative:
Easy Access System Europe Oü, 16879218
Address: Mustamäe tee 50, 10621 Tallinn, Estonia
Email: gpsr@easproject.com Tel: +358 40 500 3575

FSC
www.fsc.org
MIX
Paper | Supporting responsible forestry
FSC® C140396

Printed in China
for ACC Art Books Ltd., Woodbridge,
Suffolk, UK

www.accartbooks.com
www.gxnu.edu.cn

ACC ART BOOKS

THE ARTS BRIDGE